The Paranormal Surrounds Us

THE PARANORMAL SURROUNDS US

Psychic Phenomena in Literature, Culture and Psychoanalysis

Richard Reichbart

Foreword by Mikita Brottman;
Afterword by Michael Prescott

McFarland & Company, Inc., Publishers
Jefferson, North Carolina

The following articles originally appeared in the *Journal of the American Society for Psychical Research* and are published here with permission from the American Society for Psychical Research, Inc. (ASPR), 5 West 73rd Street, New York, New York, 10023 (aspr.com): (1976) Psi phenomena and Tolstoy. *Journal of the American Society for Psychical Research*, Vol. 70 (3), July 1976, pp. 249–265; (1976) The Navajo hand trembler: Multiple roles of the psychic in traditional Navajo society. *Journal of the American Society for Psychical Research*, Vol. 70 (4), October 1976, pp. 381–396; (1978) Magic and psi: Some speculations on their relationship. *Journal of the American Society for Psychical Research*, Vol. 72(2), April 1978, pp. 153–175; (1990) E.M. Forster's "Passage to India": Psi, culture and causality. *Journal of the American Society for Psychical Research*, Vol. 84 (2), April 1990, pp. 145–154; (1998) Jule Eisenbud: Explorer. *Journal of the American Society for Psychical Research*, Vol. 92(4), October 1998, pp. 427–431.
The following article originally appeared in the journal *Parapsychology Review* and is published here with permission of the Parapsychology Foundation, P.O. Box 1562, New York, NY 10021–0043: (1981) Western law and parapsychology. *Parapsychology Review*, Vol. 12 (2), (March-April), pp. 9–11.

ISBN (print) 978-0-7864-9536-8
ISBN (ebook) 978-1-4766-3368-8

LIBRARY OF CONGRESS CATALOGUING DATA ARE AVAILABLE

BRITISH LIBRARY CATALOGUING DATA ARE AVAILABLE

Front cover: (left to right) William Shakespeare, Sigmund Freud and Ingmar Bergman (National Archives of the Netherlands); background image by Yuri Arcurs (iStock)

Manufactured in the United States of America

McFarland & Company, Inc., Publishers
Box 611, Jefferson, North Carolina 28640
www.mcfarlandpub.com

In memory of Nikki

Table of Contents

Acknowledgments

This book owes its genesis to the inspiration of the late Jule Eisenbud, M.D., my first psychoanalyst, whose love of life and openness to experience has informed both my life and career. I also thank the late Laura Dale, who was the editor of the *Journal of the American Society for Psychical Research* (*JASPR*) at the time that I— a neophyte—submitted my first parapsychological article. Laura was the consummate editor, knowledgeable in her own right, precise, demanding and encouraging. In addition, I am thankful to Paige Hooper-Reichbart, whose interest in this field dovetailed with my own and who was always supportive in those early years.

I would not be writing this book had the Clinical Psychology Doctorate Program of the City University of New York not accepted me, a more or less lapsed attorney in his early thirties, with a series of parapsychological articles and a one-year newly minted M.A. degree in psychology from a distant University of Northern Colorado to his credit. I am not sure I realized at the time what a chance they were taking, given this unusual background, but take me they did, for which I am deeply grateful. I also thank the late City University of New York researcher and parapsychologist Gertrude Schmeidler, who was familiar with my parapsychological work and encouraged and recommended me. I thank my second analyst, the late Joyce Steingart, who helped me to personally integrate seemingly very disparate life experiences that have led in part to this book; as well as my supervisor Janice Lieberman, who was willing—at a crucial time—to entertain psi phenomena in the process of supervision of a case. And I am further grateful to the psychoanalysts of the New Jersey Psychoanalytic Society, who have always proved supportive and created an atmosphere where one could be oneself. In addition, my own psychoanalytic institute, the Institute for Psychoanalytic Training and Research (IPTAR), where I eventually became a fellow and then president, has provided a place where the love of and fascination with psychoanalytic work flourishes.

But most immediately this book would not have happened, had it not been for a blog. In trolling the internet at one point, when I had separated myself from parapsychological writing but was curious about how Jule Eisenbud's work continued to be received, I stumbled on Michael Prescott's blog (Michaelprescott.typepad.com). It contained as insightful a recounting of Eisenbud's work, in fact of parapsychology in general, as anything I had read, although Prescott is neither a parapsychologist nor a psychoanalyst; and it inspired me to pursue this book. The chapter here on G.K. Chesterton and Ingmar Bergman (Chapter Four) was one immediate consequence—sparked initially by a passing comment to me by Eisenbud many years ago about Bergman's film "The Magician" and then resurrected for me by Prescott's commentary on his blog about Chesterton (http://michaelprescott. typepad.com/michael_prescotts_blog/2011/02/mirabile-dictu.html). Michael Prescott has generously provided an afterword to this book.

Others who have helped me to re-find my parapsychological roots include the psychoanalyst Mikita Brottman, who has been a new, articulate and unremitting exponent of Eisenbud's work, in both her articles and her book, *Phantoms of the Clinic* (Karnac, 2001), and who graciously provided the foreword to this book; Stephen Braude, colleague and friend of Jule Eisenbud's and an outstanding (and outspoken) modern parapsychological thinker; the gracious Tom Beck, Chief Curator, Special Collections, Albin O. Kuhn Library, University of Maryland, Baltimore County, who granted me access to the "Jule Eisenbud Collection on Ted Serios and Thoughtographic Photography"; Ruth Rosenbaum of the National Psychological Association for Psychoanalysis (NPAP), a colleague, who has recently been promoting the study of parapsychology and psychoanalysis; and Julian Gilbey for his editorial assistance. And thank you to my friend Thrae Harris, who has read much of this work with a sympathetic eye, and to Michael Moskowitz, who has been a source of comfort during difficult times.

Thank you also to Patrice Keane, the executive director of the American Society for Psychical Research, for permission to reproduce articles originally published in the *Journal of the American Society for Psychical Research* and for her continuing interest in this project. In addition, I thank Nancy Sondow also of the American Society for Psychical Research for her help. Without the encouragement and care of Layla Milholen of McFarland, I could not have written this book. I also am grateful to the most wonderful and thorough indexer, Nancy Gerth.

My patients have inspired me and contributed to this book with their openness and courage through the years.

Thank you to my son, David, who has had to endure more absence from me than I would have wanted. And thank you particularly to my companion of the last twenty years, Nansie Ross, who has always been there with her humor, understanding and encouragement despite the many times that I spent weekends at the office completing chapters. Without her, this book would never have been completed. And last, thanks to members of my family, who have quietly inquired and been supportive: Brent, Carmel, Jeff, and Ophira as well as those younger ones who make me laugh and take me out of my preoccupations—Leyna, Sada, Mazie, Oona, Iris, and Axel.

Foreword

by Mikita Brottman

In a world that increasingly rewards narrow specialization, Richard Reichbart is a cultural polymath. This collection contains essays on psychoanalysis, western law, anthropology and magic, as well as the work of Shakespeare, Tolstoy, James Joyce, G.K. Chesterton, E.M. Forster, and Ingmar Bergman. In addition, all the essays consider such issues as connections between the minds of people who are emotionally bonded; mysterious associations between the dreams of strangers; shared associations and memories; intuitive and uncanny insights, and the way patients in psychoanalysis communicate with one another, unknown to themselves, through the medium of the analyst.

These are brave, heady subjects, and it is striking to find a Freudian psychoanalyst with such an open mind and so many different fields of interest (and it is striking to find a psychoanalyst of any kind who uses such lucid and satisfying prose). Reichbart's unusually broad array of knowledge may have been facilitated by his early experiences. After training as a lawyer, he lived and worked on a Najavo reservation as a legal services attorney, an experience he recounts in his essay "The Navajo Hand Trember: Multiple Roles of the Psychic in Navajo Society." During this time, he became fascinated by the Navajos' uncannily accurate use of shamanic divination to find lost objects and diagnose problems.

Although Reichbart found that belief in the work of the Navajo shamans was not taken seriously outside the reservation, many people in the West today are happy to believe in the healing spiritual action of prayer, mindfulness, meditation, yoga, and any aboriginal or native ceremonial practice (especially those that involve circles, chanting, and the worship of nature). Yet when it comes to what Reichbart refers to as "the psi hypothesis"—"the idea that our thoughts, even if unconscious, can have the equivalent of a sensorimotor impact on the world"—then, as Reichbart observes, "otherwise sensible, even sensitive observers of human nature" are regularly overtaken by a "strange resistance."

This reluctance to discuss these odd and often inexplicable phenomena is a recurrent theme in this book. Reichbart explains how, in the psychoanalytic world, Freud's intriguing parapsychological writings have been ignored, denied, and swept under the proverbial rug. Beyond this, Reichbart saw first hand what happened to the greatest of all modern parapsychologically informed psychoanalysts, his friend and mentor Jule Eisenbud. As Reichbart explains in his poignant and illuminating essay, "Jule Eisenbud: Explorer," he was led to Eisenbud as a patient, knowing nothing about the man, after a failed love

1

affair had led him to a suffer a type of breakdown. His analysis continued for over two and a half years, beginning at six days a week, with an eight-month hiatus. Reichbart was, as he recounts, transformed by the process, and by Eisenbud, who, when they first met, had recently published the account of his experiments with Ted Serios, the Chicago elevator operator with the "thoughtographic" mind. Reichbart held dearly to intellectual honesty. Later, Reichbart and Eisenbud became friends and colleagues, and Reichbart witnessed first-hand how Eisenbud was ostracized and abandoned by the psychoanalytic establishment for his work on parapsychology, and finally, after his work with Serios, said to have "fallen off the deep end."

Reichbart tells a very different story. "I believe that Jule's work in parapsychology," he writes, "particularly the psychic photography data produced by Ted Serios, and his theories concerning how psi functions in daily life, to be far and away the most important evidential and theoretical work in the history of parapsychology." Standing some distance from the center of the hurricane, Reichbart, in his smooth, luminous prose, gives us a clear and depressing account of Eisenbud's experiments with Serios, the bad publicity that plagued the pair, and the angry accusations of gullibility and fraudulence. Incidentally, Reichbart's essay on Eisenbud in this collection contains the best description I have ever read of Serios's amazing and uncanny "thoughtographs," and the ridicule and resistance they provoked in Eisenbud's detractors.

In February 2011, I wrote an article for *The Chronicle of Higher Education* about an exhibition of Ted Serios images organized by Stephen Braude at the University of Maryland, Baltimore County. When the article came out, it was attacked by James Randi, who wrote, "Brottman shows clearly that she has accepted uncritically as true, everything that Eisenbud wrote or said about these silly photos." I have often wondered if, in his use of the word "silly," James Randi was reacting unconsciously to the homophonic resonance of Ted's last name. While the images themselves could not be more serious, Serios himself, by all accounts, was something of a clown. A hopeless alcoholic with a flair for drama, Ted needed his motor to be charged with whisky in order to rev up his psychic powers. Sometimes it responded; sometimes it did not. Shabby and semi-literate, he was not the kind of person scientists would consider reliable when it came to obeying stringent experimental controls. It is not surprising he was regularly taken for a charlatan. As Reichbart explains in his essay "Magic and Psi," "we are too frightened to look closely at psi, and we often will do everything in our power to entertain more comfortable and more familiar 'magical' hypotheses—hypotheses that explain things in physical terms rather than in psi terms."

In fact, as Reichbart usefully clarifies, only recently have we tried to separate magic and "genuine" psi. Many talented psychics have had a flair for the dramatic, like Serios, or have been psychotic, or have relied on tricks or charlatanism to jump-start their psychic powers, just as Ted relied on alcohol. Stringent laboratory test-conditions are not conducive to the emergence of psi, nor is logic, linear order, nor perfect manners. Shamans and preliterate people, as Reichbart understands from his work with the Navajo, can know something is a trick and yet believe in it at the same time, without contradiction (This reminds me of the philosopher Slavoj Žižek's anecdote about the quantum physicist Nils Bohr, who, when asked why he had a horseshoe above his door when he surely did not believe in the old superstition that it drove away evil spirits, replied, "Of course not, but I've heard that it works even if you don't believe in it"). There is no clear dividing line between charlatan and psychic, between psychic and psychotic. The simple fact is, that certain individuals possess greater control of psi processes—or have greater access to them—than others do, for reasons that we do not (and perhaps will never) understand.

"In their knowledge of the mind," wrote Freud of creative writers in "Delusions and Dreams in Jensen's *Gradiva*" (1907), "they are far in advance of us everyday people, for they draw upon sources which we have not yet opened up for science." This statement of Freud's is never very far from the surface of Reichbart's essays on literature, in which he identifies parapsychological themes that, if they have been previously observed, have been considered linguistic or intertextual allusions, stream of consciousness unions, symbolic or metaphoric connections. By considering these themes from the perspective of parapsychology, Reichbart allows us to see the texts in which they appear in a new way. For example, his essay "Hamlet: The Tragedy of a Parapsychologist" shows us how *Hamlet* tests a series of timeless questions concerning the phenomena of an apparition: Whence does it come? What does it represent? Is it "real"? Is the information it imparts accurate? Is it evidence of a departed soul that still exists somewhere? Is it a fantasy, a visual hallucination, an example of psi phenomena, a shared hallucination, an example of folie à deux, a figment of the imagination? Can the experiment be repeated? If not, what are we to conclude? After all, as we learn from Reichbart's essay on E.M. Forster's *A Passage to India,* there is a very unpredictable relationship between psi phenomena and causality. However we might struggle to express or make sense of the mysterious events experienced by Adele Quested, we can never completely fit them into a logical system or pattern. Psi appears and disappears. Instead of resisting and shying away from its unreliable presence, we need to stop trying to predict its pattern and simply let go of our expectations and let out minds go where they will, as in the analytic session.

My own mind began to stray as I read "Telepathy and Connection in James Joyce's *Ulysses,*" Reichbart's essay about the unconscious communication between Bloom and Dedalus, a psychic connectedness that is caused by, among other things, the trauma of daily life and early death. Reichbart's reference to Leopold Bloom's dead son Rudy, who lived for eleven days and was buried in a wool coat, was a sudden painful reminder of an orphaned baby raccoon that I had found six weeks earlier, while staying on a farm in upstate New York. I took him in, warmed him up and nursed him back to health. I set my alarm for every two hours in the night to microwave the sock full of rice I was using to keep his body temperature elevated. But at some point in the morning I slept through my alarm, got up half an hour late, and found that the raccoon had died in the night.

I buried him stoically and went back to bed. His death was nothing to me at the time. For some reason, however, it has become enormously painful in retrospect. As I read about Leopold Bloom and Rudy I began to acknowledge that my guilt at my failure to care properly for the raccoon cub, and my projection on to him, was connected to an identification with my own mother, who was not especially maternal, and to my recent hysterectomy, which had made my choice not to have children final and irreversible.

Then I turned the page and read the subtitle: "Psi correspondences among my patients: the raccoons." A strange feeling came over me, as if I was in a dream. I read on. Reichbart describes two of his patients who describe specific dreams of raccoons, and a third who dreams of a raccoon-like animal. The dreams, according to Reichbart, are connected to the themes of parents and children, and the patients are linked psychically to one another, and through him. "But as intriguing as these seeming psi links are—and however closely they resemble the type of linking that Joyce does in *Ulysses* in which the reader knows the psi associations even though the characters themselves do not—I could think of no way to use them." My own raccoon dream—albeit a daydream about a real event—had provided an extra link in the chain, another psi association, through me, of which the characters I had been reading about in the case study, including Reichbart, were unaware. And yet apart from reminding me of what I already knew, and reminding me that psi phenomena are a common occurrence, the connection seemed to have no "function." It could not be used, or harnessed, or marshaled. In fact, in some ways it was so trivial I am even reluctant to mention it. It could, after all, be just a coincidence.

Here, again, is that familiar resistance. Sometimes we resist because the implications of an event are too terrifying to believe; at other times we hold back because the instance of psi seems too trivial, too personal, too awkward or embarrassing; it involves something we should not have been doing or thinking about, something we do not want to discuss. It is built up from the smallest, most seemingly irrelevant details. Often, what emerges is often exactly what a person has been keeping secret, even from themselves. This, of course, is also a feature of dreams, and of the unconscious in general, as are so many elements of psi—wordplay, puns, allusions, inversions, repetition, and metaphor. It is not unusual, then, that psi so often emerges where the unconscious is allowed free play: in the psychoanalytic session, and in literature, as Richard Reichbart's bold and original essays amply testify.

Mikita Brottman is a psychoanalyst and a professor of humanities at the Maryland Institute College of Art in Baltimore. The author of books and articles on the history of psychoanalysis, the uncanny, aesthetics and literature, she wrote Phantoms of the Clinic *(2011) and* The Maximum Security Book Club *(2016).*

Introduction

Forewarning

This book is about psychic phenomena and the way that they appear in a variety of studies and settings and in our lives. I do not set out here to "prove" the existence of psychic phenomena. For that, I will in the course of this book refer the reader to a variety of other sources. What I do try to do here is to challenge the reader by exploring—often through a psychoanalytic lens—how "psi phenomena" appear in our literature, in cultures, and in clinical psychoanalysis. Much of the material here is either generally little known—from my speculations on the relationship between magic and psi to my discussion of the Navajo hand trembler—or entirely new, such as my focus on *Hamlet* as a parapsychologist or a different view of a famous case of Freud's, the Forsyth Case. These speculations derive from the fact that I am a psychologist, a parapsychologist, and a practicing psychoanalyst. For those of you whose interest is piqued and who are inclined to step through the door into this arena, I hope you will find much that is new and exciting here.

Words in this field can be confusing. Psychic phenomena have many names: paranormal phenomena or parapsycholgical phenomena or "psi phenomena" or simply "psi" (the term that I tend to use and is favored by parapsychologists). Sometimes the very term "parapsychology" (introduced years ago by J.B. Rhine) is also unknown to people, who are unfamiliar with the study of psychic phenomena. In addition, there are other terms that appear with regard to it, including "the occult" and "the uncanny," which—while exciting—I do not use because I believe they are misleading. And there are many different terms for the various type of phenomena that are embraced within psi—such as telepathy, precognition, and apparitions to name only three. For the reader new to this field, even for those who are familiar with it, the multiple terms for the same phenomenon can be confusing. For that reason, I have included a brief glossary at the end of this book which may be helpful.

The Genesis of This Book

This collection of articles, some of which were written forty years ago or so and others which are new, is curious in a number of ways. For one, it is personally curious: I am rather amazed that I have written these articles at all and now this book. Years ago, I did not have an interest in parapsychology or for that matter psychoanalysis. They were foreign subjects to me, about which I knew nothing, No one in my family, although well educated, ever expressed a desire for me to pursue a psychoanalytic career. Parapsychology itself would have been even more beyond the pale. In fact, I had other professional dreams, which I was pursuing when—seemingly out of nowhere—my path changed.

What happened? I had graduated from Yale Law School in 1968 and was working in Northern Arizona, on the Navajo reservation, as an Office of Economic Opportunity attorney for Dinebeinna Nahilnah be Agaditahe, Inc. (DNA, Inc.) which translates as "Attorneys who work for the economic revitalization of the Navajo people." It was a wonderful experience, living and working among the Navajo and Hopi, in the high and beautiful semi-desert, filled with great open expanses and surreal canyons and rock formations, including Canyon de Chelly and Monument Valley. I loved the experience, found the Navajo and Hopi people and cultures fascinating—as I had previously found Black southern culture fascinating, living for one summer with a Black family and working as a civil rights worker in a small Southern town, Fort Valley, Georgia, for Martin Luther King's Southern Christian Leadership Council. I had learned that cultures themselves—their details and the theories of causality that obtain to each one—had a special hold on me.

But I was not in the best psychological shape, so after a year and a half, I left, and I went to Denver, where I entered psychoanalytic treatment with a New York educated analyst, originally out of New York Psychoanalytic Institute, by the name of Jule Eisenbud. And here is where the path I had thought I was on, to be a civil rights attorney, which had become progressively more problematic for me as I increasingly found the actual practice of law intellectually boring and at times ethically tortured, fell suddenly and completely away. Psychoanalysis filled a great and yawning gap in the way that I knew the world, a gap that I did not even know was there. It explained not only memory and personality and development, but it also dovetailed with my appreciation of great literature—I had been an English major in college and briefly pursued a career in playwriting as a graduate student at the University of California at Berkeley. I took to psychoanalysis as if I had been shown a new land, with a bountiful harvest: I cavorted in it and gorged on it, reading on my own. It was a delight. Eventually, I dropped out of law, drove a cab, opened an art gallery, and then pursued a Master's degree in psychology at the University of Northern Colorado in Greeley, Colorado. I was determined to become a psychoanalyst.

But there is another part to this story, and that is that Jule Eisenbud, the Denver psychoanalyst whom I had been directed toward by a psychiatrist in Albuquerque—a psychiatrist who did not know him personally but may have known his writing and who never forewarned me nor ever explained his choice—was also a foremost parapsychologist. To this day, I do not know why things happened in this way nor can I explain the fact that the one attorney I knew in Denver, Harris Sherman (he had been representing Native Americans as I had been doing). I then discovered was a close friend of Eisenbud's family. In fact, I found out about Eisenbud's work as a parapsychologist, when I visited Harris after seeing Eisenbud for the first time, and Harris showed me a copy of Eisenbud's recently published book, *The World of Ted Serios*, a famous study of a psychic photographer (about which I will elaborate frequently in this book). More importantly, Eisenbud's integration of parapsychology and psychoanalysis became as fascinating to me as did psychoanalysis itself. It was an exciting and rarely explored portion of this vast new world of psychoanalysis that I had discovered. I made it a point of going through as many of the references in *The World of Ted Serios* and Eisenbud's book *Psi and Psychoanalysis* as I could get my hands on; in effect these books and references, and my psychoanalysis, constituted my early psychoanalytic training.

Fast forward, a number of years after this rather brief (and first) psychoanalysis: I was writing some of the parapsychological/psychoanalytic articles that you will find here and that were published in the *Journal of the American Society for Psychical Research*. I was teaching Parapsychology at the Honors Program at the University of Colorado, and ultimately enrolling for my doctorate at the Clinical Psychology Program at the City University of New York.

Being interested in parapsychology as a psychoanalyst has never been exactly safe professionally. Early on, I knew this, my knowledge based on the career and experience of Eisenbud, who had been a darling of the New York Psychoanalytic Institute, until he was considered a black sheep as a consequence of his interest in parapsychology. He had never been made a Training Analyst (upon the publication of his first parapsychological article in a prominent psychoanalytic journal, an immediate movement to oust him from the New York Psychoanalytic Society was begun but did not succeed; nevertheless he was informed that he would never be allowed to become a Training Analyst there [Eisenbud, 2010])and his parapsychological work, most particularly the psychic photography investigation of Ted Serios, to this day is taken as a sign of how far he went off track. Despite my enthusiasm for parapsychology, I learned early on in my own training as a psychology graduate student and then as a candidate at a psychoanalytic institute, to keep my head down, so to speak. It might be said that I kept my head down a lot. I graduated from a foremost New York psychoanalytic institute, the Institute for Psychoanalytic Training and Research (IPTAR), eventually became a Fellow and Training Analyst (I was determined not to suffer the same fate as Eisenbud), a Fellow of the International Psychoanalytic Association and a member of the American Psychoanalytic Association, and President of the New Jersey Psychoanalytic Society, all the while keeping my head decidedly down. I developed my psychoanalytic practice for adults and children and adolescents in a small suburban town in New Jersey. I did not write anything parapsychological (although I kept notes on psi events that occurred when seeing patients) for decades.

The private practice of psychoanalysis is dependent in part upon one's reputation among fellow analysts and in the psychoanalytic community. It was only when I was elected President of my psychoanalytic institute, that I felt professionally safe enough to return to my interest in parapsychology in terms of publishing and speaking. Even then, at my institute, a demanding and sometimes conservative training institute, it has not been until recently that I have felt I can speak out readily about my findings or understanding of parapsychological process. (For another, and even more curious reason for my ambivalence about speaking out, see the Appendix article entitled "Cloak and Dagger Psi Mystery Story.")

Filling the Gap

Which brings me to where I began this introduction, that this collection of my writings is curious in a number of ways. Parapsychological articles and books of this nature are curious because they are neither fish nor fowl. They tend to fall into the large gap that exists between parapsychology and psychoanalysis. They disappear and are forgotten. For example, periodically, clinical observations on psi phenomena similar to those made many years ago are announced by psychoanalysts, psychoanalysts courageous enough to publish them in psychoanalytic journals or in books. Unfortunately, too often they do so without a full awareness of past discoveries, and thus they tend to state their findings as newer than they are. And then these findings in turn tend to disappear from awareness as well. The fact is that psi data themselves, when looked at psychoanalytically, straddle the field of parapsychology and psychoanalysis, and thus are likely to be marginalized in the psychoanalytic world. And on top of that, the data are resisted because they so very much challenge our Western understanding of causality—a dynamic which I will expand upon in this book. When the data are particularly good, in the sense of being earth shaking, ironically they seem to be even more likely to be opposed and to disappear.

Let me expand further about that gap into which a book of this nature falls. Parapsychologists are not generally psychoanalysts nor are they psychoanalytically trained. They tend to be research psychologists and laboratory creatures. They want to capture psychic phenomena or "psi" in some way, as in a repeatable experiment; they contrive experiments to do so; they deal with statistics and tight protocols. They are often somewhat wary of psychoanalytic thinking (if not in some instances opposed to it), although they are often familiar with such thinking. In part, this is because parapsychologists are much more interested in harnessing psi than being concerned about dynamic process. In addition, their interest in psi phenomena is likely to be much broader than the psychoanalyst's. That is, they do not confine their interest to the limited type of phenomena that a psychoanalyst might conceivably find when working with a patient, such things as telepathy, telepathic dreams or even precognitive phenomena. In addition to these things, parapsychologists interests are broad, encompassing such things as remote viewing, psychokinesis, clairvoyance, apparitions, hauntings, psychics, healing, laying on of hands, poltergeists, reincarnation data, telepathic drawing experiments, mediumistic productions and so forth—an entire panoply of phenomena that the psychoanalyst, sitting quietly by his analytic couch listening to a patient, is not as likely to encounter (although a lack of openness on the part of the psychoanalyst makes it unlikely that a patient who has one or more of these experiences will share them or that a psychoanalyst will recognize their importance). Last, parapsychologists want to encapsulate psi phenomena. Spontaneous reports by psychoanalysts outside the laboratory, even though such reports may explain dynamically how psi functions for an individual, are not what parapsychologists consider "hard" experiments; and in that sense, parapsychologists often give these reports short shrift.

On the other hand, the psychoanalyst tends to be wary of the panoply of alleged experience the parapsychologist may investigate. She may go as far as entertaining the possibility of telepathy, which Freud himself entertained if ambivalently—which she may experience with her patients, and which she may courageously write about in psychoanalytic journals. But as the data expand outward, she is very likely to resist them; even precognition—which can be encountered in the psychoanalytic setting—may be further than she can venture, as it seems to defy our normal (one might say Newtonian) expectation of how the world works.

One might think that psychoanalysts would want to know about these other phenomena, beyond contending that they are all simply superstition, on the off chance that there may be something there. After all, these are phenomena that some patients will undoubtedly bring to them, during the course of a practice; things that such patients may believe in or experience or be struggling to understand. In fact, in the course of this book, you will hear a number of pleas from analysts who have ventured into the parapsychological world, including me, that patients who bring in psi material, sometimes disturbing to them, need to be accepted and listened to, in the same way as we listen to all patients, and not labeled in effect "delusional" or "crazy." But in the psychoanalytic world, particularly in the training world of psychoanalysts characterized by psychoanalytic institutes, there is a healthy fear of what Freud called "omnipotence of thought," a healthy fear of psychotic process. Of course, in many ways this is understandable: it is difficult to treat and heal someone whose "reality testing" is fragile, whose psychotic process extrudes their internal thoughts to the outside world so that the line between two becomes unclear. It can be scary and frustrating; and in some cases, as with schizophrenia, it is likely that the patient cannot be reached in usual psychoanalytic ways, if he can be reached at all. Yet patients who bring in psi phenomena, and this is the point, are *not* bringing in psychotic process. Instead, they exhibit run of the mill symptoms and diagnoses, including depression and anxiety, and for all practical purposes can be entirely "normal." In fact, because they are so confused, those patients who suffer psychotic process are considered to be *less* likely to offer good examples of psi (despite what the patients may believe about the examples they offer) than those who are healthier and close to "normal."

But more than this: psychoanalysts are afraid to admit to a variety of things *personally* for fear that to do so will compromise the sense of their own stability as psychoanalysts to other psychoanalysts. Psychoanalysts have a way of casting aspersions on each other and to say that one's reality testing is amiss is probably one of the greatest. As a consequence and unfortunately, to admit to even curiosity about psi process is too often a tendency that they carefully avoid.

What then is this collection of articles about and to whom is it addressed? As I indicated at the beginning, these articles accept the existence of psi, particularly spontaneous psi, which I have experienced in my life and my work with patients. I believe that psi phenomena are a regular part of life, which we too often choose to ignore, even though I believe there is more than enough spontaneous evidence to convince us, as it has convinced the greatest creative writers, playwrights and filmmakers that we have known and whom we celebrate, as evidenced in their work. Although in the article on the history of parapsychology and psychoanalysis, I allude to some of the experimental findings that confirm the existence of psi to which the reader so inclined may turn, my focus in this collection is not (again as I previously indicated) to convince the reader of psi based on this type of experimental evidence.

What I *am* trying to do in this book is simple: to shake and surprise both groups, the parapsychologists and the psychoanalysts. I attempt to intrigue psychoanalysts who are willing to venture into this field by providing not only a more contemporary history of psi and psychoanalysis, with particular focus on theoretical statements that have been made, but by expanding their view, in terms of culture and the arts, of how psi phenomena exist and how it is portrayed. Similarly, I hope through my focus on the arts, to get the parapsychologists to recognize how the phenomena they study has been recognized and portrayed by great Western writers, playwrights, and—in one case—a film maker.

Another group that I am hoping to reach, frankly, are the literary critics and academicians who have so often failed to incorporate in their study of great literature, a recognition of how insightful great artists have been in depicting psi phenomena, how these artists contend that such phenomena are important to our lives, and how they are not speaking to us in metaphors but in realistic depictions of parapsychological process. Freud said that we can learn from great literature and plays about psychological functioning. We can learn, too, about parapsychological functioning. I should mention here that one literary academician Nicholas Royle bravely stepped into this field in 1991, in a book entitled Telepathy and Literature (Royle, 1991), but his work, although intriguing and taking much from the philosopher Derrida, is from a parapsychological and psychodynamic viewpoint abstruse, failing to explain parapsychological phenomena in dynamic depth.

Last, I am hoping in this collection, to resurrect the work of Jule Eisenbud, which I have already mentioned, as embodied in those two outstanding studies of psi phenomena, *Psi and Psychoanalysis*, (Eisenbud, 1970) and *The World of Ted Serios* (Eisenbud, 1968, 1989). The Serios books present the psychic photography of a Chicago bell hop, who was able to influence through his mind Polaroid camera film. Psychoanalysts, even those who have written in this field, have either ignored or minimized how monumental is Eisenbud's study of the role that psi phenomena play in psychoanalytic treatment. And most psychoanalysts simply will not take that extra step, out of the psychoanalytic consulting room, to even read about Ted Serios, much less explore, the wonderful and psychodynamically presented findings of Eisenbud's book on the subject. For that matter, Eisenbud's study of Serios also has been given unnecessary short shrift by parapsychologists themselves, who prefer a repeatable experiment or something less messy than the free-wheeling interactions and events that characterized Serios's mode of production.

In attempting to present and resurrect Eisenbud's work, I am indebted to three people who have been attempting to do the same for many years and who are as knowledgeable as I am about his work—the foremost parapsychologist Stephen Braude (who knew Eisenbud professionally and was his friend), the psychoanalyst Mikita Brottman, and a fiction writer with the nom de plume of Michael Prescott, who maintains a blog that has been an inspiration to me. They have on their own presented on Eisenbud's work in heartfelt ways. I am glad to be in their company.

And finally, I have tried to write these pieces so that they are enjoyable to read. I hope that they are entertaining. Dry and academic articles do not do justice to the excitement of this field, for it is truly a fascinating one.

The Outline of This Book

I have divided this book into three parts: I. Psi Phenomena in Western Literature; II. Psi Phenomena and Psychoanalysis; and III. Psi Phenomena and Culture. These sections are necessarily interconnected, so that for example there are references in I. Literature to aspects of psychoanalysis discussed in the second section. I begin with Psi Phenomena in Western Literature because I believe it is the most accessible to the general reader, and because I make some observations about great works that are an intimate part of our Western culture—by Shakespeare, by Tolstoy, by James Joyce—as well as compelling works by E.M. Forster, G.K Chesterton and the filmmaker Ingmar Bergman.

I next provide a rather idiosyncratic and contemporary view of the history of psi phenomena and psychoanalysis, trying to bring the reader up to date, in terms of current psychoanalytic thinking about parapsychology, while at the same time strongly indicating that the discoveries of the past with regard to psychoanalysis and psi are too often ignored. For the psychoanalytic clinician, I address some of the historical findings of those who have clinically explored psi; and I also provide here (as I do in other sections of this book) examples from my own clinical practice of the exploration of psi in the consulting room.

Finally, I travel to the place of psi phenomena and culture, by providing a look at how one culture, the Navajo, takes individuals who are believed to be psychic and makes them part of an elaborate medical system, and how psi is an intimate part of the causal philosophy of the Navajos. After this chapter, I provide a chapter on the relationship between magic (meaning sleight of hand and other procedures designed to make the audience believe that something psychic is taking place) and actual psi manifestations; and I suggest that magic plays a different role in tribal cultures than in Western culture, despite a common ancestry. And then I also provide a highly speculative piece about the relationship between Western law and parapsychology, and how our Western society has decided to contain psi.

I hope that the reader will find in this assortment of subjects, things that will startle him and make him curious to explore psi further. This book is titled *The Paranormal Surrounds Us* because I believe that we live and breathe psi phenomena without awareness. It is the sea around us. It is all we know—so integral to how we survive and relate to one another and the world and yet we cannot quite get a hold of it. It is ubiquitous and elusive at the same time. Intriguingly, Derrida said that it was "difficult to imagine a theory of what they still call the unconscious without a theory of telepathy" (Derrida, 1988, p. 14). He also said, that "everything, in our concept of knowledge, is constructed so that telepathy be impossible, unthinkable, unknown" (Derrida, 1988, p. 21). This book challenges that construct.

References

Derrida, J. (1988) Telepathy. N. Royle (trans.) *Oxford Literary Review*, 10, 3–41.
Eisenbud, J. (1967) *The world of Ted Serios*. New York: William Morrow.
Eisenbud, J. (1970) *Psi and psychoanalysis*. New York: Grune & Stratton.
Eisenbud, J. (1989) *The world of Ted Serios* (2nd edition). Jefferson, NC: McFarland.
Eisenbud, J. (2010) My life with the paranormal. In R. Pilkington (ed.) *Espirit, men and women of parapsychology*, volume 1. Pp. 8–18. San Antonio, TX: Anomalist Books.
Royale, N. (1991) *Telepathy and literature: Essays on the reading mind*. Oxford: Basil Blackwell.

ONE

Hamlet: The Tragedy of a Parapsychologist

Hamlet, the Shakespearean play, is central to Western sensibility. It is emblematic of how Western culture thinks about issues of life, death and existence, and has come to symbolize modern man's existential dilemma. And thus, it has always struck me as passing strange that countless commentaries on this great play provide little insight into the extent to which Shakespeare anticipated in it the discoveries made by psychic researchers four centuries later.[1]

Perhaps it is not surprising that Shakespeare intuitively knew about psychic phenomena and depicted them in a way far superior to most dramatists of his time or for that matter subsequent times. What renders Shakespearean drama great in general and *Hamlet* in particular, aside from stagecraft and poetry, is its incredibly cogent depiction of human nature—and psi phenomena after all are an integral part of human nature. It has been my contention and those of many parapsychological investigators that psi phenomena are a common occurrence with everyone (a fact which becomes most apparent in the examination of the dreams that patients relate during in-depth psychoanalytic treatment) but that in general such phenomena are either overlooked or resisted. Certain talented individuals possess greater control of psi processes—or have greater access to them—than others do, for reasons that we do not understand and which defy any characterological category, but these individuals (whom we often refer to as "psychics") do not play a part in *Hamlet*—although they do in other Shakespearean dramas such as *Macbeth*, *Richard III*, and *Julius Caesar*. But in *Hamlet* the psi phenomena that takes place occurs to "ordinary" people of various stripes and various degrees of experience and education. Unerring as Shakespeare is in portraying human personality and these personalities in particular, he is unerring in portraying the manner in which an attribute of human personality, psi phenomenon, functions.

Shakespeare's insightful embrace of psi in *Hamlet* is ignored by the best of commentators. For example, no less a contemporary authority on Shakespeare than the Pulitzer Prize winning scholar Stephen Greenblatt proceeds to minimize Shakespeare's depiction of ghostly presences and psi phenomena, by contending that Shakespeare employed the ghost in *Hamlet* mostly as a form of stagecraft—designed to exist only in the theater—rather than as a depiction of reality. Shakespeare's ghosts, according to Greenblatt, are "staged ghosts in a spirit of self-conscious theatricality. That is, his ghosts are figures who exist in and as theater; figures in whom it is possible to believe precisely because they appear and speak only onstage" (Greenblatt, 2001, p. 295). In this regard,

Greenblatt is in good company. Earlier, Freud himself stated that Shakespeare can take us into a "purely fantastic" world of his own creation and if he chooses to "stage his action in a world peopled with spirits, demons and ghosts" as he does in *Hamlet*, we must "bow to his decision and treat his setting as though it were real for as long as we put ourselves into his hands" (Freud, 1919, p. 230). For that matter, subsequent psychoanalytic writers on *Hamlet*, such as Lacan (Lacan, 1977) and Eissler in a monumental book (Eissler, 1971) followed in the footsteps of Freud in their complete disregard of parapsychology.

In his detailed exploration of the relationship of *Hamlet* to the religious beliefs concerning Purgatory at the time Shakespeare was writing, Greenblatt simply leaves out the unique characteristics of psi phenomena—of reality—that adhere to Shakespeare's ghostly depictions. In a later work, he is somewhat gentler, suggesting that Shakespeare—while not outwardly religious—tapped into the concepts of death that the Reformation and Protestantism forbade "The official Protestant line in Shakespeare's time," remarks Greenblatt, "was that there were no ghosts at all" (2004, p. 320) but in which the public although now deprived of ritual still passionately believed and with which he too struggled at the time of the death of his son, Hamnet. As another commentator, Mayer, challenging Greenblatt's invocation of secularism, has said: "…belief in apparitions was common at almost every social level" in the 16th century. (Mayer, 2006, p. 50).

But what commentators such as Greenblatt tend to overlook—even if they acknowledge that Shakespeare appealed to a general public's belief in ghosts of his time—is that throughout the play, the character Hamlet fulfills the role of a parapsychologist, although of course that scientific occupation did not exist at the time.[2] He is a sixteenth century psychical researcher looking for data and devising parapsychological experiments. Admittedly ambivalent and tortured, nonetheless he is driven by what can only be called, scientific desire. In other words, in this respect too he is a poignant representative of contemporary man. In fact, his scientific nature contributes to the indecisiveness so often laid at his doorstep. What Hamlet and the play itself really do is present a series of hypotheses concerning the phenomenon of an apparition—Whence does it come? What does it represent? Is it "real"? Is the information it imparts accurate? Is it evidence of a departed soul that still exists somewhere? These are the questions that have attended any serious investigation of an apparition. Although in *Hamlet* they are explored within an historical framework that is not accessible to the public today, the timelessness of the questions is quite striking.

I mentioned here the "indecisiveness" which is so often attributed to Hamlet. Often it has been overemphasized because modern commentators tend to not take seriously the exploration of psychic phenomena so central to the play. If one does not treat the ghost of Hamlet's father seriously, and prefers to think of the ghost as conceit or metaphor or sign of psychic distress, then Hamlet's indecision seems more pronounced. But when we take the phenomena themselves more seriously, then part of Hamlet's hesitation seems more in the nature of a scientific quest that has occupied parapsychologists since the beginning: to pin down the psi data, which unfortunately by its very nature so often defies certainty or clarity.

For Hamlet, the question is not only *whether* the ghost which sets in motion the action of the play, is "real" (and the meaning of the term "real" is explored in a variety of ways in the drama) or—even if Hamlet grants that the ghost is "real"—whether it is the "spirit" of his father. The equally crucial question is *whether the data which the ghost imparts—which it is solely the ghost's to impart, as no one present (other than his murderer the present King) knows the data—are accurate*. And the data are very specific, as so often happens when psi phenomena occur in reality. In fact, data of exactly this sort have often been sought by people when deceased personalities seem to appear in séances or when ghosts appear—that is, veridical data that supposedly only the deceased personality could know and others present could not. If the data are found to be accurate, some people conclude that the ghostly manifestation really must be a spirit, although in fact there are other psi hypotheses to explain this.

Put differently, Hamlet is struggling with two separate hypotheses in the play—the first, whether the ghost is in some way a spirit of his father and the second, whether the information the ghost imparts about his father's death is accurate information, information that clearly could not be acquired through sensorimotor means. These two questions are the same questions that have occurred in the history of parapsychological research whenever there have been ghostly manifestations or spirit manifestations accompanied by seeming veridical information imparted by the "spirit." However, despite the fact that historically the two questions have often been linked, it is not true that the answer to the second question proves the answer to the first, although this is generally Hamlet's assumption. That is, if the phenomenon—the ghost—*does indeed* appear to communicate some secret information seemingly known only to the deceased person and not to those present, that does not necessarily confirm that the ghost *must* be a fragment of a deceased soul. There are more economical, some would say more probable explanations, invoking unconscious telepathy between living persons rather than manifestations of deceased personalities, to explain such phenomena (which I explore later on).

As to Shakespeare's personal need to explore these phenomena in *Hamlet*, it is understandable. Numerous authorities point out that Shakespeare was struggling with what happens after death because three years prior to the composition of *Hamlet*, he lost his eleven-year-old son. Revealingly, his son's name was Hamnet. In addition, at the time of the writing this drama, Shakespeare's father, John Shakespeare, was dying. These facts add poignancy to the evidentiary search that Shakespeare's hero undertakes to ascertain whether a ghost is related to a deceased person's spirit. The importance of the ghost to Shakespeare receives further confirmation from the additional historical circumstance that Shakespeare himself is believed to have played the ghost in the production of the play. Thus, *Hamlet* the play is none other than a musing and a cogitation about the nature of death, so much so that one scene takes place in a graveyard during which the poor dead Yorick is questioned. However, in sharp and ironic contrast to the more loquacious King's ghost, Yorick refuses to speak to Hamlet at all.

As I have suggested, the play proceeds very much like a scientific research report, in which a series of hypotheses (not just the two key ones I have mentioned) are invoked concerning the phenomena of the ghost, and then each one is carefully examined, until Hamlet finally arrives at a fatal "scientific" conclusion. Here, in somewhat didactic form (which while emphasizing the structure does not focus on the wonderful poetry of the play), I outline the different hypotheses as they appear.

Hypothesis One: The Ghost Is a Shared Hallucination

Initially, the ghost is a shared phenomenon, seen by others before Hamlet is summoned to see him and not a phenomenon seen by only one person, as for example in the case of the ghost of Banquo in *Macbeth* (for this reason the ghost of Banquo is more easily thought of as the product of a guilty and unstable mind, rather than as a shared apparition as here). In fact, the first person summoned to see the ghost is not Hamlet but Horatio. When the play opens, the guards Bernardo and Marcellus have seen the apparition twice, and have now requested the more learned Horatio to share their watch in the hope that he too will see it and will understand it. At this point, the ghost has not communicated anything; it has only appeared and has not spoken. Thus, the first hypothesis introduced concerning this phenomenon is that the ghost is a visual hallucination, albeit a shared one, in other words a "folie à deux" of the two guards. Marcellus introduces this hypothesis: "Horatio says 'tis but our fantasy/And will not let belief take hold of him." And then when the ghost in fact does appear briefly to all three of them, Bernardo challenges this initial hypothesis, saying to the now trembling and pale Horatio: "Is now this something more than fantasy?" To which Horatio revealingly responds, as so often happens with psi phenomena, about the evidence: "I might not this believe/Without the sensible and true avouch/Of mine own eyes" (*Hamlet*, Act I. Sc.1, lines 67–69).

And so the first hypothesis introduced by Shakespeare is dismissed in this scene. In addition, during the scene the first active investigation of the phenomenon—the attempt to intervene in some way to ascertain the nature of the phenomenon—begins. It takes place when Marcellus beseeches Horatio to speak to the ghost "Thou art a scholar; speak to it, Horatio," he implores. As one commentator says, "we are given a bit of that Elizabethan belief that conversation with a spirit was the proper occupation of a learned man" (Yellen, 1970, p. 279). Of course, Horatio has no success in his attempt.

Hypothesis Two: It Is a Ghost with Motivation to Appear

The second hypothesis that Horatio, Marcellus and Bernardo entertain is that the phenomenon is a ghost, the soul of a dead person. But in addition, enlisting the beliefs of his time concerning apparitions, Horatio hypothesizes that the ghost has a specific motivation to appear before them which the ghost can be compelled to communicate to them. He suggests a number of possible reasons for a ghost to appear: it can appear to warn people, as a harbinger of calamity (and here Horatio uses the example of omens that occurred when Julius Caesar died—an interesting reference as Shakespeare's play on Julius Caesar [the play which immediately preceded *Hamlet*] is replete with omens including the ghost of Caesar which appears to Brutus); it can appear because it is troubled by an extorted and hidden treasure of which only the deceased knew; it can appear with the desire for the living to do something to comfort it. In effect, they hypothesize that the ghost may be a troubled soul in a Christian Purgatory which must needs communicate to the living to assuage its self-torture. Regardless, their concerted attempt to address the ghost in the hope that it will speak to them, which it does not do, is an intervention to explore the ghost's motivation.

Hypotheses Three and Four: The Ghost Is a Spirit, Evil or Good in Nature, or the Deceased King Who Desires to Speak to His Son

The third hypothesis, stated by Hamlet when he first sees the ghost and is astonished, is that the ghost is either a "spirit of health or goblin damn'd" which comes either from heaven or from hell. As becomes clear, this hypothesis—particularly the ghost as a devil from hell—remains in Hamlet's mind throughout much of the play. Closely following this, is the fourth hypothesis: that the ghost is indeed the spirit of his father the King. Hamlet tries to get the ghost to speak and thereby to state his purpose, but the ghost is silent initially, beckoning Hamlet to follow him.

Hypothesis Five: The Ghost Is in a Purgatory and Asks Revenge for His Death, the Circumstances of Which Only He and His Murderer Know

The fifth, and of course the crucial hypothesis of the play, is that the King's ghost is in torment and has appeared so that his murder, of which only he and his murderer know, may be revenged. But this hypothesis can only be entertained by Hamlet and Hamlet alone, because the ghost now speaks only to him. And Hamlet at this time does not even tell Horatio what the ghost has said to him keeping the knowledge entirely to himself (he does tell him later). The ghost describes his Purgatory vividly as a harrowing "prison-house" where he is confined for a "certain term" in the day time to "fast in fires" and in the evening "to walk the night." But the most important aspect of what he tells Hamlet is his death at the hand of Hamlet's uncle and the method of that death. He was not stung by a serpent when sleeping in his orchard as everyone believes. Instead, when he was asleep as was his custom in the afternoon in the orchard, "thy uncle stole, with juice of cursed hebona in a vial, and in the porches of my ears did pour the leperous distilment" (*Hamlet*, Act I, Sc. 4, lines 67–70).

(To add another element, although the ghost is a shared visual phenomenon for all four men, the visual is linked with an auditory phenomenon *only* for Hamlet, to whom the ghost speaks his story; the other three men, also experience an auditory phenomenon [the stage directions say "Ghost cries under the stage"] but they do so separate from the visual, when the visually departed Ghost tells them repeatedly to "Swear" to keep their experience secret.)

Now for the moment, let us pause. Imagine that the vision of the ghost is an actual and shared experience of Hamlet and the three men accompanying him, not a metaphor, but an *experience* which would test anyone's credulity. And that the crucial aspect of that experience, reserved for Hamlet alone, is the information about how his father actually died and the admonition to exact revenge which the ghost imparts to Hamlet.

For a good part of the rest of the play, Hamlet—the tortured parapsychologist—attempts in various ways to test this last hypothesis. He could, of course, just believe the apparition and wreck revenge on his uncle as the ghost demands. Clearly, he is emotionally distraught by the whole thing, but it is not just emotional distress that leads him to hold off. What he wants to do is to institute a "scientific" experiment to determine whether the ghost is speaking the truth? Further, he is driven nearly mad and rendered unsure of what is "reality" not just by the injunction of the ghost to exact revenge, not just by the enormity of what the ghost has imparted to him, but by the fear that he is out of touch with reality because he has seen and communicated with a ghost. He is having the reaction which in one form or another occurs to many people who experience an apparition or a mediumistic communication in Western culture.

A Scientific Experiment: The Play Within the Play

Of course, the carefully devised scientific experiment is the "Mousetrap," the play within the play that Hamlet orchestrates, with which he hopes, in one fell swoop, to prove that the ghost is indeed the soul of his father and that, on top of that, the information the ghost has imparted about how Hamlet's father died is true. And the proof will reside in the reaction that the King has to the play, whereby his guilty conscience will give rise to some action that will give him away. However, Hamlet has not forgotten his prior hypothesis that the ghost may be the devil. Thus, in his first long soliloquy before the play, he specifically states: "The spirit that I have seen/May be a de'l, and the de'il hath power/T' assume a pleasing shape" (*Hamlet*, Act II, Sc. 2, lines 586–588).

In addition, Hamlet sets out in detail how his hypothesis will be proven, very much as a scientist might do, listing a series of events, which if they take place, will prove his cause. In that soliloquy, he states:

> I have heard
> That guilty creatures sitting at a play
> Have by the very cunning of the scene
> Been struck so to the soul that presently
> They have proclaim'd their malefactions
> … … I'll have these players
> Play something like the murther of my father
> Before mine uncle. I'll observe his looks;
> I'll tent him to the quick. If 'a do blench,
> I know my course.
> —*Hamlet*, Act II, Sc. 2, lines 576–586

In setting up the experiment later on, he enlists Horatio's aid as a fellow experimenter and observer, telling him what he is looking for as proof. Thus, he says to Horatio:

> There is a play to-night before the king.
> One scene of it comes near the circumstance
> Which I have told thee of my father's death.
> I prithee, when thou seest that act afoot,
> Even with the very comment of thy soul
> Observe my uncle.
>
> …
>
> Give him heedful note,
> For I mine eyes will rivet to his face,
> And after we will both our judgments join
> In censure of his seeming.
> —*Hamlet*, Act. III, Sc. 2, lines 75–83

That is, like a good scientist, he asks that there be an independent observer, beside himself, and that after the experiment, they compare notes.

In the midst of his careful instruction to Horatio, he states alternatively that the other hypothesis, the ghost as an evil entity, would be proven if the King has no reaction:

> … If his [the uncle's] occulted guilt
> Do not itself unkennel in one speech,
> It is a damned ghost that we have seen …
> —*Hamlet*, Act. III, Sc. 2, lines 75–77

And now the denouement: at the crucial point, when the nephew of the player King pours the poison in the player King's ear, the real King suddenly rises up, calls for lights, and departs precipitously. Hamlet and Horatio now do compare notes, and the first thing Hamlet says is: "I'll take the ghost's word for a thousand pounds. Dids't perceive?" To which Horatio agrees, and Hamlet adds: "Upon the talk of the poisoning?" To which Horatio also agrees, saying: "I did very well note him" (*Hamlet*, Act III, Sc. 2, lines 292–296). Thus, Hamlet, the tortured parapsychologist and his assistant Horatio have successfully completed their experiment.

Or have they? For Shakespeare is too wily a playwright and too insightful a human observer, to make matters so simple for us or for Hamlet. What he does next is brilliant and even more truthful to psi phenomena than what has proceeded it. Hamlet takes the information he has learned from the ghost—and confirmed experimentally—to his mother; and he confronts her with that information: what his uncle has done, and by extension what his mother unwittingly has done in marrying the man who killed her husband. He verbally attacks his uncle the King to his mother and then accuses her as well with the most violent words, such as: "to live in the rank sweat of an enseamed bed, stewed in corruption, honeying and making love over the nasty sty" (*Hamlet*, Act III, Sc. 4, lines 101–104). Over and over, his mother—now realizing she has married her husband's murderer—entreats her son to accuse her "no more": "O Hamlet, speak no more! Thou turn'st mine eyes into my very soul: And there I see such black and grained spots as will not leave their tinct" (*Hamlet*, Act III, Sc. 4, lines 97–100).

And it is now that the ghost enters once again and for the last time, entreating Hamlet to be less cruel to his mother. But this time, it is different, because this time the ghost is *not* a shared apparition. Whereas before, when there were three or four people present, the ghost was seen by everyone and thus was taken not to be the product of a hallucinating mind but to be "real" (just because it was a shared apparition); this time with two people present only Hamlet sees it. His mother neither sees nor hears it. And so she concludes that the original hypothesis suggested in the play *does* apply to the ghost: it is an hallucination and not even a shared one. Even further, she concludes that the ghost is a symptom of Hamlet's madness. This is the exchange in which Hamlet, again like a scientist, explores both the verbal and visual aspects of the experience he is having:

> The Queen: To whom do you speak this?
> Hamlet: Do you see nothing there?
> The Queen: Nothing at all; yet all that is I see.
> Hamlet: Nor did you nothing hear?
> The Queen: No, nothing but ourselves.
> —*Hamlet*, Act III, Sc. 4, lines 148–149

The ghost, to Hamlet's anguish, then departs while Hamlet implores his mother to see it as it leaves. And the Queen can only conclude: "This is the very coinage of your brain: This bodiless creation ecstasy is very cunning in" (*Hamlet*, Act. III, Sc. 4, lines 153–155).

How ironic and for two reasons. The first is that the interchange that precedes her conclusion about Hamlet's madness is all about "seeing." In trying to persuade his mother of her perfidy and her unwillingness to see what the King his uncle has done and what she has done, Hamlet asks her repeatedly: "Have you eyes?" He says it has been as if she is playing blind man's bluff or "hoodman-blind." He elaborates further that she has "Eyes without feeling, feeling without sight." And in emotional torment, she finally does confess to her son that she has been unseeing and in denial. And then, all of a sudden, the ghost appears. And this, this she truly *cannot* see.

And how ironic again because up until this point, Shakespeare has built an argument in which Hamlet scientifically explores the phenomenon of the ghost and learns information from the ghost in the process. The ghost and the information the ghost imparts to Hamlet drive the drama. And it is with this ghostly communicated information, verified by the play-within-a-play experiment, that Hamlet confronts his mother and does so in such a manner that she believes the information, although unaware that it was imparted to Hamlet by the ghost. And then Hamlet finds to his distress that the *phenomenon that drove him and the drama forward changes at the penultimate moment:* the ghost appears once again but now no longer a shared phenomenon! His mother does not perceive it. Worse, his mother accuses him of being mad *for* seeing it, whereas at the beginning the shared apparition was accepted by Horatio and the two soldiers. One is reminded here of how elusive psi phenomena can be, how it defies the repeatable experiment. For example, the Serios phenomena—the psychic photography of a wonderfully talented psychic— suddenly changed and ceased to take place after being accepted by many observers and explored scientifically.

As previously stated, one can understand why Hamlet would wonder about his sanity, even as he plays with the concept of being mad—wonder about it not only because of the emotional distress that comes from realizing that his uncle has killed his father and bedded his mother—but because the ghostly phenomena (phenomena which lead Hamlet as it would anyone to question what he sees, not knowing whence they come) seem at one minute true and capable of being shared with others, and the next minute seemingly unsharable and therefore unverifiable, and more in the nature of an halluci- nation that emanates solely from his distraught imagination.

Hamlet, 19th-Century Psychic Research and Tyrrell

In 1882, the Society for Psychical Research proposed a massive "census of halluci- nations" which was conducted years later. The number of collectors involved in the census was 410 and 17,000 people answered the census. Each person was asked "Have you ever, when believing yourself to be completely awake, had a vivid impression of seeing or being touched by a living being or inanimate object, or of hearing a voice; which impres- sion, as far as you could discover, was not due to any external physical cause." Roughly 10 percent of those questioned (1,684) replied "yes." Details of each of these cases was acquired. For example, there were 1087 cases of visual hallucinations; in only 95 of these cases however was the visual hallucination collectively perceived (out of a total of 283 cases in which the visual hallucination was perceived while someone else was present). Each case was then examined. The amount of effort that took place to garner this infor- mation was formidable and has never been equaled.

As a consequence of this effort, three seminal works on hallucinations have been published. The voluminous *Phantasms of the Living* by Gurney, Myers and Podmore; the equally voluminous *Human Personality and Its Survival of Bodily Death*, by F.W.H. Myers; and a small gem of a study (using the data from the census and the two books) by G.N.M. Tyrrell—with an introduction by the psychologist Gardner Murphy—and entitled very simply *Apparitions*. The first of these works deals—as its title suggests—with telepathy and apparitions of the living (there are many examples of these as ghosts are not actually just of the dead); the second deals with apparitions of the dead.

The hypotheses concerning the nature of these hallucinations in these three works were various (just as *Hamlet*'s hypotheses were various). But there is one hypothesis concerning apparitions of the dead which does not appear in *Hamlet*, but which is crucial and that is (for want of a better word) the "super-telepathy" hypothesis, favored by Tyrell but not by F.W.H. Myers. In *Hamlet*, one could apply the "super-telepathy" hypothesis in a number of ways. The most obvious would be that the uncle who killed his brother felt guilty for the deed and that as a consequence he unconsciously communicated to the King's son Hamlet, through an unconscious orchestration that involved others as well, that he had murdered his father. The ghost was the result. Or one could hypothesize that Hamlet's father at the point of being murdered communicated unconsciously to his son through a similar orchestration, and that subsequently a "deferred" apparition of the father appeared to Hamlet. These hypotheses obviate the need to think of the ghost as an actual "spirit" entity. It may be that there is something unsatisfying from the point of view of a dynamic story-line about the two variants of these hypotheses (although there is something dramatically compelling to think that the King, out of guilt, manages to communicate his crime unconsciously to Hamlet). Certainly, it is more compelling in some ways to suggest that there is at the very least a remnant of personality that survives death, what Tyrell refers to as an "idea pattern." But the most economical explanation, since telepathy appears to exist under many circumstances, is that of "super-telepathy" and the two variants of it that I have suggested. This is why it is not necessary to presume that the ghost is a spirit at all.

The Modern Day Parapsychologists

One wonders: why would not modern parapsychologists in general take as one of their references Shakespeare's *Hamlet* and even claim Hamlet as one of their own? Why would they not plumb the depths of this singular and great drama, that represents modern man, for its parapsychological aspects, and shout from the proverbial rooftop that their science is represented in this great work? Perhaps it is because such references are outside of the experimental investigations that modern day parapsychologists favor in which psychics or ordinary people seek to influence meaningless micro events. In fact, it is one of the failures of modern day parapsychology that it too often chooses to ignore what has been referred to as macro psi phenomenon in favor of the minor; and to concentrate on the small experiment for which there is little motivation to succeed on the part of the participant, whether talented psychic or ordinary person. *Hamlet*, on the other hand, *is* about macro-psi—a drama of passion in which the desire to find out the truth, on the part of the hero, is palpable and compelling, which may explain in the first place why the ghost does appear bearing its terrible and psi-mediated secret. Thus *Hamlet*, one of the central dramas of Western culture, speaks to all of us of parapsychological phenomena, but all too often we have chosen not to hear the voice of the Stratford bard.[3]

Notes

1. Two valuable and underappreciated exceptions to the tendency to treat the psychic phenomena in Shakespeare as metaphor or "poetic license" rather than reality are Sherman Yellen's article "The Psychic

World of William Shakespeare" (Yellen, 1970) and L.W. Rogers' "The Ghosts in Shakespeare" (Rogers, 1995). This chapter draws much upon their work, particularly that of the unheralded Yellen.

  2. Fifty years ago as an undergraduate and English major, I shared English classes (although not about Shakespeare) with Stephen Greenblatt, who was already a talented commentator.

  3. All *Hamlet* references are from *The Tragedy of Hamlet* in W.L. Cross and T. Brooke (eds.) *The Yale Shakespeare*, pp. 975–1024. New York: Barnes and Noble, 1975.

References

Cross, W.L., and T. Brooke, eds. (1975). *The Yale Shakespeare*. New York: Barnes and Noble.

Eissler, K.R. (1971). *Discourse on Hamlet and Hamlet: A psychoanalytic inquiry*. New York: International Universities Press.

Freud, S. (1919). The uncanny. *Standard Edition*. Vol. XVII, pp. 217–256.

Greenblatt, S. (2001). *Hamlet in purgatory*. Princeton: Princeton University Press.

Greenblatt, S. (2004) *Will in the world: How Shakespeare became Shakespeare*. New York: W.W. Norton.

Gurney, E., Myers F.W.H. & Podmore, F. (1886). *Phantasms of the living*. Volume I. London: Trubner and Co. (Reprint 2012, Lexington: Forgotten Books).

Lacan J. (1977). Desire and interpretation of desire in Hamlet. In J. Hulbert (ed.) Yale French Studies, No. 55/56 *Literature and psychoanalysis: The question of reading otherwise*, pp. 11–52.

Mayer, J. (2006). *Shakespeare's hybrid faith: History, religion and the stage*. New York: Palgrave Macmillan.

Myers. F.W.H. (1907). *Human personality and its survival of bodily death*. New York: Longmans, Green and Co.

Rogers, L.W. (1995). *The ghosts in Shakespeare*. Whitefish, MT: Kessinger Publishing.

Tyrell, G.N.M. (1963). *Apparitions*. New York: Collier.

Yellen, S. (1970). The psychic world of William Shakespeare. In Angoff, A. (ed.) *The psychic force: Excursions in parapsychology*. New York: G.P. Putnam & Sons, pp. 267–288.

TWO

Psi Phenomena and Tolstoy

Introduction

From 1873 to 1877, Leo Tolstoy wrote *Anna Karenina* (1960a). Enmeshed in the body of this work, but in such a manner that the full extent of them may entirely escape the reader's detection, are psi phenomena, including psi correspondences in dreams, psi-related hypnagogic visions, precognitive dreams, and psi-dynamic "coincidences." Further, the inclusion of the phenomena occurs in such a way to make it apparent that Tolstoy was fully aware of substitutions and condensations in dreams, of the use of residues (both prior and precognitive) taken from the experience of the individual dreamer, and of cross correspondences between the dreams of individuals. In addition, the phenomena are integral to one of the crucial denouements of the story: the death of Anna Karenina. In other words, they are an essential part of the novel's structure.

I highlighted the dates 1873 to 1877 on purpose. It must be remembered that the early investigators of psi phenomena, in the seventeenth, eighteenth, and nineteenth centuries, came to them only as an interesting spin-off of the mesmeric or hypnotic state (Dingwall, 1968). Deeper and more encompassing work appeared later: *Phantasms of the Living* (Gurney, Myers, and Podmore) not until 1886; Freud's seminal excursion into dream interpretation not until 1900 and his articles on psi two or more decades later (1922, 1933); and Warcollier's too often neglected work with telepathic drawing experiments not until 1921. Yet one can find in *Anna Karenina* many of the essential discoveries that have surfaced repeatedly in the scientific study of certain types of psi phenomena, most recently in the work of the Maimonides Dream Laboratory (Ullman and Krippner, with Vaughan, 1973). And one can find these phenomena not as characteristic of a particular hypnotic state, nor as isolated, glaring instances, but as somehow integral to the way life is put together.

That a creative artist such as Tolstoy should come upon these insights so early is not surprising. Freud himself was fond of saying that many of his psychological discoveries had been anticipated, albeit in less systematized form, in the work of great authors. What *is* surprising is that Tolstoy's work seems to have eluded modern-day parapsychologists. I suspect that the primary reason for this lies, ironically, in the fact that the novel has been so successful that it has become a "classic." As a result, it tends to be read very early in one's educational experience and before the development of an interest in parapsychology.

The psi phenomena in *Anna Karenina* focus over and over upon one theme: the nature of the suicidal death that the confused heroine eventually chooses. Near the end of the novel, in a final attempt to escape the psychological strain of living with her lover, Count Vronsky, while still married to her husband, Karenina, Anna throws herself under a moving freight train. Each instance of psi phenomena, directed toward this event, is intertwined with the other instances.

Fatal Coincidental Meeting

The first instance of psi-mediated events is the initial "coincidental" meeting between Anna and her lover-to-be, Vronsky. Anna, a vibrant society woman of nineteenth-century Russia, meets Vronsky, a horseman in the Russian guard, at a railroad station in Moscow. She has been sharing her train compartment "by chance" with Vronsky's mother; in turn, Vronsky and Oblonsky (Anna's brother), awaiting the arrival of the train, meet "by chance" at the station, and they greet both passengers. As they leave together, people are rushing through the station and it is evident something is wrong. A guard has been run over. Vronsky and Oblonsky go to view his mangled body, returning with the news that he was the sole support of a large family and his widow in her grief has flung herself on his corpse. Anna becomes noticeably agitated and asks if anything can be done for the widow. Upon hearing Anna's question, Vronsky goes off to the stationmaster to give money for the widow. Thus, the first meeting of Anna and Vronsky is intimately connected with an accidental railroad death which occurs at the same time and place.

Premonition

In fact, the whole incident has an immediate and pronounced effect upon Anna. As she leaves the station in a carriage with Oblonsky "her lips were trembling and ... she was holding back tears with difficulty.... 'It's a bad omen,' she said." Then she asks Oblonsky questions about her new acquaintance, Count Vronsky.

Years later, when Anna is living unhappily with Vronsky while separated from her husband (in a Russia which was hardly sympathetic to the concept of divorce), she is at the end of her emotional tether. Seeing that Vronsky's ardor for her has cooled, she alternates in increasingly violent fashion between despairing thoughts of revenge upon him and thoughts of passionate love for him. In the midst of one of her despairing moods, she finds herself at the Obiralovka railroad station after traveling by train from Moscow in needless and panicky pursuit of Vronsky. At this point, when everything to her seems blackest, she sees a means of escape:

> And suddenly as she recalled the man who had been run over the day she first met Vronsky, she realized what she had to do. With a quick, light stride she descended the step that went ... to the rails and stopped next to the train that was passing right beside her.... There—right in the middle! I'll punish him and escape from everyone and from myself ... [Part 7, Ch. 31].

And she throws herself under the passing freight train.

To bring matters entirely full circle, Vronsky rushes to the railroad station only in time to view her mangled corpse laid out on a table in a railway shed, a sad reminder of the mangled corpse that he viewed at their first meeting.

The connection between Anna's initial meeting with Vronsky, the premonition which accompanied it, and her final suicidal death is made explicit by Tolstoy and can hardly be missed. But Tolstoy has been a careful craftsman and in numerous ways he has never let go of the psychic innuendo in that first fatal meeting.

Hypnagogic Vision

For example, when Anna leaves Moscow by rail, after meeting Vronsky for the second time at a dance, she dozes in her seat and has a hypnagogic vision in which the people in the train undergo a transformation:

> [The] peasant in the long coat started gnawing something on the wall, the old woman began stretching her legs out the whole length of the carriage and filling it up with a black cloud; *then something squeaked and pounded in a terrifying way as though someone were being torn to bits* [emphasis mine]; a scarlet flame blinded her eyes, and everything was hidden by a wall. Anna had felt as though she were falling all the way down. But it wasn't at all terrifying, it was gay. The voice of the bundled-up, snow-covered man shouted something just above her ear. She stood up and came to her senses; she realized that they had come to a station and that this was the conductor [Part 1, Ch. 29].

This vision of something squeaking and pounding as if someone is being torn to bits is a further suggestion of the manner of Anna's own impending death. What is revealing is that she feels "gay" when such a vision might more appropriately have a terrifying affect.

Psi Correspondences in Dreams

Tolstoy then adds another psychic feature to the already determined fate of his heroine. Vronsky, living alone, lies down on a sofa after lunch and becomes drowsy:

> Five minutes later the recollection of the grotesque scenes he had been present at during the preceding week were jumbled up and mingled with images of Anna and of the peasant who had played an important part in the bear hunt as beater. Vronsky fell asleep; he woke up in the dark, trembling with fear, and hastily lighted a candle. What was that? What was it? What was that terrifying thing I saw in the dream? Yes, yes…. I remember that beater, the peasant, a dirty little fellow with a matted beard, bending over doing something; suddenly he started saying some peculiar words in French. Yes, that was all there was in the dream, he said to himself; but then why was it so horrifying? He vividly recalled the peasant again and the incomprehensible French words he had pronounced; a chill of horror ran down his spine.
> What nonsense! thought Vronsky, and looked at his watch [Part 4, Ch. 2].

As yet, the significance of this dream does not appear, either to Vronsky or to the reader, and Tolstoy lets the sleeping dog lie until the next chapter. But Vronsky's reaction to the dream is quite interesting: First, he exhibits the typical denial reaction of one who is threatened by the idea that a dream may be determined in some way and more than meaningless fantasy. Second, he is troubled by the riddle posed by the dream: Why should a muttering peasant be terrifying?

In the next chapter, comes a partial denouement. Anna, very upset, speaks to Vronsky of her feeling that she shall die and thus provide a solution to her problems:

> "I'm going to die. I had a dream."
> "A dream?" Vronsky repeated; in a flash he recalled the peasant in his own dream.
> "Yes, a dream," she said. "A dream I had a long time ago. I dreamed I was running into my bedroom, where I had to get some-thing, or find out something; you know how it is in dreams," she said, her eyes opening wide with horror, "and there was something in the bedroom standing in the corner."
> "Oh what rubbish! How can you believe—"

But she didn't let herself be stopped; what she was saying was too important for her.

"This something turned around; I saw it was a peasant with a matted beard, small and terrible-looking. I wanted to run away, but he stooped over a sack and began fumbling about in it with his hands—"

She showed how he fumbled about in the sack. Her face was full of horror, and Vronsky, recalling his own dream, felt the same horror filling his soul.

"He fumbled about and muttered something in French, quickly, quickly, and you know, rolling his r's: 'It must be beaten, the iron, pounded, kneaded.' And I was terrified, and I tried to wake up, wake up, but when I woke up I was still in a dream. I began asking myself what it all meant. And Korney said to me: 'Childbirth, childbirth, you're going to die in childbirth, ma'am.' Then I woke up...."

"What rubbish, what rubbish!" said Vronsky, but he felt himself that his voice lacked all conviction [Part 4, Ch. 3].

Truly, this is a remarkable document. To begin with, Tolstoy makes the dream a recurrent one, which is a sign of a dream's significance both psychoanalytically and parapsychologically. Then, he has a deft example of psi correspondence in the two dreams; not too close a correspondence, but a correspondence of some elements:

Vronsky	Anna
A peasant	A peasant
With a matted beard	With a matted beard
Little fellow	Small
Dirty	Terrible looking
Bending over doing something	Stooped over a sack
Speaking peculiar	Muttering in French,
incomprehensible French	quickly, rolling his r's
The peasant is the beater	Saying, "It must be beaten, the iron, pounded, kneaded."

Certain aspects of this psi correspondence deserve pinpointing, for they indicate that Tolstoy had an intuitive grasp of some important features of the subconscious since noted by parapsychological or psychoanalytic investigators. First, the correspondences in the dreams are based on unique data available to each individual: that is, Vronsky's bear beater, which is a residue of his day's events, shows up in his dream and corresponds to the peasant in Anna's dream who, while in her bedroom, speaks about beating. Second, a "beating in the bedroom"—from a psychoanalytic viewpoint—represents a classic distortion of what is referred to as the "primal scene," where a young child, as witness to parental intercourse and so predisposed by temperament and circumstance, may undergo the type of trauma which ultimately leads to suicide in adulthood. Third, what to me is most interesting, the feeling of terror associated with the muttering peasant in Vronsky's dream is not decipherable without knowledge of the content of Anna's similar dream (in which the interpretation is that Anna will die). This last characteristic of psi correspondence in dreams has been noted in particular by Eisenbud (1970) and used by him in the process of understanding the dynamics in the relationship among psi-mediated dreams of psychoanalytic patients.

Precognitive Dreams

These ominous dreams have a very tight fit into the final chapter of Anna's story. To begin with, Anna almost does die in childbirth: she is so seriously ill that Vronsky and Karenina rush to her bedside entertaining thoughts that they are at her deathbed. She recovers. Thus, while the dream is precognitive of grave illness during child-birth, the interpretation in the dream that Anna will die in childbirth is wrong.

Instead, the prediction in the dream comes to fruition with a vengeance on the day of Anna's suicide. That morning she awakens from having dreamt again of the little old man beating the iron bar. Tolstoy explicitly states that she has had this nightmare "even before her liaison with Vronsky." She does not know what the old man is doing with the iron bar but it is "something dreadful." (Analytically, this is easily interpreted as fear of the phallus during intercourse.) That evening, when on impulse she decides to join Vronsky at his mother's estate, she gazes out of her train window as she awaits departure from the Moscow station and sees a peasant resembling only too closely the stooping peasant in her dream:

> A grimy, hunched-over peasant in a cap, from under which his tousled hair was sticking out, passed by this window, stooping over the carriage wheels. There's something familiar about that misshapen peasant, thought Anna. Then she recalled her dream, and shuddering with fear she went to the opposite door [Part 7, Ch. 31].

Then a couple enters her compartment, a husband and wife who begin conversing with each other in French. The mutual and self hatred that emerges from their conversation appalls Anna and she sees them as a tortured pair bent upon injuring each other. However, one sentence that the wife speaks in French catches her ear: "Reason was given man to help him escape his anxiety." This phrase fills her thoughts and she uses it as a spring-board for her suicide attempt. It should be remembered that the peasant in the dreams spoke in French as well.

When Anna arrives at the Obiralovka station, still thinking along these lines, she realizes how she can escape her troubles. Here she is about to commit suicide:

> [S]he didn't take her eyes off the wheels of the second car, which were coming nearer. And just at that moment, when the middle point between the wheels drew level with her, she flung aside the red hand-bag and drawing her head down between her shoulders she fell underneath the car on her hands, and with a light movement, as though she were preparing to get up again at once, she sank to her knees. And just at this moment she was honor-struck by what she was doing. Where am I? What am I doing? Why? She tried to get up, to throw herself back, but something huge and implacable struck her on the head and dragged her down. "Lord, forgive me for everything!" she murmured, feeling the impossibility of struggling.... *A little peasant was working at the rails muttering something to himself* [emphasis mine]. And the candle by which she had been reading that book that is filled with anxiety, deceit, sorrow, and evil flared up with a brighter flame than ever before, lighted up everything for her that had previously been in darkness, flickered, dimmed, and went out forever [Part 7, Ch. 31].

There is the final psi connection: A little peasant muttering something to himself. One might further hypothesize that the beating of the iron and the sound of the rolling r's in French, in her dream, referred to a klang association to the sound of a freight train. In other words, not only were the dreams telepathically related, they were both precognitive as well.

Comparing the elements of the dreams with the elements of the suicide, one gets the following psi correspondences:

Dreams	*Future Events*
A peasant	A peasant at the Moscow station; a peasant on the rails at Obiralovka
Dirty	Grimy peasant at Moscow station
Terrible looking	Misshapen peasant at Moscow station

Dreams	Future Events
Little	Little peasant at Obiralovka
Bending over doing something; stooped over a sack	Peasant at Moscow stooping over wheels; at Obiralovka working on rails
Muttering	Muttering peasant on rails at Obliralovka
Speaking French	Fellow passengers speaking French
Peasant is bear beater; peasant is beating iron	Peasant working on rails at Obliralovka; sound of train
Prediction of death in childbirth	Nearly fatal illness at childbirth; subsequent suicidal death

This condensation of a number of future events into a dream seems to be a characteristic of precognitive dreams just as it is a characteristic of dreams which take remnants of past days' events and fuse them together. In addition, Tolstoy seems well aware of a fact that parapsychologists have learned through the years: that psi and precognitive phenomena are usually built up from the smallest, seemingly irrelevant details. The construction of the two dreams illustrates this, nowhere more so than in the dream detail of the muttering peasant which so inexplicably terrifies Vronsky and Anna. Only at the last moment does Tolstoy play this, his ace card, throwing it out without comment as if it were an afterthought.

It is hardly likely that the appearance of the peasants and the couple speaking French is just an accident of the writing. Tolstoy was an infuriatingly painstaking writer; he revised repeatedly to the extent of reworking what were supposed to be final proofs so that the page became an almost illegible scrawl. A contemporary editor, working with Tolstoy to prepare a separate edition of *Anna Karenina,* commented:

> Leo Nikolaevich firmly defended every last word he had written and did not agree to what seemed to be the most innocent changes. From his explanations, I became convinced that he values his language to an unusual degree, in spite of the apparent nonchalance and unevenness of his style. He thinks about every single word, every turn of phrase, no less than the most punctilious poet [Strakhov, 1970, p. 753].

Tolstoy's attention to fine detail combined with an admirable subtlety have made his depiction of psi phenomena remarkably lifelike. In fact, there is an added benefit: the phenomena tend to register subconsciously rather than consciously upon the reader, as such phenomena tend to do in reality. As a result, Anna's act of suicide has a convincing sense of logic and inevitability.

Precognition of Tolstoy's Death

There is an irony to the appearance of the precognitive phenomena in Anna Karenina: 33 years after writing the novel, Tolstoy died under circumstances which have a remarkable resemblance to the death of his heroine. He did not throw himself under the wheels of a passing train, but he did expire at a railroad station and how he got there is a revealing story. In other words, aspects of the fictional death envisioned by Tolstoy were precognitive of Tolstoy's own death, or, put in another fashion, the very writing of the novel seems to have been part of a process which suggested to Tolstoy "how to die." Such juxtapositions between an artist's work and his future life have been cited many times before (Greenhouse, 1971; Tenhaeff, 1972) but what is somewhat unique about this instance is that we have available a vast storehouse of data which permits us to more readily comprehend the psychological dynamics in Tolstoy's life that helped to determine his manner of death.[1]

However brilliant Tolstoy was in his novels, as a man he was egomaniacal and tortured. No doubt, one of the determining factors in his personality was the death of his mother from illness less than a month before his second birthday. This abrupt departure of his mother (who apparently was very much devoted to her youngest son) at such a dependent time during his life seems to have afflicted Tolstoy with a lifelong ambivalence toward mother figures and women in general. As will be seen, nowhere is this more evident than in Tolstoy's relationship to his wife.

On January 5, 1872,[2] a year before beginning *Anna Karenina,* Tolstoy had a revealing impulse, the desire to see the dead body of a woman. The woman, the mistress of a neighbor of Tolstoy, had committed suicide upon discovering that her lover had decided to marry his children's governess. She threw herself under a freight train at the little station of Yasenki on the Moscow-Kursk railway line. Before she did so, she sent a note to her lover: "You are my murderer. Be happy, if an assassin can be happy. If you like, you can see my corpse on the rails at Yasenki." Out of curiosity, Tolstoy went to see the autopsy, which was performed in a railway shed at Yasenki station (Troyat, 1967, pp. 343–344). Evidently this incident had a marked effect upon Tolstoy: it sparked the writing of *Anna Karenina* and became one of its central motifs; in fact, Vronsky's viewing of Anna's body in the railway shed at Obiralovka is taken directly from Tolstoy's experience. It is not hard to see to whom Tolstoy must have associated upon seeing the corpse.

What is further interesting is that Tolstoy's creativity, which was at its height in the writing of *Anna Karenina,* occurred at a time when he was surrounded by death. For 11 years prior, no death touched the Tolstoy household, but within three years, 1873 to 1875, during the writing of the novel, Tolstoy lost three children and two dearly loved aunts due to a variety of ailments—all expiring within the Tolstoy house. The aunts represented, by Tolstoy's own admission, one of his last contacts with the memory of his mother.[3] His reaction to all this was to mention the deaths as minor incidents in the most cursory fashion, to be annoyed at the inconvenience of the funerals, and to throw himself with deeper conviction into his work of creation: *Anna Karenina.*[4] One can ascribe various theories to what lay behind his behavior, including the theory that his need to plunge himself into creative work represented extreme sublimation of his grief, or even the theory that his need to begin a work of devoted creation at this time resulted from some subconscious, precognitive perception that death was about to take a fantastic toll. Or one could go even a step further, for the dynamics here are suspiciously similar to those which Eisenbud (1975) has recently observed in the psychology of the writer Florence Marryat, who seemed to create personalities not only of paper and ink but of ectoplasm. That is, Tolstoy may have had a strong strain of "Typhoid Mary" in him, his need to create being compensation for a need to destroy those closest to him through subconscious, psychokinetic aggression. In light of what eventually became Tolstoy's very conscious desire to preside over the destruction of his wife, this theory becomes less far-fetched.

Regardless, Tolstoy had an overwhelming passion to control the processes of life and death.[5] After writing *Anna Karenina,* this neurotic need to control began to take on characteristics of pathological proportions. Having in his novel created a celebration of life filled with all manner of sensuality, Tolstoy increasingly devoted himself to a life of asceticism and to a denunciation of the "immoral" work he had labored to create. Just as he created and destroyed the central feminine character of his novel, he seemed bent on creating and then through his denunciations destroying the novel itself.

His increasing asceticism took many forms: wealthy and living on his own estate, he preached a doctrine of sacrifice and self-imposed poverty and wrote numerous religious tracts (Tolstoy, 1960b). He interposed a political fanatic by the name of Chertkov into his family life and defended the cause of a religious sect known as the Dukhobors who were persecuted by Tsar Alexander I. Their doctrine resembled his: they advocated chastity, vegetarianism, abstinence from tobacco and alcohol, pooling of all goods and property, and non-violence. While Tolstoy in the midst of his asceticism did accomplish certain magnanimous, even brave, deeds and openly challenged the Tsar's authority at a time that the winds of revolution were in the air, make no mistake about where the brunt of his self-denial lay: against his wife.

Two examples of this will make the point. In August 1906, Sonya—Tolstoy's wife—was critically ill at the Tolstoy estate with a fibroma and an eminent surgeon, Professor Snegirev, came to the estate to operate on her. Tolstoy, however, was overwhelmed by the spiritual beauty of his wife as she faced death and furious at the idea of not permitting her to meet her maker "in a sublimely religious state of mind." As peritonitis set in, the surgeon, who had been hesitating, decided that he must operate and asked Tolstoy's permission. Tolstoy initially refused and when the surgeon protested that without an operation she would surely die, he angrily said, "Do as you please." The operation was a success, but Tolstoy saw it differently: "My God! What a dreadful thing! Why can't they let people die in peace! A poor woman lashed to her bed with her stomach cut open and no pillow! It's torture!" (Troyat, 1967, pp. 594–595).

The second example is equally vivid, but lies in another psycho-logical area. In 1889 Tolstoy completed *The Kreutzer Sonata* (Tolstoi, 1929), an adaptation of an unfinished short story of his called "The Man Who Murdered His Wife." The story, which is a first-person confession by a train passenger on how he murdered his wife, contains paeans to the virtues of sexual abstinence and attacks upon the institution of marriage. The fact is that many of the incidents are taken from the marriage relationship of Leo and Sonya Tolstoy. Troyat (1967) nicely summarizes the background of this story:

> [Tolstoy] unhesitatingly offers up to the public the secrets of his periods of rut, his quarrels, his loathing; he flings open their bedroom door. And he knew perfectly well that his readers, who were accustomed to the autobiographical element in his writing, would identify Sonya with the victim, and that some would pity her and others mock her. How was it that he, who professed to be filled with loving kindness for his fellow creatures, who was continually afraid of inadvertently hurting anyone's feelings, did not imagine what an unspeakable humiliation he would inflict upon his life-partner by publishing this book?
>
> Whether unwittingly or out of conscious cruelty, he did more than merely publish it: he gave the manuscript to her to read and copy in her own hand. On July 4, 1889, he wrote in his diary, "Sonya is copying it and is very much affected by it!" Singular gift for a silver wedding anniversary [p. 478].

Tolstoy, who in *Anna Karenina* pleaded the glory of marital affection, not only painted a different picture in his later work but in his later life. Chastity became the ultimate self-denial. Whenever he could not maintain this ideal, he became furious with himself. In his diary he repeatedly wrote about having "fallen" in the night, that is, having had sexual intercourse with his wife. For example, "The devil fell upon me.... The next day, the morning of the 30th, I slept badly. It was so loathsome, as after a crime."[6] And, writing to his translator, Alymer Maude: "I was myself a husband last night but there is no reason for abandoning the struggle. God may grant me not to be so again" (Simmons, 1946, pp. 493–494).

The destructive need which underlies Tolstoy's actions in the sexual arena can be seen from a number of perspectives. The most obvious one is that the logical consequence of universal chastity is the destruction of the human species. Tolstoy—never one to do things, even chastity, in moderation—was more than willing to accept this. If it was God's will, so be it. Nothing daunted, he wrote, "What is it that revolts men in the idea that righteous life will also bring the race to an end?" (Lavrin, 1948, Ch. IX). But while Tolstoy's aggressions may appear nicely democratic, they are most particularly visited upon his wife in her role as a mother figure. Tolstoy's wish to deny her his penis represents the desire to punish her as surrogate mother for what subconsciously he perceives as her "betrayal" in dying. The constellation of characteristics that make up the internalized concept of the "mother" initially derives from the mother's breast upon which the infant is dependent. Thus, Tolstoy's subconscious equation, in the *lex talionis* style to which the subconscious inevitably subscribes, reads: "I will withdraw my penis from you to punish you for your withdrawal of your breast from me."

The variety of instances I have recounted should not obscure the basic fact that Tolstoy's asceticism is the product of constant posturing. This posturing results from Tolstoy's almost unbearable anxiety in the face of death, an anxiety which, growing out of the sudden traumatic death of an early and deeply loved object, more and more afflicted him as he approached another death: his own. Thus, the increase in his posturing as he got older is a reaction in large part to what must have been his growing realization that his own creative powers, physical, artistic and sexual, were gradually and inevitably declining (Crankshaw, 1974, pp. 171 ff.). In fact, he was never to produce on the same scale a work which approached the artistic magnitude of *Anna Karenina*, completed when he was 49. Unable to stem the inevitable tide, Tolstoy seems to have settled on the course of pretending to control it by making a virtue out of the loss; in effect, he determined to preside at his own funeral.

Sonya Tolstoy

Tolstoy's wife, Sonya, who entirely subordinated herself to her husband and family: "I am so used to living not my own life but the life of Lyova and the children," she wrote in her diary (S. Tolstoy, 1928[?], p. 247), performed herculean tasks: she bore 13 children; managed the household and estate; acted as her husband's secretary, editor, and even publisher; looked after the children's education, and in times of illness nursed her family—including Leo (Asquith, 1961). But as she found her control of Tolstoy slipping away and her way of life threatened by his desire to give up material wealth, she panicked. She wrote an answer to *The Kreutzer Sonata* (1929), which she almost published, called "Who Is to Blame?," in which she depicted her husband as a sensual brute; she copied out the diaries of Tolstoy's youth, working herself into rages of jealousy over his numerous sexual adventures before they were married ("Marriage cannot be happy after the husband's debauchery," she wrote. "He doesn't realize my purity alone saved us from perdition" [S. Tolstoy, 1928(?), p. 262]); she cultivated a platonic relationship with a young pianist and repeatedly invited him to the estate (the third party in *The Kreutzer Sonata* was a violinist) until Tolstoy, intensely jealous, threatened divorce; and most of all, she became progressively more nagging, more given to hysterical scenes and outbursts, and more inclined to attempt to control her husband's every action (A. Tolstoy, 1953). Finally, at her wit's end as her prize inevitably followed his inclinations (he has "again taken the bit in his teeth," she once wrote when Tolstoy went for a walking tour [Simmons, 1946, p. 428]), she began to threaten and make numerous suicide gestures to rein him in. In this strangely dependent, tragic-comic, love-hate relationship, nothing—as we have seen—was more likely to reach to the core of Tolstoy's anxieties.

Tolstoy's Finale

The relationship with his wife came to a head as Tolstoy approached the time of his death. After many thoughts of doing so, and tentative attempts, at the age of 82 Tolstoy decided to leave his wealthy estate and his wife of 48 years. With his personal physician, he surreptitiously left one night in 1910 and took a train to a monastery. Finding this an uncertain refuge, and fearful that Sonya would discover him there, he again left three days later by train with an undefined destination. He fell ill on the train, and had to be removed at a tiny, obscure railroad station on the Moscow-Tula line: Astapovo. No hotel was in the town, but the stationmaster offered Tolstoy a room in his house facing the station. Here, Tolstoy's condition rapidly worsened and he expired within a week, mourned as if a saint by an entire nation. Meanwhile, his wife was denied entrance into the death house by the doctors and various family members (and Tolstoy, who requested the presence of others, including his followers, did not request hers) on the grounds that she would upset her husband too much. She had to stay in a nearby railway car until her husband was unconscious, unable to recognize her, beyond hope of recovery, and at the very point of death (S. Tolstoy, 1962; Troyat, 1967, pp. 668–696). His wife had acted as secretary in the many rewritings of *Anna Karenina*, sometimes working all night to copy out Tolstoy's almost indecipherable scribbling. And so, on November 7, 1910, Tolstoy died at a railroad station, estranged from the woman he had lived with most of his life, in a manner only too poignantly reminiscent in some of its details of that in his own novel: a death marked, it seems to me, by mutual cruelty between husband and wife not unlike the doomed relationship of Anna and Vronsky.

The psychological logic of this end should not be missed. For the fact is that Tolstoy never "worked through" in the psychoanalytic sense the death of his own mother, death being equated by the sub-conscious with leaving and betrayal. Thus, Tolstoy progressively left his wife sexually, until he achieved his ultimate desire: to leave the surrogate-mother figure, Sonya, through death in a manner that was punishment for the mother's original leaving. In effect, the oft-debated motto to the beginning of *Anna Karenina*, "Vengeance is mine; I shall repay," was epitaph to Tolstoy's own life.

Conclusion

The manner of departing apparently suggested by the death of the neighbor's mistress and elaborated upon with parapsychological insight in the writing of *Anna Karenina* was ultimately acted out by Tolstoy. For our purposes, what is most interesting is that it was acted out with certain psi factors coming into play: How could Tolstoy know through sensory means that the stationmaster would put him up in his house? That his wife would be confined to a railway car at the station?[7] The extent to which his manner of death fit his psychological needs and the extent to which it resembled the original railroad death he had viewed, all this is intriguing evidence of the creative mechanism of the subconscious. More particularly, it suggests that the creative mechanism may in some way explain the existence of precognitive phenomena. Through the years, parapsychologists have noted instances in which a person has predicted his own death or someone has picked up precognitive data concerning another person's death (see, e.g., Saltmarsh, 1934). But the piling up of instances reaches a point of diminishing return (except for the skeptic who will never be convinced that such phenomena exist). The challenge, it seems to me, is to explore in depth the individual psychology which might help to explain the predictions.

Of course, we have little difficulty in determining that someone who commits suicide has orchestrated his manner of death, and psychiatrists are constantly peeling away psychic layers to reveal that certain seemingly "accidental deaths" were a product of an individual's desire to expose himself to a dangerous situation. But Tolstoy's precognition of his own death is intriguing evidence that precognitive psi phenomena are part of an orchestration by the sub-conscious whereby (given the physical limitations of the world, whatever they may be) that final event to which each of us looks with a mixture of dread and fascination is in some of its dynamics determined by us.

Notes

1. The material on Tolstoy is voluminous (his complete works alone compose 90 volumes). Tolstoy was an inveterate diary keeper as was his entire family and he has been well-biographed since. I would hesitate to venture into this thicket if not for the fact that I have nowhere seen the particular dynamics that I am emphasizing, although Troyat (1967) does everything but take the final plunge. Troyat has been criticized for inaccuracies (A.L. Tolstoy, 1968), but his psychological insights seem to me far superior to those of other commentators.

2. I am using here the Julian calendar, which was employed in Russia until after the 1917 revolution. The Julian calendar is 12 days behind the Gregorian in the nineteenth century and 13 days behind in the twentieth.

3. On November 9, 1873, his youngest son Petya died at a year and a half; on June 20, 1874, his Aunt Toinette—who had become a mother to him after his mother's death—died in the Tolstoy house; on February 20, 1875, the last born son Nicholas, 11 months old, died; on October 30, 1875, Tolstoy's wife Sonya gave birth to a baby girl who died within an hour; on December 22, 1875, another aunt, Pelagya Ilinishna Yushkove, a rival to Aunt Toinette who had moved into the household from a monastery after Aunt Toinette's death, died (Troyat, 1967, pp. 347–351).

4. Polner (1945) makes a telling observation: "*Anna Karenina* has two hundred and thirty-nine chapters. Only one of them has a title—the twentieth chapter of the fifth part. And it is called 'Death'" (p. 112).

5. Tolstoy experienced other deaths and departures of parental figures early in his life which doubtless contributed to his already established sense of inconsolable loss in the face of death. His father died when he was a few months short of nine years old. He was then left in a family consisting of the parental grandmother, an Aunt Aline, and the woman who largely fulfilled the role of mother to him since the death of his own mother, Aunt Toinette. The grandmother died a year later. Aunt Aline died when Tolstoy was 13; simultaneously, Aunt Toinette was replaced by a rival aunt, Aunt Pelagya, who obtained custody under Russian law.

6. Here are echoes of the primal scene, a reminder of another crime: the "beating in the bedroom" in Anna's precognitive dream.

7. Not only was Sonya Tolstoy present, but a whole panoply of witnesses overflowed the Astapovo station: reporters, cameramen, the clergy, Tolstoyans, the curious. They filled every available space: railway cars, the station, the restaurant in the station. Even the restrooms became sleeping quarters. After his death, the name of the railroad station was changed from Astapovo to Leo Tolstoy Station (Simmons, 1964, p. 768). It might be remarked that Sonya Tolstoy was clearly part of the psi interaction with Tolstoy in determining aspects of

the death scene: she had at one time in contemplating suicide set out to throw herself under a train, as Anna Karenina had.

References

Asquith, C. (1961). *Married to Tolstoy.* Boston: Houghton Mifflin.

Crankshw, E. (1974). *Tolstoy: The making of a novelist.* New York: Viking Press.

Dingwall, E.J. (Ed.) (1968). *Abnormal hypnotic Phenomena: A survey of nineteenth-century cases* (Vols. 1–4). New York: Barnes and Noble.

Eisenbud, J. (1970). *Psi and psychoanalysis.* New York: Grune and Stratton.

Eisenbud, J. (1975). The case of Florence Marryat. *Journal of the American Society for Psychical Research,* 69, 215–233.

Freud, S. (1900). The Interpretation of Dreams. In *The basic writings of Sigmund Freud.* New York: Random House, 1938, pp. 181–549.

Freud, S. (1922) Dreams and telepathy. *Standard Edition,* 18. London: Hogarth Press, 1955, pp. 195–220.

Freud, S. (1933) Dreams and occultism. *Standard Edition,* 22: Ch. 30. London: Hogarth Press, 1964.

Greenhouse, H.B. (1971). *Premonitions: A leap into the future.* New York: B. Geis.

Gurney, E., Myers, F.W.H., & Podmore, F. (1886). *Phantasms of the living* (Vols. 1–2). London: Triibner.

Lavrin, J. (1948). *Tolstoy: An approach.* 2d ed. London: Methuen.

Polner, T. (1945). *Tolstoy and his wife.* New York: Norton.

Saltmarsh, H.F. (1934). Report on cases of apparent precognition. *Proceedings of the Society for Psychical Research,* 42, 49–103.

Simmons, E.J. (1946). *Leo Tolstoy.* Boston: Little, Brown.

Strakhov, N.N. (1970). Memoirs of N.N. Strakhov—summer, 1877. In G. Gibian (ed.), *Anna Karenina.* New York: Norton, pp. 752–753.

Tenhaeff, W.H.C. (1972). *Telepathy and clairvoyance.* Springfield, IL: Thomas.

Tolstoi, L.N. [Leo Tolstoy] (1929). The Kreutzer sonata. In *The works of Lyof N. Tolstoi* Vol. 19. New York: Scribner's, pp. 58–154.

Tolstoy, A. (1953). *Tolstoy: A life of my father.* New York: Harpers.

Tolstoy, A.L. (1968). *The real Tolstoy: A critique and commentary on the book "Tolstoy" by Henri Troyat.* Morristown, NJ: Henry Evans.

Tolstoy, L. (1960a). *Anna Karenina.* New York: Bantam Books.

Tolstoy, L. (1960b). *Lift up your eyes: The religious writings of Leo Tolstoy.* New York: Julian Press.

Tolstoy, S. (1928[?]). *The diary of Tolstoy's wife, 1860–1891.* New York: Payson and Clarke.

Tolstoy, S. (1962). *Tolstoy remembered by his son.* New York: Atheneum, 1962.

Troyat, FL (1967). *Tolstoy.* Garden City, NY: Doubleday.

Ullman, M., & Krippner, S., with Vaughan, A. (1973). *Dream telepathy.* New York: Macmillan. Warcollier *La telepathie.* Paris (Republished in English translation and with additional material by the Boston Society for Psychic Research in 1938, under title of *Experimental telepathy*).

THREE

E.M. Forster's *A Passage to India:*
Psi, Culture and Causality[1]

In 1924, the British author E.M. Forster published the fifth and arguably the best novel of his career, *A Passage to India,* a work that was immediately acclaimed as enduring literature; almost 60 years later it was adapted to movie form. As fate would have it, this was Forster's last novel. Although he continued to participate in the world of belles lettres for another 45 years as critic, biographer, and occasional short story writer, the creative well he so successfully tapped in *Passage* suddenly had run dry.

Passage is a sometimes subtle, sometimes heavy-handed attempt to capture the inter-action of the peoples of two cultures, Britain and India, at a time when British rule still flourished on Indian soil. Its sympathies are decidedly on the Indian side; indeed, the work was inspired by Forster's own experiences in the 18 months he spent in India and his life-long friendship with Syed Masood, an Indian adopted by an Anglo-Indian as a child whom Forster first met as a tutor. The work created a furor when first published—its intercultural insights and political liberalism often attracting as much attention in both countries as the beauty of its writing (Furbank, 1978, Vol. 2, pp. 123–130).

Amid all these acclaims, no critic has fully addressed a central feature of this novel: the intuitive handling by Forster of psi phenomena. (For that matter, a movie version [Brabourne, Goodwin, & Lean, 1984] left out the core event of the story with its psi dynamics, replacing it with a mystical episode, and as a consequence rendered the story line incomprehensible.) This is not surprising. Contemporary scholars of science and letters have other and more striking examples of such scotoma to their credit. For instance, they honor the themes and genius of a work such as Shakespeare's *Hamlet,* but they dismiss as hallucination or superstition the very core of that play—the psi phenomenon of a shared (as seen by Marcello, Horatio, and Hamlet) and unshared apparition, the latter of which provides Hamlet with a key fact about his father's death—that poison was poured in his ear—which presumably Hamlet could not have learned through sensorimotor means (in fact, the entire play can be viewed as one man's frantic struggle to determine whether psi data are accurate); or they honor the Oedipus myth in the work of Sophocles, raising it to the cornerstone of a psychoanalytic theory, while letting lie fallow and unex-plored the famous predictive psi elements of the myth.[2] Short of outright ignoring psi phenomena in its literature, modern Western culture sugarcoats it with the nomenclature "poetic license"—transforming a ghost from a fact into a metaphor, as critic Leslie Fiedler says in another context (Fiedler, 1975, p. 496). This is the defense so often taught to our children in high school and college, when great literary works are studied; and it reflects the power of Western culture's resistance to the psi hypothesis. The reason this is an unfortunate state of affairs is that we could often profit from the intuitive graspings of poets, novelists, and playwrights who sometimes anticipate by many years the more systematic findings of the scientists—now called parapsychologists—who devote themselves to the field. Certainly, this was the case in the early Russian novel *Anna Karenina,* written in 1874, which preceded by a half-century or more the theories of parapsychologically oriented psychoanalysts such as Freud (1922/1955, 1933/1964), Eisenbud (1970), and Fodor (1947), and which intertwined parapsychological data in events, dreams, and hypnagogic imagery in a subtle and unobtrusive fashion and in the day-to-day life of the main characters. Yet at the same time, the psi phenomena introduced by Tolstoy were crucial to the ultimate denouement of the novel, predicting in various very specific if disguised ways the details of the suicidal death of the heroine (Reichbart, 1976b). To summarize briefly: Details occurring just before or at the moment of Anna's death when she threw herself under the wheels of a train—a couple arguing in French in her train compartment, a little peasant worker bending over the rails muttering to himself as she died— appear in altered but recognizable form in a repetitive precognitive dream of Anna's, in a striking veridical dream of her lover Vronsky, and in a hypnagogic vision of hers. In addition, the first meeting of Anna and her lover Vronsky takes place at a train station where a worker is accidentally run over and killed. All these events are so skillfully interwoven into the story, on a day-to-day basis, that some of them no doubt register unconsciously with the reader, making the ultimate death seem all the more determined and logical.

This subtle, day-to-day portrayal of psi phenomena is equally true of their introduction into *Passage.* What is particularly informative about *Passage* is that the psi phenomena interweave in the mental disturbances of the central character, Adela Quested, providing one of the foci of the novel. Forster suggests that psi phenomena may appear in conjunction with a dissociated state of mind, and he further suggests that the phenomena can bring up questions of causality that are not fathomable by Eastern mysticism or classic Western reasoning. In addition, he highlights the psychological stresses that occur to people when two cultures, one upholding a belief in psi phenomena and the other not, come together—a subject which, as I have indicated when writing about American Indians, is sorely neglected in cross-cultural psychology studies (Reichbart, 1976a).

The Story

To explain to what I am referring in *Passage,* I must first give a brief synopsis of aspects of the story. Adela Quested as portrayed by Forster is an angular, physically unattractive British woman with a forthrightness that tends toward literal-mindedness, yet with an underlying sensitivity. She arrives in the city of Chandrapore to visit her friend Ronny Heaslop, the new City Magistrate. He intends to propose to her, hoping she will remain with him in British India, and he has asked his mother—Mrs. Moore—to bring her from England so that both of them might see him in his new surroundings. But from the beginning there is tension. Ronny has begun to act the role of the typical Anglo-Indian bureaucrat, disdaining the Indians he governs, and Adela finds him unpleasantly changed.

Adela and Mrs. Moore—rebelling against the exclusively Anglo atmosphere and prejudices of the Chandrapore Club—become curious about Indian life and arrange to meet some Indians in a more congenial atmosphere at the home of Mr. Fielding, an Anglo principal of a local high school who lives away from the British administrative compound. Here they chat in particular with Dr. Aziz, an attractive Moslem medical doctor—only to have Ronny come bursting into the formal setting to rudely drag Adela away to watch polo. For her, this is the final straw, and she blurts out to Ronny immediately afterward that she now finds she cannot marry him. Crestfallen, he agrees with typical British rectitude that they will remain friends instead; and then—as if to demonstrate his tolerance—he accepts an invitation from a wealthy Indian, the Nawab Bahadur, to take them for a ride in his automobile.

The Introduction of Psi

On this ride on the Marabar road, a minor accident occurs that marks the major introduction of psi phenomena into the dynamics of the story (and is entirely eliminated in the recent movie). Sitting in the back seat while the Nawab Bahadur naps in the front and the chauffeur drives, Ronny and Adela find that their hands touch and they do not withdraw. Then a bump, a swerve, a sudden stop: an accident. The Nawab Bahadur, startled from his sleep, is almost hysterical. But Adela has seen the cause of the accident: some "hairy animal" hit the car. Curious, even excited, Adela and Ronny attempt to discover with a flashlight what the animal was. "Steady and smooth ran the marks of the car [in the dust]," relates Forster,

> ribbons neatly nicked with lozenges, then all went mad. Certainly some external force had impinged, but the road has been used by too many objects for any one track to be legible, and the torch created such high lights and black shadows that they could not interpret what it revealed. Moreover, Adela in her excitement knelt and swept her skirts about, until it was she if anyone who appeared to have attacked the car [pp. 89–90].

Hyena, buffalo—they cannot quite determine what it was. But as a consequence of this adventure, their mood changes, they feel closer to one another, and they decide unexpectedly to marry after all. Yet this seemingly minor accident, with its dramatic social consequences, becomes stranger and stranger, for when Adela remarks about it to Mrs. Moore, who in her old age has grown somewhat mystical, Mrs. Moore responds under her breath: "A ghost!" "What made you call it a ghost?" asks Adela later on. "Call what a ghost?" "The animal thing that hit us. Didn't you say 'Oh, a ghost,' in passing." "I couldn't have been thinking of what I was saying." "It was probably a hyena, as a matter of fact" (p. 97).

Meanwhile, however, it appears that the Nawab Bahadur had entertained just such hypothesis, as a consequence of specific circumstances that could not have been consciously known by the others: Nine years previously, when he first had a car, he had driven over a drunken man and killed him, just at this spot on the Marabar road! Thus, Forster presents some curious questions of causality vis-à-vis what at first appears as an explicable incident. To complicate matters further, this incident appears to be related in an equally curious manner with the central event of the novel, the incident of the Marabar caves and the riddle of what happens there.

Sexual Fantasies and Psi

Adela, Mrs. Moore, and Fielding have arranged with Dr. Aziz to go on an expedition hosted by Aziz to see the real India—the Marabar caves in the Marabar hills outside Chandrapore. It is the kind of adventure that the typical Anglo-Indians disparage, being outside the well-regulated confines of their colonial lives. Climbing up the rocks to the caves with Dr. Aziz, Adela is filled with thoughts and plans about her upcoming marriage, when she suddenly thinks to herself: "What about love?" Forster's narrative continues:

> The rock was nicked by a double row of footholds, and somehow, the question was suggested by them. Where had she seen footholds before? Oh yes, they were the pattern traced in the dust by the wheels of the Nawab Bahadur's car. She and Ronny—no, they did not love each other [p. 152].

Realizing this, Adela is horrified but keeps her emotions under control, wondering whether she should break off the marriage, and then thinking that perhaps love is not necessary to a successful union. Then, turning to her attractive companion Dr. Aziz, she asks him about his wife and family (in fact, his wife is deceased, but he feels vulnerable and defensive with this inquisitive Anglo woman and finds it more fitting to pretend his wife is alive)—and she muses on how handsome he is. In her ignorance of Indian custom, and an unconscious expression of a wish of her own, she next inquires whether he has more than one wife. Aziz, an educated Indian Moslem, is appalled by such an ignorant question, and he escapes to hide his discomposure and anger by entering the nearest cave. Adela, absorbed and not noticing exactly where she is, enters an adjoining cave. Here, she believes that Aziz sexually molests her.

She flees back to Chandrapore, Aziz is arrested, and the stage is set for the denouement of the novel: the trial of Aziz. On one side of this pivotal social situation are arrayed the Anglo-Indians, self-righteously contending that Aziz's actions were the inevitable, tragic consequence of a too-close mingling of the races; on the other side are Aziz, the Indians in general, and Fielding, the only Anglo-Indian to believe in Aziz's innocence and in the existence of some terrible mistake. At the trial, Adela is placed on the stand and begins to testify about what happened at the Marabar caves, reliving the events in her mind as the prosecutor, Mr. McBryde, questions her. To her own surprise, and certainly that of the audience, under the impact of McBryde's questions, she suddenly realizes that Aziz did not follow her into the cave. She admits her mistake, and the case is dismissed. Needless to say, there is uproar: The Anglo-Indians, angry and embarrassed, consider Adela now to be persona non grata. Ronny terminates his engagement to her and she has no one with whom to talk, certainly not the Indians who are furious with her for leveling her charges in the first place.

Hints at the Workings of Psi

There is only Fielding who after his initial anger listens to her with interest and admiration for her honesty as she attempts to puzzle out what happened to her. What did happen? Apparently, she suffered a hallucination in the cave. She explains that she felt as if she were ill, "living at half pressure," since her visit to Fielding's; and that she had had a buzzing in her ears, which she refers to as an "echo," ever since her entrance into the caves—a buzzing sound that went away when she testified that Aziz did not molest her. Fielding suggests a hallucination, and she picks up on it:

Living at half pressure expresses it best. Half pressure. I remember going on to polo with Mr. Heaslop at the Maidan. Various other things happened—it doesn't matter what, but I was under par for all of them. I was certainly in that state when I saw the caves, and you suggest (nothing shocks or hurts me)—you suggest that I had an hallucination there, the sort of thing—though in an awful form—that makes some women think they've had an offer of marriage when none was made.

Fielding agrees and then adds

"My belief—and of course I was listening carefully in hope you would make some slip—my belief is that poor McBryde exorcised you. As soon as he asked you a straightforward question you gave a straightforward answer, and broke down."

"Exorcise in that sense. I thought you meant I'd seen a ghost."

"I don't go to that length."

"People whom I respect very much believe in ghosts," she said rather sharply. "My friend Mrs. Moore does."

But then they both agree that there are no such things as ghosts, and Forster adds: "There was a moment's silence, such as often follows the triumph of rationalism" (pp. 239–241). But later on, returning to the incident, they try again to puzzle it out without success:

"Let us call it the guide [who accompanied them to the cave, says Adela].... It will never be known. It's as if I ran my finger along that polished wall [of the cave] in the dark, and cannot get further. I am up against something, and so are you. Mrs. Moore—she did know."

"How could she have known what we don't?"

"Telepathy, possibly"

The pert, meagre word fell to the ground. Telepathy? What an explanation! Better withdraw it, and Adela did so. She was at the end of her spiritual tether, and so was he. Were there worlds beyond which they could never touch, or did all that is possible enter their consciousness? They could not tell [p. 263].

Analysis of Passage

Forster is too much of a craftsman to leave anything entirely clear about the underlying causality of the accident on the Marabar road or the subsequent events, for what is most striking about psi phenomena in real life is the ambiguity that seems to attach to them: how people entertain the hypothesis, as did Adela and Fielding, and then shy away from it, an observation that Eisenbud has repeatedly made in connection with the resistance to psi that persists in the minds of members of Western culture (Eisenbud, 1972). But Forster's depiction suggests the following dynamics to the brief hallucination, or psychotic episode, that Adela Quested went through: Uncertain and confused about her proposed marriage, and sexually both frightened and frustrated, she perceives that Ronny Heaslop has changed in a manner obtuse and unpleasant. But when she tells him that she does not want to marry, the prospect of coming out to India only to return alone and empty-handed is too difficult for her to accept. In this state, she is particularly vulnerable—and here, the incident on the Marabar road, the accident with the mysterious hairy animal, occurs. One might note how this incident fits into the unconscious needs of the participants: how the Nawab Bahadur is obsessed by the death he caused on the road and how Adela needs something to make her feel close to Ronny Heaslop. But it is at this exact point that Adela begins to lose touch with reality, being unwilling to accept her true feelings about Ronny Heaslop.

It appears to me that what happens at this moment, which resembles the beginning of a brief psychotic episode that culminates in Adela's hallucination of Dr. Aziz molesting her (her unconscious wish breaking through to replace reality), is that Adela becomes more open to psi phenomena, much as the literature reveals that in extreme cases of dissociation, such as the multiple personalities of Sally Beauchamp (M. Prince, 1913) or Doris Fischer (W.F. Prince, 1915, 1916), psychic manifestations often become more apparent. The mix of features in the parapsychological manifestations as depicted by Forster is interesting.[3]

First, he explicitly brings up the issue of repressed sexuality, which appears to be a major determinant of Adela Quested's psychotic episode and of the surrounding psychic manifestations. It has been remarked by a number of commentators that repressed sexual wishes, and sometimes outright sexual acting out, have often intertwined with psi phenomena (e.g., Eisenbud, 1970, pp. 190–194; Fodor, 1959, Chap. 16). In addition, there is the combination of a ghostly manifestation with telepathy, in which Mrs. Moore suspects, in a barely conscious way, that a ghost has been involved in the accident on the Marabar road. For that matter, in many cultures, hairy animals are viewed as a sign of the existence of malevolent psi or witchcraft—and it was a "hairy animal" that supposedly caused the automobile accident. Still further, in the attempt to understand what happened on the Marabar road, Forster recounts Adela's investigation of the incident in a particularly brilliant manner: Her investigation of the incident seems to change things in itself, or to suggest the peculiar difficulties of investigating a psi event of which we are a part, and in the end, it appears as if Adela herself had "attacked the car." In terms of psi causality in which Adela's unconscious aggression may function as a cause, Forster's suggestion is that there may be some truth to this.

Interestingly, the subsequent attempt to determine causality through Western legal thinking in the trial scene is doomed, as are legal attempts in relationship to psi in general (Reichbart, 1981). As successful as the trial is in determining what did not happen at the Marabar, it fails to fathom fully what did happen, to tie together the events at the cave with the previous accident, or to examine why they occurred. Only Adela and Fielding pursue these problems after the trial, for Western law is not directed toward understanding psychological or psi causality. In fact, it is as if the Western legal system by virtue of the limitations in what it considers as evidence of causality encourages the type of accusations Adela makes in the first place, as well as their ultimate denouement, while the possible underlying psi determinants of events go unnoticed.

What did happen? The accident on the Marabar road is connected in Adela's mind to the supposed molestation by Aziz in the caves; the two events represent the beginning and then the humiliating end of her thoughts of marrying Ronny Heaslop. The connection is definitely spelled out in her observation of the double row of nicks in the rock near the cave reminding her of the nicks in the dust of the road at the time of the accident; and this is coupled with her realization that although she decided to marry Heaslop at the time of the accident, she does not love him. Momentarily, unconsciously, she wishes that Aziz, physically attractive and climbing with her, could be her husband instead, and she invests this terrific wish, as compensation for her feeling of loss, with overwhelming hallucinatory power. In some sense, combined with this psychotic episode, there is a ghost with intent, and it is as if in the peculiar susceptibility of her state on the Marabar road, Adela makes a sudden psi connection with this personality who was deprived permanently of life and of any sense of earthly fulfillment at just that spot, or alternatively she connects telepathically with the thought of just such a person in the guilt-ridden mind of Nawab Bahadur as he travels the road, even though asleep, wishing the person alive. In the long run, the dead person can no more be alive than Adela can create love in her relationship with Ronny Heaslop. But when the accident occurs, she magically tries to resurrect her love, and it is as if the dead person's wish for resurrection or the wish of Nawab Bahadur for such resurrection has dovetailed with her wish or has helped to create it. (Once one begins to explore psi relationships in this fashion, it is not a very far step to suggest the further possibility of some kinds of animal psi, and there is the seemingly symbolic fact that this animal, though hit, escapes miraculously, as would have been equally nice for the man once hit at the same spot, or for the mortally threatened love of Ronny and Adela.) When she is reminded about the impossibility of it all by the double nicks at the Marabar caves, she *cannot* let go, and desperately, out of her poignant unconscious needs, she hallucinates the wish to be physically touched by the attractive Dr. Aziz in place of Ronny Heaslop. And finally, only when confronted directly at the trial does her psychotic-like state, the "living at half pressure" and the buzz, suddenly pop like a bubble bursting—and she comes back to reality. Revealingly, this moment is associated with exorcism by Fielding, who has no knowledge of the death on the Marabar road, as if he unconsciously sensed that the wish for a dead person to be alive had helped to create or influence Adela's state of mind, and that this wish also lost its psychic power when Adela was directly confronted by reality.[4]

Conclusion

As I have indicated, Forster does not come out in a flatfooted fashion for a parapsychological causality for the events he describes in *Passage,* but in an artistic fashion, he focuses on the manner in which parapsychological events seem to flit in and out of real life situations; and he suggests that these flittings are central to an understanding of the patterns of our lives. In addition, in a masterly manner, he depicts the typical Western defense of entertaining briefly the psi hypothesis and then veering quickly away, as if it were too hot to touch, and the Eastern defense of entertaining the hypothesis in an amorphous and mystical form but refusing to pursue any detailed, dynamic investigation of psi events. There is even a caricature of a Hindu mystic in the novel, a Professor Godbole, who entertains all such hypotheses in a mystical soup of "God is love." What is remarkable about Forster's depiction is that it was published in 1924, and although the novel itself has been widely recognized, the accurate, subtle, and intuitive portrayal of psychic manifestations and perhaps causality in daily life, and the struggle to comprehend them, particularly in a country where different cultures survive together, has gone all but unappreciated. In this respect, the critical evaluation of Forster's A *Passage to India* has mirrored the events described in the novel itself in which the crucial psi determinants generally escape the attention of the participants.

Notes

1. I gratefully thank Paul Gorrin for his help and encouragement.
2. True, the oracular element in Greek tradition is almost universal. Nevertheless, the Oedipus complex—the "cornerstone" of classical psychoanalytic theory—might be better understood if it included the psi elements inherent in the myth yet ignored by almost all psychoanalysts—a point I hope to make in a future contribution.

3. Forster professed himself not to know for certain what happened in the cave: "In the cave it is *either a* man, or the supernatural, *or* an illusion. And even if I know! My writing mind therefore is a blur here—i.e., I will it to remain a blur, and to be uncertain, as I am of many facts in daily life." He did see the event, however, as springing "straight from my subject matter," the theme of India. "I wouldn't have attempted it in other countries, which though they contain mysteries or muddles, manage to draw rings round them" (Furbank, 1978, Vol. 2, pp. 124–125). Ten years after, he had second thoughts and regretted making this "muddle" the central event of the novel (Furbank, 1978, Vol. 2, pp. 124–125n2).

4. To add to this resurrectionary motif, it should be noted that Dr. Aziz himself wishes his wife alive when he pretends to Adela that he is married.

References

Brabourne, J., Goodwin, R. (Producers), & Lean, D. (Director). (1984). *A passage to India* [Film]. Burbank, CA: Columbia Pictures.

Eisenbud, J. (1970). *Psi and psychoanalysis: Studies in the psychoanalysis of psi-conditioned behavior.* New York: Grune & Stratton.

Eisenbud, J. (1972). Some notes on the psychology of the paranormal. *Journal of the American Society for Psychical Research, 66,* 27–41.

Fiedler, L.A. (1975). *Love and death in the American novel.* Briarcliff Manor, NY: Stein & Day.

Fodor, N. (1947). Telepathy in analysis. *Psychiatric Quarterly,* 21, 171–189. Also in G. Devereux (Ed.), *Psychoanalysis and the occult.* New York: International Universities Press, 1953, pp. 283–296.

Fodor, N. (1959). *The haunted mind.* New York: Garrett Publications.

Forster, E.M. (1952). *A passage to India.* New York: Harcourt Brace (Original work published 1924).

Freud, S. (1955). Dreams and telepathy. In J. Strachey (ed. and trans.), *The Standard edition of the complete psychological works of Sigmund Freud* (Vol. 18, pp. 195–220). London: Hogarth Press (Original work published 1922).

Freud, S. (1964). Dreams and occultism. In J. Strachey (ed. and trans.), *The standard edition of the complete psychological works of Sigmund Freud* (Vol. 22, pp. 31–56). London: Hogarth Press (Original work published 1933).

Furbank, P.N. (1978). *E.M. Forster: A life* (Vol. 2). New York: Harcourt Brace Jovanovich.

Prince, M. (1913). The *Dissociation of a personality: A biographical study in abnormal personality.* 2d ed. New York: Longmans, Green.

Prince, W.F. (1915). The Doris case of multiple personality, Part I. *Proceedings of the American Society for Psychical Research,* 9, 1–700.

Prince, W.F. (1916). The Doris case of multiple personality, Part II. *Proceedings of the American Society for Psychical Research,* 10, 701–1332.

Reichbart, R. (1976a). The Navajo hand trembler: Multiple roles of the psychic in traditional Navajo society. *Journal of the American Society for Psychical Research,* 70, 381–396.

Reichbart, R. (1976b). Psi phenomena and Tolstoy. *Journal of the American Society for Psychical Research,* 70, 249–265.

Reichbart, R. (1981). Western law and parapsychology. *Parapsychology Review,* 12(2), 9–11.

FOUR

G.K. Chesterton and Ingmar Bergman: Artists of Magic and Psi Whose Intimations Proved Too Real

I have chosen to tell a story here in a seemingly roundabout way, traveling to different countries and different historical times, which deposits us in the end in Denver, Colorado, more or less in the present, and then—in a short epilogue—in an obscure campus library in Baltimore, Maryland. It is a tale of the rarely discussed relationship between two phenomena, magic and psi. By magic I mean the imitation of actual psi phenomena by sleight of hand or other physical means that escape ready detection from an audience.

In Chapter Nine, "Magic and Psi," I discuss in more developmental detail the relationship between these two phenomena. Here I tell a story—a story which begins with the remarkable insights of seemingly very different artists, who intuitively understood aspects of the relationship between magic and psi in Western culture, and who then plumbed that relationship poignantly and accurately in two wonderful tales. The story then finishes in modern times with a recounting of a series of real events that resemble in some respects only too closely the fictional tales of these artists, particularly in the difficulty that people in Western culture experience accepting the existence of psi phenomena. The story is in many ways a sad one, for it suggests that we are too frightened to look closely at psi, and that we often will do everything in our power to entertain more comfortable and more familiar "magical" hypotheses—hypotheses that explain things in physical terms rather than in psi terms.

Let us begin in Gotesburg, Sweden, in 1934 when the City Theater was constructed. It still stands today. It is a large modern rectangular structure, built in a style variously referred to as Nordic Classicism or Swedish Grace, with Art Deco features, by the architect Carl Bergsten—who also gained fame for his interior and furniture design. Thirteen years after it was built, in March 1947, a drama called *Magic: A Fantastic Comedy* ran for thirty performances at the theater. *Magic* was the first play written by G.K. Chesterton, the prolific British essayist, novelist, poet, short story and mystery writer (the author most famously of the Father Brown detective series) who was somewhat of a tortured soul and who eventually converted to Catholicism, about which he frequently and subsequently wrote. *Magic* had been written in response to a challenge from Chesterton's good friend, the playwright and atheist George Bernard Shaw who differed with him entirely—and frequently formally debated him—on all matters political and religious. In a 1908 letter, Shaw had threatened Chesterton: "I shall repeat my public challenge to you; vaunt my superiority; insult your corpulence [Chesterton weighed almost 300 pounds]; … if necessary, call on you and steal your wife's affections by intellectual and athletic displays, until you contribute something to the British drama" (Shaw, 1972, p. 759).

Magic, written by Chesterton in 1913, was the result. The Swedish production of the play in 1947 at the City Theater was directed by none other than Ingmar Bergman, who was to become the great filmmaker (Steene, 2005, p. 534). In fact, Bergman was so intrigued with *Magic* that a decade later in the late 1950s, when he wrote and directed such film classics as *The Seventh Seal*, *Wild Strawberries*, *Smiles of a Summer Night*, *Virgin Spring*—he created the film *The Magician* (originally called *The Face*) which was derived— although vastly different—from the Chesterton play. *The Magician* is a brilliant work which explores that strange and disturbing mixture of magic and psychic phenomena touched upon (but with a light touch indeed) by Chesterton in his play. *The Magician*, however, is darker than Chesterton's play by far and it is placed in an earlier time when Mesmerism was popular.[1] But the insights of Bergman—and Chesterton before him— are central to the understanding of psychic phenomena in Western culture; and the lessons that can be inferred from their works (if only we were inclined to listen for them) continue to apply today.

As a young man, in what Chesterton called a "period of madness" which "coincided with a period of drifting and doing nothing" and unable to settle down to regular work, he "dabbled" in Spiritualism. He and his brother played with a planchette or Ouija board. Apparently, whatever happened (he never explains) frightened him. He felt—to use his own words—that he was "playing with fire; or even with hell-fire." He elaborated by suggesting that perhaps unconscious human force was at work, although not sure of this possibility: "I saw quite enough of the thing to be able to testify, with complete certainty, that something happens which is not at all natural, or produced by normal and conscious means. Whether it is produced by some subconscious but still human force, or by some powers, good, bad or indifferent, which are external to humanity, I would not myself attempt to decide" (Chesterton, 2006, p. 88). In other words, he worried about the Devil being at work in the Ouija board manifestations.

Despite his fear and ambivalence, despite his oscillation between a deep psychological hypothesis to explain psi manifestations or the alternative hypothesis of external malignant forces at work, Chesterton remained fascinated by psychic phenomena which he thought of as miracles. Further, he understood what to this day has been hard for scientists, indeed for parapsychologists themselves, to appreciate: that the psychological nature of psi phenomena makes it difficult to investigate them in prototypical scientific fashion. He thought it futile to try to confine psi phenomena in the strait jacket of a scientific method that left out the essential ingredient of the motivation of the people involved.[2] Thus, in 1908—five years before he created his play *Magic*—he wrote in his book *Orthodoxy* (Chesterton, 2012):

> One may … surely dismiss that quite brainless piece of pedantry that talks about the need for scientific conditions in connection with alleged spiritual phenomena. If we are asking whether a dead soul can communicate with a living, it is ludicrous to insist that it shall be under conditions in which no two living souls in their senses would seriously communicate with each other. The fact that ghosts prefer darkness no more disproves the existence of ghosts than the fact that lovers prefer darkness disproves the existence of love….
>
> It is just as unscientific as it is unphilosophical to be surprised that in an unsympathetic atmosphere certain extraordinary sympathies do not arise. It is as if I said that I could not tell if there was a fog

because the air was not clear enough, or as if I insisted on perfect sunlight in order to see a solar eclipse [p. 96].

And later on, Chesterton added to his defense of psi in reference to "swindling mediums":

I hope we may dismiss the argument against wonders attempted in the mere recapitulation of frauds of swindling mediums or trick miracles. That is not an argument at all, good or bad. A false ghost disproves the reality of ghosts exactly as much as a forged banknote disproves the existence of the Bank of England ... [p. 96].

These astute and prophetic observations of Chesterton's about scientific attempts to investigate psi phenomena are central to—and anticipate—my argument in this essay, and I will return to them. But first to Chesterton's answer to Shaw, who had little use for either miracles or psi phenomena,[3] as embodied in the play that Chesterton wrote as a result of Shaw's goading, and which he so aptly named: *Magic* (Chesterton, 1913). *Magic* is an English drawing room drama, that takes place in the country home of a Duke, who is a genial if somewhat vacuous host, given to social compromise. His guests are the local Rev. Cyrus Smith, and a local doctor, Dr. Grimthorpe, who trade alternate views of what is important in life; and in addition, the Duke's young and beautiful niece, Patricia Carleon, bohemian in quality, and prone to being enchanted by the ethereal and mystical. A further and late arriving guest is the Duke's young nephew, Morris Carleon, an American, a businessman, who presents as self-assured, impulsive, practical and self-important. Enter into this mix: a Conjuror, a tall, dark, mysterious man who has been invited by the Duke to perform for this audience (he has performed even before the King), and who immediately becomes enthralled with the beautiful niece, as she does with him.

The Conjuror is mysterious about his powers. Impulsively and immediately enamored of the beautiful and elegant Patricia, he wants so to impress her, but he feels unworthy of her. In class, he is not her equal, condemned to stay at fifth rate lodgings and travel in third class carriages, as he displays his performances ("new tricks, new patter, new nonsense," he says [Chesterton, 1913, p. 25]), which appear to be part magic and part psi, from town to town. And even more importantly, he does not think of the psi part of his abilities as being wonderful and beautiful as the faeries, with whom Patricia desires to communicate. Instead, he is haunted. Like Chesterton with the Ouija board, the Conjuror is afraid his psi powers are not only dark but derive from the Devil.

This strange amalgam of patter, trick, and psi, are more than the young American Morris can take. He will have none of it, and he is further incensed by the apparent affinity between his beautiful cousin (whom he wishes to protect) and the Conjuror. Over and over, he goads the Conjuror, denying that psi exists and saying that he knows how the Conjuror produces each and every effect (the furniture moved because of a "sliding plank" for example) even though he struggles with some of them to find a logical explanation. Finally, however, the Conjuror has apparently had enough. He psychically turns a distant light from a lamp in the garden from red to blue. The entire drawing room contingent becomes silent. They do not know how he did this.

The consequence is that Morris becomes distraught because he cannot determine how the "trick" was done, so distraught and obsessed that the doctor and the reverend become concerned about his health. And now here is the rub. Everyone tries to prevail on the Conjuror to tell the truth, to explain to Morris by what legerdemain, through the use of what magic trick, he managed to get the light to change color. They hope that in this way, Morris (who appears to have a predilection for mental instability) will rise up from his bed, where he is being treated by the eminent doctor, and will become well again.

The problem of course is that there was no "trick." In one impassioned plea to the clergyman, the Conjuror laments the clergyman's effort to persuade the Conjuror to speak to Morris:

> Conjuror [violently] ... I want you to bear witness to your own creed. I say these things are supernatural. I say this was done by a spirit. The Doctor does not believe me; he is an agnostic and he knows everything. The Duke does not believe me; he cannot believe anything so plain as a miracle. But what the devil are you for, if you don't believe in a miracle? What does your coat mean, if it doesn't mean that there is such a thing as the supernatural? What does your cursed collar mean if it doesn't mean that there is such a thing as a spirit? [exasperated] Why the devil do you dress up like that if you don't believe in it? [Chesterton, 1913, p. 47].

And the Reverend Smith confesses, after a pause, "I wish I could believe" to which the Conjuror, replies paradoxically, "Yes, I wish I could disbelieve" (Chesterton, 1913, p. 47). Finally, the Conjuror (rejecting incidentally a sum of money which the Doctor presses on him to tell the "truth") to appease everyone and to help restore Morris's equilibrium, tells Morris a made-up-story so that Morris will think that the change of the light was simply done by sleight of hand. As he explains to the Doctor "I am going to tell that poor little lad a lie ... I have managed to think of a natural explanation of that trick." To which the Doctor enthusiastically responds, "I think you are something like a great man" (Chesterton, 1913, p. 54). The Conjuror does so, Morris is immediately restored to health, and everyone is pleased except the Conjuror, who is saddened not only because he has had to take part in a fabrication, but because the woman, Patricia Carleon, who so instantly enchanted him and with whom he fell so magically in love, could not abide the thought that psi phenomena may not all derive from light and tenderness, but might sometimes come from something darker.

I know that the reader may be perplexed that I am devoting such attention to this confusing amalgam of legerdemain and ostensibly true psi phenomenon as well as explanations for psi that embrace spirits and the Devil but if he can tolerate some ambiguity for the moment, I believe that the compelling lessons of Chesterton's drama—what it teaches us about the nature and social matrix of psi in Western culture—are worthy of thought. For Chesterton suggests that the established representatives of societal institutions and customs are all threatened by the possibility that psi exists. Scientist, clergyman, politician, romantic, all the other characters in the drama aside from the Conjuror, not only cannot tolerate ostensible psi, but go so far as prefer a patently false explanation that favors a magic trick and then prevail upon the Conjuror to join in this explanation to assuage their own anxieties about psi. Although in reality turning a distant light from red to blue, as far as I am aware, as a psi phenomenon does not exist in the anecdotal or experimental record, it does not matter. (However, when the ghosts of those whom King Richard III murdered, haunt him in his sleep, he relates that the "lights burned blue" in the dream. The Yale Shakespeare annotates this with an observation about Elizabethan customs during Shakespeare's time: "There was an old superstition to the effect that spirits signified their presence by causing lights to ... burn blue" [Shakespeare, 1993, p. 607, V.iii, 198]. Perhaps Chesterton was familiar with this belief.) Chesterton wishes to show that the fear of psi phenomena experienced by societal representatives is so great that they insist at any cost (even at the expense of truth) upon a magical or sleight of hand explanation instead.

Certainly, the film director Bergman (who saw himself as a conjuror with a "magic lantern" often at odds with the forces of science, religion, and politics) was fascinated with Chesterton's story. Hewing closely to the dynamic heart of *Magic*, he proceeded to construct a powerful film, dramatically different as to its details and of much greater darkness, although allegedly a comedy. He set it in the mid–1800s. in the time of Mesmer, depicting as a tortured hero the figure of a Dr. Vogler, a Mesmerist, who alters his appearance through makeup and a beard to look particularly sinister to his audience and who travels by carriage as a performer with a small troupe through the isolated towns of Sweden. Vogler has lost much of his hypnotic ability apparently, and is bitter and hopeless. He travels with his grandmother, a mysterious and frightening woman with her apparent psychic ability intact, who can "get furniture to move" but who has a variety of "magic" potions that she has concocted from herbs and mushrooms and assorted things that she gathers in the countryside, and then sells to customers that the troupe finds along the way. In addition, there is an androgynous figure, Aman, Dr. Volger's wife, who is disguised as a man, and acts as an assistant to her husband and who still believes in his psychic ability to cure, as well as a blustery, barker kind of figure, Tubal, a stage manager, who is in charge of publicity and getting invitations for the performances of "Vogler's Magnetic Health Theater." The premise of all this may escape the film viewer, because the distinction between mesmerism and psychic phenomena on the one hand, and magical tricks on the other, is not part of many people's vocabulary—but the premise is that the healing mesmeric and psychic activity that Vogler sometimes practices is forbidden by the authorities, just as Mesmer and his followers were often hounded by the scientific establishment in reality.[4]

In fact, the findings of some of Mesmer's followers were not just those of hypnotic cures of physical ailments (originally believed to be aided by the introduction of magnets) through the use of suggestion. For our purpose, what these followers did was to explore the use of mesmeric trance as a facilitator of psi phenomena. For example, in 1784 one of Mesmer's foremost disciples, the Marquis de Puységur, reported "clairvoyant" powers in an uneducated mesmerized peasant; in 1819, H.M. Weserman reported five successful attempts through the use of mesmerism to influence the minds and dreams of friends at a distance; in 1823, Dr. Alexandre Bertrand verbally commanded an entranced mesmeric subject to do one thing, while willing her to do the opposite resulting in increasing agitation of the subject. The list goes on: Dr. John Elliotson, a celebrated professor of medicine at the University of London, published in the volumes of Zoist for thirteen years beginning in 1843 reports of psychic phenomenon, particularly that hypnotized subjects experienced the same sensation as Elliotson at a distance; Dr. James Esdaile in 1846, claimed to have hypnotized patients at a distance; Dr. William Barrett, a Dublin professor of physics in 1875 reported something similar. And these reports of telepathic phenomena associated with medical hypnosis continued all the way to the great psychologists Liebault and Pierre Janet (Eisenbud, 1970, pp. 54–60). But the earliest Mesmerists, unlike the later medical hypnotists, were an undisciplined lot and the psi phenomena that apparently sometimes took place was not closely reported. One commentator (Eisenbud, 1970) states:

> such was the bewildering array of weird manifestations described by the mesmerists, with their hysterical group séances in which magnets, tubs, rods, musical instruments and other paraphernalia played dramatic parts, that little notice was taken of these fringe [psi] effects. They were shrugged off

as little more than especially odd twists in the extravagant fancies of these part mystic, part charlatan and part, for all that, strangely effective healers who claimed nothing less than that they were calling upon resident powers of the universe itself to restore the sick [p. 54].

In fact, they were looked upon with such disdain and fear by the established medical profession of the time that the Faculty of Medicine of the French Academy of Sciences (on which incidentally Benjamin Franklin, then ambassador to France, sat) published a report in 1784 that concluded that mesmerism was "nothing more than the clever exploitation of the powers of imagination (and sex) among unbalanced individuals" (Eisenbud, 1970, p. 55).

   Bergman seems to have been strikingly aware of this background in creating *The Magician*. For when the members of Vogler's little troupe in the carriage make their way through the forest to the next town, hoping to perform in public, they find themselves immediately detained by the police as they enter the town and then escorted to a country manor. Here they are confronted not only by the wealthy owner Consul Egerman, but by the Chief of Police, and by Dr. Vergerus, "Royal Medical Counselor," who are determined to put Volger and his motley crew to the test. And so Bergman has managed to transform Chesterton's work to a different time and place but with similar features: Chesterton's august representatives of society (doctor, clergyman, wealthy society host) become a Royal Medical Counselor, a wealthy consul and a chief of police. For that matter, even the romantic love interest appears when Consul Egerman's pretty and emotionally vulnerable wife (who has recently lost a child) becomes fascinated and enamored with the "magician," hoping he will tell her why God took her child. She invites him to her bedroom that evening, although he turns back her seduction.

   The three establishment men take it upon themselves to investigate Vogler and in the process to humiliate him. They do so when they first meet the troupe, by questioning the members in the manor's drawing room and then they insist that the troupe perform privately for them the next day before they appear before the public in the town. From the beginning, the medical doctor, Vergerus, makes it clear what he thinks of Mesmer's animal magnetism: "I know the method well. It is completely worthless" (Bergman, 1960, p. 304). To protect themselves from charges that Vogler actually has some psychic abilities which the troupe fears will be looked upon as dangerous if confirmed, Vogler, Aman and Tubal now are compelled to pretend that everything Vogler does is based solely on harmless "magic tricks" (a homage to the underlying drama of Chesterton). Dr. Vergerus correctly observes that Vogler's own activities are strikingly divergent:

   First we have the idealistic Doctor [said sarcastically]Vogler who practices as a physician according to Mesmer's rather doubtful methods. Then we have a somewhat less than idealistic magician who arranges all kinds of hocus-pocus according to entirely home-made recipes. If I've grasped the facts correctly, the activities of the Vogler troupe range unscrupulously between these two extremes [Bergman, 1960, p. 306].

He is far from accepting there is anything to the hypnosis part, however, exhibiting a virulent and nasty skepticism. Even though he offers to be a guinea pig, challenging Vogler personally to produce frightening visions in him through his hypnotic ability, and then becomes clearly frightened; and even though Vogler then hypnotizes the wife of the Chief of Police who proceeds to talk about how disgusting she really finds her husband with his pig-like habits, completely unaware of what she has said, Vergerus persists in denying that there is anything to what Vogler does. At one point, slightly inebriated, he has this exchange with Aman, now revealed to be Manda by name, Vogler's wife:

VERGERUS: When you first came into the room, I immediately liked you. Your face, your silence, your natural dignity. This bias on my part is very deplorable and I wouldn't be telling you if I weren't slightly intoxicated.

MANDA: If you feel like that you should leave us in peace.

VERGERUS: I can't do that.

MANDA: Why?

VERGERUS: Because you represent something which I most abhor.

Manda looks questioningly at him.

VERGERUS: The unexplainable.

To which Manda replies:

MANDA: Then you can immediately stop your persecution, Mr. Vergerus, because our activities are a fraud from beginning to end.

VERGERUS: A fraud?

MANDA: Pretense, false promises, and double bottoms. Miserable, rotten lies throughout. We are the most ridiculous scoundrels you can find [Bergman, 1960, p. 339].

But as Bergman himself remarks in his autobiography, although Manda must pretend that everything is a magic trick, she actually continues to believe in the previous psi abilities of her husband: "Manda represents the belief in the holiness of human beings. Vogler, on the other hand, has given up. He is involved in the cheapest kind of theater, and she knows it. Manda is very open in her talk with Vergerus. The miracle happened once, and she herself carries it. She loves Vogler in spite of being fully aware that he has lost his faith" (Bergman, 2007, p. 167).[5]

Interestingly, in contrast to Amanda, whose inner turmoil is apparent, Bergman also presents the old grandmother (Vogler's mother) whose psychic abilities allegedly persist but who is perfectly content to hide them entirely. Throughout the film, she criticizes her son for being reckless in exhibiting his psi abilities. Instead, she chooses to make money in mercenary if somewhat questionable ways. We see her at the beginning gathering stones, herbs and plants from the forest which she packages as cure-alls and love potions later in the film. As Bergman (2007, p. 170) says of her:

She is … a witch, who can make candleholders topple over and glasses explode. She is an authentic old sorceress with roots in ancient traditions; at the same time she is the smartest one in the troupe. She sells concocted love potions and saves the money that she earns from her sorcery, planning to retire and become harmless.

The denouement of the questioning of Vogler and his troupe, after much Sturm und Drang in which through a series of magic tricks Vogler does manage to frighten Vergerus and make the police chief look silly, is that Vogler himself ends up being humiliated by all. Without his make-up, shorn of his costume, at the end he is reduced to pleading to everyone for money for his performance and to beseeching the Consul's wife, who—like Patricia Carleon—now turns upon him. They ridicule how powerless he looks and insist that if he wants help he should return to his magician costume. And then, at the last minute, there arrives at the mansion, three black carriages; and suddenly the entire yard is filled with constables and police. Everyone expects that finally they have come to arrest Vogler.

But no, not at all: there is an announcement that Vogler is being summoned to the Royal Palace in Stockholm so he might perform before the King! (Apparently a count—

to whom they had previously presented and who, enthralled with Amanda, had made what they took to be an empty promise to get the troupe an audience with the King—had actually come through.) And so, amid a flourish of trumpet sounds, the troupe rides off in triumph to their appointment with royalty.

—◦◦◦—

I began by saying that we would travel to Denver, Colorado, and that is where we are now turning, seemingly far away from England or Sweden, and pushing forward by decades to the modern day. For now comes a true story of the most evidentiary modern psi event and its dismal fate. And this modern event proclaims itself as if the two parables of what happens when psi occurs—the tales of Chesterton and Bergman—came to life. And yet this is not fiction: the acceptance of psi suffers in reality and in the present and on a grander scale the same dismal fate as it does in the fictional stories of these two masters.

The actual event or series of events are the work of the psychiatrist and psychoanalyst Jule Eisenbud, whom I cited above from an unrelated work of his, with a talented psychic called Ted Serios from the years 1963 to 1967. For those who do not know the story, it is an amazing tale; and for those who do—at least from the unfortunate publicity that subsequently plagued the Serios phenomenon—I ask that they listen afresh and without preconceptions. Ted Serios was an unemployed Chicago bellhop, in his mid–40s, alcoholic, not well educated, impulsive, at times somewhat sociopathic but with the uncanny ability of projecting images from his mind onto Polaroid camera film. He would often work himself up into a state, after many drinks, concentrating intently, exhibiting signs that resembled having an intense bowel movement, sometimes removing his shirt, and having a Polaroid camera pointed right at him or holding one himself, and finally—snapping the picture with a flash. When there was a "hit," what developed was not at all what one expected. The Polaroid photograph when pulled away from its paper setting showed neither Ted nor his surroundings. Instead, an image appeared that not only had not been before the camera, but was unreproducible from reality. This last point is crucial. Ted would get images, particularly of buildings (which seemed to be a favorite subject of his) which *did* exist somewhere, but the images were conflated or different from reality: brick walls would now show as stone, perspectives would be impossible to reproduce, aspects of the building would be from a past era whereas other aspects were from the present, striations appeared on structures that were not there in actuality, different existing structures were melded together in impossible ways, an image of a statue showed an arm position that did not exist in reality, a building with lettering on it showed a misspelling that did not exist, and so on. These images would come after many often futile tries and sometimes not at all. Sometimes there would be more than one camera snapped by participants, with Ted at a distance from the cameras; sometimes prints would appear with impossible juxtapositions and dislocations—for example, the camera would reveal a picture from where Ted was sitting, but the camera actually had been triggered by a participant in another location; or photographs would reveal people in another room. In addition, Ted sought to get images of target pictures that participants brought to sessions in sealed envelopes (so that Serios could not know what they were) and sometimes the images he produced on film were related to those targets, presumably as a consequence of a telepathic connection, and sometimes not. It should be emphasized that Ted did not have to have any contact with the camera for these things to happen.

Here is Eisenbud describing what it was like:

> In the usual situation, with others manning the camera and gismo [more about this later] more than a foot away, neither Ted's hands nor any other part of his body would be in contact with the camera (and sometimes the gismo) and he would indicate by gesturing to the person holding it … just how he wanted it angled … so that he could stare directly into the lens…. Sometimes Ted would deploy one person to hold the camera, another to trigger it, and often a third to hold the gismo…. Finally with everything the way he wanted it, he would begin squirming in his chair, his eyes staring wildly and his hands running frenziedly through his hair. If he were standing … he might simply keep his hand … or hands poised to snap. This would keep up until he exploded with his "Now!" usually snapping his finger or fingers as a signal to the triggerman to trip the shutter release. Then he might continue snapping his fingers and incanting, in best crap game fashion, sometimes with a chorus of children and adults chiming in, "Be there, baby, be there." This might keep up—unless Ted had, in his frenzy, demanded that someone hand him another camera—for the ten or fifteen seconds the print was developing [Eisenbud, 1989, p. 79].

And here, more or less at random, is another type of example from Eisenbud's book:

> In five different sessions, Ted's separation from the camera was effected by a physical barrier in addition to the distances that were involved. One of these took place in the laboratory of physicist James A. Hurry who provided for the occasion a small (about 9 by 7 by 7.5 feet) room known as a Faraday cage. A fine mesh wire screen was wrapped completely around the room to screen out long wave radio and radar waves. Hurry … provided the film and camera and arranged the test conditions, which he supervised. Ted was kept inside the cage … but was permitted to keep a gismo with him…. Hurry remained outside the cage with cameras and another gismo.
>
> Hurry wrote that: "When Dr. Eisenbud held the camera and I held the gismo. When I held the camera, Dr. Eisenbud held the gismo" [Eisenbud, 1989, p. 86].

And despite the distance, despite the Faraday cage, psychic photographs were obtained, including one of three standing men apparently in uniform from the back and side as if observing a parade. (Eisenbud neglected to note that this experiment took place on February 22, 1966, George Washington's birthday which was a national holiday in the States at that time [it was only subsequently on January 1, 1971, that the Uniform Monday Holiday Act became effective and proclaimed that Washington's birthday would be celebrated on the third Monday of February; eventually the holiday was melded with Lincoln's birthday of February 12 to create President's Day and Washington's actual birthday was generally forgotten] all of which might explain the appearance of the soldiers.)

What was most impressive were the observers and participants who took part when Serios produced his pictures. They were scientists and scholars, from a variety of fields, who delighted to be present when these seemingly magical events occurred. They were assembled by Jule Eisenbud, who was also an Associate Professor at the University of Colorado Medical School, from the Denver community and beyond, to be at sessions with Ted. One of them would be assigned to write the events as they occurred at the session. Each "hit" photograph would be numbered and signed and the circumstances of its production recorded. These scientists and academics, who signed as witnesses to the production of one or more of these pictures, included: *fourteen* professors at the University of Colorado Medical School (from assistant, through associate, to full professor); a physicist at the National Center for Atmospheric Research; another (also a full professor) at the University of Denver; a third who was chief of research at the Veteran's Administration hospital and a fourth from the research division of a private company; a professor of botany at Colorado State University; a curator of archaeology at the Denver Museum of Natural History; a famous professor of astronomy at Northwestern University; as well as two physicians in private practice; and the Chief Physicist at a private company (which provided the Faraday cage mentioned above). One would think with this degree of gravitas as well as expertise that their views would lead to a serious consideration of the Serios phenomena, strange as the phenomena were.

But the lessons that obtain in the work of Bergman and Chesterton bore bitter fruit. Even before Serios, Jule Eisenbud had become something of a persona non grata in his personal field, psychoanalysis. He had been a brilliant and rising star at the premiere psychoanalytic institute in New York City, the New York Psychoanalytic Institute, conceivably on his way to becoming a training analyst. But then his interests turned to parapsychology. He took to heart the observations made by Freud (who himself once said that if he had to do it all over again he would become a parapsychologist) about how telepathy between a patient and others in his life or between a patient and the psychoanalyst might express itself. Most of the followers of Freud, who too often treat each word that Freud wrote with the veneration that one would accord the pronouncements of a deity, have found reasons to ignore, deny, and sweep under the proverbial rug, Freud's parapsychological writings and insights; it is almost as if these psychoanalytic followers are ashamed of their founder for these comments. In the alternative, they seek various ways of emphasizing Freud's ambivalence about the reality of psi phenomena (an ambivalence he clearly felt) and thereby ignore his astute clinical hypotheses as to how telepathy might function if it existed.

Eisenbud in a series of psychoanalytic articles in the 1940s and 1950s, including a striking exchange with Albert Ellis (then a psychoanalyst but who years later actually left the psychoanalytic fold to create his own brand of therapy, Rational Emotive Behavior Therapy), suggested the importance of psi phenomena in dreams and in life and in psychoanalysis. Although there were a number of other psychoanalysts at that time who joined in the exchange or who sought to explore psi phenomena in psychoanalysis themselves, Eisenbud was preeminent. His road to becoming a training analyst blocked as a consequence (at one point years later a leading light of the institute, the New York Psychoanalytic, Charles Brenner, claimed as one of his achievements that in opposing Eisenbud he had single-handedly thwarted any further publication about psi phenomena in all "reputable journals" [Brenner, 1987], presumably including the hallowed publication, the Psychoanalytic Quarterly, of that institute—in which Eisenbud's work had once appeared). But Eisenbud, remained committed to parapsychological study, particularly in his involvement with the American Society for Psychical Research. He moved his psychoanalytic practice to Denver (as did a number of New York psychoanalysts at the time) and affiliated with the University of Colorado Medical School. For most psychoanalysts, he continued to be thought of as having fallen off the deep end. And then his involvement with Ted Serios confirmed for them that indeed he was long lost. (In the Appendix, there is my published a tribute to Eisenbud which discusses him in more detail.)

And yet, the photographs of Ted Serios, what is often called "thoughtography" were truly amazing. In 1967, Eisenbud published *The World of Ted Serios: "Thoughtographic" Studies of an Extraordinary Mind*, which recounted in brilliant detail what it was like working with Serios and which contained tens of the pictures that Serios produced. In addition to recounting the Serios phenomena, the book is a tour de force of psychoanalytic insights and speculations concerning psi phenomena and the psychological associations in Serios's mind that may have given rise to the thoughtographic pictures; and it contains philosophical and historical insights as well. This aspect of things was perhaps too highflying for many parapsychologists themselves, who are not generally psychoanalytic, and felt wary of such material, not believing it scientific enough in appearance. However, for me, the book and particularly the psychoanalytic and speculative aspects of it, were inspiring and wonderful (again refer to my comments in "Jule Eisenbud: Explorer" in the Appendix). In a second edition, published in 1989 by McFarland, Eisenbud left out some of these speculations; and elaborated in greater detail about the thoughtographic pictures themselves, the categories of psi anomalies that occurred in them, and the particularities of their production.

And now the denouement, in this case in reality rather than in fiction. One would envision and hope that at the very least contemporary parapsychologists would have been and continue to be delighted by the psychic photography of Ted Serios and that, in the canons of their field, the work would be put forward as the most important to ever have occurred. For the fact is that one has, in the Polaroid photographs that Serios produced, the tangible evidence of psi phenomena at work. But parapsychologists generally did not entirely rejoice at the Serios phenomena. Their reactions ran the gamut. Some were incensed that Serios himself was not a nicer subject—dissolute, often seemingly on the edge of self-control, foul mouthed—and that the setting was not as pristine and dry as a laboratory. It is as if they were affronted in a moral way by Serios and thereby decided the phenomena he produced could have no possible merit. In other words, like Patricia Carleon in Magic they would only acknowledge psi phenomena if it were a seemingly wondrous work of sweetness and light—fairy dust—rather than dark and messy. In terms of their need for sterile surroundings, these commentators entirely ignored Chesterton's powerful insight that it "is just as unscientific as it is unphilosophical to be surprised that in an unsympathetic atmosphere certain extraordinary sympathies do not arise." Others understandably wanted to see for themselves if the phenomena would occur in their own laboratories, and although Eisenbud arranged for Serios to be examined in other laboratories, by other researchers than those assembled in Denver, the results were intriguing but not as striking.

The whole matter came to a head in a manner straight out of Chesterton and Bergman, a non-fictional enactment that never fails to astonish me in recounting it. Enter now two professional photographers, David B. Eisendrath and Charles Reynolds, from Popular Photography—a monthly magazine, largest of its kind with hundreds of thousands of subscribers—(both of whom were amateur magicians) and a professional magician and sleight of hand artist, specializing in cards (a seemingly wayward but brilliant youth in his late 20s who was only now attending college and who subsequently became a renowned professor of statistics at Stanford University, discoverer of the randomizing effects of card shuffling—Persi Diaconis). The professional magician Diaconis in fact was financed on his trip to Denver by Martin Gardner, an editor of Scientific American and a notorious skeptic of all things parapsychological. It was now June 3, 1967. At this point, Ted had produced over 400 ostensibly paranormal prints in 3 years time, since he began with Eisenbud on April 3, 1964. *The World of Ted Serios: "Thoughtographic" Studies of an Extraordinary Mind*, the first edition of Eisenbud's compelling books on the Serios phenomenon, had just been published by William Morrow. It would seem that matters were moving along particularly well.

That Wednesday, the three amateur magicians arrived at Jule Eisenbud's home in Denver. They had come with the intention of determining whether Ted's use of what he referred to as a "gismo" could account for the results he got. The "gismo" was a half-inch cut section of the plastic tube that carried the chemically impregnated piece of hard foam—which one used like a squeegee to fix the Polaroid print after it developed. Often Ted held it between his thumb and one of his fingers, placing it flat against the lens of the camera, to help him concentrate and supposedly to keep his fingers away from the lens. Although using the device really made little sense, Ted's sometimes need for it appeared to be like the need for the little repetitive ritual that an athlete finds essential, for example when he serves the ball in tennis or bats in baseball or putts in golf. Nevertheless, as Eisenbud noted, this device "never failed to arouse darkest suspicions on the part of uninitiated observers"—their hypothesis usually being that Ted placed a piece of film or picture into the "gismo" which accounted for the images he received. Never mind that Ted got images to appear when separated from the camera and when other people held the camera and that sometimes he did not use the "gismo" at all. (More than three dozen pictures were obtained with Ted at varying distances from cameras and gismos operated by others, at nine different locations and at twelve occasions; there were thirteen people other than Ted holding and triggering the camera [Eisenbud, 1989, p. 78].) Never mind that he often received different images one after the other, as people observed his movements closely. Never mind that the psi pictures themselves had significant and seemingly impossible distortions or apparent additions (sometimes from different historical times) or seemingly impossible perspectives. Never mind that Ted was sometimes so inebriated when he was really "hot" that it would have been difficult for him to perform any smooth, surreptitious maneuver, much less something requiring the dexterity of a sleight of hand in front of his audience. Never mind that sometimes the images he produced were distortions of people in the room, strange perspectives and juxtapositions, for which it would have been impossible to prepare in advance. Never mind that he was never discovered with anything inside the "gismo," which was often observed closely when he used it, it being entirely empty. And never mind that even were all the scientists who observed him easily distracted and somehow missed observing that Ted placed some object into the gismo each time he got a "hit," no one had succeeded in producing under normal conditions the type of sessions that Ted held when he was "hot," one hit after another, unpredictable variations on who held the camera or which camera was used, and unpredictable images—cumulative psi and procedural phenomena that are so challenging. Never mind these things, for the two photographers and amateur magicians and the professional magician financed by an arch skeptic and scientific editor of a major publication, were all loaded for bear. They were determined to find by what normal means Ted produced his pictures.

However, after two hours of fruitless attempts, Ted had produced no images—not the first time this had happened—which left him irritable and frustrated. And at this point, slightly inebriated after consuming quantities of beer, he "sullenly refused to hand over the gismo for inspection when asked to do so by Diaconis" (Eisenbud, 1989, p. 223), contending that there was no point because he had not gotten any pictures. The three investigators left seemingly empty-handed either in seeing images produced or in finding fraud. Something psychologically must have been set in motion within Ted after this visit, however. Twelve days later, at another session with a Swedish photojournalist present, Ted kept on getting "blackies" (a blackie showed no image and only a black surface where one would naturally expect at least an image of reality and while technically evidentiary that something was at work, a blackie had none of the excitement of a thoughtographic image), which frustrated him to such an extent that he exploded. Angrily, he demanded that the journalist turn the back of the camera to him, at which point he brought his fist down hard on the camera, and said "Develop *that* now." The print that was pulled showed a curtain.

And indeed, it was "curtains." What Eisenbud had always feared—that Ted's psi abilities might stop as mysteriously as they had begun—had come to pass: "What we didn't realize, but what seems obvious in retrospect, was that the curtain symbolized 'The End' just as plainly as the fifth act curtain of *Hamlet*," wrote Eisenbud 20 years later in the revised edition of *The World of Ted Serios* (Eisenbud, 1989, p. p. 217). For years after June 3, 1967, Ted attempted to get images and none came, other than blackies or whities (completely white fields), which while inexplicable had none of the power to amaze that psi images possess. And so, just as happened to the magician in Bergman's movie, Ted's psi power waned. He spent the rest of his life in doomed attempts to recapture the magic that had once existed.

The sequel though is crueler by far than just this disappointment. In October 1967, the two amateur magicians and photographers published in Popular Photography a damning article, claiming that not only did Ted refuse to show them his "gismo" but that when he pulled away from Diaconis who had reached for the gismo, Ted *could* have dropped something into his pocket from inside the gismo. They had not seen anything in the gismo, but it *could* have been there (Eisendrath, 1967; Reynolds, 1967)

And now the lessons conveyed by Chesterton and Bergman in their fictional dramas played out in a harsh reality. Remember how large the circulation of Popular Photography was, and remember too how the resistance to psi phenomena among established society was so chillingly depicted by both artists. This combination proved lethal. One would think that anyone investigating the phenomena would read Eisenbud's work in full or at least Eisenbud's book, before taking the opinion of a two hour session with three men (published in a popular journal rather than a scientific one and devoid of scientific protocol), none of whom make reference in a meaningful way to what the existing psi-mediated prints show or the number of people who observed Ted close at hand.

However, the publicity from the October 1967 *Popular Photography* article caught on like wild-fire, and the description that the three magicians provided then began to morph into something else entirely. Thus, in 1972, Reynolds changed his story, stating that he *had* observed Ted dump a gimmick into his pocket when asked to turn it over. Then in 1987, Reynolds returned to his original version, stating that he had *not* seen Ted drop a gimmick into his pocket, but that unexplainable images *could* have been made with the use of a hidden gimmick. (Clarke, 1985)[6] Diaconis did not publish anything until over ten years later (he actually remained anonymous until that point); now a recognized mathematician he wrote an article in Science in which he stated that "[o]n one trial I *thought* I saw him secretly load something into the tube [my emphasis]" (Diaconis, 1978, p. 132). Twenty years later, in an interview in New Scientist, this description had morphed into a statement that he *had* seen Serios load a marble with a photo attached to it into the tube (Mullin, 2007, pp. 52–53).

But the most pernicious invader against scientific and even-handed assessment of the Serios phenomenon was a professional Canadian-American magician who had turned his knack for publicity into the debunking of psi: James Randi, who went by the stage name "The Amazing Randi," but whose original name was Randall James Hamilton Zwinge. The vitriol that attached to Randi's attacks on Eisenbud—combined with untrue statements concerning Eisenbud's reports—are for a dispassionate observer something to behold: they seem exactly like the snarl of the Royal Medical Councilor Vergerus in Bergman's Magician who stated that he abhorred what Dr. Vogler practiced because it represented the unexplainable. The writer Michael Prescott nicely summarizes that vitriol in discussing the Serios case as it appears in Randi's book *Flim-Flam* (whose subtitle, *Psychics, ESP, Unicorns and Other Delusions*, is in itself demeaning). "(I)t is interesting to take note of Randi's style of argument," says Prescott. "(His) relatively brief treatment [of the Serios case] includes the following snipes at parapsychology":

> simple little minds … silly … delusions. You'll *never* be a parapsychologist at that rate…. Isn't para-psychology just grand, folks? … the psi nuts … any parapsychologist will hesitate to look too carefully … the irrationality of his kind … inane … preposterous … nonexistent are the powers of Serios and the objectivity of those who investigated him … naivete … duped … [Eisenbud] will carry his delusions with him to the grave … perhaps Dr. Borje Lofgren had it right when he described parapsychology enthusiasts as "decaying minds" with "thinking defects and disturbed relations to reality" … Dr. Eisen-bud is not rowing with both oars in the water [Prescott, 2006].

One would have thought—given the utter and complete nastiness of Randi, the inaccuracy of his summary of the Serios material and his failure to duplicate Serios's productions by sleight of hand (despite his elaborate protestations that it would be possible to do so, he then refused to take up the challenge [Eisenbud, 1975])[7]—that an enlightened world would greet Randi in regard to the Serios phenomenon with opprobrium, as it would if he had ventured forth with such sloppy accusations and unscientific attributes into any other field of scientific inquiry. Far from it, however. In fact, the exact opposite.

Since his attacks on Serios, showman and debunker Randi, has been heaped with public praise. For example, in 1986, he received a John D. and Catherine T. MacArthur Foundation Fellowship—sometimes referred to as a "genius" award—of $272,000 dollars, as an "educator." Admittedly, in 1986 Randi had done a celebrated and accurate investigation of a charlatan by the name of Popoff, who was a television psychic and showman of some renown who appeared before large audiences and apparently performed feats of extraordinary telepathy (accompanied by healings and predictions) with audience members. Randi showed that assistants planted in the audience transmitted information to Popoff about audience members by the perfectly ordinary means of radio transmitters so that Popoff could then appear to "psychically" know about them when he called upon them. Randi demonstrated these transmissions, which he had intercepted and recorded, on The Johnny Carson Show, with the result that Popoff lost his followers and quickly became bankrupt (although he now has revived his career) (Randi, 1989, pp. 139–181).

Unfortunately, this useful type of debunking was very different than Randi's inability to investigate the actual psi phenomena produced by Serios, phenomena evaluated by a sophisticated and in no way mercenary psychic researcher, Eisenbud, and by the Ph.D. and M.D. professionals who assisted him. For the fact is that Randi took on the Serios phenomena in a manner that belied any pretense to accuracy by anyone who has examined the Serios material in any detail.

—⁓—

At the beginning, I mentioned that we would end this story in an obscure campus building in Baltimore. In 1999, Jule Eisenbud passed away at the age of 91 (Serios himself died in 2006). There was a question of what to do with the remarkable Serios data—the Polaroid photographs, the notes, the story of what is the most evidentiary psi event in all of our history. Due to the intervention of Dr. Stephen Braude, a noted parapsychologist, who had a professorship at the University of Maryland in Baltimore and remains one of the few parapsychologists to promote Eisenbud's work with Serios—as well as the fortunate openness of Tom Beck, Chief Curator of the Special Collections at the Albin O. Kuhn Library at the Baltimore campus of the University—the University of Maryland accepted all of Eisenbud's work (courtesy of Eisenbud's son Eric) and housed and catalogued it at the library in Baltimore.

The library is in a forbidding, almost factory-like building of stone and glass. A number of years ago, I spent days at the library, looking at the Serios photographs, courtesy of the affable Tom Beck, a middle aged man of pleasant appearance—exact, modest, and evenly modulated as a librarian would be expected to be—and yet enthusiastic in his desire to champion his Serios collection. As in all well-kept archives, one has to wear white gloves so as not to damage the documents and photographs; only pencils not pens are permitted on one's person, also as a protective measure. It is very quiet and library assistants softly and graciously bring boxes of the photographs, all carefully catalogued by year. Thus, I got the opportunity to hold in my hand the original pictures that are reproduced in Eisenbud's books on Serios and his journal articles.[8]

I had been looking forward to this visit with great anticipation for a long time. After all, I could now touch a photograph that could only have been produced, in its strange details, through psi phenomena, as one might touch a piece of a comet from outer space that had, in its meanderings, come to rest on earth. I thought I would be emotionally overwhelmed. But looking at a picture which only could have been obtained through psi, is not the same thing as seeing the picture produced in real time. There was neither Chestertonian nor Bergmanesque drama here. There was no magical moment, no internal thunderclap—as when the Polaroid paper was peeled away from its backing and something appeared that seemed simply impossible, while Serios drank or commented or smoked or went on to produce yet another impossible picture. There were no impassioned intonations of "Be there, baby, be there." I was disappointed. Intellectually I could wonder about the privilege of holding in my white cotton gloved hand such a psychic photograph, but emotionally each photograph seemed to be just an old Polaroid print—albeit more often than not strangely constructed.

These prints sit largely untouched in this antiseptic archive, a place rarely visited and far from the attention of the world. And thus, there is no deus ex machina to end this story, no unexpected summons from the King that rescues these strange and wondrous players—the scholarly and brilliant Dr. Eisenbud, and his often drunken and even more amazing charge, the psychic Ted Serios—from the cynical assaults of self-appointed debunkers; or brings to the archives in a nondescript building on a Baltimore campus, the attention of a modern audience: the acclaim that *should* come when a small—and intellectually frightening—fragment breaks off from the universe, a fragment that silently challenges us to question everything (just as Chesterton and Bergman suggest we do)—everything we thought we knew about how our world is constructed.

Notes

1. I am grateful to the late Jule Eisenbud who alerted me over forty years ago to the significance of Bergman's *The Magician*.

2. Arthur Conan Doyle, a contemporary of Chesterton's who of course also wrote detective stories, made the same point in a more dramatic way when he attacked psychic researchers referring to them as "those

meticulous researchers who insist upon tying up a medium until the poor creature resembles a fowl trundled for roasting, and who … ruin their own results" (Conan Doyle, 1926, p. 93). Toward the end of his life, Conan Doyle abandoned the ways of his alter ego, Sherlock Holmes, and became a proselytizing Spiritualist, whose indiscriminate appreciation of mediumistic productions left much to be desired … and whose adoption of Spiritualist beliefs, over and above his interest in psi phenomenon itself, left G.K. Chesterton dismayed.

3. Although Shaw—unlike his orthodox and more traditional friend Chesterton—was acerbically opposed to organized religious belief and very much in favor of scientific progress including the theory of evolution, his relationship to the paranormal was more complicated than one might suppose. Weekly, Shaw's mother organized a séance and Shaw contended she introduced the first planchette into Ireland; she also believed in "spirit photos"—the precursor to the Serios phenomenon (Shaw, 1972, p. 280); Frank Podmore (who became so influential at the Society for Psychical Research and co-wrote *Phantasms of the Living*) was a fellow Fabian, and Shaw attended with him meetings of the Society for Psychical Research (Henderson, 1911, p. 127); in 1908, the same year as his taunting letter to Chesterton, Shaw published a play, *Getting Married*, which featured in a positive light an aging woman clairvoyant (Shaw, 1990); and at one point Shaw stayed with T.E. Lawrence and others at a haunted house but had a nightmare from which he awoke feeling he was grappling with a ghost and became so frightened that he fled the house. In 1941, he recounted to the psycho-analyst/parapsychologist Jan Ehrenwald an incident of apparent telepathy, that he believed had occurred to him: He had been thinking of Maurice Baring, a British man of letters, from whom he had not heard in years, and then the very next day received a letter from him. He also contended to Ehrenwald that he had been vic-timized by a physically debilitating "telepathic curse" from an enemy, although the example he provided might as readily be construed in another light—as an unconscious recognition of the presence near him of this enemy and then a self-induced self punishment (Ehrenwald, 1941, pp. 38–39).

4. The relationship between magical tricks or magic and psi phenomena is explored more fully in Chapter Nine. There I suggest that magic was developed as an effective psi-conducive technique by shamans, only to subsequently play a diametrically different role in Western culture where the stage magician through magic now helps to relieve the audience that psi exists.

5. Bergman's "magician" reminds one of the shaman, who practices sleight-of-hand maneuvers to create a belief in psi phenomena in his audience. I explore this in Chapter Nine, on "Magic and Psi," contrasting the original use of sleight-of-hand magic as a psi-conducive technique to its subsequent development in Western society as a method of dealing with the anxiety that psi creates by denying that it occurs. Another movie that plays with this juxtaposition is *Leap of Faith*, in which a charlatan faith healer, named Jonas Nightingale (of course an overdetermined choice) played by Steve Martin, unwittingly and to his surprise cures a partially paralyzed child at one of his events and as a result abandons his life as a con man (Manheim, Picker & Pearce, 1992). A consultant to that movie, incidentally, was the sleight-of-hand magician Ricky Jay.

6. Reynold's final changed version occurred in the British television series hosted by Arthur C. Clarke. In addition to an interview with Reynolds, the video contains footage of an attempt by Eisenbud and Serios, ten years after the curtain fell, to once again have Serios produce thoughtographic pictures. The effort they go through for hours on end, without results, is quite striking (similar to the lengthy effort when things *did* work out). Equally striking (and distressing) is the extent to which Eisenbud encourages Serios to drink liquor (what Eisenbud refers to as Serios' "film juice" [the video begins with their visiting a liquor store]) in the hope that Serios's more intoxicated state would facilitate the thoughtographs as in fact it often did in the past. Now, though, nothing happens, although Ted is convinced each time a picture is snapped that a psychic pho-tograph will appear. In their determination to conjure the elusive but very real "magic" that once existed, a weathered Serios (like an athlete past his prime) and his once successful coach poignantly try to recreate the past.

7. As Serios said, "I'd be happy to get pictures by trickery, if only someone would just show me how" (Eisenbud, 1975, p. 96).

8. I had one session with Ted Serios and Eisenbud at Eisenbud's home in Denver in the mid–1970s with Paige Hooper-Reichbart also in attendance, at a time when Serios was no longer producing images. It was uneventful in terms of images appearing although there were some "blackies," that is complete blackness where ordinarily an image would appear—evidentially as significant but unfortunately not nearly as con-vincing.

References

Bergman, I. (1960) *Four screenplays of Ingmar Bergman*. L. Malstrom & D. Kushner (trans.) New York: Simon & Schuster.

Bergman, I. (2007) *Images: My life in film*. M. Ruth (trans.). New York: Arcade Publishing.

Chesterton, G.K. (1913[?]) *Magic: A fantastic comedy*. UK: Dodo Press.

Chesterton, G.K. (2006) *The autobiography of G.K. Chesterton*. San Francisco: Ignatius Press (Originally pub-lished 1936).

Chesterton, G.K. (2009) *Orthodoxy.* Lexington: Popular Classics.

Clarke. A.C. (1985) Fairies, phantoms, and fantastic photographs (May 22, Episode 8) In *Arthur C. Clarke's world of strange powers.* Visual Entertainment Network (DVD).

Conan Doyle, A. (1926) *The land of mist.* London: Hutchinson.

Ehrenwald, J. (2010) An autobiographical fragment. In R. Pilkington (ed.) *Esprit: Men and women of para-psychology, personal reflections, volume 1.* San Antonio: Anomalist Books, pp. 36–44.

Eisenbud (1967) *The world of Ted Serios: Thoughtographic studies of an extraordinary mind.* New York: William Morrow.

Eisenbud, J. (1970) *Psi and psychoanalysis: Studies in the psychoanalysis of psi-conditioned behavior.* New York: Grune & Stratton.

Eisenbud (1975) On Ted Serios's alleged confession. *Journal of the American Society for Psychical Research,* 69 (1): 94–96.

Eisenbud (1989) *The world of Ted Serios: Thoughtographic studies of an extraordinary mind.* 2d ed. Jefferson, NC: McFarland.

Eisendrath, D. (1967) An amazing weekend with Ted Serios: Part II. *Popular Photography* (October): 85–87, 131–133.

Henderson, A. (1911) *George Bernard Shaw: His life and works.* Cincinnati: Stewart & Kidd Co.

Manheim, M., & Picker, D.V. (Producers) & Pearce, R. (Director) (1992) *Leap of faith.* [Motion Picture] United States: Paramount,

Mullin, J. (2007) Interview: The chance of a lifetime. *New Scientist,* 193, Issue 2596, March 24, 2007, pp. 52–53.

Prescott, M. (2006, August 1) Re: Let's get Serios [Web log comment]. Retrieved from: http: //michaelprescott. typepad.com/michael_prescotts_blog/2006/08/lets_get_serios.html.

Randi, J. (1982) *Flim-flam! Psychics, ESP unicorns and other delusions.* Buffalo: Prometheus Press.

Randi, J. (1989) *The faith healers.* Amherst, New York: Prometheus Press.

Reynolds, C. (1967). An amazing weekend with Ted Serios. Part I. *Popular Photography* (October): 81–84, 136–40, 158.

Shakespeare, W. (1993) *The Yale Shakespeare: The complete works.* W.L Cross & T. Brooke (eds.). New York: Basic Books.

Shaw, B. (1972) *Bernard Shaw: Collected letters, 1910.* New York: Dodd. Mead & Co.

Steene, B. (2005) *Ingmar Bergman: A reference guide.* Amsterdam: Amsterdam University Press.

FIVE

Telepathy and Psychic Connections in James Joyce's *Ulysses*: A Window into the Psychoanalyst's World

Psychic Connections in Ulysses

One of the greatest novels of the twentieth century, emblematic of modern times, is James Joyce's *Ulysses*. This densely written and experimental tour de force, first published by Sylvia Beach in 1922, recounts a day in the life of Leopold Bloom in Dublin—June 16, 1904. The other main character is Stephan Dedalus, an intellectual and haunted young man, plagued by guilt and Jesuit self-doubt, who is an alter-ego of Joyce himself. The novel recounts the interior life of these two very different characters as they go through this one day; and the plot, such as it is, shows how these two main characters not only share mutual concerns and dynamics but how they meet on June 16. In effect, the novel depicts an elaborate and internal psychic dance that takes place between Bloom and Dedalus, much of which they themselves are unaware but to which the reader is privy, that brings them together.

There are many ways of commenting on this magnificent work, but for our purposes what is remarkable about it (and yet generally unremarked by both parapsychologists and psychoanalysts alike) is the thesis of unconscious communication between people as represented by Bloom and Dedalus—of a substratum that at seemingly erratic intervals connects people's unconscious minds as they go through life. As Tolstoy did with the psi elements in Anna Karenina, Joyce depicts unconscious psi-mediated communications, not so much highlighting them but rather embedding them into the work, often with subtle clues, albeit much more elaborate than the Russian master attempted. In both cases, and fascinatingly, unless one is determined to follow the hints and clues very much as a detective, the reader may not even notice many of these psi elements. Their connectedness will tend to register on *the reader's* unconscious, very much as it appears that psi phenomena register on people's unconscious in real life.

In effect, in *Ulysses*, Joyce articulates a thesis of how the world is put together. Put differently, Ulysses is an elaborate dissertation on the role that psi phenomena play in daily life. There is no other major work of fiction that does this to such an extent, and although there have been many observations about Joyce's use of stream of consciousness, few commentators have focused on the theoretical underpinnings of this work. Perhaps the greatest exception is a criticism that all but matches Joyce's brilliance: John Rickard's "Joyce's Book of Memory: The Mnemotechnic of Ulysses," published in 1999. What I present here uses Rickard's work as the principle point of reference, from which I attempt to add psychoanalytic and parapsychological adumbrations.

Joyce and His Environment

The relationships Joyce made often reflected the general interest in parapsychology that existed among the intellectuals of Trieste and Zurich (two cities in which Joyce lived) in the early twentieth century. For example, Joyce's closest friend in Trieste at that time was Ottocaro Weiss, a cultured man familiar with music and literature who was the brother of the Italian psychoanalyst Edoardo Weiss. Ottocaro knew both Freud and Jung whom he discussed with Joyce. In addition, Joyce's other very good and earlier friend in Trieste was Ettore Schmitz, an uncle of the same psychoanalyst Edoardo Weiss. Ettore under the pen name Italo Svevo wrote novels that Joyce resurrected and then actively promoted, including the later work *Zeno's Conscience*, published in 1923, which has been described as the first psychoanalytic novel and features (and ridicules) a mediumistic table turning scene (Svevo, 2003). In fact, Schmitz is often believed to be the model for Leopold Bloom himself, and certainly Joyce relentlessly plumbed both Weiss and Schmitz about Jewish customs and characteristics, which he then added to the attributes of Bloom in *Ulysses* (Ellman, 1982, pp. 272, 395–396).

With Ettore and then Ottocaro, Joyce shared his thoughts, his readings, and his drafts of passages of *Ulysses* and spent time in each city, going to operas and concerts together. To add to the mix the psychoanalyst Edoardo Weiss, Ottocaro's brother and Schmitz's uncle and now considered to be the father of Italian psychoanalysis, was very much in favor of the study of parapsychological phenomena. With Emilio Servadio, who became Weiss's analysand and who ultimately became a foremost parapsychologist/psychoanalyst in his own right, Weiss participated in experiments with the medium Ereto in Naples in 1932. When Freud was told by Weiss of his interest, Freud stated:

> Contemptuous rejection of [parapsychological] ... studies without any experience of them would really be to imitate the deplorable example of our opponents.... [T]o take flight, in a cowardly fashion and behind the shelter of disdain, from the allegedly "supernatural" shows very little confidence in the trustworthiness of our scientific Weltanshauung [Weiss, 1991, p. 70].

My basic point, however, is that the milieu in which Joyce found himself was heavy with parapsychological and psychoanalytic thought.

Despite Joyce's closeness at least by association to Edoardo Weiss and Joyce's familiarity with psychoanalysis, Joyce remained highly skeptical of and ambivalent toward psychoanalysis itself throughout his life. One of his patrons, Edith McCormick, tried to convince him to go into analysis with Jung but he refused (Ellman, 1982, p. 466–469): "I want no expurt nurses symaphy ... I can psokonaloose myself any time," he wrote in *Finnegans Wake* in apparent reference to the incident (Joyce, 1939, 522.34–35); in turn, for whatever reason, Jung himself apparently did not initially have a particularly good impression of Joyce, and at one point wrote a critical piece on *Ulysses*, saying that it could be read as easily forward as backward (Ellman, 1982, p. 628). He was ambivalent however. Thus, subsequently he wrote to Joyce that despite the disagreeableness of *Ulysses* he had learned a great deal from it, and that he admired Joyce's understanding of women, which he felt was greater than his own.

In later years, the serious mental illness of an especial woman, Joyce's daughter Lucia, brought the two men more closely together, when Joyce in desperation sought out Jung to treat her, after failed attempts by literally nineteen other therapists. At the beginning, Jung established a good rapport with Lucia but the treatment eventually broke down. Unfortunately, Joyce appears to have had difficulty recognizing at times the extent of Lucia's mental illness; he over-identified with her, believing her to be particularly clairvoyant—parapsychology appearing again—and to be talented as a writer, and he appeared to have great difficulty realizing that her way with words (similar to his own) in her case betrayed a loss of reality rather than brilliance (Ellman, 1982, pp. 675–681).

One might think that given the extent to which Jung embraced parapsychological phenomena, sometimes under the concept that he developed of "synchronicity" and at other times accepting of psychokinesis (during an argument with Freud about psi phenomena, Jung contended that the sudden knocking sound in a bookcase was a sign of psychokinesis—he called it a "catalytic exteriorization"; the skeptical Freud a seeming "poltergeist"—[Jung, 1989, pp. 155, 361–362]), and the extent to which he believed in a kind of universal unconscious—that he and Joyce might in more substantive ways make reference or allude to their similar beliefs about psi. However, this apparently never happened. Nor for that matter, although familiar with some of Freud's writings, does Joyce ever make mention of Freud's parapsychological speculations. And although Freud had a particular love of literature, acknowledging the work of many authors, he never wrote about James Joyce's contributions and this despite Joyce's frequent references to dreams and levels of consciousness in his work.

Ulysses and Hamlet

Ulysses is a study of the memory of its two main characters and how those memories determine their day and their ultimate psychic connection. Those memories are marked by mourning for the death of loved ones. These two very different men, Bloom and Stephan Dedalus, on June 16, 1904, are dressed in mourning black. Bloom is dressed in black funeral clothes because on this day he attends the funeral of a friend, Paddy Dignam. In addition, Bloom is still mourning the death of his son, eleven years ago who lived for only 11 days (the number 11 appears repeatedly in Ulysses and symbolically is used to bind together the characters which I will show shortly). And Stephan is dressed in the obligatory black of mourning because of the death of his mother a year ago. Each character feels guilty about the death that attaches to him, the agnostic Stephen because he refused his mother's wish to pray when she asked him on her death bed; and Bloom because he believes his son's sickliness was a consequence of a lack of masculine potency on his part. What *Ulysses* is largely about is both characters attempting to "work through" their separate mournings, which culminates in their meeting each other near the end of the day.

In fact, the deep parapsychological connection that takes place between these two characters is determined by these respective traumatic events. Joyce, as the other authors and playwrights discussed in this book, suggests that trauma can give rise to psychic connectedness (almost as if there is a desperate unconscious psychological reaching out by the traumatized individual). This seems to be a common unstated theme in great works of fiction that invoke psi. Thus, psi events happen to Hamlet, upon his father's death; to Anna Karenina, when Vronsky leaves her; and to Adela Quested, E.M. Forster's heroine in *A Passage to India* who is lonely and very much charmed by Dr. Aziz and who attempts to put down her growing awareness that she does not love her fiancé, Ronny Heaslop—a different kind of loss, but a loss nonetheless.

In this list, I began with *Hamlet* with a particular intent. Joyce was an ambitious man. Although *Ulysses* takes its name and its continual symbolic references from Homer's *Odyssey*, the other continual references and allusions are to Shakespeare's work, and specifically to the play *Hamlet*. In effect, Joyce plumbs in this epic book, two of the most celebrated literary works of the Western world, *The Odyssey* and *Hamlet*. Moreover, and here is the point, what engages Joyce is exactly what Shakespeare attempts to explore in *Hamlet*—the workings of psi phenomena. Moreover, Joyce is acutely aware of the great playwright Shakespeare himself and the fact that he wrote *Hamlet* after the death of his son Hamnet—another trauma that Joyce suggests led to the depiction of psi phenomena by Shakespeare in his play. In effect, Joyce is addressing in literary terms the exact same things that I have addressed in speaking of *Hamlet* in Chapter One. That is, he takes seriously the ghostly manifestations that occur in *Hamlet* the play, is fascinated by the relationship of the play to the life of Shakespeare and the death of his son Hamnet, and is much closer in his novel to the sense of the play *Hamlet* as a parapsychologically informed work than are most literary commentators or even parapsychologists. Taking the ghost of Hamlet's father as psi phenomenon rather than metaphor, he weaves this phenomenon into a fabric which depicts psi communication in general. When I chose to write about *Ulysses*, I had a vague sense of the role of psi in the novel, but it has been a revelation for me to discover the extent to which Joyce, is clearly fascinated by psi, and places it at the very center of this great work.

Thus, what binds all these "characters" together, including Shakespeare and Hamlet, are death and unresolved mourning. That is, Bloom mourns the death of his son Rudy; Stephen Dedalus mourns the death of his mother; Hamlet the death of his father; and Shakespeare himself the death of his son Hamnet. The culmination of this appears in the final "Circe" section of Nighttown when Bloom and Stephan, having encountered each other at a whorehouse, see in a mirror the face of William Shakespeare, "beardless ... rigid in facial paralysis" (*U* 15:3822) and Shakespeare hallucinatorily speaks to them; and when Stephen's mother appears to both of them also hallucinatorily (like a ghost) with aspects of her that seem to arise from Bloom's own life rather than just Stephen's. In addition, one of the conclusions of their meeting at the whorehouse, is that Bloom in effect rescues Stephan from the establishment, which has taken much money from him, and acts fatherly toward his new charge (which has much meaning given the focus on fathers and sons in Joyce's work and given the fact that Bloom has lost his real son).

But this culmination is proceeded by frequent instances of telepathy and similar memories between the two characters as they unknowingly and slowly approach each other during the day. Put differently, the Circe scene involving Shakespeare's appearance is the penultimate and intermingling point of their unconscious associations during the day. In other words, as in *Hamlet*, psychic phenomena are crucial to the structure of the novel.

Here is Rickard's description of this process (Rickard, 1999):

Bloom and Stephen share many strange coincidences of thought and memory in Ulysses, seemingly telepathic exchanges that imply the ability of one mind to draw on the experiences of another. Some of these shared memories are very recent thoughts or events that occur to one character appearing in the mind of the other only hours later.... Other shared memories go much deeper, allowing the characters to access more distant memories, events that happened years ago but still have a crucial significance for Stephen and Bloom on June 16, 1904 [p. 91].

And here again:

The widespread interest in telepathy and shared mind among Joyce's contemporaries provides a context for the telepathic exchanges between Stephen and Bloom, shared memories that suggest mysterious and complex bonds between the characters, allowing a sense of destiny, of importance, to build up around their meeting and to prepare for the climactic "Circe" episode in which memories and symbols relevant to one character's experience become available and useful to the other [p. 92].

Let me give three examples of this. They are filled with hints and associations that are difficult to unravel but in this regard, they resemble those tantalizing but hard-to-pin-down connections so often characteristic of dreams and events that have psi elements in real life.

1. Stephen's Dream of Haroun al Rashid

Stephan struggles to remember a dream of his from the night before. He gets fragments:

Wait. Open hallway. Street of harlots. Remember. Haroun al Rashid. I am almosting it. That man led me, spoke. I was not afraid. The melon he had he held against my face. Smiled: creamfruit smell. That was the rule, said. Come. Red carpet spread. You will see who [U 3:365–69].

When later in the day, he finds himself in Nighttown, the dream appears precognitive to him: "Mark me. I dreamt of a watermelon.... It was here. Street of harlots.... Where's the red carpet spread?" (U 15. 3922 and 3930–31). At the same time, Haroun al Rashid (in actuality he was the author of A Thousand and One Nights) appears in one of Bloom's fantasies and then when Bloom leaves the prostitute's house, one of the prostitutes, Bella, impressed by him, asks him who he is: "Who. Incog." He does not answer but he invokes Haroun al Rashid, as Stephen did before; imagining himself to be Haroun al Rashid, he: "draws his caliph's hood and poncho and hurries down the steps with sideways face. Incog Haroun al Raschid he flits behind the silent lechers and hastens on ... with fleet of a pard [a leopard]" (U 15.4324–26). And for that matter, the pard itself appeared earlier in one of Stephen's fantasies, when he thought of a dog digging in the sand on the beach as a "pard ... vulturing the dead" (U 3.363–364). The symbolic significance of digging up the dead is related to the theme of the entire novel Ulysses itself. Digging up the past is a constant concern for both characters and at one point, Stephen describes himself as one who wishes to "wrest old images from the burial earth" (U 10.815). In addition, as now becomes apparent Bloom *also* struggles to remember a dream of the exact same night as Stephen's! He thinks: "Dreamt last night. Wait. Something confused. She had redslippers on. Turkish. Wore breeches. Suppose she does? Would like her in pyjamas." The "her" here is his wife Molly. He wonders whether he would like her in pants and then thinks of her in petticoats.

Thus, both dreams, Stephen's and Bloom's, on the same night evoke the exotic East, with similar (red carpet and redslippers) if not exactly matching elements.[1] Lastly, with regard to the melons so vividly recounted in Stephen's dream, Bloom famously thinks of Molly near the end of *Ulysses* in terms of melons. When they are in bed, he kisses the "plump mellow yellow smellow melons of her rump, on each plump melonous hemisphere, in their mellow yellow furrow, with obscured prolonged provocative melonsmellonous osculation" (*U* 17; 2242–43). In so many ways then, Stephen and Bloom psychically and very specifically connect around a sensuous theme.

Exactly how are these two dreams related psychodynamically? Poor Bloom, whose wife is cheating on him with her lover Boylan, which he knows about, tends to facilitate the relationship between the two in a masochistic fashion. Into this masochistic tendency of Bloom's walks another man as well: Dedalus. Here, I cite Nabokov, whom I discovered soon after writing this section had also been intrigued about these linked dreams:

> So on the night of 15 June to 16 June, Stephan Dedalus in his tower at Sandycove, and Mr. Bloom in the connubial bed in his house on Eccles Street dream the same dream. Now what is Joyce's intention here, in these twin dreams? He wishes to show that in his Oriental dream Stephen foresaw a stranger offering him the opulent charms of his, the dark stranger's, wife. This dark stranger is Bloom [Nabokov, 1980, p. 328].

The wife of course is Molly.

2. Rudy

Bloom's son, who only lived for 11 days, was named Rudy. He was buried in a "little wooly jacket" (*U* 18/448) or a "fair corselet of lamb's wool" (*U* 14/269) knitted by Molly, Bloom's wife. Yet early on, before we learn this, Stephen sees two old women descending steps to the beach on which he is walking, one of whom is holding a bag. He imagines them to be midwives and thinks: "Number one swung lourdily her midwife's bag…. One of her sisterhood lugged me squealing into life. Creating from nothing. What has she in the bag? A misbirth with a trailing navelcord, hushed in ruddy wool" (*U* 3: 32–37). If the reader is observant, he will catch this unmistakable psi connection (ruddy wool and Rudy in a wool jacket) between Stephen's fantasy and Bloom's sad reality. If the reader does not, it will nonetheless register unconsciously.

3. Bloom, Stephen and Shakespeare: The Number 11

These midwives are not to be so easily forgotten. We are later told that in the midwife's bag there are actually "eleven cockles" (*U* 10:1275–76). The number eleven links together Bloom, Stephen and Shakespeare. For one, Stephen has a haunting disquisition on Shakespeare contending (as other commentators have done) that Shakespeare played the part of the Ghost in the production of *Hamlet*. Stephen is troubled by the poignancy of this. He says:

> It is the ghost, the king, a king and no king and the player is Shakespeare, who has studied Hamlet all the years of his life which were not vanity in order to play the part of the spectre. He speaks the words to Burbage…: Hamlet, I am thy father's spirit, bidding him list. To a son he speaks, the son of his soul, the prince, young Hamlet and to the son of his body, Hamnet Shakespeare, who has died in Stratford that his namesake may live for ever [*U* 9.165–173].

As Stephen points out, Hamnet lived for 11 years; and he posits that Shakespeare's mourning attaches to the character Hamlet, in some way interchangeable for his own deceased son Hamnet. As mentioned before, Bloom's son, Rudy, lived for 11 days (and died 11 years ago). Added to all of this is the fact that Stephen is enthralled by a poem involving the number 11, which he associates to the death of his mother. The poem is:

> The fox crew, the cocks flew,
> The bells in heaven
> Were striking eleven.
> 'Tis time for her poor soul
> To go to heaven

Thus, the mourning Bloom, the mourning Stephen are associated with the mourning Shakespeare; and the eleven cockles actually in the midwife's bag just add to the psi connections.

Complex, yes, and difficult to follow or untangle. But Joyce presents a definite model here of how people interact parapsychologically—that is they often have psi connections that are outside of their conscious awareness. Their psi communications are experienced subliminally. For example, tracing how the number 11 occurs in the thoughts and events of both Stephen and Bloom, Rickard (1999) says: "Eleven thus takes on suggestive power for both Stephen and Bloom *that exceeds their own awareness of the connections between them* [my emphasis], bringing them together unconsciously through shared, but buried, associations and memories" (p. 150). This is an important aspect of the Joycean model. It is in fact the reader that becomes part of this interaction, not just for the number eleven, but throughout the novel. As Rickard (1999) says in another place:

> Just as the similarities between characters lie beneath the surface of the novel, available to the careful reader but not, for the most part, to the characters themselves, so the shared memories serve to link the characters subconsciously rather than consciously, giving us access to a deeper level of significance than the characters are consciously aware of ... [p. 96].

If one were to tease out the theme that lies behind the shared memories for both characters it would be their mutual trauma concerning loss and feelings of guilt toward the lost object.

Reality and the Model of Psi in Ulysses: Relevance to Psychoanalysis

This model presented by Joyce of how people relate parapsychologically may seem very far removed from most people's experience. The fact that the two main characters in *Ulysses* are—more often than not—unaware of their psi connections (and only the reader is, and even then, only to some extent because he may not consciously pick up on the subtle threads that Joyce intertwines) may seem to many people to have little counterpart in real life, and regardless it would seem almost impossible to investigate or verify such connections in real life since neither party tends to know about them. So Joyce's construction may appear to some to be precious or phantasmagoric or both.

However, what is most intriguing is that there is one (and only one) endeavor where one may discover and explore a real world that seems to match Joyce's exposition—and that is the psychoanalytic endeavor. The psychoanalyst who leaves him or herself open to the psi hypotheses when treating patients may find himself in the same world as the reader of *Ulysses*. As he becomes aware of the internal processes of his many patients, he may then find that *unknown to themselves* they are communicating telepathically with each other, through the medium of the analyst. As the psychoanalyst Eisenbud explained, using as an example two patients who were in a "telepathic rêve à deux":

> One of the most interesting aspects of telepathic behavior occurs when two or more individuals who are unknown to each other effect a psychological relationship in their seemingly separate dreams which seems to transcend the conventionally conceived barriers of time, space and ordinary sense perception. Such dreams appear to be by no means rare and are occasionally seen during the course of analyses, where the analyst may be privileged to explore the conditions of such an occurrence with greater or less success [Eisenbud, 1947, p. 39].

These interactions very much resemble those that Joyce invents in *Ulysses* between Stephen and Bloom. In fact, it is amazing that Joyce had the imaginative insight to all but recreate what a psychoanalyst experiences in these situations. Put differently, psychoanalysis verifies Joyce's hypotheses about how the unconscious of various people may communicate, and it is psychoanalysis which confirms Joyce's view of how the world is constructed. There is one difference however and that is that the psychoanalyst, who actually is more or less in the place of the reader of *Ulysses*, recognizing the psi connections between characters of which they themselves are unaware, plays an important *dynamic* role in the psi interactions of his patients (which of course the reader of *Ulysses* does not). That is, patients unknowingly and unconsciously compete with each other for the psychoanalyst's attention by producing these psi interactions; and—to make it more intriguing still—in the process more often than not they unknowingly tap into the psychoanalysts own thoughts, feelings, wishes, and life events.

   This aspect of psi in psychoanalytic treatment I discuss in more depth in Chapter Six, where I provide an abbreviated history of psychoanalytic findings on this subject, since Freud's first papers telepathy, and draw the reader's attention particularly to the work of Eisenbud. But here let me give some examples of these dynamically determined psi connections that take place in treatment, often unbeknownst to the patients unless the analyst intervenes to point them out. I will provide two examples, the first from the work of the psychoanalyst Eisenbud, who provides many instances of this; and the second, from my own psychoanalytic work.

Psi Correspondences Among Eisenbud Patients

"The Dark Skinned Lady"

   There are literally scores of examples that appear in Eisenbud's works, from which I could choose, so that this one rather than being unique is simply presented as illustrative. Eisenbud (1970) tells of three patients who present similar dreams at the same time. Thus, Mrs. S., who is pregnant and near term, dreams:

> I am on a large lake or ocean, where I am somehow rescuing a dark skinned Spanish lady. With one hand I am grasping the dock, and with the other fondling her breasts. Off to one side, is a Cuban boy in a row boat.

The second patient, Mr. L., dreams:

> I am on a steamship named the S.S. Egypt, apparently plying between New York and Egypt. On board there was a sort of dive, and in it I was watching a beautiful dark skinned girl tap dancing. She danced so that now and again we would catch sight of her thighs and her vagina.

The third patient, Mr. F., dreams:

> I am in a rowboat with you, fishing. You hooked a large fish which you then left me to struggle with and reel in. The fish had a terrifying yet beautiful mouth and set of teeth ... [my ellipsis] You went off to a smaller rowboat where you sat in a huddle with a woman who was probably another patient. When I finally caught the fish it turned into a dark skinned lady from Haiti who spoke Spanish and whom I couldn't understand ... [p. 184].

These dreams are interrelated in their manifest and latent content, and also attach to events that took place in Eisenbud's life that evening when a friend of his, at a dinner engagement, expressed the fantasy that his next child would be born with a "full set of teeth," which appalled rather than amused his also-pregnant wife, who recognized his aggression. The correspondences in the three dreams latent meaning and their association to an event in Eisenbud's life make for what Eisenbud says is "something as complicated as chess," reminding us of how complex Joyce's psi correspondences are in *Ulysses* itself. For example, and here I am simplifying from Eisenbud's account for the sake of the argument, we are told that the first dreamer, Mrs. S. has a persistent masturbatory fantasy of being a tap dancer who reveals her vagina to her dance master (one here might read analyst) in the course of a high kick. Thus, Mr. L. in effect is unconsciously competing with Eisenbud to be the one to observe Mrs. S.'s charms. Mr. F., the last dreamer, too wants to be part of this interaction having caught "a fish that turned into a dark skinned lady," this time from Haiti. Perhaps the "hate" aspects of this has some meaning, for indeed there is much in these dreams to suggest not only a birth "fantasy"—actual birth and being rescued from water—but oral aggression. Eisenbud suggests that Mrs. S.'s latent desires are to provoke sexual desire in men and then to deny them.

Eisenbud observes all of these interactions but in this case, there is no indication that he makes his patients aware that they are involved in an elaborate cross-correspondence of dreams and real events (at other times, he does do so, as I explain in Chapter Six). Thus, Eisenbud is in the role of the reader of *Ulysses*, an omniscient observer. Unlike the reader, however, upon learning from these patient's psi associations the force and power of their desires, he may be able to fashion interventions or interpretations toward each one in the course of their psychoanalyses. Such interpretations or interventions, from his point of view, will have to incorporate hypotheses of why each patient unconsciously invoked psi. In addition, there is always the strong possibility that these psi connections are related to something in Eisenbud's dreams or in his life, as happened here, which also he will have to take into consideration in determining his patients' motives.

Psi Correspondences Among My Patients

"The Raccoons"

In 1998, I published a memorial article about Jule Eisenbud in the *Journal of the American Society for Psychical Research*, which I entitled "Jule Eisenbud: Explorer" and which I have also included in the Appendix (Reichbart, 1998). At the end of the article, I recounted what had happened when a patient said to me that he thought of himself as a polar bear who would maim and kill me if I got too close to him. Immediately after my patient left, I sat down to read a psychoanalytic article by Per Anthi, in which he examined the thoughts of Amundsen, the discoverer of the South Pole, when he had been attacked by a polar bear, and miraculously escaped. It seemed that my patient's fantasy was a precognition of my reading this article; and his unconscious invocation of psi, seemed to be his way of staying in contact with me—despite his aggressive feelings toward me (which given the Per Anthi piece might also suggest the hope that I might miraculously escape my patient's aggression)—after he left his session.

The *Journal of the American Society for Psychical Research* is a very obscure journal, with as of yet no online presence, and all but obsolete in terms of current publishing, so it is highly unlikely that any patient of mine subsequently would have had access to my article on Eisenbud. And yet in 2011, thirteen years later, Mr. H., a professional man in his early sixties, dynamic and articulate and always impeccably dressed, who is in twice a week treatment on the couch, begins a session by telling me that he has been reading an article about Amundsen, the explorer. He tells me, which he has not previously mentioned, that Amundsen is a favorite of his and when he was younger *he* dreamt of being an explorer like Amundsen. I am somewhat on the alert now. Despite his impeccable dress and suave appearance, Mr. H *is* somewhat of an adventurer I think to myself, in terms of his physical activities out West. In this regard, I say to myself, he resembles Jule Eisenbud, who did somewhat similar adventurous things also out West where he lived, to those of Mr. H. and who was also often suavely dressed. I wonder whether Mr. H, psi-wise, is saying "I am an explorer too." He then tells me that he had the following dream, which he describes as "particularly vivid": "I am walking in the woods and I see a raccoon that is eating the dead body of an opossum. I give it a wide berth as I walk by."

Now it is fairly easy for us to work with this dream, at least by itself. Mr. H. has been going through a painful divorce of a wife of thirty years. As we have discovered, he married someone very much like his mother who was much less engaged in life than he is. Passive and subject to depression, his wife rendered his marriage torturous and then she became distressingly lifeless. Thus, we conclude that the meaning of the dream is that he wishes to express his rage at the "passive" opossum, who not only is "playing dead" in the dream but is actually dead. Mr. H., however, has a distinct aggressive streak, sometimes verging on the sadistic, at least in his fantasies toward women, no doubt because of his unresolved (and unacknowledged) feelings toward his mother, who while not as compromised as his soon-to-be-ex-wife, was less-than-giving toward her son when he was growing up. Much of his therapy, in fact, is directed toward his starting to acknowledge this fact.

While I discuss this with Mr. H, I am acutely aware of the parapsychological elements of his dream, over and above my thoughts about my long-ago patient and the article on Eisenbud I published, because, unknown to Mr. H. my previous patient, Ms. Y, had been talking this day, and in her previous session before today's as well, about the fact that *she saw two raccoons coming out of a hole in the top of a garage next door, and she has been wondering, somewhat obsessively, whether she should tell the owners of the house to which the garage belongs.*

Why does there then seem to be this psi connection? I wonder. Is Mr. H competing unconsciously with Ms. Y, saying "I am a true adventurer. She may see two raccoons but I can bring you a psi event and talk about Amundsen?" Is there some "pun here" on the "wide berth" Mr. H gives the animals in his dream and are the two raccoons coming out of the hole in the roof like a birth? Perhaps Mr. H. is reacting to Ms. Y's passivity toward telling her neighbors, warning them in effect, which may reflect the failure of anyone to protect her from years of sexual abuse from a family member.

Then just to complicate things further, my next patient, Ms. X, also in analysis (who just prior to entering treatment divorced her husband, the father of her two elementary school children because she experienced him as cruel and sadistic) comes in and tells me the following dream: "I am observing my ex-husband with a woman supervisor of mine. He is supposed to do contract work for her. But he suggests that as part of the work he can kill four pairs of animals that she wants killed."

Again, it is difficult for me, in thinking of Mr. H's dream, in which he in effect kills off an "opossum" through the agency of a raccoon, not to link it with Ms. Y's experience of seeing a "pair" of raccoons, emerging from her neighbor's roof, and now with Ms. X dream of having pairs of animals killed. Is Ms. X through her dream saying that *she* can imagine solving the problem of the two raccoons by simply killing them, although through the agency of her ex-husband? In thinking about her dream, Ms. X associates the animals in pairs to her own two children, for whom she feels her ex-husband is an emotional danger. She is in some ways right about this—and "contract work" certainly suggests killing on top of that. But she herself is often not the best with these children, so that the aggression expressed toward them in the dream is also hers. Meanwhile, Ms. H who sees the two raccoons being "born" out of the roof is herself childless and unmarried. Her own ambivalence toward having children is in fact considerable.

Seeing these associations, it is possible to recognize dynamics in which each patient is struggling with his or her own sense of aggression and asking for attention about it from me by unconsciously evoking psi. Certainly, the dream of Mr. H. sets that stage, particularly given the link to Amundsen where the issue was the aggression of a polar bear, and my own writing, years before about another patient whose aggression also had a psi link to my reading about Amundsen's polar bear. But as intriguing as these seeming psi links are—and however closely they resemble the type of linking that Joyce proposes in *Ulysses* in which the reader knows the psi associations even though the characters themselves do not—I could think of no way to use them. In retrospect, I might have hazarded something with Mr. H. in particular because my sense was that characterologically he would have been the most open to entertaining the psi hypothesis, least threatened by it, and even intrigued by it.

Unlike Eisenbud, who often sketched out these links for his patients during treatment, contending that to do so revealed dynamics to them which the patients otherwise might not have been able to accept, I tend to do so much less frequently, as I further indicate in Chapter Seven, "Psi and Psychoanlysis II: Rescuing Sisyphus Today." And so, I am left very much in this case in the position of the reader of *Ulysses* who becomes aware of the detailed and very particular psi connections of the characters, many of which the characters themselves have no idea.

Conclusion

Let me end with what continues to seem so passing strange to me. Here we have *Ulysses*—one of the emblematic English literary works of our times, one to which we frequently allude in our modern life—just as we have the great works of Shakespeare, particularly *Hamlet*, written in the 16th century, to which every schooled person in Western civilization can make reference. These two works in particular are part and parcel of our modern consciousness. We may make easy reference to "to be or not to be" (which has an especial poignancy given the existence of the ghost in *Hamlet*); we may feel we know Bloom and Dedalus or celebrate Bloomsday by a public reading of all of *Ulysses* at the Y in New York City. And yet, and yet—we too often seem unaware that both these emblematic works are in part cogitations on parapsychological phenomena, cogitations by two of the Western world's greatest literary thinkers; or for that matter, that one of the driving forces behind the writing of *Ulysses* was Joyce's wish to explore the parapsychological dynamics depicted in *Hamlet*. Put differently, Joyce—unlike so many other commentators—was aware that Hamlet (and in a sense Shakespeare) was internally tortured by things parapsychological. How is it possible that we so steadfastly refuse to register these facts? How is it possible that we do not acknowledge that these two literary masters are plowing the same ground and that Joyce is consciously addressing a similar sense of psi-connectedness that Shakespeare addressed in the play *Hamlet*, in fact that Joyce is invoking Shakespeare for this very reason? Why do our literary and philosophical critics who touch upon *Ulysses* or *Hamlet* fail to embrace this aspect of these works, much as psychoanalytic commentators fail to pursue the parapsychological findings in Freud's writings? And why so uniformly prefer to fit the psychic connections and the ghosts that appear in the writings of Joyce and Shakespeare (and Tolstoy and Foster and so many others), into the framework of poetic license or metaphor rather than into parapsychology?

We celebrate Joyce and Shakespeare for their intuitive and dynamic insights into human nature. And we celebrate *Hamlet*, the play, and *Ulysses*, the novel, for the representative way these great works reflect Western understanding of human experience. What will it take for us to recognize that these two great artists enlist the very same intuitive insight they bring to human emotions in general to also explore psi processes, and by so doing, that they contend that these processes are embedded in our experience?

Notes

1. In her book *Phantoms of the Clinic*, Mikita Brottman (2011, p. 30) makes a reference to Nabokov who, in lectures published in 1981 but given during the 1940s and '50s at Cornell and Wesleyan, commented on the linked dreams in Tolstoy's Anna Karenina of Vronsky and Anna (Nabokov, 1981, p. 162). Five years before Nabakov's publication became available, I also discussed in detail the linked dreams in *Anna Karenina*, which now appears as Chapter Two of this book. In tracing this down still further, I recently turned to another lecture of Nabakov's in the two-volume series of his lectures, this one published in 1980, only to discover that in writing about Joyce's *Ulysses*, Nabokov says: "Nobody has noticed yet … no commentator has noticed yet that as in Tolstoy's *Anna Karenina* there is in *Ulysses* a significant double dream; that is, the dream seen by two people at the same time" (Nabokov, 1980, p. 326). It is very nice to know that, without having any awareness of Nabokov's writing on this subject, I have ended up plowing the same ground as did he.

References

Brottman, M. (2011) *Phantoms of the clinic: From thought transference to projective identification*. London: Karnac.
Joyce, J. (1939) *Finnegan's wake*. London: Faber & Faber.
Joyce, J. (1986). *Ulysses*. New York: Random House.
Nabokov, V. (1980). *Lectures on literature*. New York: Harcourt.
Nabokov. V. (1981). *Lectures on Russian literature*. New York: Harcourt.
Eisenbud, J. (1947). The dreams of two patients in analysis interpreted as a telepathic Reve à Deux. *Psychoanalytic Quarterly*, 16: 39–60.
Eisenbud, J. (1970). *Psi and psychoanalysis*. New York: Grune & Stratton.

Ellman, R. (1982) *James Joyce*. Oxford: Oxford University Press.

Rickard, J. (1999). *Joyce's book of memory: The mnemotechnic of Ulysses*. Durham: Duke University Press.

Roazen, P. (2005). *Edoardo Weiss: The house that Freud built*. New Brunswick: Transaction Publishers.

Weiss, E. (1991). *Sigmund Freud as a consultant: Recollections of a pioneer in psychoanalysis*. New Brunswick: Transaction Publishers.

SIX

Psi and Psychoanalysis I:
Rescuing Sisyphus

One who accepts the evidence in support of telepathy and clairvoyance as conclusive would only praise Freud's open-mindedness on the subject and also his inclination to adopt a positive attitude toward the conclusions drawn from it, as one more example of his far-sightedness and willingness to contemplate the improbable.—Jones, 1957, p. 374

I am ... prepared to believe that behind all occult phenomena lies something new and important: the fact of thought-transference, i.e., the transferring of psychical processes through space to other people.—Freud in Weiss, 1991, p. 69

Perhaps the problem of thought-transference may seem very trivial to you in comparison with the great magical world of the occult. But consider what a momentous step beyond what we have hitherto believed would be involved in this hypothesis alone. What the custodian of [the basilica of] Saint-Denis used to add to his account of the saint's martyrdom remains true. Saint-Denis, is said, after his head was cut off, to have picked it up and to have walked quite a distance with it under his arm. But the custodian used to remark: "Dans des cas pareils, ce n'est que le premier pas qui coûte." [In such instances only the first step is hard] The rest is easy.—Freud, 1921, p. 192

The history of the exploration of psychic phenomena by psychoanalysts is remarkable, not only for the discoveries but for the continual need of the psychoanalytic establishment to deny those discoveries or, in the alternative, to bury them, so they are unearthed anew, rediscovered, and supposedly for the first time decades later. In other areas of psychoanalysis, gradual change has often occurred, as aspects of development or of attitude have given way to new, less biased understanding. Thus, for example, Freud's view of women and their development, with its phallocentrism, has been challenged and his theory drastically revised; or his failure to fully recognize pre–Oedipal and early childhood determinants of development, has been noted, resulting in an increased focus on attachment and characteristics of separation-individuation; or the pathologizing of homosexual object choice has been discontinued; or the greater appreciation of countertransference and enactment has supplanted the judgmental constraints that formerly attended clinical treatment, resulting in a refreshingly more open and human interaction between analyst and analysand. These theoretical changes have tended to bring together contemporary analysts who speak with each other and struggle together as part of a mutually agreed upon effort to further the clinical understanding of the psychoanalytic endeavor, and sometimes are even able to do so when their theoretical orientations—

relational, object relational, contemporary Freudian, Jungian, Lacanian and so on— differ.

None of this is the case in the attempt to understand the intersection of psychic (or what is referred to by parapsychologists as "psi") phenomena and psychoanalysis. The discoveries that Freud himself made about the dynamics of psi are ignored (in favor of an emphasis on his admitted ambivalence toward the psi hypothesis) and sometimes even when alluded to, they are minimized; the psychoanalytic articles on psi that graced the American psychoanalytic journals from the Psychoanalytic Review to the Psychoanalytic Quarterly in the 1940s and 1950s (and most famously collected in George Devereux's book collection of these articles, *Psychoanalysis and the Occult*, published in 1953)—have too often been forgotten; and the great insights to the field of psychoanalysis and parapsychology by such analysts as Emilio Servadio, Jan Ehrenwald, Jule Eisenbud, Montague Ullman, and Nandor Fodor (to name a few) are overlooked. More often than not, those unfamiliar with this area believe that Jung must represent the principal contributor to it as a consequence of his theory of "synchronicity" as well as his theory of the "collective unconscious," despite the fact that his psychodynamic contributions to the field were actually very limited and his work was not integral to the discoveries made by the analysts I have just named, including Freud. (I do pay tribute to his concept of the collective unconscious when I discuss Joyce's *Ulysses* [Chapter Five]; and for a fuller discussion of Jung and parapsychology see Main, 2012; Jung, 1977; Cambray, 2002.) Whereas Freud was fascinated by psychic phenomena, he was less open to phenomena beyond telepathy than Jung and also skeptical of Jung's tendency to mingle the investigation of psychic phenomena with mysticism; nor did he hold out much hope of successfully exploring mediumistic productions in séances because he believed the darkness that invariably attended these events and the lack of control of the medium precluded scientific protocol (Weiss, 1991, pp. 13, 69). Nonetheless, Freud's dynamic discoveries concerning telepathy and the principles he suggested as part of these discoveries were groundbreaking.

It also is rather amazing that the early history of psychic phenomena prior to Freud, as well as contemporaneous to him which touches upon psychoanalysis is obscured in most psychoanalytic reports. That history travels from Mesmer and his followers through hypnotists to such illustrious figures as Janet, Einstein, Upton Sinclair, William James and Walter Franklin Prince—to simply name a few—to say nothing of the vast data (700 cases) relevant to telepathy published in *Phantasms of the Living* by Gurney, Myers and Podmore in 1886. Again, whereas psychoanalysts are aware of aspects of psychological history by therapists prior to Freud (such as Charcot) they seem unaware or minimize the parapsychological history pertinent to psychoanalytic understanding of psychic phenomena that preceded Freud's first articles on telepathy—and of which Freud himself, a member of the British Society for Psychical Research and an honorary member of the American Society of Psychical Research, clearly was aware, although he admitted to being uncomfortable with exploring beyond telepathy.

In addition, there is the problem I alluded to in my introduction to this book: the literature here tends to fall into the gap between parapsychology and psychoanalysis, and those in these respective fields often have little interest in or are reluctant to venture outside their realms. Psychoanalysts associated with psychoanalytic investigation of psi phenomena, in addition to Freud, are often strikingly important figures—Balint, Burlingham, Bion, Ferenczi for example—but parapsychologists are unlikely to recognize these figures in the same way as psychoanalysts would recognize them; nor have psychoanalysts integrated their collective work into an ongoing and organic history of psychoanalysis and psi. The consequence is that little on-going discussion takes place. For example, for years there has been a proposal before the American Psychoanalytic Association to have a Discussion Group at their annual winter meeting to discuss parapsychology and psychoanalysis. Despite the fact that briefly, under the auspices principally of Elizabeth Lloyd Mayer (more of which later), such a group had previously existed, and despite the fact that the members proposed for the discussion group are in other respects prominent analysts (Susan Lazar, Ira Brenner, Ruth Rosenbaum) the decision of the American has been to consistently refuse to grant this Discussion Group a venue. Recently, a smattering of excellent articles, most strikingly in the relational journal *Psychoanalytic Dialogues* and in *American Imago*, as well as some books on psi and psychoanalysis have appeared but they cover ground previously explored by earlier analysts, particularly of the 1940s and '50s referred to above. As interesting as these contributions are, often the authors make mistaken assumptions about psi, not fully aware of the history of psi and psychoanalysis, and generally appear disinclined to explore the broader findings of parapsychology itself. However, because this recent trend in *Psychoanalytic Dialogues* and *American Imago* is encouraging, and a tribute not only to these authors' courage but to the foresight of the editors of these journals who have opened their pages to articles dealing with telepathy (something which historically preeminent psychoanalytic journals for a period of time since the 1960s refused to do). I synopsize some of the articles in the chapter following this one.

Perhaps the most striking aspect of all this is the extent to which the discoveries of one psychoanalyst, Jule Eisenbud, who built upon the findings of Freud, tend to be forgotten, marginalized, or dismissed, most particularly the data and exposition concerning psi that appear in his groundbreaking book *Psi and Psychoanalysis*, published in 1970 (Eisenbud, 1970) as well as subsequent books such as *Paranormal Foreknowledge* (Eisenbud, 1982) and *Parapsychology and the Unconscious* (Eisenbud, 1983a). (Many of Eisenbud's articles appeared originally in the *Journal of the American Society of Psychical Research*—my articles appeared there as well—once a dynamic and important publication with fascinating contributions and discussions. Unfortunately, it does not have an online presence and it became moribund in 2004, making it particularly difficult for researchers to access it and even less likely for those outside of parapsychology such as psychoanalysts to do so.) Whereas earlier papers of Eisenbud's are often cited, whereas Devereux's *Psychoanalysis and the Occult* (in which a few of Eisenbud's earlier papers appear) is sometimes seen by commentators as seminal, the achievement of the book *Psi and Psychoanalysis*, which is infinitely broader in scope, is missing from most contemporary psychoanalytic accounts. What is equally curious is that contemporary authors consistently attribute to other psychoanalysts the discovery of certain types of psi data or the revealing of the analyst's dream or personal life as it intersects with such data, despite the fact that Eisenbud so prolifically provided examples of exactly these things in his 1970 book and thereafter. Perhaps this is partly attributable to the fact that *Psi and Psychoanalysis*, long out of print, is difficult to locate; but even then, those commentators who apparently have located it, give it unusually short shrift. Or it may be attributable to the fact that Eisenbud's other explorations went far beyond telepathy itself, including precognition and psychokinesis, which has served to frighten off those psychoanalysts who have ventured into parapsychology from even considering Eisenbud's less controversial telepathic data. Ultimately, however, the overall tendency in psychoanalysis to excise or diminish important work in this field gives one pause, as happens when one finds that history favors some thinkers over others, as well as some theories over others, despite their inherent worth or groundbreaking nature. We are fortunate when long forgotten creative achievements which have been buried are rediscovered and resurrected, whether it be a ground-breaking monograph on peas or a novel concerning a white whale, but unfortunately this is not what always happens. Perhaps this chapter may help in some way to correct the tendency to obscure Eisenbud's and others' achievements and encourage interest in a remarkable but threatened field.

The reader should be forewarned that my purpose in this chapter (and the next one) is *not* to summarize the experimental parapsychological studies that have been done that show the existence of psi phenomena nor to recount the extensive history of scientific psi investigation. Parapsychology is an enormous field and any psychoanalyst at all curious about it will find a plethora of phenomena that have managed to escape incorporation into our psychoanalytic literature as well as innumerable scientific studies. For a sense of this, I would recommend two large compendiums of articles, Edgar Mitchell's (the astronaut who subsequently became a parapsychologist) *Psychic Exploration: A Challenge for Science* (Mitchell, 1976) and Benjamin Wolman's *Handbook of Parapsychology* (Wolman, 1977).

Nor is my purpose in this chapter to provide a complete history of psi as it intersects with psychoanalysis. Again, the history here is extensive. Summations of it have been attempted by others, to which I refer the reader (see, e.g., Eisenbud, 1970; Eshel, 2006). What I *do* try to do in this chapter is present specific discoveries that have been made in the field of parapsychology that touch upon psychoanalysis, particularly with regard to the most ubiquitous of the phenomena and the one most likely to be encountered clinically—telepathy, before, during and after Freud; and then to allude to other psi phenomena that have been explored psychoanalytically. Rather than relate a detailed history of these discoveries, I focus on three things—*Freud's historical place* in parapsychological investigation; the *principles of psi functioning* that were first articulated by him and then expanded upon by other pioneers in the fields of parapsychology and psychoanalysis; and *significant subsequent contributions* that have been made by certain analysts (and one philosopher) in this field (this third category carries on into the next chapter). In effect, I try to show how psi manifestations have been understood psychoanalytically, how they appear in psychoanalytic treatment, and what we have learned, in a psychological and psychoanalytic sense, about them when they manifest themselves. In doing so, I try to address misconceptions that tend to result when an analyst or an analyst's patient has a telepathic experience and then the analyst extrapolates from that single experience without adequate reference to the extensive psi and psychoanalysis literature; or when an analyst accepts the popular understanding of psi phenomena, which he then attributes to superstition, without any awareness of other hypotheses concerning the data. At the end, I share some examples of psi phenomena that have appeared in my own clinical practice over the years.

In providing this idiosyncratic history, as well as an even more contemporary history in the chapter following this one, with its emphasis on principles, I am trying to fashion a parapsychological foundation to which a psychoanalyst might turn. A psychoanalyst who reads this and who then comes upon data or dreams or events that seem psi-determined in her clinical work, hopefully will have the benefit of this background. And as a result, perhaps she will not feel compelled to single-handedly push the Sisyphean rock up from the base of the mountain but will recognize that what she has found has been discovered and discussed previously, and the principles already isolated. The Sisyphean rock, to continue this admittedly forced metaphor, actually has come to rest today on a slender perch at least half way up. Thus, this chapter is designed to encourage the psychoanalyst to incorporate the principles of psi discovered by past and contemporary psychoanalysts so that an organic understanding of this field can flourish. Put differently, I would like to ensure that no contemporary report of psi phenomenon in psychoanalytic work begins with the inaccurate statement that "Little has been written in this area..." or "This is the first report of..."

On "Unconscious Communication"

The term "unconscious communication" between analyst and analysand has become popular in recent years in the psychoanalytic literature. Much is communicated between analyst and analysand that is not just attributable to the manifest words spoken, despite the emphasis in classical clinical theory on talking and interpretation (in the past, reports of psychoanalytic sessions often read like transcripts of a court proceeding in which everything was squeezed out of the interaction between the two parties except the words spoken). Thus, the trend toward discussing what occurs unconsciously between patient and analyst is a positive one. But the term "unconscious communication" is often loosely defined and broad, subsuming within it communication of one's intonation, body posture, glances, hesitations, tendency to think in similar ways or unconsciously recognized ways as a consequence of identification with the other or projection or manifestations of transference and countertransference. And along with these important, even subliminally registered, communications, sometimes psi phenomena are included but often not by that name. The difficulty here is that the specificity of psi communication, the remarkable nature of telepathic dreams or telepathic communications that have been so clearly recounted in past reports, as well as the principles which I will elaborate here, are subsumed within the term "unconscious communication"—often with a kind of amorphous generality—and then largely ignored. It is as if many psychoanalysts prefer to use a term they consider less loaded and less dangerous than telepathy, and do not wish to explore how the specifics of telepathy work, which entails speculating about psychodynamics, much less acknowledge nor reference those psychoanalysts who have examined telepathy. And just as importantly in the process they also entirely avoid entertaining other types of psi phenomena beyond telepathy.

(Here let me note that, as I indicate in the glossary, I also eschew the term "the uncanny" favored by Freud in one of his papers in which he incorporates a grab-bag of unrelated phenomena and which as a term unfortunately has become popular among some psychoanalysts to describe psi phenomena. Equally questionable, and also commented about in the glossary, I try to avoid the term "occult" used by Freud and others such as Devereux. It is a misleading term, since it means "unknowable," and I do not use it because I do not believe any psychological phenomenon is unknowable. Admittedly these two terms are exciting; however, when applied to psi phenomena, they incorporate deceptive assumptions: most particularly they fail to recognize the specificity of psi phenomena on the one hand and its general ubiquity in our lives on the other, much greater than most psychoanalysts [or others] seem prepared to realize. This latter characteristic is an aspect of the phenomena which I stress in this chapter. The terms "occult" and "uncanny" are designed to create shivers of fear and mystery in the reader. My hope is to lead the reader to realize that psi phenomena are a regular feature of daily life which our Western culture has walled off from consideration, denying their existence, or when doing so, denominating them in such a way that they seem strange and unusual. In this regard, even the term "paranormal" implies that there is something beyond "normal" that takes place when psi occurs, which I believe is inaccurate [one of my Navajo informants made a similar point (Reichbart, 1976, p. 393)]. Nonetheless, I do use the term "paranormal" as simply less misleading than the others.)

In fact, I believe the trend with regard to using the term "unconscious communication" is similar to what happened in parapsychology itself, when the term "anomalous experiences" (yet another nomenclature I find misleading) was introduced over forty years ago by some parapsychologists to replace parapsychology, on the understanding that parapsychological phenomena would be subsumed within the term. The hope was that this would make things sound more scientific. But the term often became so broad and undefined, in the same way as "unconscious communication" has become for psychoanalysts, pulling within it so many different things unrelated to psi phenomena that the findings of parapsychology have been jeopardized and the scientific categories and nomenclature of various psi phenomena have been forgotten. I made this argument with Stevenson, a pre-eminent parapsychologist, years ago when the term was first introduced, when a new journal was founded to subsume all type of exceptional phenomena, and when Stevenson sought to fold "parapsychology" into broader fields, such as personality studies (Stevenson, 1988; Reichbart, 1990). (At that time, Stevenson laid a scorched earth attack on *both* parapsychology and psychoanalysis, linking them with phrenology and homeophathy, that have "been refused recognition and have withered" [Stevenson, 1988, p. 314].) My concerns about this tendency in my opinion has been justified. As I said then it is "naive" to hide parapsychology within the "folds of other disciplines." Just because parapsychology struggles as a scientific pursuit, there is no reason to vitiate it by using other language or by allying it with all manner of other and unrelated studies.

From the therapeutic viewpoint, the clinician may not particularly care to pin down whether an "unconscious communication" is telepathy or something else. As part of any on-going therapeutic process, it often may not be appropriate to mount an investigation or it may be a distraction to do so. After all, the psychoanalyst is positioned to heal the patient not to be a parapsychological researcher. However, at other times, the specificity of telepathic messages, as Freud himself suggested, requires looking at those messages in the same way one looks at the specifics of a dream or of any communication in order to dynamically analyze why it occurred. One common—if unconscious—dynamic motivation of telepathic communication is that the patient seeks to gain the attention of the analyst, whom he feels is not giving him enough thought or consideration, by unconsciously invoking telepathy. It certainly serves to bring the analyst up short, particularly when the communication attaches to some hidden feature of the analyst's own life. It invariably leads the analyst to ask himself why the patient—at that moment—sought attention in this fashion. Failure of the psychoanalyst to recognize telepathy and its specificity may sacrifice the import of the psi communication in a clinical sense.

However, today, it is almost as if many psychoanalysts *would* prefer the sometimes mystical sense of a shared "unconscious communication" between analyst and analysand rather than recognizing the possibility of telepathy. Bach has suggested that there is a continuum of "unconscious communication" where telepathic communication appears at an extreme end of the spectrum (personal communication, 2017). Perhaps most interestingly, Brottmann has wondered whether psychoanalysts unconsciously settled on the concept of "projective identification," derived from Melanie Klein and much favored by psychoanalysts after the 1950s (when psychoanalytic investigation of psi, once at its height, waned) to replace an interest in telepathy in part because it was a safer concept. "Projective identification" is a rather turgid term—"mired in uncertainty" says Brottman (Brottman, 2011, p. 100) in trying to trace the various ways in which it has been employed since its introduction in 1946 (Klein, 1946, p. 99). Klein suggested that the infant "expelled" destructive feelings, anal and urethral in origin, "into the mother." As a consequence, the mother came to "contain" bad parts of the self and she was "not felt to be a separate individual but to be the bad self." In analysis, it was felt something similar could take place between patient and analyst. The patient could project parts of himself into the analyst, to such an extent, that the analyst would be perceived by the patient as having acquired those characteristics (Segal, 1964, p. 126). It was further suggested that the analyst could be so affected that he would find himself acting in a manner congruent to those projected elements. Some commentators, such as Meissner find the term can often be used as a justification for a countertransferential reaction by the analyst (Meissner, 1980). Regardless, the term is used to describe a sense of deep mutual identification between analyst and patient that sometimes can take place in analysis.

I am not sure that I agree with Brottman's suggestion that projective identification became a more acceptable substitute for telepathy and thus accounted for the dearth of articles on telepathy after 1950. However, it is striking that psychoanalysts seem more than willing to use such metaphorical concepts in relation to identification as "expelling" feelings "into" another person, and to give these concepts valence, despite their mystical sense. Thus, although there may not be the direct correlation that Brottman suggests, the use of "projective identification" as well as "unconscious communication"—mysterious, mystical, even unclear in nature—has proven more acceptable to psychoanalysts than the (ironically) more explicit but forbidden concept of telepathy, which depends for its verification on identifiable and specific details of correspondence as opposed to an amorphous sense of connectedness.

Eshel (2006), similarly, suggests that the shift away from telepathy, was because psychoanalytic thinking moved increasingly "towards feeling-transfer and emotional influences between patient and analyst" after 1970. She emphasizes not only the turn toward the concept of projective identification but the new emphasis on "countertransference" initiated by Paula Heimann and Racker as well as Bion's emphasis on the patient's unbearable experiences being transferred into the analyst where they are modified (Eshel, 2006, p. 1611). Again, many of these concepts rely upon metaphors that are much more amorphous and mysterious than the specifics of telepathy or telepathic suggestion. In an even broader sense, de Peyer summarizes a series of psychoanalytic thinkers each of whom employs his own concept to suggest unconscious attunement between analyst and patient—the "container and alpha functioning" (Bion, 1959), "potential and transitional space" (Winnicott, 1975), "symbiotic relatedness" (Searles, 1973), "reverie" and its interplay between subjectivity and intersubjectivity (Ogden, 1997), "thought unknown" and "receptive unconscious" (Bollas, 1987, 1992), the embeddedness of "unformulated experience" (Stern, 1997) "twilight space in which the impossible becomes possible" (Bromberg, 1996). At the end of this list, she asks tellingly, even plaintively: "So why within psychoanalysis the need to persist with the divide between these methods of attunement and possible paranormal or telepathic attunement?" (Depeyer, 2016, p. 160).

Freud's Contributions Were Essentially About Telepathy

Although Freud was well aware of other aspects of parapsychology (mediumistic productions, poltergeist activity, apparitions, hauntings and precognition for example), his discoveries were only about the phenomenon of telepathy. "You will see" he says at one point, "that all my material touches only on thought-transference. I have nothing to say about all the other miracles that are claimed by occultism" (Freud, 1921, p. 193). It is this principally about which he wrote, side-stepping in one instance clinical material he introduced about apparitions but then refused to comment upon (Freud, 1922). Of instances of putative precognition, or prophecy, he had a parochial view—attributing to it the popular assumption that it necessarily involved a kind of magical time-travel and thus was impossible. He therefore attributed all instances of "prophetic dreams" for example to mis-remembering when the dream actually took place. He asserted that "the creation of a dream after the event, which alone makes prophetic dreams possible" (Freud, 1900, p. 625) was the model to explain precognitive dreams. (His explanation for some prophecies of fortune-tellers while denying precognition did contend that predictions could have been explained as a consequence of telepathy from the sitter.) Thus, the principles which he announced, allude only to telepathy.

Similarly, of hauntings and ghosts, he had a parochial view. One of the most unfortunate of his papers from the point of view of psi and psychoanalysis is "The Uncanny" (Freud, 1919) to which I referred above and in which (as I indicate in the glossary) he throws in everything but the kitchen sink (loss of one's eyes, the double, epilepsy, severed hands, automatons that appear human, the evil eye, resurrection of the dead) as examples that lead one to an uncanny feeling. And into this mix, he adds ghosts and haunting indicating that these phenomena are superstition. It does not occur to him that apparitions might be explained in terms of the telepathic hypothesis or "super-telepathy," which I discussed in more detail in the chapter on *Hamlet*. Those psychoanalysts skeptical about psi, tend to turn to "The Uncanny" paper as representative of Freud's views on psi, without sufficient recognition of the work that Freud did pursue on telepathy in his other papers.

And yet, curiously, Freud was painfully aware that once one acknowledged the possibility of unconscious telepathic communication between individuals—mind to mind connection—the world theoretically opened up to a plethora of phenomena far beyond telepathy. In fact, it was this in part which concerned him about publicly endorsing telepathy. In addition, it has become clear in recent years the extent to which Freud's published work on parapsychology did not reflect his more positive and more impassioned assertions about parapsychology in private. Before I elaborate further, let us turn to the history in which Freud's discoveries were embedded.

Early History of Psi: Mesmerism, British Studies, Telepathic Drawing Experiments

A vast amount of data preceded Freud's first venturing into this field or took place contemporaneously with his early efforts. The most complete summation of this period, beginning with the findings of Mesmer's followers, and proceeding through large statistical gathering of information by British psychical researchers as well as fascinating telepathic drawing experiments is contained in the lengthy Chapter Six of Eisenbud's *Psi and Psychoanalysis*, entitled "The Psi Hypothesis" (Eisenbud, 1970, pp. 41–98). Freud himself was aware of many aspects of parapsychological study, certainly of the British psychical researchers. Here I will focus on three aspects of this, mesmerism and hypnosis, the British Studies, and telepathic drawing experiments. I am leaving out a vast amount of historically studied parapsychological phenomena, most strikingly mediumistic productions, because I want to make accessible to psychoanalysts some of the history most relevant to clinical work.

Mesmerism and Hypnosis

The study of psi phenomena began centuries ago with Mesmerism, the precursor of psychoanalysis itself, rather than, as is sometimes contended, the study of mediums and spirit communication that was ushered in by the Fox sisters in 1848 in Hydesville, New York. It was discovered that psi phenomena sometimes took place with subjects who were treated with Mesmerism. In these cases, telepathy appeared spontaneously when a mesmeric trance was elicited. It was not sought; rather it was a "side effect" of what was believed to be a healing procedure, although at one point it was called "the higher phenomena" of mesmerism. And when the elaborate mechanism of magnets, tubs, rods and other paraphernalia that characterized Mesmerism was dropped in favor of the simpler and more refined inducing of a hypnotic trance—often by hand movements over the body—psi phenomena continued to be in some instances an apparent side effect. The first well-reported instance of this phenomenon occurred in 1784, when Marquis de Puységur, who considered himself a follower of Mesmer, but had already modified the procedure, induced a trance in an apparently retarded peasant named Victor Race who not only then conversed fluently and intelligently (in more than one language) but exhibited psi phenomena, including "suggestion at a distance"—that is the mesmerist could suggest at a distance that Victor fall into trance, which would then happen. In addition, Victor appeared when in trance at times to be in telepathic communication with Puységur.

This early history leads to Freud himself. After Puységur, a series of hypnotists continued to find at times that when in trance the subject exhibited telepathy or went into trance as a consequence of "suggestion at a distance." In 1819, H.M. Weserman reported five successful experiments with telepathy of patients who had been mesmerized, one in which a patient dreamed of a funeral procession, at the time Weserman attended a funeral procession, but the patient made the "error" of seeing the corpse as Weserman himself (an early example of how dreams work in terms of both aggressive wishes and transference). This type of example continued: in 1823, Dr. Alexandre Bertrand (Bertrand, 1823), in 1837 Dr. John Elliotson, Professor of Medicine at the University of London (who greatly influenced Dickens and Thackeray, Dickens to the extent that with one afflicted friend, he acted for many years as a practicing mesmerist employing "suggestion at a distance" [Kaplan, 2015]), in 1846 James Esdaile, in 1876 William Barrett, a Dublin professor of physics before the British Association of Science—all wrote about similar parapsychological experiences with mesmerized individuals (Eisenbud, 1970, pp. 54–63). For those who wish to go further, not only Eisenbud's summary but Eric Dingwall's monumental compilation *in four volumes* of historical reports of abnormal hypnotic phenomena, European country by country, supplies overwhelming data (Dingwall, 1968). Curiously, for reasons that are unclear, these early mesmeric studies disappeared from the consciousness of clinicians, only to be resurrected forty years later when Charcot began his work.

Which now of course brings us to Freud. From October 13,1885 until February 28, 1886, Freud spent a total of four and a half months in Paris (with the exception of a brief break for the new year holiday) at the Saltpetriere with Charcot, the brilliant showman and hypnotist, who so influenced him that Freud decided to leave research and become solely a clinician. Freud was not in any sense in Charcot's inner circle during this brief visit, although he did translate Charcot's work into German. Nonetheless, for Freud the experience was transformative. What is equally fascinating is the variety of outstanding intellectual mental health professionals who clustered around Charcot from countries throughout the world at that time and it was during that time, in particular, that Charcot and others (tilling the same ground as the Mesmerists before, although they had forgotten the earlier work) began to again connect parapsychological phenomena to the hypnotic state (Ellenberger, 1970; Taylor, 2009). For example, on November 30, 1885, Paul Janet delivered for his nephew Pierre, a paper before the Society of Physiological Psychology with Charcot in the chair, in which he described his nephew's investigations into Leonie, a naive peasant woman, whom Pierre had gone to Le Havre to study. Leonie was particularly susceptible to hypnotic suggestion, could be put under trance "at a distance" and in subsequent trials, could apparently when in trance respond to "suggestions at a distance." Charcot was so impressed with Janet's report—which eventually became part of Janet's dissertation and then a book—that he subsequently traveled to Le Havre to investigate Leonie. Liebault and Bernheim, two famous medical hypnotists of the rival Nancy school, went there as well (Taylor, 2009, p. 32). Again, in the winter of 1885, four other papers on telepathic hypnosis were read before the Society of Physiological Psychology (also with Charcot presiding) (Eisenbud, 1970, pp. 58–59). Although Freud does not mention these developments, clearly the atmosphere in which he was working at Charcot's Saltpetriere was rife with speculations and reports about psi phenomena associated with hypnotic trance at the very time he was there. Rather than telepathy being a quirky addendum to Freud's interests, as some psychoanalysts would have one believe, early on in his career—at the time when he became aware of the power of the unconscious through his contact with Charcot—Freud simultaneously became aware that unconscious process apparently could reveal or facilitate psi phenomena.

And the fact is that subsequent contemporary studies by parapsychologists have shown that the hypnotic state can indeed facilitate psi phenomena. Reviewing a vast amount of such psi experiments in 1977 for example, Charles Honorton concluded: "To summarize these studies comparing psi performance in waking and hypnosis conditions, it is clear that hypnotic induction procedures enhance psi accuracy" (p. 447).Hypnosis and other psychological states that bring one closer to unconscious process, are referred to as "psi-conducive" states by parapsychologists.

The British Studies

Charcot's hypnotic studies—acting as a "magnet" in their own right to doctors, psychologists, and other professionals throughout the world—attracted many to come visit him and hear his lectures. Among those present before Freud was the American psychologist William James, who subsequently was involved with psychic research in the United States, in investigating Leonora Piper, a medium, and was one of the founders of the American Society for Psychical Research in 1884. In addition, it was actually Charles Richet, who was later to win the Nobel Prize in physiology, who first introduced Charcot himself to hypnotism in 1878 by allowing the hypnotist Burq into the Saltpetiere to treat patients (Taylor, 2009, p. 20). And in fact it was Richet who did the research that connected Charcot's hypnotism with the early work of the Mesmerists, such as Puyseqer, reestablishing the link from forty years and more previous which had been forgotten by Charcot and others. For many years thereafter, Richet was a prominent psychic researcher (Taylor, 2009, pp. 20–21).

Charcot's work led to more organized parapsychological investigations of another kind. A group of British researchers who eventually formed the backbone of the British Society for Psychical Research were also part of this mix of people drawn to Charcot. Not only did Charcot travel to Le Havre to visit with Janet and observe the peasant Leonie, but so did F.WH. Myers and his brother Henry Sidgwick coming from England. These men, with Frank Podmore, William James, Edmund Gurney and others subsequently formed in 1882, the British Society for Psychical Research, the original model for the American version (for an earlier history of the psychical researchers, see Crabtree, 1993, pp. 266–280). In 1886, Gurney, Myers and Podmore published *Phantasms of the Living*, the seminal survey of spontaneous cases of apparitions of living persons. (I discussed this significant book in Chapter One on *Hamlet*, in which I indicate that apparitions or ghosts—a common feature of all cultures—do not require a hypothesis of "soul" or "spirit" but can alternatively be explained as an elaborated form of telepathy.)

In 1889, Janet's dissertation was completed and presented at an historic event, the First International Congress of Physiological Psychology, in which the importance of the unconscious was stressed. The conference was originally organized by Charcot, but everyone came: F.W.H. Myers, Henry Sidgwick, William James, Binet, Bernheim, Schrenck-Notzing, and Morton Prince, for example. And in addition, Sigmund Freud was there, having come to discuss one of his patients with Bernheim (Taylor, 2009, p. 34). Note too, that the first person to subsequently introduce Freud and Breuer's work to the American public was none other than William James in 1894, who described it as a continuation of the discoveries of Janet.

Again, the point of all this is that Freud was very much exposed to the field of psychic research from early on (not incidentally as a consequence of Jung's interest in these subjects) and psychic research was in many ways an integral part of his early discovery of the unconscious. Although as I indicated he failed to consider apparitions in depth, for example, he certainly would have known of the work from the British Society for Psychical Research. And in fact, many years later, in 1911, he did join that society; and in 1915, he also accepted honorary membership in the American Society for Psychical Research. (Jones, 1957). (Both societies in 2017 are still extant.) For that matter, in 1922, when writing of telepathic dreams, he states that he is aware of "the abundant store of telepathic dreams that have appeared in the literature of the subject. I should not have far to seek, since the publications of the English as well as the American Society for Psychical Research are accessible to me as a member of both societies" (Freud, 1922, p. 199).

Freud's Psi Discoveries

That Freud was ambivalent about pursuing his interest in psychic phenomena is apparent. Ernest Jones constantly warned him about the dangers of doing so, for the future of the profession of psychoanalysis, because an interest in psi might jeopardize its acceptance; and Freud himself wavered and waffled, being very circumspect in what he wrote, not committing himself definitively to a belief in the phenomena (except one could argue near the end) and yet stating at one point in a letter to the psychic researcher Hereward Carrington that if he had to do it over again, he would become a psychic researcher—and then forgetting that he had ever written the letter (!), an example he admitted of his resistance to the subject. He was clearly fascinated by the possibilities of telepathy in particular. His communication with his close and younger colleague the Hungarian Ferenczi, who was involved in investigating psychic phenomena, reveals his enthusiasm; he encouraged Ferenczi's explorations, particular with a psychic named Frau Seidler, and in fact Freud did a series of experiments with his own daughter Anna.

We are indebted to Ernest Jones, who despite his strong disagreement with Freud, devoted in a somewhat even-handed manner an entire chapter to Freud's interest in para-psychology, entitled Occultism, in his biography of Freud, including some of his communications with Freud on the subject. (However, Jones was not above slyly introducing this discussion by referring to Freud's tendency to be superstitious about the meaning of dates and numbers, as in his interactions with his colleague Fleiss, thereby implying that Freud's work on telepathy was "magical thinking" cut from the same cloth, an argument I have heard from more than one psychoanalyst.) Of the frequent summations of Freud's attitude and writing on the subject of telepathy, most recently Eshel composed a succinct and well-researched example which I would recommend (Eshel, 2006).

In terms of publication, Freud published four articles on the subject (plus a brief note). (I have left out his paper on "The Uncanny" which is often included because, as I mention in the glossary, it throws in everything but the kitchen sink and is from the point of view of exploring telepathy uninformative.) Here the four are with a summation of each.

(1921) Psycho-analysis and Telepathy, Standard Edition, 18, pp. 177–193

This is Freud's first publication, in which he discusses two prophecies of fortune teller's, and which also suggests an important principle. Freud comments on a fortune teller's prophecy concerning crayfish poisoning of the brother-in-law of a patient who sat for the fortune teller. The prophecy did not come true, but in fact the brother-in-law, unbeknownst to the fortune teller, had previously experienced crayfish poisoning. Freud hypothesizes that his patient had aggressive wishes toward his brother-in-law that he be poisoned again, which the fortune teller telepathically received, but attributed to the future. The principle in effect is that *telepathic messages can be shared but that one can make false assumptions about their meaning; the popular way in which they are understood can be wrong, but that does not deny the fact that they may be examples of psi.* This is an important observation which (as I will show) can be expanded in many ways beyond what Freud anticipated. A second example, also announcing the same principle and to which Freud returns in other articles, again suggests that a prophecy of a fortune teller, was actually a product of telepathy, rather than precognition. Years ago, the patient had consulted a fortune teller who, in predicting the future of the patient, apparently picked up telepathically on the history of the mother of the patient The patient wished to have a life similar to her mother's, particularly to have two children before she was thirty— and in many respects subsequently did (thus the sense of precognition by the fortune teller) and what the fortune teller was in touch with telepathically was the patient's wish to be like the mother. Note that in both instances Freud seeks to discount the possibility of precognition (indeed in these instances he is probably right to adopt the most economic explanations) by invoking the proposition that secret wishes can be telepathically shared. (Ehrenwald and then Brottman in a wonderful observation, state that the seemingly prophesying Witches of Thane in *Macbeth* might equally be considered to have telepathically picked up on Macbeth's desire to be king and thus this too fits into Freud's examples [Ehrenwald, 1975, p. 110; Brottman, 2011, p. 99]!)

Freud ends this article by expressing another principle, the implications of which he himself avoided and which subsequent commentators have frequently cited. It might be called the "slippery slope principle," which I also cite at the beginning of this chapter. He says of the thought-transference hypothesis:

> But consider what a momentous step beyond what we have hitherto believed would be involved in this hypothesis alone. What the custodian of the [basilica of] Saint-Denis used to add to his account of the saint's martyrdom remains true. Saint Denis is said, after his head was cut off, to have picked it up and to have walked quite a distance with it under his arm. But the custodian used to remark: "Dans des ces pareils, ce n'est que premier pas qui coute." The rest is easy [Freud, 1921, p. 193].

In other words, in these matters, it is the first step that counts. Indeed, this principle underlies the entire field of parapsychology; it represents the slippery-slope that Freud feared but could not help but point out to his readers. Once one admits to telepathy, a variety of other phenomena are necessarily pulled in—suggestion at a distance being the most obvious but others too—which are disquieting to explore. In broader context, telepathy challenges our Western assumptions of how the world is constructed by calling into question how "mind" operates in the sensual world.

(1922) Dreams and Telepathy, Standard Edition, 18, 197–220

This second article of Freud's announces some important principles with regard to a possible telepathic dream that a father has concerning the birth of his daughter's twins that occurs at a distance from him. The initial principle announced is that *the sleeping or dream state facilitates psi*. The second, and a very important one, is that *a telepathic message, unconsciously received, can be transformed in the manifest content of a dream in the same way that a "day residue" sensorily experienced is transformed*. I will elaborate on these two principles shortly.

In addition, Freud takes the opportunity to dismiss, rather gratuitously, seemingly telepathic messages concerning the death of a brother at a distance, which do not involve a dream, as well as the phenomena of an apparition and a knocking sound announcing a death. He attributes all these latter reports to mis-remembering by the subject (the unfortunate and common fallback which can take place when a psychoanalyst is skeptical about psi phenomena). Freud does not explain why in these instances he favors mis-remembering as an hypothesis, but does not do so in other instances.

Freud also makes some personal observations. He states of himself: "I have never had a 'telepathic' dream" (p. 197). The twin-birth telepathic dream that he analyzes is not from his own practice; it is recounted in a letter from the dreamer. In fact, Freud observes that during "twenty-seven years of work as an analyst I have never been in a position to observe a truly telepathic dream in any of my patients" (p. 199). (This applies only to telepathy in dreams; as we will see, he recounts an incident of putative telepathy by a patient during a session but unrelated to the dream state.) He is aware of the "abundant store of telepathic dreams that have appeared in the literature of the subject" and is equally aware of "publications of the English as the American Society for Psychical Research (that) are accessible to me as a member of both societies" (p. 199).

(1925) *The Occult Significance of Dreams, Standard Edition, 19, 125–138*

This very short article repeats the fortune teller's prediction about the woman who subsequently had two children before she reached thirty (as her mother did), stressing the oedipal dynamics of the wish because the patient was close to her father. There are no other examples of psi provided. However, Freud does speak much more openly and positively about his own telepathic experiences and suggests that telepathic "transfer" is not unusual. He says:

> I have often had an impression, in the course of experiments in my private circle, that strongly emotionally coloured recollections can be successfully transferred without much difficulty. If one has the courage to subject to an analytic examination the associations of the person to whom the thoughts are supposed to be transferred, correspondences often come to light which would otherwise have remained undiscovered. On the basis of a number of experiences I am inclined to draw the conclusion that thought-transferences of this kind comes about particularly easily at the moment an idea emerges from the unconscious, or in theoretical terms, as it passes from the "primary process" to the "secondary process" [Freud, 1925, p. 138].

The principle hinted at here is that *telepathy is not so unusual; it can occur to anyone and it does not require dramatic or traumatic circumstances for that occurrence,* although Freud suggests that strong emotional memories are more easily transferred. In his last article, Freud will more explicitly say that telepathy is commonplace.

(1933) *Dreams and Occultism, Standard Edition, 22, 31–56.*

This posthumously published article is perhaps the most significant of the four articles Freud published. It contains the Forsyth case, the only reported case of Freud's involving telepathic material that took place during a patient's session with Freud. (The two prophecies discussed by patients in the 1921 article were presented in session but they did not involve telepathy in vivo, so to speak, nor apparently did Freud share with either patient his thoughts about the dynamic reason for the telepathy.) But in the Forsyth case, when telepathy seemed to occur in the session, Freud mentioned it immediately to the patient, Herr P., and analyzed the reasons for the telepathy with him. Of this example, Freud says it was "the one which left the strongest impression on me" (p. 47). In fact, the Forsyth case was supposed to be included in the earliest 1921 article, but because of what Freud calls his own "resistance," he mislaid his write-up of the case at the time; and only found it later.

In effect, three principles were expounded in this case. The first was that: *patients can invoke telepathy as a result of unconscious competitive feelings toward other patients, using telepathy to observe some aspect of the other patient's life and to gain the analyst's attention in preference to the rival patient.* The second and related principle, is that *patients can invoke telepathy by touching upon the analyst's own life often with similar motivation.* The third principle which has been expanded upon by subsequent analysts is that *the analyst can break the analytic frame and inform the patient of the events or dreams he has telepathically (and unconsciously) picked up from the analyst's or other patient's life. In this way, the patient is provided with additional dynamic access to these psi-mediated associations or dreams or productions of which he would not otherwise be aware.*

In a broader sense, Freud states an overarching principle, citing a prior 1926 paper by Helene Deutsch. It is that *telepathy can be determined by the transference relations between patient and analyst.*

These principles are very important. However, conservative psychoanalysts are wary of recognizing them because they challenge the model of doing treatment to which they subscribe. It is particularly difficult for the psychoanalyst who is more classically trained, and whose model of treatment is to say little about himself, so as to encourage the patient's transference to the analyst as a loved object—father, mother, sibling, to recognize that Freud himself when it came to telepathy abandoned that model. It is even more of a stretch for such an analyst, in working with a psi connection, to inform a patient about another patient, despite the fact that this is exactly what Freud did. An analyst who follows a less conservative model, such as the relational, which permits and encourages the analyst to reveal more of himself to the patient of his feelings or perceptions than the classical model would be more comfortable with Freud's willingness to explore telepathic communications as he did. Perhaps this explains why the largely relational psychoanalytic journal, *Psychoanalytic Dialogues*, as opposed to other publications, has recently been at the forefront of publishing articles that invoke telepathy. However, the interesting thing is that in the past when it came to telepathy many classically trained psychoanalysts have in effect followed the example of the Forsyth case and shared telepathic material, breaking the frame, even though classically trained. (Eisenbud, classically trained at New York Psychoanalytic, as I will show has been the primary exponent of this tendency.) The extent to which this has happened with classically trained analysts in the past has also been minimized by many commentators.

In addition, in this article, Freud explicitly states the principle, which he hinted at in the short article on the occult significance of dreams and that is "if telepathy is a real process, we may suspect that, in spite of its being hard to demonstrate, it is a quite common phenomenon" (p. 55).

Last, Freud speculates that telepathy is the "original, archaic method of communication between individuals" which was replaced in the course of evolution by signals that could be picked up by the sense organs (p. 55). This leads him to wonder about the mental life of children who feel that their parents know their thoughts. He then turns to a paper of Dorothy Burlingham's, a child analyst (and companion of Anna Freud) whom he calls a "trustworthy witness." She recounts how a mother spoke in her analytic session of the part a gold coin played in her early childhood, only to have her ten-year-old son bring her a gold coin (which he had been given two months earlier on his birthday) as soon as she returned home; and then her son requested the gold coin back from her just at the point two weeks later when she sat at her writing-desk to write about the incident. Freud goes so far as to say if her observations can be "confirmed" they would "put an end to the remaining doubts of the reality of thought-transference" (p. 60). However, he neglects to comment about an even more compelling and disturbing example from the same paper by Burlingham where a boy attempts to throw hot water on his sister, apparently picking up telepathically on his mother's wish to throw boiling water on someone with whom she is angry.

Of all Freud's papers, this one—his last—is his least ambivalent about the telepathic hypothesis.

Freud's Letters Reveal His Continual Struggle and at Times Greater Belief in Telepathy Than Revealed in His Writings; However, They Do Not Contain Clinical Findings

The wish to believe [in telepathy] fought hard with the warning to disbelieve. They represented two fundamental features of his [Freud's] personality. But here he was truly wracked; little wonder he bewailed that the topic "perplexed him to distraction."—Jones, 1957, p. 406

As I have indicated, we are very indebted to Jones who, despite his passionate skepticism about psychic phenomena, devoted an entire chapter in his biography of Freud to Freud's interest in telepathy and psi, drawing upon his discussions with Freud and their letters to each other on the subject. In fact, the letters of Freud, Ferenczi, Jung and Jones (and Weiss) with regard to this subject have often been discussed by psychoanalytic commentators. The correspondences are historically interesting and reveal the struggle that all parties had in whether to publicly pursue a discussion of psi and psychoanalysis. But unfortunately, the letters do not add to the clinical principles that Freud suggested in his written work with regard to telepathy in psychoanalysis, nor do they incorporate psi phenomena in general into clinical theory. For that reason, I will only touch upon them briefly. (For a fuller discussion, cf. Eshel [2006] and Gymensi [2009]; Gymensi in particular provides an excellent synopsis of both Jung and Ferenczi's interest in psi phenomena.)

Very recent research reveals that Jung and Ferenczi communicated in person and by letter *before* Ferenczi even introduced himself to or met with Freud, and they discussed parapsychological phenomena in particular. Even before they contacted each other, both Jung and Ferenczi already had an interest in this subject. As early as 1899, Ferenczi wrote a paper in an Hungarian medical journal discussing various psi phenomena (including spirit photography, a precursor to the psychic photography practiced by Serios which I elaborate on in Chapter Four) and advocated that scientists "should not shrink from sitting down at the moving table or from visiting spiritistic gatherings of lay people" as a means of investigating psi both sociologically and materially (Ferenczi, 1963, p. 143). Similarly, Jung completed his dissertation on psychic phenomena.

In 1906, Jung started a correspondence with Freud whom he then met in person for the first time in March 1907. After this meeting in Vienna, Jung continued on to Budapest, where he met Ferenczi, also for the first time and thereafter the two men started their correspondence, in which their mutual interest in the paranormal played an essential part. They exchanged at least five letters prior to Ferenczi himself meeting Freud almost a year later for the first time on February 2, 1908. And as Keve (2015) notes: "It is clear … that Ferenczi and Jung were discussing the paranormal and the occult from the very beginning of their relationship. We should note that psychical research was an acceptable, even respectable scientific field at that time…" (p. 96). For example, on September 11, 1907, Jung wrote Ferenczi that he had been made an Honorary Fellow of the American Institute for Scientific Research (which eventually became the American Society for Psychical Research) as a consequence of his dissertation that dealt with mediumistic activity. Subsequently, Ferenczi apparently wrote to Jung about his experiments with thought transference, which began before he met with Freud and which Jung encouraged. The correspondence about parapsychology continued between the two after Ferenczi became close to Freud (Keve, 2015).

1. The Letter to Hereward Carrington

The single most famous vignette of Freud's struggle with telepathy, which I previously mentioned, is his having written a letter to Hereward Carrington, a prominent British psychical researcher, on July 24, 1921. Freud stated:

> I am not one of those who from the outset disapprove of the study of the so-called occult psychological phenomena as unscientific, as unworthy or even as dangerous. If I were at the beginning of a scientific career, instead of as now at its end, I would perhaps choose no other field of work in spite of all difficulties [Freud, 1957, p. 12; also Jones, 1957, p. 392].

However, Freud proceeded to entirely forget that he wrote this, even denying he did so, until the evidence was obtained 8 years later by Nandor Fodor, an American psychoanalyst and parapsychologist. As Jones and others have remarked, his forgetting is evidence of Freud's considerable resistance to the subject.

2. Communication with Jung

Jung's interest in psi phenomena arose "quite independently" of Freud as a consequence of his personal background. It was understood by his mother's family that family members possessed psychic ability, including "second sight, forebodings" and visions; and in 1902, four years before meeting Freud, he published his dissertation, "On the Psychology and Pathology of Occult Phenomena," involving investigation of a medium who in actuality was his first cousin, Helene Preiswick (Jung, 1977b). At various points, Jung expressed an interest in psychic phenomena beyond Freud's focus on telepathy, interest sometimes derived from personal experience, which included apparitions, spiritualistic communications, precognition, psychokinesis, out of body experiences, and UFOs (Main, 2012; Jung, 1977a). He generally rejected and yet at one point appeared to reluctantly consider the hypothesis of a "spirit" as an entity. In one famous incident in 1909, when having a disagreement with Freud about whether parapsychological phenomena existed, he believed that two sudden loud knockings in Freud's bookcase, the second of which Jung predicted would occur, were a result of telekinetic force (Jung used the term "catalytic exteriorization phenomenon"; Freud characterized it as poltergeist activity) (Jung, 1989, p. 155). Freud, while startled, subsequently preferred to attribute the loud knocks to natural creaking sounds that happened to take place when Jung was present. Of poltergeists, Freud added in his letter to Jung at the time discussing the incident, "it strikes me as quite unlikely that such phenomena should exist" (Freud, 1994, p. 104).

In two instances, one involving the unlikely appearance of a dead Kingfisher (a bird that Jung claimed was unusual in his vicinity and which had figured in a previous dream of his) and another involving a scarab beetle (the latter at the window just after a patient was speaking of an Egyptian scarab) (Jung, 2010, pp. 109–110), Jung believed that psi— or to use his term "synchronicity"—had played a part in their appearance. (These examples incidentally are not unlike a later and similar psi example involving birds, the famous incident in the mid–1950s when Eisenbud contended that the unusual appearance of a worm-eating warbler in New York City's central park had been predicted in a patient's precognitive experience, possibly a dream; it was this "unusual appearance" which Charles Brenner subsequently contended was not so unusual and thus did not constitute a psi experience at all [Eisenbud, 1955, 1957; Brenner, 1957]. I discuss this below, but what has never been remarked upon by commentators is that a second bird that appeared to Eisenbud's patient in a similar precognitive manner was none other than a Kingfisher!

Time-wise, in terms of publication dates in English, Eisenbud's and Jung's Kingfishers both appeared in 1955.)

In February 1911, Jung wrote to Freud with enthusiasm that he had been accepted as a corresponding member to the (British) Society for Psychical Research (Freud himself also became a corresponding member in 1911) (Freud, 1979, p. 176) and by May, he was writing to Freud that "Occultism is another field we will have to conquer" (Freud, 1979, p. 183). Freud's response was curiously encouraging. He wrote back: "I know that your deepest inclinations are impelling you toward a study of the occult and do not doubt that you will return home with a rich cargo. There is no stopping that, and it is always right for a person to follow the biddings of his own impulse." Yet, he added a caution, saying that "you will be accused of mysticism" and then requested Jung not to "stay in the tropical colonies too long" (Freud, 1979, p. 184). Only a month further on, in June, Freud wrote to him that in "matters of occultism, I have become humble" and that his "hubris has been shattered" as a consequence of hearing of Ferenczi's psi experiences. And he hoped that Jung and Ferenczi would act "in consonance, when one of you is ready to take the perilous step of publication" in this area (Freud, 1979, p. 187). In May, on the other hand, Freud wrote Ferenczi rather explicitly saying how dangerous writing about psi would be and that he could not get involved:

> Jung writes that we must also conquer occultism and requests permission to undertake a campaign in the realm of mysticism. I see that both of you can't be restrained. You should at least proceed in harmony with each other; these are dangerous expeditions, and I can't go along there [Brabant, Falzeder & Giampieri-Deutsch, 1993, p. 374].

3. Interaction with Ferenczi

Freud's interaction with Ferenczi on this subject eventually was much more intimate and involved attempts at psi investigation and experiments by both men, which Freud never publicly acknowledged. In 1909 Ferenczi consulted a psychic, Frau Seidler, whom Freud concluded had a "physiological" gift for telepathy, something which peculiarly he described as not psychological in nature, but "somatic." Although Freud was impressed, "You have begun to discover something big" he wrote to Ferenczi, he also swore him to silence (Jones, 1957, p. 385). (It is generally believed that Freud and Ferenczi visited Frau Seidler together in Berlin in the process of returning from America [Jones makes this assertion (Jones, 1957, p. 384) and others have followed it] but the letters between them at the time appear to belie this assertion [Brabant, Falzeder, &Giampieri-Deutsch, 1993, pp. 77–81].)

In 1910, Ferenczi conducted a series of parapsychological thought experiments with a homosexual patient. He believed that he could explore the transference relationship by doing so, although it is difficult to follow his reasoning. In fact, he thought he had discovered the beginnings of a new psychoanalytic technique. The model he followed was not unlike what takes place in telepathic drawing experiments and in the dream studies conducted half a century later by Ullman, and which psychoanalytically inclined parapsychologists have generally followed: by free associating, there was an increased possibility that one would find "hits" between two people's thoughts. The patient was asked to think of something and then Ferenczi free associated to himself—and subsequently determined whether his associations matched what the patient was thinking about. For example, the patient thought of the managing director of a bank and Ferenczi thought of paper, scissors, desk and then among other associations, editing and the director of a newspaper office. At the end, he said to the patient, "Director" (Brabant, Falzeder, & Giampieri-Deutsch, 1993, p. 235). Extremely enthusiastic about his experiments, in November 1910, Ferenczi wrote to Freud that "I am a great soothsayer, that is to say a reader of thoughts!" and that when he visits Freud in Vienna, he will introduce himself as "court astrologer of the psychoanalysts" (pp. 235–236). In October 1911, Freud sent a letter at Ferenczi's request to the (British) Society of Psychical Research, of which Freud himself was already an honorary member to help Ferenczi gain membership, half a year after Jung became a member of the same institution.

The correspondence was more or less quiescent on this issue for almost fifteen years until a circular letter from March 15, 1925, in which Freud wrote: "Ferenczi was here recently on a Sunday. The three of us carried out experiments with thought-transference. They were remarkably good, particularly those in which I played the medium and then analyzed my associations" (Jones, 1957, p. 393). Although subsequently, Freud again urged caution, it was this experience that made him most firmly convinced of the reality of telepathy. I think what is most interesting and generally not noted was that Freud compared his determination to pursue the study of telepathy to his determination to embrace psychoanalysis itself, despite critical outside forces, over thirty years previously. Thus Freud wrote to Jones (a year almost to the day from the circular letter) after conducting telepathic experiments with Ferenczi and his daughter Anna, the details of which we do not know but which he found successful and where he contended he was a rather good medium that:

> *...my own experiences with Ferenczi and my daughter won such a convincing force for me that the diplomatic considerations on the other side gave way. I was once more faced with a case where on a reduced scale I had to repeat the great experiment of my life: namely, to proclaim a conviction without taking into account any echo from the outer world* [my emphasis] [Freud, 1993, p. 597].

This is poignant. Those analysts who have explored psi phenomena, such as Eisenbud, have had a similar sense of the need to "go it alone" and thereby have allied themselves with Freud at his intransigent and determined best, despite his subsequent waffling—the type of intransigence and determination that gave birth to psychoanalysis itself, the "great experiment" of Freud's life. Such psychoanalysts have felt they had no choice but to go forward, as Freud did if only momentarily. The irony is that it has been fellow psychoanalysts themselves, such as Brenner (see below), often considerably more condemning than even Jones, who have too frequently attempted to scorch their path.

A Detour: Telepathic Drawing Experiments

A short detour into the phenomena of telepathic drawing experiments might be helpful at this juncture, before we turn in more detail to the principles that Freud suggested, because telepathic drawing experiments are particularly accessible to psychoanalytic thinking as well as psychoanalytically informative. (There are innumerable parapsychological experimental protocols, from random number generators to remote viewing to Zener cards; telepathic drawing experiments are only one but they represent an early dynamic procedure.) It is not clear whether Freud was familiar with these experiments, but they took place during his lifetime and for a time were considered important in parapsychological literature. They are also fascinating. And they touch on what Freud suggested in his second telepathy article and privately when he enigmatically spoke of doing his own telepathic experiments with his daughter and Ferenczi (although we do not know what he meant exactly), because they involve simple connections that lend themselves to free-associative formulations. There are two famous series of telepathic drawing experiments, those of Rene Warcollier and those of Upton Sinclair. These experiments, without going into elaborate detail, essentially are arranged in this way: one person, at a distance from another, draws a picture, which the other tries to reproduce.

This may in itself seem straightforward. It is not quite so easy however. Remember that Freud assumed that a telepathic communication between two individuals, at least that manifests itself in a telepathic dream, would be subject to distortion as it passed from one person's unconscious to another person's unconscious and then into the manifest dream. What I want to emphasize about telepathic drawing experiments is that the same holds true in these experiments. Whereas Freud could posit psychodynamics to explain the distortion that took place when a man dreamt of his wife rather than his daughter (the actual mother) giving birth to premature twins, it is hard to find the dynamics in telepathic drawing experiments, but the distortions themselves do take place. Further, the question which often plagues parapsychologists or other investigators in these instances is: What constitutes a "hit"? Let us say, for example, you draw a bunch of grapes with a stem and focus on it, and at a distance, your best friend or spouse or even someone whom you do not know who is supposed to be the recipient of your telepathic message, then draws a bottle and labels it "wine." Is that a "hit"? It does not resemble at all the shape in your drawing, but clearly a wine bottle suggests the *thought* of "grapes." Or let us say the receiver or percipient draws a picture that resembles almost exactly your grape drawing, but then he says that it is a bunch of balloons, not grapes, and what appears to be a stem is actually a string attached to them. Is that a hit? It does not resemble your thought, but it *does* match exactly your drawing. It is as if the percipient saw your drawing and said, "those remind me of balloons." We could of course go on in this manner, because the associations of the percipient might also be important. For example, in this case, let us say the percipient draws a ghost when the "sender" drew grapes. There seems to be no connection whatsoever. In other words, not a "hit" at all. But in talking with the percipient and asking him about what he drew, let us say he answers: "I drew a wraith." And when we ask him, "Do you associate anything to a wraith?," he responds. "Well, yes, it's kind of silly, but I now think of Steinbeck's Grapes of Wrath, which I have been rereading." So now the question is: Do we have a hit or not? Just to make matters worse, we might also want the associations of you, the "sender," who might conceivably think of the grapes in another way, let us say in terms of Italy, particularly Pisa, from which you have recently returned. If the percipient drew a picture of a leaning tower, in no way like the grapes, would that be a "hit"? It is clearly a problem that those who wish to pin down psi in a confined, exact manner might wish would simply go away.

This problem is not new. Shakespeare touches upon it a number of times, in prophecies in his plays. The most famous, of course, is when the third apparation says:

> Macbeth shall never vanquish'd be until
> Great Birnam Wood to high Dunsinane Hill
> Shall come against him

It is only when Macbeth sees that enemy soldiers are using tree branches to disguise their advance upon him, creating the appearance of a forest moving, that he discovers what seemed to be an impossible "hit" is actually one. It might not be exact, but it is close (and as a result terrible) enough.

Two extensive series of telepathic drawing experiments were conducted in the 1920s and 1930s. The first, conducted over a period of years beginning in 1921, was by Rene Warcollier, a French chemical engineer, In 1938, his writings on the subject were collected in a work, *Experiments in Telepathy*, with a foreword by the psychologist Gardner Murphy, in which Murphy said of Warcollier: "(H)e has concerned himself not with the question of marshaling masses of evidence, but with the question of the mental processes which characterize those who 'send' and those who 'receive' impressions." Incidentally, distance did not seem to matter in these experiments; whether the sender and percipient were separated by a room or by an ocean, the results were similar. But to give an example of the type of "hit" of which I am speaking, taken somewhat at random, the sender drew a picture of a spider web, a seven-sided geometric figure, with concentric lines, leading to a center, and a spider pouncing upon a fly near the center. The percipient thought of "feet descending a spiral staircase, trigonometry" and then drew a bug with six legs (Warcollier, 1938, p. 180). There was neither spider nor web, but it is hard not to think of this as a "hit." Of course, we do not know, and will never know, why the idea of a "spider and fly" translated this way to the percipient or why the spider web became a harmless geometric figure not incorporated into the drawing of the bug. Perhaps the percipient unconsciously sought to rescue the fly. The point though is that image and thought telepathically reached the unconscious of the percipient and were transformed in the manifest content, while still revealing a dynamic connection to the material sent.

In *Mental Radio,* by the novelist Upton Sinclair, published in 1930, the same phenomenon takes place in a series of telepathic drawing experiments: the material sent telepathically presumably to the percipient's unconscious is transformed in the manifest content of the percipient but necessarily remains related. In this case, Upton Sinclair (or sometimes his secretary) was the sender and the percipient was Upton Sinclair's wife, Mary Craig Kimbrough, referred to as "Craig" in the book. The preface to the book by Albert Einstein (1962) states in part;

> I have read the book of Upton Sinclair with great interest and am convinced the same deserves the most earnest consideration, not only of the laity, but also of the psychologists by profession…. If the facts here set forth rest not upon telepathy, but upon some unconscious hypnotic influence from person to person, this also would be of high psychological interest. In no case should the psychologically interested circles pass over this book heedlessly [p. x].

Here is an example of the type of "hit" of which I am speaking. Sinclair's secretary draws a heart, and Craig, the percipient, draws just the double crescent of the top of the heart (somewhat like the letter M) but she then adds beneath it drops of blood (Sinclair, 1930, p. 104). This certainly appears to be a hit, but why the heart shape dropped out is not clear or why Craig drew drops of blood, almost like tear drops—did it signify a "broken heart"?—is unclear. (I have a particular preference for this example as I have written about the derivation of the stylized "heart shape," in which I emphasize that the double crescents are breast symbols [cf. Reichbart, 1978], as well as having written about the phenomenon of the "broken heart" [cf. Reichbart, 2013],—although both of these are really other stories.) Again, rather amusingly, Upton Sinclair draws a picture of an Alpine hat with an upright feather in the hatband, a very masculine item; but Craig draws a shape that resembles exactly that of the hat, but without the feather—although a feather-like shape now floats above the hat shape. (p. 115). And Craig says of the hat shape that it is a "chafing dish"! We cannot know why the transformation, although a "chafing dish" is perhaps a more feminine association and "chafing" is a loaded word, given its other meaning of "irritating"; and then severing the feather from the hat, perhaps has catastrophic significance. (All of this is of course speculative, and would require an interview of Craig, but I am simply trying to show how things might work dynamically.) In addition, not commented upon by Sinclair, there are two crescent shapes in this drawing of Craig's, one under the other, distantly looking like the "hat" itself, but making it tempting—given the breast significance of crescent shapes—to posit some desire on her part to transform the masculine Alpine hat into a feminine symbol. Nevertheless, such speculations aside, my main point—and I could have chosen any number of examples from Mental Radio to make it—is that when there is a psi connection—unconscious to unconscious—there are transformations, mediated by associations and repression, which take place before the content becomes manifest.

(Parenthetically, although the studies of Warcollier and Sinclair are old, they do continue to be referenced in parapsychological experiments. Thus, Ullman, when introducing contemporary dream telepathy experiments he conducted, makes the interesting observation that the fragmentation of the symbols that took place in these earlier drawing experiments [as occurred with the double crescents or the floating feather] resembles what happens when an individual is shown a tachistoscopic image of a symbol and asked to draw what he has seen. A tachistoscope shows an image for a very short time, and then when the percipient is asked to draw what he sees, a fragmentation of the image takes place. Ullman suggests that "the neurophysiological pathways involved in the processing of telepathic transfer may be the same as in normal visual perception" [Ullman, 2003, p. 27].)

I do not want the reader to think that in these experiments there are not at times "hits" that are more exact. But I have emphasized these two studies of telepathic drawing experiments because one can extrapolate from them that when patients have psi-determined dreams or when they talk about something in the analyst's life of which they could have no conscious knowledge or when they touch psychically upon something in another patient's life, that their productions are subject to *all* the associative dynamics that psychoanalysts consider part of unconscious process in general. We do not expect *exact* "hits" in these psi connections, and in fact we can and should examine why the "hits" may not be exact, what dynamically accounts for the changes, just as we would when a "day residue" differs from the manifest content of a dream. Everything is necessarily mediated by the associative material of each individual and by the repressive tendencies of both sender and percipient. The great artists, as I show in the chapters on literature, such as Tolstoy, Shakespeare, and Joyce, knew this instinctively, elaborated upon it in their works, and in fact, made these phenomena central to those works. It is clear from his writings, that Freud knew it as well.

The Principles in Greater Depth

Let me now expand upon the principles that Freud articulated in his four articles. I am wary of being overly didactic, but I think it will be helpful to state them in more detail, and to expand upon them in light of findings after Freud. I do not quite use the exact same formulations that I used in discussing Freud's papers, but the principles are in essence the same.

Principle: Psi Phenomena Is a Part of Everyday Life *Not* Just a Consequence of Traumatic Events in the Past or Early Separation Anxieties

As we have seen, Freud did not consider telepathy unusual, rather he considered that it must be "a common phenomenon." Too frequently, psychoanalysts who write in this area appear to have ignored this hypothesis by Freud. And all indications from the parapsychological field is that Freud was right, as well as from the many examples of previous psychoanalytic writings. My personal experience and my experience with patients have been similar.

However, psychoanalysts who do venture into this field often contend that telepathic ability occurs *primarily* as a consequence of developmental trauma, a reaching out of a patient or a person under extraordinary circumstances or great stress in the past, which has continued into the present in the person's functioning. They also often contend that individuals, based on early loss or trauma, in which they sought to maintain a psychic connection to a loved object whom they experienced as distant, are those who exhibit parapsychological manifestations during psychoanalytic treatment. It is a compelling argument and can indeed apply to understanding the psychodynamic determinants of psi manifestations in the treatment of certain individuals. And it makes psychoanalysts more comfortable, frankly, if they can attach psi manifestations to a psychoanalytic dynamic formulation such as this. But it ignores the history of the exploration of psi, both in parapsychology and in psychoanalysis, as well as the broader implications of psi in the universe. To put it bluntly, it simply is not true.

Whereas it may be possible to trace in certain individuals that their psi abilities continued into adulthood, or manifested as a child as a consequence of trauma, and there is fascinating historic and present material that shows psi ability with certain disassociated individuals (such as Ira Brenner's account which I have summarized below) the bulk of analytic reports suggest that telepathic manifestations in treatment are not necessarily related to this dynamic, and that individuals of all stripes and diagnoses and developmental histories can exhibit psi, although they may be unaware of it. Freud implied as much when he ventured his remark. True, those who have exhibited exceptional psychic ability, of which they are aware, sometimes have a traumatic developmental history or history of separation anxiety, but again, we have no evidence that this is a necessary correlation. On the other hand, as I show in the chapter on the Navajo hand trembler, some cultures—more so than Western culture today—accept and identify those with exceptional psychic ability. If Western culture were to encourage rather than marginalize those who exhibited psychic ability, we might find that—as with any ability that touches on unconscious process—such as the musical ability of say a Mozart for example—we have talented psychic people in our midst who do not have histories of developmental stress.

Eshel contends that each of five patients who exhibited telepathy during treatment had a common experience in early childhood: each had a

> mother who was emotionally absent-within-absence, due to the absence of a significant figure in her own life. The primary traumatic loss was imprinted in their nascent selves and inchoate relating to others, with a fixation on a nonverbal archaic mode of communication. The patient's telepathic dream is formed as a search engine when the analyst is suddenly emotionally absent... [Eshel, 2006, p. 1603].

Eshel then reports on such a case. Eshel's report is compelling and so is the concept that such early developmental trauma accounts for the tendency for telepathy in some individuals when they mature. However, parapsychological data indicates that a variety of individuals, with all types of personalities, exhibit telepathy and psi functioning and that such phenomena are not exclusive to those who have suffered early developmental trauma or loss.

Principle: The State of Sleep May Facilitate Telepathy

Freud was particularly interested in telepathic dreams. As he stated of the study of psychic phenomena or "occultism," that it was:

> most probable that there is a real core of yet unrecognized facts in occultism round which cheating and phantasy have spun a veil which it is hard to pierce. But how can we even approach this core? at what point can we attack the problem? It is here, I think, that dreams come to our help, by giving us a hint that from out of this chaos we should pick up the subject of telepathy [Freud, 1933, p. 36].

He then went on to proclaim that "the state of sleep seems particularly suited for receiving telepathic messages. In such cases one has what is called a telepathic dream..." (p. 37).

In this way, Freud announced his awareness that certain states of consciousness, such as the dreaming state, can facilitate psi:

> All of this has only this much to do with dreams: if there are such things as telepathic messages, the possibility cannot be dismissed of their reaching someone during sleep and coming to his knowledge in a dream. Indeed, on the analogy of other perceptual and intellectual material, the further possibility arises that telepathic messages received in the course of the day may only be dealt with during a dream of the following night. There would then be nothing contradictory in the material that had been telepathically communicated being modified and transformed in the dream like any other material [p. 137, psychoanalysis and telepathy].

Principle: Telepathic Data Can Be Transmitted to a Person's Unconscious and Can Be Transformed in the Same Way as a "Day Residue" Would Be Transformed in the Manifest Content of a Dream

Perhaps Freud' most important hypothesis concerning telepathic communication was his understanding of the relationship between the manifest dream content and what we refer to as the latent content, as it pertains to telepathic communication. It is most striking in the twin-birth dream that a man wrote to Freud about. He dreamt:

> my wife had given birth to twins. I saw two healthy infants quite plainly with their chubby faces lying side by side. I did not observe their sex; one with fair hair had distinctly my features and something of my wife's, the other with chestnut-brown hair clearly resembled her with a look of me. I said to my wife, who has red-gold hair, "Probably 'your' child's chestnut hair will also go red later on." My wife gave them the breast [Freud, 1922, p. 200].

In fact, his wife was deceased. It was his daughter at a distance who gave birth to twins prematurely.

Freud concludes:

> A telepathic message will be treated as a portion of the material that goes to the formation of a dream, like any other external or internal stimulus.... In our example, it is evident how the message with the help of a lurking repressed wish, became remodelled into a wish-fulfilment ... [Freud, 1922, p. 207].

In other words, a telepathic message from one person to another will be transformed in the manifest content of a dream, very much as a day residue would be transformed. If this man had the same manifest dream, after actually being informed of his daughter giving birth prematurely to twins, we would have no trouble psychodynamically understanding why the manifest content—in which his wife gives birth to twins rather than his daughter—was different than the reality, and would attribute the change to his repressed incestuous wish. Here the data ostensibly traveled telepathically from his daughter to his unconscious—and was treated by Freud in the same way as a "day residue" would have been treated in the formation of a dream. As he states: "One forms the conviction that the telepathic news has played the same part as any other portion of the day's residues and that it has been changed in the same way by the dream-work and made to serve its purpose" (Freud, 1933, p. 37).

Principle: The Analyst Can Share Telepathic Data of Which the Patient May Not Be Aware to Make an Interpretation

Exactly what the analyst is to do when it becomes apparent to him that the patient's productions, whether in dreams or in associations, suggest telepathy? This technical issue has actually been a question from the beginning. Despite misapprehensions by some who have written about it, the fact is that from Freud onward, analysts have tended to let patients know that something they have presented suggests telepathy and, in many cases, suggests telepathic access to the analyst's own life. Freud as we have seen let his patient, Dr. Forsyth know. On what basis, a psychoanalyst, trained to withhold personal information or to minimize providing it, on the supposition that too much personal data about the analyst will interfere with the development of the transference, or make the transference more difficult to disentangle from the therapeutic relationship, is an open question, which Freud did not explore. Many psychoanalysts who followed Freud provided personal information to an even a greater extent than did Freud as a consequence of a patient's telepathic link to the analyst (or to the analyst's other patients) and some attempted to grapple in more depth with the question of what it might mean to provide this information to the patient. (I will discuss this technical issue in greater depth later.) But nonetheless, it was Freud who was first to "break the frame" by providing one patient with a telepathic link of which the patient was not at all aware.

The case in question, as I indicated above, is referred to as the Forsyth case. In 1919, a foreign doctor who had just arrived from London came in to see Freud in the hope of arranging treatment with him. His name was Dr. Forsyth. Freud did not have time to speak with him but took his card and arranged a time to talk later on, in the strong hope that he could acquire an excellent new patient, things having been slow after the war years. Freud's next patient, whose name was Herr P., was not a particularly "good" psychoanalytic patient (as Freud anticipated he might find in Dr. Forsyth). In fact, Freud had told Herr P. he could not cure him of the sexual difficulties he presented, yet Herr P. continued to come to see Freud more or less out of social enjoyment. And now, as soon as he arrived, Herr P. proceeded to tell Freud that a pretty virginal girl, with whom he had a flirtation, liked to refer to him as "Mr. Foresight." At this point, impressed by the possible psi circumstances, Freud showed Herr P. the card of Dr. Forsyth.

There were other circumstances here, to which Freud alludes, but the dynamic interpretation which Freud makes (and which Freud shared with his patient) is that it was as if the patient were saying: "I am hurt your thoughts should be so much wrapped up in this newcomer. Come back to me; after all I am a Forsyth too—or rather only a Mr. Foresight, as the girl called me." In fact, Freud had been thinking that Dr. Forsyth would make a better patient than Herr P. And the point here is that Freud broke the frame to tell Herr P. that his communication at that point to Freud about being called Mr. Foresight must have been psi determined, and handed him the card of his recent visitor Dr. Forsyth.

Principle: One Motivation for a Patient Unconsciously Evoking Psi Is to Compete with Other Patients for the Psychoanalyst's Attention

As it was in the Forsyth Case, this dynamic is often central to the appearance of psi in patient's associations and dreams. It was expanded upon most fully years later with many examples by Eisenbud (eg.1970), but Freud was the first to articulate it.

Thus, Freud interpreted why Herr P. brought up a girl calling him "Mr. Foresight"; he was competing with the prior visitor, Mr. Forsyth, for attention from Freud and did so through telepathy. As Freud said, Herr P. was saying to him: "I'm a Forsyth too: that's what the girl calls me." And then Freud adds poignantly:

> It is hard to mistake the mixture of jealous demand and melancholy self-depreciation which finds its expression in this remark. We shall not be going astray if we complete it in some such way as this: 'It's mortifying to me that your thoughts should be so intensely occupied with this new arrival. Do come back to me; after all I'm a Forsyth too—though it's true I'm only a Herr von Vorsicht [gentleman of foresight], as the girl says [Freud, 1933, p. 51].

Almost all the examples of telepathy from my clinical practice, which I provide at the end of this chapter, involve this dynamic.

Principle: The Telepathic Episode Is Often a Function Not Only of Repression of Emotionally Charged Material by the Patient, but of Repression of Similar or Related Emotionally Charged Material by the Analyst. Thus, in Effect, Psi Is Invoked in Relation to Transference and Countertransference.

Those analysts who write about telepathic linkage with their patients invariably are impressed with the anxiety-provoking material that a patient has picked up from the analyst's own life, expressed most particularly in a patient's dreams, although of course such linkage can come up in other ways, such as the material and associations that a patient presents in session that are not dream-related. I will contend later that Freud unconsciously articulated this principle in the Forsyth case. The events from the analyst's own life can range from the truly frightening, such as deaths or accidents or concerns about pregnancy, to the more mundane, such as embarrassing situations. What is striking is that contemporary analysts who have reported on these telepathic connections, often seem unaware that there is nothing new here, and that similar reports have already been made. If one is not familiar with the literature, it may be that the analyst's experience of a particular type of telepathic communication with a patient seems not only compelling but very unique. Generally, it is not. Of course, in saying this, I do not mean to detract from the important dynamic reasons that analysand and analyst may telepathically communicate about an event. Nor do I wish to discourage continued reports of telepathic events in psychoanalytic treatment. I do wish, however, to put such reports into context, both historical and substantive. In addition, there is a tendency on the part of contemporary analysts who publish this material (and are brave enough to do so) to try to fit their seemingly singular or unique experience into a theoretical framework linked solely to that experience. I would suggest that psi phenomena, like the phenomena of dreams themselves, looked at in totality, does not lend itself readily to these particularized and confined theoretical frameworks, as appealing as it is to try to circumscribe them in this way.

Eisenbud succinctly articulated the tendency of the patient, when unconsciously invoking psi, touching upon the analyst's anxieties and thoughts. And he suggested that it was incumbent upon the analyst to "scan his own day residue and dreams" when psi seemed in these instances:

> It, soon becomes apparent, moreover, that the phenomena are both rooted in and fashioned by the observer himself to a far greater degree than what is experienced in the transference-countertransference aspects of psychoanalytic therapy. Just as Freud discovered that fortune tellers' predictions mirrored their clients' secret wishes, every clinician who invokes the psi hypothesis by way of attempting to comprehend certain puzzling occurrences will sooner or later discover that the material he is confronting mirrors what he himself is defending against. Like a bumbling detective, he finds that the fingerprints he comes upon are his own. "It is the patient who makes my slip," wrote Hollós.... It is the patient also who dreams my dream (and vice versa), acts out my fantasies and mirrors my defenses. In fact the analyst who conscientiously scans his own day's residues and other material when applying the psi hypothesis to his patient's material—a process I have termed "triangulation"—will soon find himself in a confusing gallery of mirrors [Eisenbud, 1981, 71–72].

Ehrenwald introduces the same concept somewhat humorously when he says that a patient's telepathic dream may:

> confront the therapist with a new and somewhat disconcerting situation: it shows that, despite the attitude of detachment and reserve which he seeks to maintain during the treatment, he may become more involved with his patient's problems than is allowed by psychoanalytic theory, and that, on a deeper level, his patients may themselves have a far greater awareness of his involvement than may ever occur to the analyst [Ehrenwald, 1975, p. 51].

Psi communications between patient and analyst often depend on circumstances. Hollos and Servadio for example have posited that psi is likely to be enlisted when the patient wishes to "see" the primal scene by a magical looking; Eshel, who herself recounts issues of personal loss, has found patients who suffered traumatic loss then attempt to establish contact with the analyst through psi; and many psychoanalysts, as already stated, believe that the patients psychically discover issues that the psychoanalyst himself wishes to deny or repress.

As Eisenbud states more pointedly in an early article:

> One outstanding fact which sooner or latter must emerge from the study of telepathy as observed in analysis resolves the paradox: the telepathic episode is a function not only of emotionally charged material by the patient, but of the repression of similar or related emotionally charged material by the analyst as well [Eisenbud, 1946, p. 52].

Ultimately, I contend that telepathy is part of the fabric of our lives, and obtains to all of us, regardless of developmental history, although some of us may have more ability than others and although developmental trauma may lend itself to more conscious telepathic ability.

Principle: When Psi Does Occur, Popular Explanations for Its Occurrence Need Not Be Accepted and Other Hypotheses for Its Occurrence May Be More Accurate

In effect, Freud announced this principle but then in practice he too often tended to accept popular explanations, labeling them unbelievable and then using them to discount the facts themselves. He announced this principle clearly when he investigated the premonitions of psychics. As we have seen, the prediction about crayfish poisoning, although not accurate as a prediction, nonetheless suggested to Freud that telepathy between the psychic and the "sitter" had occurred in which the sitter's unconscious aggressive wishes concerning an incident of crayfish poisoning in the past had been picked up telepathically by the psychic. Similarly, the accurate prediction by a psychic about a sitter's future suggested to Freud that the prediction could more easily be explained as a consequence of telepathy in which the psychic picked up on very specific wishes of the patient to emulate her mother.

The principle itself as articulated by Freud is very important. In fact, it exists throughout parapsychological investigations, and is familiar to parapsychologists, but this is the first time it was fully articulated by a psychoanalyst. Psychoanalysts even today may be less familiar with the principle and too often tend to revert to popular explanations for alleged psi phenomena, and then—because they find the popular explanations so unbelievable—they proceed to dismiss the data themselves as unbelievable. Similarly, and unfortunately, Freud frequently did the same. Despite the principle, he *did* accept popular explanations of various types of psi data: his version of telepathy being like a telephone connection traveling from one person to another was inaccurate or simplistic; his need to think of an apparition as a putative soul of a deceased person served to discount the phenomena and prevented him from entertaining the hypothesis that there was a telepathic explanation of apparitions of persons living or dead; and his failure to engage premonitions as a possibility resided with his apparent belief that they required a kind of time travel, which as I will indicate later on, they do not necessarily.

Some Important Commentators: Charles Brenner, Mayer and Stoller, Derrida

Here I will elaborate about some of the more important contributions to psi and psychoanalysis since the 1960s whose names are well known to the established psychoanalytic field. In terms of contributions, nothing compares to the work of Eisenbud, but the difficulty has been that the bulk of his work since that time has not been in psychoanalytic journals but rather in parapsychological journals or in books nor is he well known generally among psychoanalysts, whereas Derrida (although a philosopher rather than an analyst), Brenner, Mayer and Stoller whom I discuss here were more public figures in the psychoanalytic firmament. In my effort to bridge the gap between parapsychology and psychoanalysis, I hope that summarizing the contributions of these analysts will also inform those parapsychologists who are not familiar with the more recent psychoanalytic literature.

The Charles Brenner Paradox: An Expert on Reality

Whoever undertakes to set himself up as a judge of Truth and Knowledge is shipwrecked by the laughter of the gods.—Einstein, 1982, p. 28

On May 9, 1986, Charles Brenner, a powerful leading light of the New York Psychoanalytic Society (where Eisenbud had trained), a proponent of conflict theory, whose work was very much admired by many psychoanalysts gave the Plenary Address at the annual meeting of the American Psychoanalytic Association at the Waldorf Astoria Hotel in New York City. This was a signal honor. He presented a memoir of his many years as a psychoanalyst.

Thirty years previously, in 1957, Brenner had a battle in a psychoanalytic journal with Eisenbud with regard to whether a part of an interaction between Eisenbud and a patient had been an instance of psi phenomena.—most famously, Eisenbud claimed that a patient dreamt of seeing a worm-eating warbler in Central Park before actually doing so, suggesting precognition, and that according to Eisenbud's research this particular type of bird was completely unlikely to be at this location. Brenner countered with the claim that his own research revealed that the warbler was commonplace and thus there was nothing precognitive about the dream at all. Now in his 93rd year, Brenner took this somewhat auspicious occasion to return to that one battle, depicting himself as a hero, who had—in opposing Eisenbud in this fashion—singlehandedly managed to impede the continued publication of psychoanalytic articles concerning psi phenomena in "reputable" journals.

Bragged Brenner, of his 1957 article, "I wrote a short article which I called, 'Facts, Coincidence, and the Psi Hypothesis' … duly published in the *International Journal [of Psychoanalysis]* … As far as I know, there has not been another ESP article in a reputable psychoanalytic journal from that day to this … at least no one since has gone so far as to publicly revive a belief in psi phenomena." And then Brenner went on, clearly looking for laughs: "When it comes to an area as problematic as parapsychic phenomena, one must be doubly cautious and doubly sure of the reliability of one's evidence. I have a private rule of thumb in such matters. When a thing is impossible, it cannot be so…"

I was not at this meeting (although I am now a member of the American Psychoanalytic Association) but I have no doubt that the audience joined Brenner with laughter, reflecting the view that psychoanalysts generally have of parapsychology. In fact, the information about publication that Brenner gave his audience was incorrect. There had been tens of articles published in the intervening years, including ones by Burlingham, Schwarz, Eisenbud, Farrell, Nelson, Ullman to name just a few (to say nothing of innumerable books). Many of these, however, had been published in journals that the audience of the American Psychoanalytic Association at that time—made up almost entirely of medical analysts (it was not until two years later that the American was compelled as a result of a lawsuit to begin to accept non–MDs into its ranks)—considered less than "reputable"; they would have approved generally of the *International Journal of Psychoanalysis* [at times called the *International Review of Psychoanalysis*] (publications of the International Psychoanalytic Association), the *Journal of the American Psychoanalytic Association* and the *Psychoanalytic Quarterly* (of New York Psychoanalytic), and the *Psychoanalytic Study of the Child*, Their elitism would not have permitted them to include the *Psychoanalytic Review* (a publication of the National Psychological Association for Psychoanalysis) for example, which to its credit continued to publish articles on psi. Today, with the advent of the Psychoanalytic Electronic Publishing (PEP) in 1998, beginning with only six journals but then expanding, psychoanalysts have access to a plethora of psychoanalytic journals, including new ones that have published on parapsychology, and the elitism expressed by Brenner is less present.

I bring this up, simply so one can see how entrenched is the failure to even have Freud's ambivalent view of psi embraced by contemporary analysts (and this despite the fact that as I have indicated among others Ferenczi, Jung, Balint, Burlingham—all powerful names in psychoanalytic circles—urged a more open attitude), how unable they are to even explore this area, how quickly they make a priori judgments similar to Brenner's, and how they could not respond either with the openness of Freud himself or of a scientist such as Einstein. I am tempted to say: "For shame!" But I also know that skilled and empathic analysts, colleagues and friends of mine whose psychoanalytic judgment I value in every other respect, have simply no ability to go in this direction. And it does not help, that the attitude expressed by Brenner, which suggests that one is "disreputable" if one explores this aspect of human functioning, makes psychoanalysts afraid to step out of line. This is the fear that Stoller and Greenson speak about as we will see in the discussion that we turn to now, saying in effect: "Don't publish in this area. It will hurt your professional reputation." It may not be in keeping with what we all, as psychoanalysts, have learned from Freud—that our field depends upon honesty in the consulting room and a full reporting of what our patients and what we as psychoanalysts experience—but it is still, unfortunately, a sad professional fact.

Elizabeth Lloyd Mayer and Robert Stoller

As I have indicated, the professional psychoanalytic world, which determines so often the course of psychoanalytic knowledge, can tend (perhaps as any professional field) to be circumscribed and parochial. Thus, for a period of time, in the psychoanalytic journals, after the spate of articles in the '40s and '50s and after the publication of George Devereux's *Psychoanalysis and the Occult* in 1957, the impression in that world was that interest in psi and psychoanalysis had dwindled. Eisenbud, and other psychoanalyst/parapsychologists continued to publish however. Eisenbud's *Psi and Psychoanalysis* came out in 1970, the first edition of the *World of Ted Serios* in 1967, *Paranormal Foreknowledge* in 1982, his *Parapsychology and the Unconscious* in 1983, Ullman's *Dream Telepathy* in 1973 to give some examples. Nor were psychoanalysts aware of articles during this time in the *Journal of the American Society for Psychical Research* (such as a number of my articles reprinted here)—not that they had ever been—that continued to explore parapsychological phenomena from a psychoanalytic perspective because this journal was essentially in another professional arena entirely. The twain simply did not meet.

Thus, psychoanalysts simply turned to the psychoanalytic journal literature and found it basically empty for a period of time of articles on psi phenomena. And they had no awareness of what was happening. In addition, Eisenbud had became something of anathema after his publication of *The World of Ted Serios* and perhaps after the gratuitous bashing by Brenner. If I had ever been under the impression that knowledge proceeds in a logical and fair way, that we build upon the findings of past theorists, and that we preserve the struggles of those who came before us, this state of affairs cured me of entertaining that idea.

In 2001, fourteen years after Brenner's plenary address, a prominent psychoanalyst published an article in the *Journal of the American Psychoanalytic Association*, which apparently now awakened many in the analytic community (Mayer, 2001). There was nothing new in the material she published. But this field, like any other, has its stars: Elizabeth

Lloyd Mayer was one, and Robert Stoller, whose article, drafted in 1973, she now presented posthumously to the analytic world, had been another, as had been his prominent supervisor at the time, Ralph Greenson, who also figures in the article. The "star power" gave the article and telepathy the attention that could not have been garnered by less celebrated psychoanalysts (if in fact it would have been published at all).

Mayer presented the material somewhat unfairly, by suggesting that there was more new in it than otherwise. In fact, it was essentially a series of telepathic, if sometimes striking dreams of patients who touched upon events in Stoller's life, a series apparently initiated when Stoller had a troubling telepathic dream of his own concerning Greenson. There were dynamic formulations, but limited more to Stoller than to his patients, and no discussion of what to do technically when a patient had a telepathic dream. What *was* new or at least fascinating, to me, was how little Stoller had apparently read at the time about telepathy in psychoanalysis, how frightened he was by his psi experience, how concerned both he and Greenson were that to publish about his experience during his lifetime might jeopardize his career, and yet how the experiences actually changed Greenson and Stoller's view of the possibility of telepathy (which they never publicly admitted). Now over 40 years later, the material was finally being published by Mayer, which was positive. This reluctance to publish is further and continued evidence of the resistance to exploring psi phenomena in our psychoanalytic community.

Let me summarize the article briefly. Stoller had a dream that he told to his analyst before he met with his supervisor Greenson. He dreamt that he was back working in the emergency area of a San Francisco hospital where he had worked 20 years ago and that they brought in a medical student, with a compound commuted (that is a break or splinter of a bone into more than two pieces) fracture of his left leg. When he then met with Greenson and asked how he was, Greenson said that his son Danny, a medical student, suffered a compound commuted fracture of his left leg the day before the dream. At this point, Stoller turned white—perhaps guilt or fear as in fact Stoller had sometimes wished to be Greenson's son. He then tells Greenson his dream. And thus begins an entire series of telepathic dreams, which he recounts in this article, not between Stoller and Greenson, but between Stoller's patients and Stoller. Greenson is so moved by Stoller's initial dream, that from that time forth he apparently changes his mind about telepathy in dreams, which previously he had thought of as a mystical and unscientific concept. However, he never advertises his change of heart to the psychoanalytic community, apparently preferring to play it safe, as he advised Stoller to do.

Stoller relates a series of 19 telepathic dreams by 4 of his patients that followed this first telepathic event, in which each patient apparently cognizes events in Stoller's life as expressed in the content of the dream. Often the dreams and the linked events from Stoller's life involve anxious and somewhat catastrophic situations, such as a patient dreaming of an "older man" carrying a large object who smashes through glass, when Stoller carrying a chair, smashed through a glass door that he did not see (but is not hurt); or the patient dreaming of a house under construction where someone has put an initial in the still soft cement of a sunken bath, and in fact Stoller's house (which the patient could not have known was under construction) is vandalized and an initial has been scratched in the sunken bath (p. 639) or the patient dreaming of spilling acid, from bottle of chemicals that he is pulling in a toy wagon, onto his hand and burning it, when Stoller's son burned his hand on some chemicals from a toy set (p. 640); and so on.

Stoller's dreams represent a rather rich trove, but as I have indicated unfortunately they are not explored dynamically in the same way as other analysts, such as Eisenbud, have done with patient's telepathic dreams We do not know what is happening with Stoller's patients, and what we are faced with are the very bare bones of connectiveness between a patient's dream and the analyst's life, although more often than not the events to which the patient telepathically connects appear anxiety-provoking ones for Stoller. The most dynamic general formulation in the article is Stoller's assertion that these dreams tended to take place when there was a separation between analyst and patient ("over a weekend, after an hour was missed, or during a time when I was away for an extended period" [p. 650]), as if the patient desired to stay "magically" in touch with the analyst. Another particular interpretation relates to the fact that Stoller's mother's maiden name was "Greene" and that when his mother met Greenson, she said "My God, he looks just like my father!" (who died when Stoller was five). Greenson suggests that Stoller should say: "I am in a sense a 'Greene-son.' ... Was I not then Greenson's grandson?" and then he adds further that the telepathy stopped for Stoller for a reason: "The point is being 'my son,' you developed the telepathy—why you stopped (needing to feel like my son?), you didn't need it" (p. 638, fns. 6, 8).

There is one other curious note by Stoller, which Mayer does not pick up upon, but which those familiar with psi, would recognize. A patient has a vivid dream of a man kissing her, but when he does so, the teeth on the side of her mouth come out, down to the ridge although the root is still there. One of Stoller's sons, actually had a surfing accident on the weekend, and breaks his tooth at the root. The surfing accident was on Friday afternoon, the patient's dream on Friday night or Saturday morning; however, Stoller did not learn of the accident until *Sunday* afternoon. Despite how close in content are the dream and the event, Stoller says it might not be telepathy. He is not familiar with the ubiquitous way in which telepathy can seemingly express itself and he assumes it must go directly from his conscious knowledge to the patient. As he did not consciously know of the tooth damage until after the patient had her dream, he contends her dream might not be telepathic. But, of course, such information could flow telepathically from Stoller's son to his patient directly, or through Stoller himself. We know how patients apparently communicate telepathically without actual knowledge of each other. This type of contortion on Stoller's part, where one removes the emotional surprise of an apparent hit, by invoking the hypothesis of coincidence, can easily happen if the analyst is not familiar with parapsychological literature and the nature of psi phenomena.

But perhaps the most moving aspect of Stoller's report is his distress that he had these experiences of telepathy, which he thinks of as if they were part of a bout of an illness. He says: "I have ... hesitated to write this up because of not knowing if something right or wrong is going on in me" (!). Stoller takes responsibility for in effect generating telepathic dreams in his patients, but he does not appear to recognize the extent to which his patients also are causally part of these interactions. Regardless, if he had been familiar with the literature, he would not have been so threatened by the idea that patients tapped telepathically into things in his life (or he influenced them telepathically); nor would he have contended so strongly that telepathy was circumscribed by distress rather than a part of everyday life. As in the case of Eshel, whose work I will discuss shortly, the tendency, because the personal data of telepathic experiences may be limited, is to extrapolate solely from those experiences and pronounce that telepathy takes place only under certain circumstances. A full knowledge of the literature would mitigate that tendency, or at the very least acknowledge that telepathic communication takes place under a variety of circumstances, appears to be an everyday part of life (as Freud himself suggested) and does not necessarily arise from severe symptoms, severe distress or developmental trauma.

Now to another part of Mayer's report of Stoller's paper. Mayer states in her introduction, after listing those who have written about "thought transference," including Eisenbud's work and George Devereux's *Psychoanalysis and the Occult* that : "It is notable that almost never in those papers has the reporting analyst revealed to a patient the fact that some communication between the two of them has struck the analyst as telepathic." When I read this, which so misstates the history, even though she had cited Pederson Krag, Hollos, and Eisenbud, among others, who did exactly what she claimed had rarely been done (and neglected to mention that Freud initially did exactly that), I confessed at the time to being completely flummoxed. I sat down and wrote a letter to the editor of the *Journal of the American Psychoanalytic Association*, Arnold Richards, in which, among other things, I disputed this. Richards was going to publish my letter, as well as a kindly but it seemed to me not-to-the-point response from Mayer, and another response from me, but for some reason, it never happened. (I have included these letters in the Appendix.)

Mayer was stalwart, if in my opinion at times misleading, in her willingness to champion an exploration of certain types of psi phenomena. What had prompted her to become involved in the field, as she explained in her book *Extraordinary Knowing*, was a curious event. In 1991, her daughter's valuable harp was stolen in Oakland, California. Having no luck in finding it through normal means, she took the desperate step of contacting a dowser, Harold McCoy, over 2,000 miles away, on the other side of the country, in Kentucky. McCoy psychically determined that the harp was in a house in Oakland but miles from where it was stolen, and he located the exact address. (Note that this type of "finding" is one of the possible abilities of the Navajo hand trembler, the psychic in Navajo traditional society, whom I report upon in Chapter Eight). For the police, this hardly represented "probable cause," not enough apparently to even knock on a door, and so they simply closed the case. However, Mayer, although skeptical, figured she had nothing to lose and took the further step of posting signs within a two-block radius of the house, requesting the return of the harp; whereupon to her surprise, someone called to say he had seen the signs, knew who had taken the harp, and that he would have it returned, which he did.

As a consequence of this, and the sense of revelation that she experienced when it happened, she began to investigate on her own the field of psychical research. And then six years later in 1997, with her colleague Carol Gilligan, she created a Discussion Group at the American Psychoanalytic Association entitled "Intuition, Unconscious Communication, and Thought 'Transference.'" This group, which met a handful of times, was initially overwhelmed with requests by analysts to join the group; it was a requirement that a prospective analyst participant submit a "written account of an apparently anomalous experience, personal or clinical" (Mayer, 2007, p. 14). Numerous prominent analysts approached Mayer with accounts of such experiences, including Patrick Casement, Robert Pyles, and Susan Coates. Ultimately this publicity brought the unpublished Stoller piece to Mayer's attention through the intervention of another analyst, Carole Morgan.

Mayer's investigation into psychic phenomena was published in 2007 in a somewhat popularized book entitled *Extraordinary Knowing*. It too was published posthumously, after her untimely death on New Year's Day 2005 at the age of 57 from an intestinal disease she had for fifteen years. *Extraordinary Knowing* takes a certain circumscribed stance toward psychic phenomena, and it is clear that it owes much to Mayer's work with contemporary parapsychologists, who shepherded her through their field. And there is actually very little about psychoanalysis in the book. What she attempts to do is give a brief history of psychical phenomena and then focus on modern day research, hoping to grace the field with the mantle of "hard science." Thus she eschews the term "parapsychology" and favors "anomalous experiences" (as she did when she made it a requirement for analysts to have such an experience to join the Discussion Group)—a term which since its introduction in the 1970s, in the disingenuous hope that it would prove less publicly threatening than "parapsychology" or "psychic research" or the "study of psi phenomena"—has as I have indicated previously simply muddied the waters by encouraging the introduction of phenomena that are not in fact parapsychological or cannot be conceived of in that way. And in her review and focus on behavioral research—from Rhine Zener card studies to the remote viewing experiments at Stanford Research Institute to her speculations on the relationship of psi phenomena to quantum physics—she does not take advantage of her expertise as a psychoanalyst to show how psi operates dynamically.

It is also remarkable that there is no mention of psychic photography and the Ted Serios phenomenon. In fact, she does not mention Eisenbud at all (!) in her book nor for that matter does she mention Stephen Braude (Braude, 1986; Braude, 2000) whose comments on Eisenbud's work are crucial to hypotheses concerning telepathy and psychokinesis, although she does entertain both precognition and psychokinesis. Then, to make matters worse, she speaks approvingly of James Randi, who she says, "even received a MacArthur 'genius' award for his work in educating the public on the need for scientific rigor and a healthy sense of skepticism" (Mayer, 2007, p. 93). I have indicated how completely irrational and ethically-challenged Randi has been with regard to the Serios data (see Chapter Four on Bergman and Chesterton).

I suspect that Mayer, new to the parapsychological field, was captivated by the parapsychologists with whom she met, many of whom tend to minimize the importance of the Ted Serios data. As I have said, despite the fact that the Serios phenomenon represents the most important data we have about psychokinesis and its dynamic creation, many parapsychologists are as threatened by it as are psychoanalysts.

And yet, to Mayer's credit, after providing a synopsis of some of the behavioral findings (I do not wish to entirely minimize their importance although it is not the focus of what I am presenting in this book) she admits that—of the thousands of experimental studies she has read, that keep on trying to adjust details of experimental method, in order to experimentally elicit and control psi—

> (t)he more studies I read, the more that approach strikes me as missing the forest for the trees. Not only does it lead to more boredom—endless articles packed with methodological quibbles—but more important, it puts figuring out a way to play by the rules of conventional science ahead of asking whether anomalous mental capacities actually play by those rules [p. 265].

One would have hoped that Mayer *began* her book with this observation (which she attributes in part to William James) rather than ending it in this way. What she says was stated forcefully by Eisenbud years ago in an article entitled *Psi and the Nature of Things* (Eisenbud, 1963, reprinted 1983b) to the consternation of parapsychologists, where he questioned the use of concept of the "repeatable experiment" as applied to the investigation of psi phenomena, which most convincingly and most meaningfully express themselves spontaneously. In fact, he introduced his study of the Serios data in exactly this manner (Eisenbud, 1967, p. 11).

Derrida: Freud's Resistance to Telepathy Explored by Derrida with Some Further Elaborations

The French philosopher Jacques Derrida, wrote a turgid but haunting piece entitled *Telepathy*, translated into English by Royle—an amazing free-associative excursion into Freud's ambivalence in pursuing telepathy (Derrida, 1988). It is also a paean to the importance of telepathy. At times in the piece, Derrida writes as if he speaking as Freud, struggling with his ambivalence. As Derrida observes, all of Freud's parapsychological papers, in the service of his resistance to the very phenomena he was exploring, were lectures that in fact were never given! He calls them, provocatively, "fake lectures." Derrida summarizes these articles:

> The fake lecture of 1921 " Psycho-analysis and Telepathy," supposedly written for a meeting of the International Association, which did not take place, he never gave it, and it seems that Jones, with Eitingon, dissuaded him from presenting it at the following congress. This text was only published after his death and his manuscript included a post-script relating the case of Dr. Forsyth, and the Forsyte Saga, forgotten in the first version out of "resistance" (I quote). The fake lecture of 1922 "Dreams and Telepathy," was never given, as it was supposed to be, to the Society of Vienna, only published in *Imago*. The third fake lecture, "Dreams and Occultism" (30th lecture, the second of the *New Introductory Lectures)* was of course never given ... [Derrida, 1988, p. 18].

Derrida shows most clearly how Freud was caught on the one hand between the parapsychological experiments that Ferenczi conducted with Freud and his daughter Anna, and with the clairvoyant Frau Seidler, which Freud himself encouraged, and on the other hand with Jones's politically motivated admonitions to him not to taint psychoanalysis with discussion of anything telepathic or psychic. In 1926, Freud—now leaning toward acceptance of telepathy—wrote to Jones:

> My own experiences through tests I made with Ferenczi and my daughter won such a convincing force for me that the diplomatic considerations on the other side had to give way. I was once more faced with a case where on a reduced scale I had to repeat the great experiment of my life: namely to proclaim a conviction without taking into account any echo from the outer world. So then it was unavoidable. When anyone adduces my fall into sin, just answer him calmly that my conversion to telepathy is my private affair like my Jewishness, my passion for smoking and many other things, and that the theme of telepathy is in essence alien to psychoanalysis [Jones, 1957, p. 395; see also Freud, 1993, p. 597].

Of this, says Derrida:

> Who would be satisfied with such a declaration coming from him? ... (H)ow does one accept this disassociation pure and simple on the part of someone who has struggled with the theorization of telepathy? And then, if it is foreign to psychoanalysis, like a foreign body precisely, as though "off the subject," must psychoanalysis remain silent about the structure and the incorporation of the foreign body? [Derrida, 1988, p. 33].

What is equally intriguing about this piece is the circumstances of its publication. As with Freud's write up of the Forsyth case (which as I have noted was left out of Freud's 1921 article on telepathy and then only published posthumously), Derrida's material on telepathy was *also* left out of the book to which it was supposed to be attached, *The Post Card*, and only published separately later! The unconscious resistances which attend

writing about psi in the psychoanalytic field seem to lead to enormous resistance to actually *publishing* the material once it is written. As Freud says of his 1921 omission of the
Forsyth case, which was published subsequently in 1933: "*Postscript*. Here is the report,
omitted owing to resistance, on a case of thought-transference during analytic practice"
(Strachey, 1955). Freud is even more forceful about this when he elaborates on the circumstances of his misplacing the case report and taking instead the wrong pages: "Nothing" he says, "can be done against such a clear resistance" (Freud, 1921, p. 190).

A similar experience of resistance occurred to the psychoanalyst Farrell. He had a
telepathic dream that involved his trying not to spill a bowl of soup, milk or wine, while
being observed by a friend; the dream coincided with the unexpected cardiac attack and
death many miles away of the friend's wife, who collapsed in front of her husband, after
carefully carrying a pitcher of punch (to fill a punch bowl), which she put down without
spilling despite her distress. Farrell was determined to write up his dream and the circumstances. But, he acted very much as Freud did:

> I encountered a quite formidable resistance in myself to pursuing the investigation I had in mind as
> I had consciously intended. Several times, in fact, I misplaced the notebook with the account of the
> dream; finally, after spending several hours off and on over an entire weekend searching for the note-
> book before I found it, I forced myself to lock the notes away in the filing cabinet. Even then, I found
> myself doubting my memory—for example, convincing myself that my dream had occurred on another
> date than 2 July [the date of the death]—and avoiding checking the notes, now securely locked in the
> filing cabinet [Farrell, 1983, p. 72].

Similarly, Ira Brenner in writing about psi phenomena remarks that he had "started and
stopped writing this chapter numerous times," quickly realizing "how difficult it was to
write about working with ... patients who seem to manifest that facet of mental functioning that pertains to the realm of psi phenomena" (Brenner, 2001, p. 177). And for that
matter, Ferenczi, writing in 1932, the year before he died, poetically spoke of this resistance:

> Cases of thought transference during the analysis of suffering people are extraordinarily frequent.
> One sometimes has the impression that the reality of such processes encounters strong emotional
> resistance in us materialists; any insights we gain into them have the tendency to come undone, like
> Penelope's weaving or the tissue of our dreams [Ferenczi, 1988, p. 33].

Here I might add that I have found that I have experienced considerable personal
resistance in writing this chapter of this book and the next one. It was easier by far to
write about literature and psi, or culture and psi but writing about psychoanalysis and
psi, in a clinical framework, has proven a challenge. I know that I am reluctant to make
myself subject to the opprobrium that so often attends the announcing of oneself as a
psychoanalyst interested in parapsychology, but as importantly I have found it hard to
consciously articulate my thoughts about the data which I have accumulated and experienced over my years as a clinician, because in doing so I see how fundamentally my
view of the place of "mind" in the world differs from the views of my colleagues or of
our Western culture. If the community of psychoanalysts who accepted this material was
larger, it would of course be easier. But I have felt those echoes of the fear that others,
such as Stoller, have felt when contemplating publishing such material. I suppose I should
be grateful that it appears this work will not be published posthumously as occurred
with Stoller and with Freud's last article.

In the past, in meeting new colleagues, I invariably never mentioned my interest in
psi. At present, no longer as concerned about what putative colleagues might think (I

have reached an age and a point in my career when I care less), I *do* mention it. And then often I recognize the wariness that suddenly overcomes the colleague with whom until that point I was having a pleasant conversation and the careful distancing that takes place. I suspect I have lost out on more than one return dinner engagement as a consequence; and been dropped by more than one email correspondent who has suddenly been rendered curiously mute. Humorous as this may be, the fact is that—as in any profession—the wheels of advancement or acceptance are greased with a kind of commonality of understanding. When one steps outside that commonality, as did Eisenbud for example, the ostracism for one's views and direction can be quite palpable.

Make no mistake. Such ostracism is not confined to the psychoanalytic profession. For example, Brian Josephson, winner of the Nobel prize in physics in 1973, was disinvited from speaking at a conference on physics in 2010 by a letter from the organizers stating: "It has come to my attention that one of your principal research interests is the paranormal … in my view, it would not be appropriate for someone with such research interests to attend a scientific conference." Josephson's intended presentation in fact had nothing to do with the paranormal. Subsequent explanation from the organizers as to why it was necessary to disinvite Josephson as well as another physicist, David Peat, who had an interest in Jung's theory of synchronicity and Native American thought (which the organizers indicated was equally unacceptable) was revealing: it was that those in control of the physics profession were so prejudiced against the paranormal that belief in telepathy or other psi phenomena might disqualify one for consideration for a job. Thus, to protect young physic researchers who might attend the conference from being even remotely associated with paranormal research, it was necessary to disinvite Josephson and Peat! (Josephson, May 8, 2010). One might presume that Einstein himself, as a consequence of having written the introduction to Upton Sinclair's *Mental Radio*, would have suffered the same fate.

A Revelation: Freud's Own Psi Involvement in the Forsyth Case

Derrida's attention to the Forsyth case, prompted me to return to it once again and also to read Ernest Jones' and Freud's letters to one another with reference to parapsychology. And then I realized that there is actually much more to the Forsyth case that has not been mentioned by any other commentator. What has been missed, and what Freud himself missed, is that the ostensible psi that occurred in the Forsyth case was a product of *Freud's* unconscious, not just Herr P.'s. The unconscious motivation for psi on Freud's part was as great as was Herr P.'s motivation to unconsciously express through psi his jealousy of a new putative rival, Dr. Forsyth. Put differently, the psi in the Forsyth case was as likely created by Freud as psychological "ammunition" in the battle taking place between Jones and Freud about telepathy as it was by Herr P.; or it was in effect mutually created to fit both Freud's and Herr P.'s divergent needs. In a completely over-determined way, even beyond what one can glean from the facts that Freud presents, the psi that took place served as an answer to Jones, the inveterate English skeptic of things parapsychological who tried so hard to discourage Freud's explorations into this area. In other words, the direction of Herr P.'s psi is not so easily denominated as Herr P. toward Freud but in the opposite direction as well.

Let me explain. As Freud elaborates, Dr. Forsyth, the new rival for Freud's attention in Herr P.'s unconscious, was English, having just arrived from London. However, as

Herr P. reminded Freud, a month previous another English guest had appeared "quite unexpectedly" from London to Freud's delight, Ernest Jones himself, who interrupted *that* previous session with Herr P., and then was told to wait in the waiting room. Added to this was the fact that Herr P., referred to a recent dream of his own in English as a "mare's nest," because he had forgotten the English translation of "nightmare." To this Herr P. apparently also associated when Freud showed him Dr. Forsyth's card, dwelling upon the English culture of both people who had impinged on his sessions with Freud.

Freud picks up on this interesting "mare's nest" slip by Herr P., whose command of English in general was quite good, and wondered whether the slip was overdetermined by an unwitting psi connection by Herr P. to the Englishman Jones who interrupted his previous session. As Freud states, it was unlikely that Herr P. was aware that Jones himself was the author of a monograph on the nightmare. As to things English, Freud also mentions that at that time of the Forsyth event he was reading the English novel, the Forsyte Saga, presented to him by none other than Herr P., who had an extensive English library. Concludes Freud, it seems as if, "starting from the idea of English", derived from the English visitor, Herr P. drew in other situations that aroused jealousy in him and also drew in another Englishman, namely Jones.

What Freud does not mention is that Dr. David Forsyth, who left his calling card, was not only a London doctor (actually a pediatrician) but he was in fact a colleague of Jones whom Jones had made one of the new members of a psychoanalytic society in England. In fact, it was Jones himself who had helped to arrange *this very interview* of Forsyth with Freud, for the purpose of Forsyth getting experience as an analysand! (Freud, 1993, pp. 233, 350, 355). So Jones is intimately involved in all of these examples. And remember, over many years, Freud's argument about whether or not to publish his thoughts about telepathy and parapsychology was principally with Jones, who repeatedly warned Freud not to do so. (The quote by Jones with which I began this chapter is in fact followed by Jones's stating an exactly antithetical view, his view expressing how foolish was Freud's adventure into parapsychology.)

Thus it is more than just piquant that the Forsyth case of apparent telepathy is intimately connected with Jones. Dynamically, if one were to search for possible reasons that psi appeared to occur under these circumstances, it would not only be because of Herr P.'s jealousy of Forsyth and by extension Jones. It was as if Freud himself unconsciously took delight in making the skeptical Jones, with his staid Englishness (upon which Freud remarks with regard to telepathy) the foil for what happened in the session. As Freud writes to Jones in March 1926: "I very much regret that my views on telepathy have plunged you into new difficulties. But it really is difficult not to offend English sensibilities" (Freud, 1993, p. 596). And so, one cannot help but wonder whether Freud himself was unconsciously party to the psi that occurred, as if to say "I will show you, Jones: I will answer your sometimes insufferable fear-mongering and skepticism about introducing psi into psychoanalysis by producing an example in which *you yourself* play a part. That will turn the tables so to speak and make my point." And then, the coup de grace: "And I will publish the case with you as the foil so the world might see that telepathy does indeed exist." And thus, although it appears as if it is Herr P. who ropes in so many associations to things "English" in his jealousy and who speaks the actual words suggesting psi, who is the only one to have the motivation for enlisting psi, it is Freud himself, with his rather strong feelings about telepathy and things "English" personified in Jones, who also has more than sufficient motivation to invoke psi. Stated again: the Forsyth

Case is as much about Freud unconsciously creating psychic phenomena to answer Jones's skepticism as it is about Herr P.'s jealousy of Dr. Forsyth.

As to this aspect of the case: in general with psychic phenomena it is impossible to believe that it works like a telephone, despite the fact that Freud himself made this analogy, as if one can control in a conscious way the *direction* of the call. It is an unconscious phenomena, without such control. The psychoanalyst himself can get drawn in (as Hollos says "The patient dreams the analysts dream") and other patients can get drawn in as well. Derrida made the point beautifully and succinctly: "The ultimate naivety would be to allow oneself to think that Telepathy guarantees a destination..." (Derrida, p. 16). In effect, telepathy does not function like an arrow. When it takes place it is more like a "surround" or a "magnet" that can draw in many people's thoughts—the analyst, the patient, other patients, family members. (See my discussion of this in the chapter on Joyce, where I indicate how more than one patient can be drawn into a psi communication.) So when Freud points to his patient as the source of the telepathy, and his patient's jealousy as the determining motivating force, you can be sure—as I have indicated—that more was at work. Put differently, as Eisenbud says, the psychoanalyst who looks for psi in his patients' productions may find, like a bumbling detective, that the "fingerprints are his own."

There are some further less important footnotes to the seemingly eternally interesting Forsyth case. Whatever high hopes Freud had for Dr. Forsyth as an English adherent to psychoanalysis, did not come to fruition after all. Eventually there was a distinct falling out, with Jones and Freud, on the one hand, and with Forsyth on the other (Freud, 1993, pp., 374–376, 378, 381, 397). So Herr P.'s jealous feelings in this telepathic incident, ended up in the long run with his unconscious rival Dr. Forsyth developing a distinctly cool relationship with Freud. And the tendency for the Forsyth case to contain itself within addendums—as occurred with Freud's posthumous publication of the Forsyth case after his resistance led him to misplace the write-up of the case for the earlier 1921 article, and as occurred with Derrida's failure to add his discussion of the Forsyth case and telepathy in general to a larger work—has continued. In 1983, Maria Torok published an article "L'occulte de l'occultisme: Entre Sigmund Freud et Sergei Pankejev—Wolfman" (Torok, 1973), which was then modified to yet *another* addendum, an afterword in a book about the Wolfman (Abraham and Torok, 1986). Torok claimed in the afterword that the unidentified Herr P. must have been the Wolfman, a famous patient of Freud's, and she constructed an elaborate speculative theory concerning telepathy based on this assumption. However, her assumption proved to be wrong. For in 2009, Pierri published an article which related that he had located a missing first draft of the "Forsyth Case" among Freud's papers—like everything else in this case, the first draft also went peculiarly missing until its discovery by Pierri—and that Herr P., rather than being the Wolfman, was in fact Paul B., "a Jewish advisor ... of a company ... that traded in ferrous minerals" (Pierri, 2009, p. 752). Perhaps this will be the last of the addendums in a case that seems to have a life of its own.

Psychoanalytic Misconceptions About Telepathy

Freud's misconception, that telepathy acts somewhat like a telephone call, tends to be a common one with psychoanalysts. Derrida, as we have seen, had a better sense of how telepathy works. In fact, when things telepathic occur in the clinical setting, it often is not just as a one-way or even as a two-way street between patient and analyst or between two patients but it as if a "telepathic surround" has been established, which can draw in a number of people. That is, the psychoanalyst's anxieties or experiences may be brought parapsychologically to a patient's dream or to a patient's associations or even to another patient's similar experiences, and then a third or fourth patient may also in effect unconsciously participate, as if those patients too unconsciously desire attention from the analyst and want to be included. In this regard, it is almost as if psi acts like a search engine that focuses on an issue or an anxiety, an event or a symbol, and then taps people associated unconsciously with each other. (Eshel also uses the concept of a "search engine" to explain the telepathic process but confines it to a search for the missing "other" as a result of early loss [Eshel, 2006].) Jung had a better feel descriptively of what can happen when he posited a "collective unconscious" (although the actual concept was somewhat different and suggested a substratum of unconscious attunement that did not follow individual unconscious wishes as much as societally ingrained or mythic similarities) than did Freud.

More than any other commentator, Eisenbud recounts frequent instances in which more than one patient unconsciously participates in a dynamic way in a telepathic conversation. In Chapter Five, I summarized one such three-way correspondence among Eisenbud's patients involving a dark-skinned lady; as well as a three-way correspondence among patients of mine involving raccoons. Here is another clinical example from my patients, involving sexual wishes or prohibitions.

Honey and Oral Sex

Ms. J is a once-a-week Friday patient of long standing—resilient, intelligent, and often humorous—who for a period of time in her life, after a truly horrendous marriage to a physically abusive man, has avoided intimate male relationships. She has now to her surprise found that she is not only once again drawn to men but has taken a male lover, who is both giving and supportive. With this new lover, for the first time in her life she enjoys a full and mutual heterosexual relationship which includes oral sex. This change, which she never thought of taking place when she began treatment, has delighted her. In fact, Ms. J, who often follows her instincts, has managed in her life to have a number of lucky breaks which often have the quality of serendipity, and she believes in effect in psi phenomenon although not by that name. Nor is she particularly knowledgeable about it. In this Friday session, she tells me how after a sexual experience with her new lover, he said she was like a bee flitting around him, and they both laughed and played with the image. By seeming chance, subsequently, she saw an erotic poem on the internet, about a bee flitting around a pistil, and then at the end of the poem, there was a picture of a woman with honey dripping out of her mouth. She thinks that observing this so close to her metaphorical joke with her lover was somewhat miraculous and emphasizes the "delight" she experienced. In fact, she had thought of sending the poem to me, by email but then became anxious about doing so.

On Monday, Ms. M, an analytic patient who at the moment is not happy with her husband, tells me: *I had a dream in which my husband's penis was in my mouth, but there was no sexual sense to it, no sexual feeling. And then I dreamt that I lost a diamond from my ring.* It is not that Ms. M does not enjoy oral sex; she very much does. But clearly, her disappointment with her husband at the present time is considerable; and unlike Ms.

J, she makes a point in her dream of depriving herself of any feeling of joy with her husband or with oral sex with him. She says specifically when elaborating, "I felt no delight in my dream." It is quite a contrast with Ms. J.

And then on Tuesday, Ms. G., another long standing analytic patient, who is all but obsessed with thoughts about fellatio, because of terrible sexual abuse of her for many years as a child, feeling years later that people were convinced she performed fellatio on him (although she did not) goes on and on in session about having sampled some honey at a country fair over the weekend. She tasted it, and says that ten minutes later, she felt sick. The experience clearly has made her very anxious. Never previously has she reported such an experience with honey. The fact is that Ms. G. is completely uncomfortable with the idea of oral sex, which she has felt the need to repeatedly inveigh against over many years of treatment. She is convinced that it is something I desire of her. Unlike the other women, she has had little sexual contact with men over many years.

The first and third patient appear very much to be on the same unconscious page, as evidenced by the appearance of honey in the first patient's dream and the third patient's actual experience with honey, although with vastly different conclusions; and the second patient seems to be involved as well, emphasizing her lack of delight in an activity that generally she would enjoy and which has never come up quite as graphically in a dream of hers. What is interesting is that the first patient had thought of emailing me (something which generally she would not do) and also thought that discovering the poem by chance on the internet after her experience with her lover was particularly miraculous. Query whether, in effect, something more or less seemingly "miraculous" also occurred as a consequence of the psi connections that did take place in the correspondence with the other patients. In a sense, it was as if the first patient elicited psi as a way of competitively triumphing over the other female patients of mine—"I enjoy the honey"—indicating her delight in her sexual experience, and unconsciously appealing to me as a sexually alive woman in this way. Of course, one might also posit that my own sexual wishes, played an unconscious role in this surround.

When a patient produces a telepathic dream, the paranormal surround often gets enlisted with other patients, and I find myself frequently impressed with how the number of participants grow. It is as if psi comes in twos or threes; once invoked it draws in the unconscious of other participants or the events to which they are subject.

Incidentally, a misconception by psychoanalysts is to believe that psi is governed by popular notions such as that it is an electromagnetic wave which takes place at a particular time. There is no indication that the nature of psi connections is in the manner of waves; Serios for example when confined to a Faraday cage (which would block electromagnetic waves) produced psychic photographs nonetheless in a Polaroid camera held outside the cage. As we have seen in the telepathic drawing experiments, distance seems not to be a discernible factor, despite Einstein's belief that it should be.[1] (Osis and his associates claimed to have experimentally found a very slight time delay based on distance, but these findings have been criticized as not taking into account psychological factors that may have contributed to the delay when participants knew of the distances [Steinkamp, 2008, p. 134; Osis and Turner, 1968; see also Braud, W. (2010) for a review of this issue suggesting it is undecided].) In addition, the popular conception that one can necessarily locate psi as taking place at a particular time, is simply not true, as appealing as it is (and appealing as it was to Freud who used the hypothesis when the father dreamed that his wife rather than his daughter gave birth to twins at a distance away from him, attempting to match the time of the birth and the time of the dream, which I previously discussed). Sometimes, telepathy *does* appear to take place at a particular moment in time, as when there is an accident or a death (and of course parapsychological experiments try to confine it as well); but at other times there is no such indication. Often commentators more or less use the similarity in time as a way of verifying that telepathy must have been operating, but this, while appealing ("it must have been telepathy because the events occurred at the same time") is in no way a condition for the psi hypothesis. If one assumes that psi connections are unconsciously mediated, they can more or less be "stored" in the unconscious at any time. This is what I contend explains apparitions, that is telepathy that provides an hallucinatory experience, as I stated in my discussion of the ghost in *Hamlet*, and the same hypothesis can be used for hauntings when over time different people in a particular place have an experience that is known to others. It is not so much that an apparition attaches to the physical place, although it can very much appear that way, but that people's thoughts (people who are presently alive) about that place create a paranormal surround that can touch others when they visit the place.

More on "The Use of the Psi Hypothesis in Interpretation"

The quoted material in this subtitle is actually taken from the title for Chapter 16 in Eisenbud's *Psi and Psychoanalysis* (Eisenbud, 1970, pp. 318–329), which is intentional because many commentators neglect to mention the extent to which Eisenbud engaged the issue of how to discuss with a patient the fact that some of what the patient presents in analysis appears to be mediated by psi. The question, which applies to Freud's intervention in the Forsyth case but which Freud himself never specifically addressed, is whether to present the ostensible psi connections of which the patient is not aware to the patient at all and with what purpose or justification.

Background and context are important here; and one of the most important of them is that the analyst for therapeutic reasons is usually trying *not* to share aspects of his own life and feelings with the patient. The supposition, at least of the theories of treatment referred to as Modern Freudian (which is close to my training and my present belief), is that the analyst must not share too much of himself with the patient so that the patient can focus on his own thoughts and feelings and fantasies. The hope is that the patient will develop a transference toward the analyst, at times during the treatment, thinking of the analyst and acting toward him as he would toward a loved object (a father, a mother, a sister for example) in his developmental past, which theoretically happens more readily when the analyst's own life and experiences are *not* known to the patient. In this way, the patient can begin to work through those distressing and traumatic events that have led to interactions and feelings in the present that are neither realistic nor healthy.

Of course, there are technical variations and other theories on this, many of which focus on the way in which patient and analyst interact, with various degrees of emphasis on how much the analyst necessarily brings to the interaction with the patient, now referred to as countertransference, which has a more enlarged meaning than it did in the past (when it suggested that an analyst had to maintain a neutrality by knowing his analytic self and developmental history so well that he would never act toward the patient as he did toward a figure in his past).

Regardless, in practice, what can happen is that the analysand, in the service of the transference, and as a consequent of limited information, spins theories and fantasies about the analyst—sometimes wildly inaccurate in fact—which then can be questioned and explored. However, now we tend to believe that it is inevitable that the analyst and patient will tend to co-create an aspect of the analytic interaction, and that the analyst cannot at times help but enact, that is say things to the patient, based on his own vulnerabilities and wishes, in response to the patient's psychological affect on him. Most technical differences reside in how much the analyst shares of himself with the patient, ranging from the Classical Freudian, where such sharing is kept to a minimum to relational and interpersonal theories where the analyst will share considerably more with the patient about himself during the course of the analysis.

The attempt to limit the information the patient receives about the analyst has resulted in many technical maneuvers, some bizarre, others less so. One of the more bizarre ones was the attempt in the past of some classically trained analysts to make their offices as barren and impersonal as possible, with no hint of the analyst's personality, no attempt to personalize nor beautify, on the grounds that nothing should be known about the analyst or his tastes at all—it made for a sterile and unappealing environment to say the least. Other controlling ones in the past have been to tell the analysand not to read anything about the analyst, including his psychoanalytic writing, or to make sure that analyst and analysand do not attend the same psychoanalytic presentation, particularly one featuring the analyst. Another has been for the analyst and analysand to avoid encountering each other at the same social event or at the same restaurant. But, of course, the fact is this all tends to be rather artificial and to some extent is no longer entirely practiced by many. After all, the analysand can tell from the analytic session—from how the consulting office is furnished for example, or how the analyst dresses or how the analyst looks on a particular day or (if the office in in the analyst's house) what his house is like or his car—a great deal about the analyst. If the analysand is a candidate at the analyst's institute, he will invariably have contact with his analyst at the institute in person, or through institute announcement or list-serves. And increasingly with social media, the boundaries have become even more porous. It is not unusual these days for an analysand to Google her analyst for example.

However, psi is something else again. What do you do as an analyst, if the fiction of the analysand not knowing about your life abetted by attempts to limit information to the analysand, is really not sustainable theoretically because the analysand invariably will pick up material about you or other patients through the operation of psi? The breach here, if one wants to call it that, I believe is in fact inevitable and cannot be controlled. It is part of the unconscious communication that takes place in all analyses. The analysand does not consciously plan to tap into the analyst's life or his dreams or the lives or dreams of other patients; nevertheless, he does. Nor can the analyst control what happens unconsciously, when he may unconsciously wish to telepathically communicate with his analysand. In fact, one might say that the very structure of the analytic session, where so much is not known by the analysand about the person with whom he interacts three or four or more times weekly (or about the other patients the analyst sees) tends to call up unconscious psi, as a way to magically overcome the artificial barrier. How significant is such communication depends, of course, on the circumstances. In addition, of course, the analyst is often aware, sometimes painfully, of a psi connection but the patient is not.

As we have seen, the founder of psychoanalysis, Freud, completely avoided any discussion of how to technically handle psi, and in fact blithely told his patient Dr. Forsyth of the psi connection with the previous patient of which he would not otherwise have known, without providing justification for the maneuver, other than the fact that in this case the competitive dynamics of the patient's psi were obvious.

Similarly, Eisenbud avoids a full discussion of how revealing information obtained through psi to the patient affects the artificial barrier cultivated to theoretically preserve as best as possible the transferences of the patient. He never really engages this problem. He begins by citing Ehrenwald who stated that psi "interpretations should only be given at an advanced stage of analysis, when all aspects of the transference relationship have been thoroughly worked through and when the therapist feels safe to expose whatever hidden evidence of his own countertransference is contained in the telepathic material" (Ehrenwald, 1975, p. 283). Ehrenwald went on to suggest that psi should not be invoked when the patient is involved in a negative transference; and that for the "advanced schizophrenic" psi interpretations are not appropriate because they will only add "confirmation of his delusional trend" (Ehrenwald, 1975, p. 284). In contrast, Eisenbud is more liberal. He states: "I have yet to find a contraindication to acquainting patients with the psi hypothesis and its usefulness in connection with specific types of analytic material" (Eisenbud, 1970, p. 319).

Gillespie, who served as President of the International Psychoanalytic Association, from 1957–1961, was more cautious, opening up the question but not providing an answer. He said:

> Should the analyst keep this better understanding (as a consequence of a psi link to something in the analyst's life, in this instance between a dream of the patient and a dream of the analyst: my addition), or should he communicate it to his patient, and if so, how? ... The point in making such a communication to the patient is, of course, that without them [sic] he cannot be in a position to understand the full significance of his own dream. The technical problem is analogous to that of the interpretation of symbols, but is much complicated by the transference implications.... We are accustomed to the idea that the essential work of analysis proceeds by the analyst's unconscious making contact with that of the patient; but this has customarily been taken to involve the mediation of the ordinary senses and the use of verbal and other physical means of communication. The facts of telepathy open up quite new possibilities of a much more direct means of communication between one unconscious and another. This is surely of the greatest significance both for our theory and our practice [Gillespie, 1953, pp. 380–381].

Two Psychoanalytic Reasons Given for Resistance to the Psi Hypothesis

That there is resistance to experiencing, acknowledging and exploring psi phenomena is apparent. Given this resistance, one must ask: Why? What are the dynamic reasons for such frequent and overwhelming resistance to the psi hypothesis? Through the years, psychoanalytic writers have suggested essentially two reasons for that resistance. The first relates to boundaries and the second to aggression. They are not necessarily mutually exclusive. What these two reasons try to answer is not only why a patient might tend to resist the psi hypothesis but why, in effect, over and over the data that has been put forth, by Freud onward, have been so successfully resisted by psychoanalysts themselves (and sometimes by parapsychologists as well). Those discoveries that have been made, the data provided by psychoanalysts in the past, the manner in which psychoanalysts have used that data in clinical practice, the theories generated about the data—all of these things too often have been ignored or forgotten.

The first reason for resistance, and the one more readily accessible, is that psi phenomena appear to represent a loosening of the psychological boundaries between people, and call up early development, when the child's sense of separateness particularly from his mother has not yet been established. The analyst Dorothy Burlingham, companion to Anna Freud, first wrote about this in 1935, in speaking of child analysis. She said: "The power of unconscious forces is especially marked in the interplay between the parent and child" and then she gave a series of examples in which a child was influenced by his mother's thoughts (Burlingham, 1953, p. 188). In one, a child guesses her mother is pregnant before her mother knows; in another, a child brings his mother a gold coin the same day as the mother in her analysis speaks of an important emotional event in her childhood involving a gold coin and a few weeks later, when the mother sits down to make a note of the occurrence, the child comes in and asks for the gold coin back; and in a third, a mother in her analytic session has the fantasy of throwing a jug of boiling water over someone in a rage when an hour later her young child approaches his sister with a glass of steaming water and threatens in anger to pour it on her. Freud, citing Burlingham's article, and mentioning the gold coin example, alludes to the part telepathy might play in early development. Saying that if telepathy exists, it must be a "common phenomenon," he then turns the direction of the thought communication around and states that: "It would fit in with our expectations if we could show that it occurs particularly in the mental life of children. One is reminded of the frequent fear felt by children that their parents know all their thoughts…" (Freud, 1933, p. 56).

Similarly, Ehrenwald states that "We must assume that every telepathic incident involves the temporary fusion of two emotionally linked individuals into one functional unit, re-establishing for a fleeting moment the original mother-infant unit as it existed at an early developmental stage" (Ehrenwald, 1960, p. 53).

Thus, the fear that adults presumably feel toward entertaining the psi hypothesis is the fear of regression to aspects of that early developmental state, when the ego looses its boundaries and tends to merge with another.

The second reason for resistance to the psi hypothesis is that it frightens us about our aggression. If we can influence others with our thoughts, or affect the outside world through unconscious telekinesis with our thoughts, it is terribly troubling. No end of modern-day horror movies play with this concept. It is striking for example that when Freud approved the observations made by Burlingham, he cited the example of the gold coin, but managed to overlook (as it appears have all subsequent commentators) the much more intriguing of the parapsychological examples that Burlingham mentions, namely a boy who threatens his sister with a glass of steaming water shortly after his mother has the rageful thought of throwing boiling water on someone. It is as if the boy as a consequence of unconscious telepathy finds permission to articulate his own aggression against his sister ("You, mother, wish in anger to throw boiling water on someone; so I can surely do the same to my sister!") or that he acts out his mother's wish transformed for some reason to express anger at her daughter. (This incidentally is the exact type of situation that I explore in Chapter Ten on "Western Law and Parapsychology," where I suggest Western law is a construct about causality used to provide order to society, rather than a true exploration of cause.) To assume that early psi communication between mother and child is all positive, all an attempt to heal a rift that develops when the two are in some way separate, defies our understanding of how unconscious communication in general between people works or our knowledge of in-depth dynamics. Love and aggression are both there. Thus, when I said that the two reasons for resistance to the psi hypothesis were not mutually exclusive, fear of the potentially aggressive impact of psi is the other reason that there is resistance to the hypothesis. The mother-child or parent-child dyad is where that resistance begins which articulates itself years later in reluctance to entertain the psi hypothesis at all.

Here is an interesting example of this proposition. Years ago, under my supervision, one of my students, a 33-year-old mother, conducted a study with her 8-year-old daughter. For a period of approximately three months, she and her daughter kept dream records. Despite the fact that the mother was quite knowledgeable about parapsychology, she claimed she had never had a verifiable psychic experience; and she was convinced at the beginning of her study, that nothing verifiable would come of it. However, her anxiety about getting verifiable psi data gradually changed to another anxiety during the course of the study, when it became apparent at periodic intervals of comparison that there were a number of instances of dramatic psi correspondence between the dreams recorded by her and those recorded by her daughter, which could not be attributed—without great stretching of the imagination—to shared residual experience. To give one example, on April 10, 1977, the mother recorded a dream: "Not supposed to take (birth control) pills any more," and as if in retributive response to the mother's apparent desire for another child, the daughter recorded on the same date the dream: "My mom had quadruplets." The mother had not shared any thoughts about birth control with her daughter. So it seemed the daughter in her dream responded to her mother's dream by saying "If you want another child to replace me in your affection, I hope you get four. That will show you." The upshot of this study was that as the mother—who was psychoanalytically inclined—got closer and closer to the aggressiveness which existed between herself and her child, and simultaneously to her own relationship to her mother when she was at the age of her child, she became increasingly resistant to conducting the study at all (Reichbart, 1977). On the other hand, Schwarz in a book entitled *Parent-Child Telepathy* recounts five hundred and five possible episodes of telepathy in his family—during the time his daughter went from birth to nine years and his son from birth to seven years nine months—which he entitles "a study of the telepathy of everyday life" (Schwarz, 1971).

The proposition that the principle resistance to entertaining the psi hypothesis is the fear that one can express aggressive wishes through psi—psychokinesis is usually meant but the proposition applies as well to suggestive telepathy—was promulgated originally by Tanagras and subsequently by Eisenbud (and later Braude). Not all parapsychologists entertain this hypothesis. Psychoanalysts will generally find the concept anathema. The very center of psychoanalytic practice is that wishes are harmless, as distinguished from actions, and the road for so many patients to recovery from a harsh superego and guilty feelings, is through the patient expressing his aggressive wishes and then accepting that they are "wishes only," distinct from aggressive action, and thus they have no power to harm—and thus one need not feel guilt for them. This proposition, despite my knowledge of the aggressive aspects of psi, is one that I follow myself in clinical practice and almost always to good effect. If I am practicing a kind of "double-think," it is because I know of no other way to be helpful to patients, but from a theoretical viewpoint there is a great deal unresolved by my approach. I can only answer that—as with the Navajo system of accountability for psi actions—culture necessarily defines, and even I would suggest controls to some extent, how psi functions. Western culture seeks to control psi through a kind of collective denial, which may conceivably tend to fashion the way psi is expressed. In this sense, when Freud was troubled that by entertaining telepathy, it was only the first step that mattered, he was right. Once that step is taken, a variety of possibilities necessarily exist that are difficult to contemplate, perhaps most troubling of which is precognition (which can be explained as a consequence of telekinesis or telepathic suggestion rather than as a consequence of a momentary time travel), upon which I will elaborate in the next chapter. Even more disturbing are propositions concerning precognition of large human disasters also discussed in the following chapter. And here, in the aggressive possibilities, is where I believe lies the substantial resistance to the psi hypothesis, by psychoanalysts and by parapsychologists themselves (who somewhat obsessively become involved in small experiments, devoid of emotion, as a way to contain the understandable anxiety of these thoughts). In effect, once that first step is taken in this area, even the step that some psychoanalysts are willing to take, namely telepathy, all other phenomena involving influence from one mind to another and from mind to matter become possible.

Psychoanalysts Are Neither Taught Nor Trained to Understand Psychic Phenomena

> If we succeed in relinquishing the professional hypocrisy, projection, and idealization, surrounding parapsychological phenomena, we might get to grips with the underlying real problem, what the nature and function of E.S.P. is.—Balint, 1955, p. 35
>
> (T)he two disciplines which have the most to do with unconscious factors of human affairs, parapsychology and psychoanalysis, have so little regard for each other and play so little part in each other's thinking.—Eisenbud, 1983, p. 11

One would think that contemporary psychoanalysts, who learn through their own analyses, their control analyses, and their course work at their institutes to explore carefully and non-judgmentally what their patients say, would have the utmost curiosity about a variety of phenomena that people experience in life, in and outside of Western culture, phenomena that sometimes can affect patients deeply: out of body experiences (sometimes referred to as astral projections), ghosts or apparitions, hauntings, telepathy, precognition, psychic healing, poltergeists. But if you were to ask the usual contemporary psychoanalyst about these things, it is more than likely the psychoanalyst would say such things as that he is "not familiar with these phenomena" or that "these things never come up in treatment" or worse, that "these are delusions and signs of psychotic process" or that "these are popular superstitions."

There are gentler responses, but since the area is rarely breached, it is hard to know how often those responses exist. How many psychoanalysts today might respond, as did an experienced and skilled clinician at my institute, that she simply does not know much about this area but believes the possibility of telepathy exists? Not being at all familiar with the psychoanalytic literature on parapsychology, despite its existence, is a common theme even when the analyst might be more positively inclined. I have found, for example, to my amazement that if I mention the word "parapsychology" to some psychoanalysts, they have no familiarity with the term.

There is a danger, even when there is a much more nuanced and gentler response on the part of the psychoanalyst, especially if the patient explicitly brings psi up in treatment that goes beyond the apparent telepathy between patient and analyst. An example of this is presented by Bach, who treated a patient whose "sole reason for coming was that she had certain experiences of a parapsychological nature which dominated her thinking but which she could share with no one in the world around her" (Bach, 1985, p. 7). Let me spend a little time discussing Bach's approach in this case, because his talent as an analyst is compelling and yet, attempting to be non-judgmental and non-committal, he ultimately is dismissive about the existence of psi, which in this instance he compares to a patient's belief in an imaginary companion, which like a transitional object, may wane when it no longer serves a developmental function. In fact, he contrasts the "world of parapsychology" with the "world of reality" or the "rational world," despite his apparent care not to impose this distinction upon his patient, and despite the fact, as I have contended throughout this book, there is nothing "irrational" about psi. And he goes on to say (and here he makes my point) that because his "mind and training point in this direction," he formulated a dynamic and genetic explanation of the "meaning" of these parapsychological phenomena, while unable to accept that such phenomena might actually be part of the "real" or "rational" world.

To his credit, Bach makes it clear that he did not consider his patient psychotic—"her judgment, reality testing, reality sense and object relationship" were intact—and he never indicated to her that he disbelieved the "extraordinary occurrences" she reported. Of course, we do not know whether the patient, who conducted her own parapsychological experiments, was *actually* exhibiting psi. Bach suggests that when the patient began to think dynamically and put her parapsychological experiences into a dynamic context, it was evidence that she was getting more in touch with reality rather than "alternate worlds." But he exhibits no awareness that the proposition that psi takes place psychodynamically has been explored by many analysts, from Freud onward, and that such psychodynamic determinants are part and parcel of how psi works. Psychodynamic formulations by a patient in analysis, including relating to psi, are a sign of emotional growth; they are not necessarily a sign that psi does not exist, nor do they only take place in earnest if the patient gives up an interest in psi. We have seen for example that such psychodynamic formulations, beginning with Freud and the Dr. Forsyth case, are central to the psychoanalytic literature about telepathy encountered in treatment.

But what is particularly striking in Bach's report is that at one point the patient says, "I developed an unexposed film and it was a picture of my grandfather—you probably think that's because you're going away and I want something to remember you by." What a wonderful dynamic formulation (not unlike Eshel's and Stoller's views that often psi takes place to address loss or absence), but it does not speak at all to the phenomena being more fantasy than reality, a point which Bach misses. And of course it is more than intriguing that the patient touches upon psychic photography, in the nature of the Serios phenomena or the experiences of the early psychic photographers who allegedly *did* get images of "departed" personalities.

Bach suggests that when his patient's interest in psi and her alleged psi abilities waned, it represented a return to "real life." But query what would have happened in the treatment if Bach had been accepting of the possibility that psi *was* an integral part of everyday life, an integral part of the "real world" if little understood and little accepted, or had availed himself fully of the literature on psi and psychoanalysis? It is not clear whether the patient herself was exhibiting psi, but one cannot help but wonder whether

Bach's internal stance about psi was conveyed to her in some way. If Bach were not so ready to dismiss psi, would the patient have so readily thrown out the baby with the bathwater as she got healthier, and would she have managed to retain in a healthy way her interest in parapsychology, if less intensely? Would she have had as a consequence a broader sense of the "real world," one that incorporated the possibility of psi within it, rather than the more limited world in which Bach apparently—perhaps he would say tentatively—believes? And wouldn't that have been even more wonderful?

I focus on this particular case because I am so sympathetic to the type of analysis that Bach practices. I have said, repeatedly, that otherwise talented and accomplished psychoanalysts are unable to fully entertain psi phenomena. We have seen that Bach is not one who would necessarily attribute a belief in psi to psychotic process; but ultimately his training and the very ambiance of the psychoanalytic world that he so ably occupies (he is, among his other affiliations, a Fellow of my institute) does not lend itself to an acceptance of psi phenomena or a psychoanalytic formulation that would embrace the phenomena in the process of treating a patient.

Happily, what I have written about this case of Bach's requires an up-to-date revision. At a recent presentation (in April 2017) by S. Ellman focusing on "unconscious communication" between patient and analyst, Bach was the discussant, and, after the talk, I had an opportunity to revisit with him his point of view on telepathy. He stated that his view had changed, and he considered telepathy on a "continuum" of unconscious communication, in effect at the extreme end when there is no discernible sensorimotor way in which analyst and patient communicate, whereas other ways in which such communication takes place—similar themes occurring to both patient and analyst, intonation, barely discernible facial or bodily cues (that might register subliminally)—apparently would be on the other end of the continuum. Although this modification of view did not apply to psychic photography, it is nonetheless encouraging, but I have decided to preserve what I have written about Bach's case because the view he expressed would continue to meet with favor among most psychoanalysts.

The Particularly Pernicious Effect of Not Exploring Telepathy or Psi Phenomena with Certain Patients

As psychoanalysts or therapists, our role is to listen to patients and try to understand their experiences. Bach's case should serve to remind us of other dangers: if we label "telepathy" as delusional from the start, not having done the minimum on our parts of investigating the phenomena, then what happens when a patient attempts to speak of a psi experience? This is particularly a dilemma with patients who are aware of psi experiences and are troubled by them or patients who believe in general that they are "psychic." Powell recounts that during her training as a psychiatrist at John Hopkins, she was "taught that people who claimed to have psychic powers were psychotic" (Powell, 2012. p. 127) and then recounts the case of Ms. M, a hospitalized patient who claimed to be psychic, but whom Powell listened to carefully, declined to medicate over the staff's disapproval, and then found indeed managed to relate things about Powell that she could not have known otherwise. Powell's willingness to listen and accept her patient's abilities created a successful working alliance. As Powell says: "I have been taught from a young age that a true scientist doesn't throw away data just because it does not fit one's theory.

After meeting Ms. M., I had data I could not ignore. I just did not have a framework for understanding it" (p. 129).

Perhaps the most eloquent appeal to therapists to listen to patients who present telepathic material came from Ullman. He said:

> Those of us who have taken a public position espousing the reality of psi events are aware of a lost battalion of people who have had telepathic dreams that seemed both genuine and relevant to current issues in their lives and which left them confused and concerned often to the point where they questioned their own sanity. To share it with others would risk rebuff. People don't ordinarily go around having experiences like this. I have known of situations where the distress was severe enough for the individual to seek psychiatric help and were faced with the psychiatrists' failure to discern or consider the difference between genuine telepathic powers and the claim of telepathic powers as a symptom of schizophrenia…. One hopes that greater knowledge and a deeper understanding on the part of the therapist on the nature and reality of psi will someday save these individuals from the pain and distress of a frustrating search for help and at the same time broaden the horizon of the helping profession itself [Ullman, 2003, pp. 43–44].

Multiple Personality, Severe Trauma and Ira Brenner's Psychic Patient

> I have started and stopped writing this chapter numerous times. I quickly realized how difficult it would be to write about working with traumatized patients who seem to manifest that facet of mental functioning that pertains to the realm of psi phenomena—claivoyance, telepathy, out-of-body experiences, precognition and other paranormal phenomena.—Brenner, 2001, p. 177

Generally neglected in the recent psychoanalytic literature on parapsychological phenomena that appears in clinical treatment is Ira Brenner's report of a severely traumatized bi-racial woman whom he calls Mary Lou (Brenner, 2001). It is recounted in a chapter "Intersubjectivity and Beyond" in his book entitled *Dissociation of Trauma: Theory, Phenomenology, and Technique*. In this remarkable report, the patient with a tendency to disassociate, that is to go into a fugue like state where she heard or felt she became an alter that she called "the dead child"—appeared to have some psychic ability of which she and her family and friends were aware, and which distressed and puzzled her. Why there are not more reports of this nature is an open question. I suspect it takes an even greater willingness to explore in treatment much less report on this type of patient, than it does with a patient who exhibits some telepathic dreams or experiences but who does not consider herself particularly psychic.

Ira Brenner (no relation to Charles) follows a psychoanalytic orientation that focuses on the disassociative experiences of severely traumatized individuals. He states that in his experience "well over 50 percent (of his disassociative patients) report paranormal experience, the most frequently being an autoscopic, out-of-body sensation which may or may not be associated with information transfer." Out-of-body experiences are not in and of themselves considered to be psi experiences unless the individual *does* obtain as a consequence of his experience information that in a purely sensual manner he could not obtain. Sometimes out-of-body experiences do contain such information; at other times, they do not. (Nor are near-death experiences—which Brenner also includes—in and of themselves considered paranormal for the same reason. Incidentally, the literature on out-of-body experiences [also referred to as OBE or OOBE or astral projection] is voluminous. Perhaps most impressive is a survey and compendium of such experiences, which invariably have similar features, by Crookall, who published a score of books on the subject [e.g., Crookall, 1961; see also Alvarado, 2012, for a discussion of Crookall's work and Monroe (1971) for a different take on the phenomenon]). Thus, the context in which Brenner places his report of Mary Lou is somewhat misleading. From the point of view of exploring psi, it would have been more accurate if he had categorized more fully his experiences with patients prone to disassociation.

Nonetheless, his report of his treatment of Mary Lou is compelling. Subject to continual sexual abuse by her stepfather when she was a child, sexual abuse years later by a physical therapist, illness, as well as the birth of her own child with life-threatening perinatal complications, Mary Lou in her early twenties unraveled with suicidal symptoms, mood swings, amnestic periods and auditory hallucinations, and was hospitalized with a diagnosis of "multiple personality." Yet Brenner managed to forge a therapeutic alliance with her in outpatient five times weekly treatment. After years of therapy, thinking that she had sufficiently recovered and cutting back in treatment, she returned to intensive work. But then she had a relapse, and only then—finally (!)—did she admit to Brenner that she believed she had psychic ability that made her feel "crazy." It is a testament to how difficult it is for patients to open up about their psi experiences, that it took so long for Mary Lou, despite her alliance with her therapist, to trust him sufficiently to open up about psi.

Mary Lou exhibited apparent paranormal abilities: she telepathically picked up on an experience of death that Brenner had as a young boy; she knew when Brenner was about to catch a plane to go North to give a talk to a group of doctors on multiple personality; on another occasion she thought that Brenner was going to Stanford or Sanford because she saw a black and white sign with that name and then on that trip Brenner encountered an inept and frustrating airline ticket agent wearing a black and white name plate that said "Mr. Sanford" (a classic example of psi in which a person gets a "hit" but is somewhat wrong). In addition, she recounted that electrical equipment tended to turn on for no reason in her presence, an ability which her family recognized and accepted. (The acceptance may have also been part of her cultural background, upon which Brenner does not expand, because her family also accepted that her great grandmother had been a psychic). On more than one occasion when Mary Lou was exasperated, Brenner noticed that the lights got momentarily lighter in his office because of a power surge. She also recounted an out of body experience when hospitalized and unconscious at 6 years old, briefly given up for dead, in which she observed what was happening in the hospital room from a vantage point above and looking down.

Brenner's ability to listen and accept these experiences permitted Mary Lou to more truly and freely associate. She had been terrified that she would "be certified as totally insane if this secret" were to be found out. At the same time, she was very much afraid of the notion that she had "special powers." (This confirms Tart's report [1986] that many psychics are uncomfortable with their abilities.) One common analytic dynamic that seemed to explain when these abilities occurred in the treatment was a fear of losing her analyst and a desire to be emotionally close to him (note how she telepathically picked up on his trips away from her).

It is very important for any analyst to be open to understanding the considerable conflicts that appear to exist for such a patient, the fluctuations in the patient's confidence in her reality testing that often results from such an ability, and the stress that having an ability that, if known by skeptical others, can so often lead to questioning of the person's sanity. Brenner's openness to his patient's experiences—and his own experience during her treatment—is a testament to his courage. But this is not an easy area and it is one that is more likely than not to be avoided.

Brenner's report does not recount a new phenomenon, however. The British Society of Psychical Research at the turn of the century and the American Society of Psychical Research were fascinated by multiple personality, and one of the most interesting early multiple personality cases the American Society published was that of Doris Fischer, investigated principally by Walter Franklin Prince, a close friend of the parapsychologist Hereward Carrington (to whom Freud wrote his famous letter) as well as subsequently to J.B. Rhine, the Duke parapsychologist (Prince, W.F., 2015). The Doris case is provocative reading for anyone curious about this phenomenon (as is the other famous and somewhat earlier case, that of Sally Beauchamp, investigated by Morton Prince [Prince, M., 2012, originally published in 1906].) At that time, investigators who were interested in and attempting to treat such "disassociated personalities" (whose disassociations were recognized as having their genesis in incidents of severe early childhood trauma) also were intrigued by the idea that multiple personalities had something in common with the possession-like appearances that overcame mediums when they went into trance and were taken over by a guiding spirit, at which point they sometimes appeared to exhibit psi. And so these investigators were alert to whether multiple personalities also exhibited psi. Indeed, Doris, in one of her personalities appeared at times telepathic, for example successfully picking up at a distance when Prince was writing a letter to another investigator as well as the contents of the letter, or picking up at a distance when someone was out shopping, including the outfit she was wearing at the time, and the contents of a store window in which she was looking (Mitchell, 1920, pp. 67–68). Thus, Brenner's report of Mary Lou's telepathic abilities fits within a framework already established decades previously, even though Brenner makes no mention of this history.

On Being Psychic and Related Analytic Issues

The story of Mary Lou is one example of a patient who is aware of being psychic in a manner beyond the normal, and on a continuing basis—not just in an isolated extreme circumstance. For a period of time, her fear of telling her psychoanalyst about her psychic experiences, her need to consciously repress those experiences when she spoke to him, made it difficult for her to freely associate, which is so essential to effective psychoanalytic treatment.

I have had one patient who was aware of being psychic over a long period of time and had been accepted as such by people in his environment. Mr. S. was a health care professional, but previously and unknown to those in his field, he had been a practicing psychic. His early childhood was replete with so many traumas—a father so abusive that there were times Mr. S. was often afraid his mother would be killed—that it was remarkable that he functioned as well as he did. Initially, Mr. S. was wary of telling me of his past experience as a practicing psychic for fear of my disapproval. On top of which his ambivalence about his psi abilities as well as having used his abilities in this fashion was considerable. When he first mentioned it, he did so passingly and accompanied the revelation with minimization and denigration of what he had done.

My reaction was different than he had expected. I wondered to him why he felt the need to disparage himself, his abilities and what he had attempted to do as a practicing psychic. The extent of his surprise at this reaction became apparent over time, as he had fully expected I would neither know about this field nor accept that his abilities existed and that I would consider this part of his life as evidence of pathology or psychosis or, equally concerning to him, that alternatively I would be an advocate of New Age sensibility, admiring and undiscriminating in my assessment of his abilities.

But I saw my role differently, having very much in mind how the Navajo provide a place for the psychic in their culture, and—generally—how frequently patients of mine, particularly in the early stages of treatment, disparage an action they took when younger— running away from home rather than going immediately into college, pursuing an early passion for music although ultimately deciding to embrace a safer economic profession, falling deeply in love and suffering a broken heart and then regretting the experience (Reichbart, 2011)—which they now wall off from their present-day persona. In attempting to survive, such patients too frequently become judgmental about these early creative efforts which often touch on a libidinal core and so they then fail to integrate the considerable positive aspects of them. In effect, they feel the need to wall off a part of themselves, the part that took part in the experience, for what they believe will guarantee a safer equanimity; and then they suffer a kind of deadening as a consequence, whose genesis they usually do not understand.

In this case, Mr. S. distrusted aspects of having been psychic because it had made him too sure of himself, too prone to a sense of narcissistic certainty or omnipotence. Essential to acting as a psychic is a type of certainty that permits one to say things without the type of filter that usually applies in interactions between people. This aspect of acting as a psychic, and the fear of a grandiosity that could take over his persona, was why he wished to deny his abilities in the present. He had been trying to fashion a more rational interaction with those in his professional world, and thus he wanted to rid himself of or minimize his psychic experiences. (I am reminded here of how the psychic photographer Ted Serios, at the beginning of his abilities, was so overcome with nervousness and ill health in trying to prove them to others, and was subject to so much ridicule, that he was persuaded to go to a psychiatrist. The psychiatrist proceeded to hypnotize him, told him that the psychic photographs he was producing were all a dream and "cock-eyed" and to forget about making them. This intervention was "brilliantly successful" so that Serios *did* forget his dream, destroyed about three hundred of the psychic photographs, and for a while was convinced he had been delusional [Eisenbud, 1967, p. 219] Fortunately, he recovered from the hypnotic suggestion. But it was a loss that took place in the service of supposedly bringing Serios back in touch with reality. And what we would give for those photographs now?).

It should be added that Mr. S. could at times be strikingly psychic in his dreams (see his dream below when he touches unwittingly upon the fact that I am to undergo a colonoscopy); but at other times, he would be convinced there was something medically wrong with me, when I could find no discernible problem to match his concern. On the other hand, despite his attunement, he often missed when I *did* have a medical concern; and in one instance when a death of someone close to me occurred, he showed no psi awareness of it at all. He also, as happens with any patient, could be quite wrong when he speculated about my life in general.

I have had discussions with an established psychoanalyst in the field, who was previously a practicing psychic, and recounts how different the two states are. With those who are psychic, the peculiar state of certainty (perhaps necessary to retain confidence when what one says does not rely upon sensory input) attaches to the need to free the mind to say whatever occurs concerning the subject however strange it may be (and— as an integral condition of doing this—*not* being informed at all by the person whose reading it is of either facts or background). How very different this is to the state of mind that adheres to practicing psychoanalysis, where extrapolations occur principally from the sensory information imparted by the patient to the analyst. Of necessity, a psychic must hazard making grievous errors by his free association; this is part and parcel of the work that a psychic undertakes, sometimes resulting in statements very wide of the mark and at other times catching hold of something that does have meaning to the person who has asked for a reading. "Logic" is not engaged. An analyst functions differently and is careful what he says, attempting to monitor his countertransferential reactions, and to fashion an argument from the words, inflections and attitude imparted to him by the patient as he explores a psychological dynamic. Needless to say, the established psycho- analyst of my acquaintance would never, at this juncture, confide to his colleagues his previous background as a psychic for fear of the opprobrium that would ensue. He is acutely aware however of this different way of processing the world, although he can never convey this intriguing aspect of the world as he knows it, with its psychological characteristics, to his fellow psychoanalysts. Put in a larger context, the failure of psy- choanalysis to recognize psi phenomena and to do so in the training of psychoanalysts, holds dangers in which patients, with greater or lesser degree of conscious psychic abil- ities, are neither informatively assessed nor understood.

A Random List: Telepathic Dreams of Patients That Touch on the Analyst's Life

One way I can think to impress psychoanalysts inclined to pursue telepathy but unaware of how much has already been reported is to go through the type of events that have been reported when patients telepathically connect in their dreams with the analyst. To do so does not display the dynamics of these interactions—why the patient and analyst connected in this fashion, and what it meant that they did so, dynamics which from the psychoanalytic viewpoint can confirm the telepathic connections. But it does have the virtue of synopsizing and highlighting what has been written, even if in a concrete, one might say flat-footed fashion. I am trying to address—as I have repeatedly indicated— the tendency of psychoanalysts who venture into this field to say: "This is the first time that…" or "This is an unusual case of…" In providing this list, I have left out many exam- ples, but I believe that the reader will get the idea. As one might expect, Eisenbud presents the richest trove of psychoanalytic data of this kind presently available to us. For example, in his book Psi and Psychoanalysis, there are roughly 62 telepathic dreams of patients; in Paranormal Foreknowledge, another 51 psi-mediated dreams are presented (in both cases based on the indexes of these books). This does not include the telepathic dreams in Eisenbud's psychoanalytic articles. And this is to say nothing of other types of psi communication between patient and analyst such as statements or associations during sessions rather than in dreams. It seems to me disingenuous at best and misleading at worst to write in this area without making substantial reference to the material in both of Eisenbud's books.

I do not wish in giving these examples to minimize the extent to which patients pick up telepathically on other patients in treatment, which represents what also happens frequently, as I have experienced in my own practice and as recounted by Eisenbud and others. What I do wish to focus on is the type of events that patients have telepathically picked up in dreams from their analysts' lives. Those listed are the most dramatic connections. Last, this summary (which is in no way complete) does not touch on analysts who have reported on their own psi experiences in their dreams, exclusive of patients, as did Rosenbaum (a dream of a plane crash) and Farrell (a telepathic dream of the death of a friend that featured red punch in a bowl, and another dream of the death of his former analyst).

The List

Accidents

Patient dreams of old man going through glass door when the analyst Stoller falls through glass door (Mayer, 2001, p. 639); patient dreams of analyst's daughter having an accident in the snow and being hospitalized when analyst's daughter has sledding accident resulting in broken arm (Eisenbud, 1982, p. 41); patient dreams of her teeth on one side of her mouth being broken off at the root when analyst Stoller's son breaks tooth in surfing accident (Mayer, 2001, p. 642); patient dreams of small animals in an attic at the time that the analyst is trying to exterminate squirrels in his attic (Eisenbud, 1970, p. 153); patient dreams of spilling acid, from bottle of chemicals that he is pulling in a toy wagon, onto his hand and burning it, when Stoller's son burned his hand on some chemicals from a toy set (Mayer, 2001, p. 640).

Pregnancy

Patient dreams of analysts wife being pregnant, days before pregnancy is confirmed (Eisenbud, 1970, p. 271); patient—who has abandonment issues as a result of early maternal loss—has a series of dreams about pregnancy at a time that the analyst has decided to and attempts to become pregnant (Suchet, 2004); patient dreams of woman holding two children who upset ewers of water (which she associates to water breaking), and then realizes that the wife of the analyst must have just given birth to a child (Peerbolte, 2003).

Medical Concerns

Patient dreams of treating man's exposed intestines the night before analyst is to go for a colonoscopy (Reichbart, see next chapter); patient dreams of her husband groaning, and then waking up in the dream to find him sitting on the toilet "losing a lot of blood" when the analyst had woken the same night to find her own husband sitting on the toilet in a "frightening and identical episode of bleeding" (de Peyer, 2016, p. 167).

Funerals and Anniversaries and Events

Patient dreams of an eighth wedding anniversary on the analyst's eighth wedding anniversary (Deutsch, 1970, p. 141). Patient dreams of father's funeral when analyst attends ceremony on anniversary of father's death (Eshel, 2006, pp. 1617–1618). Patient dreams about being near the same location as the analyst had been earlier in the day, and having similar associations at the time, which coincides with the analyst's experience (Gillespie, 1953, p. 373). Patient anxiously dreams of analyst being lost in the "Black Forest" in Germany on analyst's vacation when analyst, who in fact is in the Caribbean, goes scuba diving the next day with some trepidation [his second lesson] in an area called the "Black Forest" because of the black coral—the name of which he did not discover until that very day (Cambray, 2002, pp. 422–423). Patient dreams that she and her analyst have the same dream when the analyst is thinking about the "problem of telepathy" a subject he had never been interested in before, because the day previous to the dream he had attended a lecture by Hollos on telepathy (Roheim, 1932, pp. 287–288). Patient dreams in detail of a house in a beautiful setting with a little green field on the side of it that he is not supposed to go into, when the analyst that weekend has seen an exactly similar country house on which he put a deposit for summer rental, only to discover that a grassy patch on the side of the house cannot be used by tenants. resulting in his losing his deposit in a nasty altercation with the owner (Ehrenwald, 1975, pp. 52–55).

Embarrassing Situations

Patient dreams of company coming to dinner but being concerned that there may not be sufficient silver knives and forks, or they may be a mess, when analyst worries about whether she has sufficient or good enough cutlery for a dinner party (Pederson-Krag, 1953, p. 278–279); Patient dreams of analyst in a very loud sport jacket at Atlantic City, looking "Hollywoodish" when analyst—who has been lobbying his family to go to Atlantic City—has to his chagrin recently bought an unprepossessing sport jacket, despite a salesman's suggestion to be more bold (Eisenbud, 1946, p. 57–59). Patient dreams of a "chromium soap dish" which he offers to a man, who to his surprise takes it, with a smirk, when the analyst has taken a chromium soap dish mistakenly shipped to him at the time of construction of his house, which "in a spirit of belligerent dishonesty inspired by rising costs of the house, I had no intentions of returning..." (Ulllman, 1973, pp. 50–51).

Books and Movies

Analyst reads a Maugham story, involving a boiled egg after a patient's similar dream (Eisenbud, 1982, p. 54); analyst reads a psychoanalytic article about an explorer being attacked by a bear, after an analysand compares himself to a bear that will attack the analyst (Reichbart, 1998, p. 430); patient dreams of a magic clock in a glass case, which produced the death of Socrates, at the time that analyst reads a short story by Elizabeth Bowen called "the Inherited Clock," "verging on the occult" in which a clock in a glass case is feared (Gillespie, 1953, p. 376); patient dreams of a bottle of white foamy stuff labeled "Appealing Nausea" and of a small leopard the same evening the analyst sees a movie on cats that in an experiment develop an addiction to a mixture of alcohol and milk (Ullman, 2003, p. 19).

Connection to Analyst's Dreams

Patient dreams of brownstone houses on fire the same night as analyst dreams of brownstone houses on fire (Eisenbud, 1970, p. 190); patient dreams of losing two front teeth three weeks after analyst dreams of losing two front teeth (Suchet, 2004, p. 273).

My hope in providing this list to the psychoanalytic reader has been to shake him or her sufficiently to recognize the extent to which clinical examples of psi phenomena have been recorded by psychoanalysts. It seems a fitting conclusion to a chapter in which I have been attempting to highlight the history of psi and psychoanalysis and convey the principles applying to the clinical treatment of a patient when psi occurs. In the chapter following this one, I review some of the more current literature on psi and psychoanalysis, provide fresh examples for the reader of psi from my years of clinical practice, and touch upon precognition in a fuller way than I have before. I also end with a plea directed to psychoanalysts in general, which applies to the readers of both chapters.

Notes

1. In two letters sent to Ehrenwald in 1946, Einstein indicated that he could only think of psi phenomena as being subject to considerations of distance, in effect to be in the nature of a wave. And he was more impressed with telepathic drawing experiments than "large scale statistical experiments" which he felt were more subject to "minute systematic errors." Despite his introduction to Sinclair's book, he confessed to being a skeptic, although he felt one should not "go through the world with blinders" to the possibility that psi existed. He stated that he had no personal experience of it, however. (Ehrenwald, 2010, pp. 39–40).

References

Alvarado, C.S. (2012) Explorations of the features of out-of-body experiences. *Journal of the Society for Psychical Research*, 76 (907), 65–82.

Bach, S. (1985) *Narcissistic states and the therapeutic process*. New York: Jason Aronson.

Bach, S. (2017) Personal communication. April 2, 2017.

Balint, M. (1955) Notes on parapsychology and parapsychological healing. *International Journal of Psycho-Analysis*, 36: 31–35.

Barker, J. (1967) Premonitions of the Aberfan disaster. *Journal of the Society of Psychical Research*, 44: 169–181.

Bertrand, A. (1823) *Traite du somnambulisme*. Paris: J.G. Dentu.

Bion, W.R. (1959) *Experiences in groups*. New York: Basic Books.

Bollas, C. (1987) *The shadow of the object: Psychoanalysis of the thought unknown*. New York: Columbia University Press.

Bollas, C. (1992) *Being a character*. New York: Hill & Wang.

Brabant, E., Falzeder, E. & Giampieri-Deutsch, P. (Eds.) (1992) *The correspondence of Sigmund Freud and Sandor Ferenczi, Vol I, 1908–1914*. Boston: Belknap Press.

Braud, W. (2010) Psi and distance: Is a conclusion of distance independence premature? www.inclusive psychology.com/uploads/Psi_and_Distance_-_A_Premature_Conclusion.pdf.

Braude, S.E. (1989) *The limits of influence: Psychokinesis and the philosophy of science*. New York: Routledge and Kegan Paul.

Braude, S.E. (2000) Obituary: Jule Eisenbud. *Journal of the Society for Psychical Research*, 64(1), 60–63.

Brenner, C. (1957) Facts, coincidence, and the psi hypothesis. *International Journal of Psycho-Analysis* 38: 51–53.

Brenner, C. (1987) Notes on psychoanalysis by a participant observer: A personal chronicle. *Journal of the American Psychoanalytic Association*, 35: 539–555.

Brenner, I. (2001) *Dissociation of trauma: Theory, phenomenology and technique*. Madison: International Universities Press.

Bromberg, P. (1996) Standing in the spaces: The multiplicity of self and the psychoanalytic relationship. *Contemporary Psychoanalysis*, 32, 509–535.

Brottman, M. (2011) *Phantoms of the clinic: From thought-transference to projective identification*. London: Karnac.

Burlingham, D. (1953) Child analysis and the mother (an excerpt) In G. Devereux (ed.) *Psychoanalysis and the occult*, pp. 188–191. New York: International Universities Press, pp. 188–191. (Originally published in the *Psychoanalytic Quarterly*, 5: 69–92, 1935.).

Cambray, J. (2002) Synchronicity and emergence. *American Imago*, 59 (4): 409–434.

Crookall, R. (1961) *The study and practice of astral projection*. London: Aquarian Press.

de Peyer, J. (2014) Telepathic entanglements: Where are we today? Commentary on paper by Claudie Massicotte. *Psychoanalytic Dialogues* 24: 109–121.
de Peyer, J. (2016) Uncanny communication and the porous mind. *Psychoanalytic Dialogues* 25: 156–174.
Derrida, J. (1988) Telepathy. (N. Royal, Trans.) *Oxford Literature Review*,10(3), 3–41.
Deutsch, H. (1953) Occult processes occurring during psychoanalysis. G. Devereux (trans.) *In* G. Devereux
(ed.) *Psychoanalysis and the occult.* New York: International Universities Press, pp. 133–146. Originally
published 1926 Okkulte Vorgänge während der Psychoanalyse. *Imago*, 12(2–3): 418–433.
Devereux, G. (Ed.). (1953) *Psychoanalysis and the occult.* New York: International Universities Press.
Dingwall, E. (Ed.) (1968) *Abnormal hypnotic phenomena* (4 volumes) New York: Barnes and Noble.
Ehrenwald, J. (2010) An autobiographical fragment. *In* R. Pilkington (ed.), *Esprit: Men and women of para-
psychology, Personal reflections, Vol. 1*, pp. 36–44. San Antonia: Anomalist Books (Originally published
as *Men and women of parapsychology: Personal reflections* by McFarland, 1987).
Einstein, A. (1962) Preface. In Sinclair, U. *Mental radio*, p. x. New York: Macmillan.
Einstein, A. (1982) *Ideas and opinions.* New York: Crown Publishers.
Eisenbud, J. (1946) Telepathy and problems of psychoanalysis. *Psychoanalytic Quarterly*, 14: 32–87.
Eisenbud, J. (1947) The dreams of two patients in analysis interpreted as a telepathic reve a deux. *Psychoanalytic
Quarterly*, 16: 39–60.
Eisenbud, J. (1955) On the use of the psi hypothesis in psycho-analysis. *International Journal of Psycho-Analysis*,
36: 370–374.
Eisenbud, J. (1957) Comments on Dr. Brenner's "Facts, coincidence, and the psi hypothesis." *International
Journal of Psycho-Analysis,* 38: 54–56.
Eisenbud, J. (1967) *The world of Ted Serios: Thoughtographic studies of an extraordinary mind (1st ed.)* New
York: William Morrow & Company.
Eisenbud, J. (1970) *Psi and psychoanalysis: Studies in the psychoanalysis of psi-conditioned behavior.* New York:
Grune & Stratton.
Eisenbud, J. (1975) Research in precognition. In S. Dean *Psychiatry and mysticism*, pp. 101–110. Chicago: Nelson
Hall.
Eisenbud, J. (1982) *Paranormal foreknowledge.* New York: Human Sciences Press.
Eisenbud, J. (1983a) *Parapsychology and the unconscious.* Berkeley, CA: North Atlantic Books.
Eisenbud, J. (1983b) Psi and the nature of things. In *Parapsychology and the unconscious*, pp. 149–168. Berkeley,
CA: North Atlantic Books.
Eisenbud, J. (1989) *The world of Ted Serios: "Thoughtographic" studies of an extraordinary mind.* 2d ed. Jefferson,
NC: McFarland.
Eisenbud, J. (2010) My life with the paranormal. In R. Pilkington (ed.), *esprit: Men and women of parapsy-
chology, personal reflections*, Vol. 1., pp. 7–18 (originally published in 1987 by McFarland) San Antonia:
Anomalist Books.
Ellenberger, H.F. (1970) *The discovery of the unconscious: The history and evolution of dynamic psychiatry.*
New York: Basic Books.
Eshel, O. (2006) Where are you my beloved?: On absence, loss and the enigma of telepathic dreams. *Inter-
national Journal of Psychoanalysis*, 87: 1603–1627.
Farrell, D. (1983) Freud's "thought-transference," repression, and the future of psychoanalysis. *International
Journal of Psychoanalysis* 64: 71–81.
Ferenczi (1963) Spiritism. N. Fodor (Trans.) *Psychoanalytic* Review, 50A (1): 139–144 (Orig. pub. 1899).
Ferenczi (1988) *The Clinical diary of Sandor Ferenczi.* J. Dupont (ed.), M. Balint & N.Z. Jacson (trans.) Cam-
bridge: Harvard University Press.
Freud, S. (1900) The interpretation of dreams. *Standard Edition* 6, 1–627.
Freud, S. (1901) The psychopathology of everyday life. *Standard Edition* 6, vii–296.
Freud, S. (1919) The uncanny. *Standard Edition*, 17, 217–256.
Freud, S. (1921 [1941]) Psycho-analysis and telepathy. *Standard Edition*, 18, 177–193.
Freud, S. (1922) Dreams and telepathy. *Standard Edition* 18, 197–220.
Freud, S. (1925) The occult significance of dreams. In Some additional notes on dream interpretation as a
whole. *Standard Edition* 19, 125–138.
Freud, S. (1933) Lecture XXX: Dreams and occultism. In New introductory lectures on psychoanalysis. *Stan-
dard Edition*, 22, 31–56.
Freud, S. (1957) An unpublished letter on parapsychology. N. Fodor (trans.) *In Psychoanalysis and the Future*,
pp. 12–13. National Psychological Association for Psychoanalysis: New York.
Freud, S. (1993) *The complete correspondence of Sigmund Freud and Ernest Jones, 1908–1939.* R.A. Paskauskas
(ed.) Cambridge: Harvard University Press.
Freud, S. (1994) *The Freud-Jung letters.* W. McGuire Ed. R. Mannheim & R.F.C. Hull (Trans.) Princeton:
Princeton University Press.
Gillespie, W.H. (1953) Extrasensory elements in dream interpretation. *In* G. Devereux (Ed.) *Psychoanalysis
and the occult*, pp. 373–382. New York: International Universities Press.

Gurney, E., Myers, F.W.H., & Podmore, F. (1886) *Phantasms of the living, Vol. 1.* London: The Society for Psychical Research.

Gymensi, J. (2009) The problem of demarcation: Psychoanalysis and the occult. *American Imago,* 66: 457–470.

Hollos, I. (1933) Psychopathology of everyday telepathic phenomena. *Imago,* 19(4): 529–546 (original in German. Psyhopathologie alltaglicher telepathischer Erscheinungen).

Honorton, C. (1977) Psi and internal attention states. In B.B. Wolman (ed.) *Handbook of parapsychology,* pp. 435–472. New York: Van Nostrand Reinhold.

Jones, E. (1957) *The life and work of Sigmund Freud, vol 3: The last phase.* New York: Basic Books.

Josephson, B. (May 8, 2010) http: //www.tcm.phy.cam.ac.uk/~bdj10/articles/uninvite.html*http: //www.tcm.phy.cam.ac.uk/~bdj10/articles/uninvite.html.

Jung, C.G. (1969) *Synchronicity: An acausal connecting principle.* Princeton, New Jersey: Princeton University Press.

Jung, C.G. (1977a) *Psychology and the occult.* R.F.C. Hull (trans.) Princeton: Princeton University Press.

Jung, C.G. (1977b) On the psychology and pathology of so-called occult phenomena. In *Psychology and the occult.* R.F.C. Hull (trans.) () Princeton: Princeton University Press, pp. 6–91 (Originally published in German in Leipzig, 1902).

Jung, C.G. (1989) *.Memories, dreams and reflections.* Richard and Clara Winston (trans.) New York: Random House.

Kakar, S., & Kripal, J.J. (Eds.) (2012) *Seriously strange.* New Delhi: Penguin Books.

Kaplan, F. (1975) *Dickens and Mesmerism: The hidden springs of fiction.* Princeton, New Jersey: Princeton University Press.

Keve, T. (2015) The Jung-Ferenczi dossier. *American Journal of Psychoanalysis:* 75, 94–109.

Klein, M. (1946) Notes on some schizoid mechanisms. *International Journal of Psycho-Analysis,* 27, 99–110.

Lawrence, T. (1993) Gathering in the sheep and goats: A meta-analysis of forced-choice sheep/goat ESP studies, 1947–1993. In *Proceedings of the Parapsychological Association, 36th Annual Convention, Toronto, Canada,* pp. 75–86.

Lazar, S.G. (2001) Knowing influencing, and healing: Paranormal phenomena and implications for psychoanalysis and psychotherapy. *Psychoanalytic Inquiry.* 21: 112–131.

Main, R. (2012) Anomalous phenomena, synchronicity, and the re-sacralization of the modern world. In *Seriously strange.* S. Kakar & J.J. Kripal (eds.). Viking: New Delhi, India, pp. 1–27.

Mayer, E.L. (2001) On "telepathic dreams": An unpublished paper by Robert Stoller. *Journal of the American Psychoanalytic Association,* 49, 629–652.

Mayer, E.L. (2007) *Extraordinary knowing: Science, skepticism, and the inexplicable powers of the human mind.* New York: Bantam.

McEneany, B. (2011) *Messages: signs, visits, and premonitions from loved ones lost on 9/11.* New York: Harper.

Meissner, W. (1987) Projection and projective identification. In J. Sandler (ed.) *Projection, identification, projective Identification.* Madison, CT: International Universities Press. Pp. 27–49.

Mitchell, E.D. (1974) *Psychic exploration: A challenge for science.* New York: Putnam.

Mitchell, T.W. (1920) The Doris case of multiple personality. *Proceedings of the Society for Psychical Research,* 31, pt. 69, 30–74.

Monroe, R.A. (1973) *Journeys out of the body.* Garden City: Anchor Press.

Ogden, T. (1997) *Reverie and interpretation: sensing something human.* Northvale: Aronson.

Osis, K., & Turner, M.E. (1968) *Distance and ESP: A transcontinental experiment.* New York: The American Society for Psychical Research.

Overbye, D. (2017) Nobel prize in physics awarded to LIGO black hole researchers, .https: //www.nytimes.com/2017/10/03/science/nobel-prize-physics.html.

Pederson-Krag, G. (1953) Telepathy and repression. In G. Devereux (ed.), *Psychoanalysis and the occult,* pp. 277–287. New York: International Universities Press (Originally published in the *Psychoanalytic Quarterly,* 16: 61–68, 1947).

Peerbolte, M.L. (2003) Parapsychology and psychoanalysis. In N. Totton (ed.), *Psychoanalysis and the paranormal: Lands of darkness,* pp. 47–72. London: Karnac.

Pierri, M. (2010) Coincidences in analysis: Sigmund Freud and the strange case of Dr. Forsyth and Herr von Vorsicht. *International Journal of Psycho-Analysis,* 91: 745–772.

Powell, D.H. (2012) Psi and psychiatry: In S. Kakar & J.J. Kripal (eds.), *The quest for a new scientific paradigm,* pp. 126–151. New Delhi: Viking.

Prince, M. (1905) *The Dissociation of a personality.* New York: Longmans, Green, and Company, 1905.

Prince, W.F. (2015) *The Doris case of multiple personality.* York: York Printing Co.

Reichbart, R. (1977) Psychic aggression: how culture deals with the whammy. Paper presented at the Parapsychological Anthropology Symposium, *American Anthropological Association Annual Meeting,* Houston, November 29.

Reichbart, R. (1981) Heart symbolism: the heart-breast and heart-penis equations. *Psychoanalytic Review,* 68, 75–104.

Reichbart, R. (1990) Letter to the editor. *Journal of the American Society for Psychical Research*, 84, 95–96.

Reichbart, R. (1998) Jule Eisenbud: Explorer. *Journal of the American Society for Psychical Research*, 92, 427–431.

Reichbart. R. (2005) The child's cognitive struggle to understand damage to an important object: A six-year-old's attempt to deal with the trauma of his father's epilepsy. *Journal of Infant, Child, and Adolescent Psychotherapy*, 4(1), 77–97.

Reichbart, R. (2011) The importance of a "broken heart." *Psychoanalytic Review* 98(3), 351–373.

Robertson, M. (1912) *Futility*. London: Arthur F. Bird.

Roheim, G. (1932) Telepathy in a dream. *Psychoanalytic Quarterly*, 1: 227–291.

Rosenbaum, R. (2011) Exploring the other dark continent: Parallels between psi phenomena and the psychotherapeutic process. *Psychoanalytic Review*, 98: 57–90.

Schmeidler, G.R. (1943) Predicting good and bad scores in a clairvoyance experiment: A preliminary report. *Journal of the American Society for Psychical Research*, 37: 103–110.

Schmeidler, G.R. (1945) "Separating the sheep from the goats" *Journal of the American Society for Psychical Research*, 39: 47–49.

Schmeidler, G.R., & McConnell, R.A. (1958) *ESP and personality patterns*. Westport, CT: Greenwood Press.

Schwarz, B.E. (1971) *Parent-Child Telepathy: Five hundred and five possible episodes in a family*. New York: Garrett Publications.

Searles, H.F. (1974) Concerning therapeutic symbiosis. *Annual of Psychoanalysis*,1, 247–262.

Segal, H. (1964) *Introduction to the work of Melanie Klein*. London: Heinemann.

Sinclair, U. (1962) *Mental radio*. New York: Macmillan.

Sondow, N. (2017) *Psychic dreams: Telepathic dream group and 9/11 premonitions*. Manuscript for presentation at the American Society of Psychic Research on March 2, 2017.

Steinkamp, F. (2004) ESP experiments: their past and their future. In M.A. Melbourne & L. Storm (eds.) *Parapsychology in the twenty-first century*, pp. 124–166. Jefferson, NC: McFarland.

Stern, D.B. (1997) *Unformulated experience: From disassociation to imagination*. Hillsdale: Analytic Press.

Stevenson, I. (1974) *Twenty cases suggestive of reincarnation*. Charlottesville: University of Virginia Press.

Stevenson, I. (1988) Guest editorial: Was the attempt to identify parapsychology as a separate field of science misguided? *Journal of the American Society for Psychical Research*, 82, 4, 310–317.

Suchet, M. (2004) Whose mind is it anyway? *Studies in Gender and Sexuality*, 5: 259–287.

Tanagras, A. (1967) *Psychophysical elements in parapsychological traditions*. New York: Parapsychology Foundation.

Tart, C. (1984) Acknowledging and dealing with the fear of psi. *Journal of the American Society for Psychical Research*, 78: 133–143.

Tart, C. (1986) Psychics fears of psychic powers. *Journal of the American Society for Psychical Research*, 90, 279–292.

Taylor, E. (2009) *The mystery of personality: A history of psychodynamic theories*. London: Springer.

Torok, M. (1983) L'occulte de l'occultisme: Entre Sigmund Freud et Sergei Pakeiev—Wolfman, Cahiers. *Confrontations* 10 (Autumn): 153–171.

Torok, M. (1986) Afterword: What is occult in occultism? Between Sigmund Freud and Sergei Pakeiev wolf man (N. Rand, trans.). In Abraham N & Torok, M. *The Wolfman's magic word: A cryptonomy*, pp. 84–106, R and N. (trans.). Minneapolis: University of Minnesota Press.

Totton, N. (2003) (Ed) *Psychoanalysis and the paranormal: Lands of darkness*. London: Karnac.

Ullman, M. (2003) Dream telepathy: experimental and clinical findings. In N. Totton (ed.) *Psychoanalysis and the paranormal: Lands of darkness*, pp. 15–46. London: Karnac.

Ullman, M., Krippner, S. & Vaughan, A. (1973) *Dream telepathy*. New York: Macmillan Publishing Co.

Warcollier, R. (1938) *Experiments in telepathy*. J.B. Gridley (trans.) New York: Harper and Brothers.

Warcollier, R. (2001) *Mind to mind*. Charlottesville: Hampton Roads Publishing Co.

Weiss, E. (1991) *Sigmund Freud as a consultant: Recollections of a pioneer in psychoanalysis*. New Brunswick: Transaction Publishers.

Winnicott, D. (1975) *Through pediatrics to psycho-analysis*. London: Hogarth Press.

Wolman, B.B. (1977) *Handbook of parapsychology*. New York: Van Nostrand Reinhold Company.

Žižek, S. (2008) *The sublime object of ideology: The essential Žižek*. London: Verso.

SEVEN

Psi and Psychoanalysis II:
Rescuing Sisyphus Today

In this chapter, I share with the reader some examples of psi as they have appeared in my own practice, discuss in more detail the knotty and troubling problem of precognition including mention of precognition of mass disasters (discussing some contemporary data concerning the attack on the twin towers in Manhattan on September 11, 2001) and touch upon a variety of other issues. I begin with a discussion of recent psychoanalytic literature.

The Recent Resurgence

Recently (writing in 2018) there has been a resurgence of interest among psychoanalysts in telepathy and in some cases beyond telepathy. I focus below on some of the more significant contributions in my judgment. Notably, the journal *Psychoanalytic Dialogues* as well as *American Imago* have opened their pages to articles of this nature, and there have been a number of books published that touch on psychoanalysis and psi. For example, in 2003, Totton edited a book entitled *Psychoanalysis and the Paranormal: Lands of Darkness* that contains a good introductory summary of telepathy and psychoanalysis, as well as an article by Ullman about the Maimonides Dream Study experiments, where some subjects dream while other subjects look at pictures in the hope the dreamers will pick up telepathically on the pictures. In 2012, Kakar and Kripal edited a book of articles by psychoanalysts and parapsychologists, including a discussion of Eisenbud's work in psychic photography by the psychoanalyst Brottman, a nice summary of Jung's work in the area of parapsychology by Main, and an experimental study by the parapsychologist Radin of precognition, which also contains disturbing vignettes of how parapsychological studies and those scientists interested in them have been mistreated by the mainstream scientific establishment.

By far the most valuable recent psychoanalytic book publication concerning parapsychology is Brottman's 2011 *Phantoms of the Clinic*, which, more than any other psychoanalytically informed exegisis, focuses on the work of the psychoanalyst Eisenbud with respect to telepathy in clinical treatment, precognition and psychic photography.

Psychoanalytic journal articles on the paranormal that recently have appeared include Lazar's 2001 article which included reference to scientific and parapsychological studies. Lazar questioned the technical implications for classical psychoanalysis because psi between analyst and patient appears to challenge the construct that the analyst must remain silent about his life and his thoughts. Lazar also asked about the role psi-mediated suggestion by the analyst at a distance might have on patients, in terms of a healing affect (or vice-versa if the patient was not liked), a concept that historically has been anathema to classical analysis. Lazar's work has influenced some of the younger writers in this field. In 2004, Suchet published a compelling if not well researched article in which a patient appeared in her dreams to be telepathically attuned to her attempts to get pregnant. In 2010, Rosenbaum published a well informed and daring piece in which she recounted one morning having seen in her mind "all kinds of debris falling through the air and a sort of odometer, with numbers running up very rapidly" from 000 to 346. The next morning, the newspaper announced that 346 people had been killed in an airplane crash in Paris at 1:00 p.m. the previous day, which was two hours *after* her vision. (Rosenbaum, 2010, p. 73) (Here I might note that precognition of plane crashes is not unique to Rosenbaum. Recently Van Luijtelarr summarized similar documented instances including a striking case in October 1992 at Schiphol airport near Amsterdam in which the percipient twice notified the authorities of her vision of an impending air crash there involving a "blue and white plane" compromised by a "hydraulic failure," providing the exact time of the crash. The authorities did nothing as a "blue and white aircraft" applied to a number of airlines. An El Al airplane crashed that day, fifteen minutes after take off from Schipol, scheduled to depart at the time of the vision but delayed almost an hour. What the percipient had left out—because she thought it bizarre—although she wrote it down at the time—was that she envisioned the pilot as "Fuck." In fact, the name of the pilot of the plane was Itzhak Fuks. It is this type of specificity, with its free associative even dynamic "error" in the vision, that gives this poignant instance a sense of veracity [Van Luijtelarr, 2017]). Rosenbaum's example of precognition is beyond what Freud could entertain, but on the other hand, the psychoanalyst open to listening, may find he encounters incidents just like this with his patients, and be loathe to acknowledge it publicly for fear of being criticized.

Perhaps the work that has received the most recent attention is Eshel's article entitled "Where Are You, My Beloved?: On Absence, Loss and the Enigma of Telepathic Dreams." I have already alluded to this work, which provides an excellent history, but which presents a theory about when telepathy occurs as a consequence of loss and early trauma in clinical treatment that very much circumscribes the actual appearance of telepathy both inside and outside the treatment room. The theory, based upon her experiences of the few patients who have exhibited telepathic dreams in her 30 years of practice, is that such patients have been subject to primary traumatic loss, due to the absence of a significant figure in their early childhood. (In a more recent work, Papazian makes a somewhat similar argument, linking telepathic phenomena with separation anxiety in one patient [a patient who appears more aware than Papazian that the psi connection between them is a product of Papazian's unconscious countertransference desire as much as it is of her wishes] [Papazian, 2017].) It may be that certain types of early traumatic experiences, including loss, lend one to being more likely to enlist telepathy in adulthood. But unfortunately, Eshel seems to imply that *all* telepathy is a product of this particular etiology. As appealing as it is on dynamic grounds, this thesis does not comport with the data that we have from innumerable sources that suggests telepathy is an experience of daily life, and observable with most patients, exclusive of diagnosis or early development. Is telepathy then an ability—like musical ability? And is it an ability which in our Western culture is generally not encouraged nor validated for a child, and so as a result of environmental pressure tends to be extinguished, neither recognized nor cultivated during a child's development? Are certain individuals simply more talented psychically in the same way that some of us are much more talented musically? Is this ability also more developed under other traumatic circumstances than those that Eshel presents? Ira Brenner for example implies that there is a relationship between developmental trauma that results in disassociation, and the possibility of telepathy occurring, and indeed the historical literature in which telepathy and disassociation occurred in the same person, would suggest this to be true. These possibilities are not elaborated upon in Eshel's report.

There is an irony in Eshel's report, of which she is I think unaware. She begins with a gratuitous attack on Eisenbud, who suggests that our resistance to entertaining the psi hypothesis in general is because we become frightened by the possible aggressive aspects of psi phenomena. She takes this somewhat personally, rather than acknowledging that it is an hypothesis that tries to address why it is that psi phenomena has a history of being denied and ignored, and then she contends that this fear never occurred to her. Seemingly unaffected by such a resistance, she states that she would go on a serendipitous process or journey with her patients through feelings of deadness, disassociation, sleepiness, petrification, yearnings and longings into the depths of perversion and on to telepathic dreams. But Eshel manages to ignore all the other aspects of psi to which Eisenbud alluded in fashioning his hypothesis, including precognition and of course psychokinesis. She does not begin to venture to these places. And in an email communication with me, she denied the possibility that a report of mine might have a precognitive element to it, largely I think because she does not want to entertain precognitive data. She would never consider this as resistance, I am sure, but my exchange with her reminds me very much of my exchange with Elizabeth Lloyd Mayer, who denied the impact of Eisenbud's work. Those that explore this field, including parapsychologists themselves (see Charles Tart, a foremost parapsychologist, for his articles on fear of psi [Tart, 1984, 1986]), are as likely to be resistant to the acceptance of certain events as are those who do not even venture as far as the telepathic. I do not doubt that Eisenbud's work with Ted Serios (to which Eshel nowhere alludes) would be met with the same dismissal by her as it did from Mayer. And I would contend that Eshel's gratuitous opening attack in her article on Eisenbud's hypothesis of why this field in general lends itself to such resistance, is evidence in fact of the very resistance she denies.

Gymensi (2009) conveys a succinct history of the exploration of psi by Freud with a particular emphasis on Freud's fear of Jung's mysticism as well as Freud's view about the unconscious as compared to Fredric Myers theory of the subliminal self. Gymensi attempts to show that there is a demarcation between the rational consideration by Freud of telepathy and the exploration of the "occult" in more spiritualist forms. In this she addresses the concerns of many psychoanalysts, particularly those who follow Freud, who react all but viscerally when they hear about psi because they immediately think of Jung or the abstruse or mystical tendency that too often take place in writing in this field. But what Gymensi fails to do is to present the rational explorations in the area beyond telepathy that *have* taken place, of which she seems unaware, and which have a history of their own, particularly the ground-breaking work of Eisenbud, who is not mentioned.

Massicotte (2014) provides an informed short summary of the history of psi and psychoanalysis emphasizing spiritualism and Freud's attempt to differentiate his own interests in telepathy from that background. However, there is much missing from her discussion of clinical telepathic discoveries by Freud and others; again, Eisenbud's *Psi and Psychoanalysis* is not mentioned to say nothing of his other books. As a consequence of the omission, one gets a distorted impression of what has been accomplished in this field; nor does she isolate the principles derived from Freud that I have enunciated in Chapter Six.

In a commentary to Massicotte, de Peyer (2014) turns her focus on the experimental evidence for telepathy from parapsychological research, citing the work of Radin and Honorton and others. Particularly interesting is her suggestion that psychoanalysis in its classic form—that is four times weekly with the analysand on the couch—lends itself more readily to the existence and exploration of telepathy, by both analyst and analysand, than once or twice weekly psychotherapy which is more prevalent today in many psychoanalytic practices. She suggests that the analyst who is not rushed is more likely to be relaxed and thus attuned to picking up telepathic connections. In a later article, de Peyer (2016) falls victim to a distortion that has plagued this field, when she states that "Contrary to the Jungian tradition, early Freudian-based acknowledgement of uncanny phenomenon [again that unfortunate term] remains relatively sparse (p. 161)." As I have tried to indicate, this is simply untrue. Freud provided a dynamic construct for his work in telepathy, ambivalent as he was, which Jung failed to do, although Jung was more liberal in entertaining ideas beyond telepathy; Devereux's collection, cited by de Peyer, contains twenty-three early articles by fourteen analysts more Freudian than otherwise, favorable to telepathy. She also, like Massicotte, seems unaware of Eisenbud's *Psi and Psychoanalysis* and his other books; and there are a plethora of analysts, from Ehrenwald to Meerloo to Schwarz whose work she does not cite. In addition, she is wrong when she states that "comparably little has been reported until recently on psi transmissions that occur during wakefulness." There are four *entire* chapters in *Psi and Psychoanalysis* (published in 1970) in which Eisenbud deals with psi and "waking state behavior," the last chapter entitled "The Psychic Pathology of Everyday Life," a play on Freud's paper on "The Psychopathology of Everyday Life." As he says, "the most fruitful field for the application of the psi hypothesis to human behavior is not necessarily in the area of dreams but in the ordinary transactions of daily life" (Eisenbud, 1970, p. 234). By my rough count, there are more than 30 incidents of "waking state" psi connections in these chapters, each elaborated dynamically over many pages, from Eisenbud's clinical work with patients. And, of course, one of the best early examples of psi, the Forsyth case of Freud's, is a "waking state" psi connection.

De Peyer's point does have some valence with reference to my own presentation in this very chapter, however. In focusing on Freud's principles, most of which involve dream work, I have presented only a limited number of "waking state" references (for example, Rosenbaum's waking reverie that seemed psi-connected to a plane crash; Schwarz's book of psi experiences between parent and child), which may give the reader the wrong impression about how psi functions.

De Peyer provides a nice example of just the kind of psi-mediated slip that Eisenbud discusses frequently in *Psi and Psychoanalysis* when she mistakenly says Tuckahoe to a patient when she consciously means Timbuktu. As it happens, Tuckahoe had a particular significance to the patient, Jordan, who was contemplating visiting a friend in New Mexico who was born in Tuckahoe (something de Peyer could not have known). Later on in the treatment, this same patient, had a telepathic dream which reproduced almost exactly a medical emergency that happened to De Peyer's husband the previous night; the patient all but stood in the place of De Peyer, who had to treat her ill husband, but in the dream it was the patient's husband who was sick, a very convincing example of telepathy that resembles other emergency medical events, such as those cited by Stoller. It is unclear how De Peyer technically handled this chilling psi connection with her patient.

All in all, many of these brave contemporary works suffer because they fail to include the findings of Eisenbud that appear in his many books and articles. As can so often happen in the psychoanalytic field, a trend gets started, or psychoanalysts of a certain persuasion promulgate a similar sense of things or a similar history. In fact, these matters in academic writing, where one journal article writer refers to the work of another, tend to have a life of their own and what is missing in an initial article then becomes serially ignored. The scotoma is perpetuated. (To be specific, the latter articles, appear to represent more of the "relational" persuasion than otherwise—as articles do in general in the journal *Psychoanalytic Dialogues*—yet to the considerable credit of that orientation, the openness to psi data today appears greater than from a more traditional orientation, despite the fact that the earlier history of psi and psychoanalysis was created by more classical analysts.) Whereas these recent contributions and contributors are courageous, much as Elizabeth Lloyd Mayer was previously as discussed in Chapter Six, they fail as she did to fully acknowledge aspects of the field that have already been explored. Assailed as it is by skeptics, and with few adherents, psi and psychoanalysis as a field cannot afford to have its history minimized, not even by those contributors who are sincerely disposed to its findings.

Avoiding Popular Misconceptions

Parapsychology is a broad field, but the difficulty that psychoanalysts often have who come upon psi phenomena in their practices or who are open to the possibilities of the exploration of psi, is that they can only go so far in their exploration. As we have seen, usually the subject that entices psychoanalysts is telepathy which seems to occur in the clinical setting between analyst and patient, or between different patients, or expresses itself in a patient's dreams. But to go beyond these phenomena becomes increasingly difficult for the psychoanalyst to do, despite the vast data of which parapsychologists at least are familiar. In a sense, like Freud, most psychoanalysts are painfully aware that in accepting telepathy, one necessarily is on a slippery theoretical slope and, like Freud, they attempt magically to prevent themselves from sliding down further, by simply refusing to look at additional data or refusing to recognize the implications of the acceptance of telepathy as a phenomenon. For example, as we have seen, despite the fact that telepathy carries with it the possibility of suggestion at a distance (as in Burlingham's example of a child who appears to telepathically pick up on his mother's aggressive thought of boiling water and then acts upon it toward his sister [as discussed in the previous chapter]), those psychoanalysts who do entertain telepathy, generally do not want to touch much less explore this idea. This is to say nothing of their taking further steps beyond this idea, such as entertaining the data of precognition on the one hand, which can often occur in clinical treatment, or ghosts on the other, which are probably a more common phenomenon, particular in the cultures of some patients, than psychoanalysts seem prepared to accept.

One of the primary reasons for this is that psychoanalysts, unfamiliar with the parapsychological field, are prone to accepting commonplace and popular explanations for such phenomena as precognition and ghosts (as well as other phenomena such as out of body experiences that seem to resemble the "soul" rising above a person as a popular explanation although parapsychologists have suggested that they are telepathic phenomena accompanied by hallucinatory images). Just as we have seen that psychoanalysts can mistakenly assume, as did Freud, that telepathy acts like a telephone call that goes in only one direction or travels only between two people or takes place at a particular, verifiable time which can be conclusively identified (rather than remaining in the unconscious for a period of time to be accessed at a later date), they also assume that ghosts must be "spirits" of the departed, or that precognitive phenomena must mean that Time is actually overcome in a kind of momentary time travel. They jump reflexively to popular hypotheses that supposedly explain these phenomena rather than simply sitting with the phenomena themselves (and the intriguing fact that these phenomena are universally reported in various cultures). And then they proceed to reject the popular hypotheses, mistakenly believing they are the only explanations for the data, attributing the hypotheses to superstition, magical thinking, delusion, or—worse—psychosis.

As a result, analysts often foreclose themselves from examining the data at all, that is the vast amount of scientific gathering of spontaneous reports of these phenomena. Nor do they let themselves explore dynamically how the phenomena may function in clinical examples. Having so automatically jumped to popular explanations of the data, analysts abandon curiosity (one of the outstanding attributes of analysts at their best) about the phenomena, to say nothing about curiosity about *other* possible hypotheses. In other words, they throw the baby out with the proverbial (one might say "popular") bathwater. In contrast and unlike psychoanalysts, many parapsychologists, familiar with the data, do not necessarily accept the popular explanations for their existence. For example, many parapsychologists, who believe the data about precognitive phenomena to be strong, nevertheless do not believe that one can actually travel forward in Time or that Time can actually be affected when precognition takes place; and one might hazard "most" parapsychologists, do not necessarily believe that "spirits" of the deceased actually account for the phenomena of ghosts or apparitions—which incidentally can take the appearance of persons very much alive (see my discussion of apparitions in Chapter One on *Hamlet*). There are other and better and, I might add, wonderfully intriguing explanations for these phenomena.

Of course, one would hope that psychoanalysts, fascinated with a person's psychological functioning, would be open to listening fully to these phenomena. The enriching aspect of psychoanalysis, its play upon the intellect and heartstrings of the analyst, lies in listening *without being judgmental,* in effect letting oneself wonder and experience curiosity about how the analysand thinks and feels. Those of us who as therapists are fortunate enough to work with children are perhaps more use to permitting childhood logic and explanations to play themselves out, without interruption from supposedly rational judgment; one can find this approach as well in the magnificent work of Piaget in talking to children about their reasoning processes and how they are developed in Western culture. (This reveals a bias of mine, that psychoanalysts who treat adults should have the experience of treating children as part of their training, because it is so informative about the importance of play and childhood development, particularly the development of causal thinking [Reichbart, 2005].) In the same way, it has always seemed to me, one must listen for experiences and associations, of oneself as an analyst and of the adult analysand, without preconceived notions or without questioning those notions that do arise. In other words, to listen for telepathy, precognition and apparitions, without a priori assumptions that these phenomena do not exist, is eminently psychoanalytic.

The unfortunate acceptance of popular explanations by psychoanalysts is not the only reason there is resistance to the psi hypothesis. Alleged phenomena that go beyond telepathy are too often simply too much for most psychoanalysts. As I have discussed, psychokinesis, the ability to influence matter through mind rather than just communicate from mind to mind, *is* usually far beyond the ability of most psychoanalysts to entertain, although as so often happens (once again) they simply have not studied the parapsychological data. (I have already alluded in the previous chapter to one of the reasons for this particular resistance—fear of aggression). Similarly, a psychic's ability to find a missing object as occurred to the renowned psychoanalyst Elizabeth Lloyd Mayer (as explained in the previous chapter) and set her on the path to exploring psi (note that this is one of the roles of the psychic—the Navajo hand trembler—in traditional Navajo society; see Chapter Eight), may also be beyond the outer edge of what most psychoanalysts might consider, although one can easily put this in the framework of super-telepathy.

The failure to recognize the full panoply of psi phenomena is not confined just to those psychoanalysts who are skeptical of telepathy to begin with; it applies (as I have indicated) to some of those psychoanalysts who *have* entertained telepathy. Thus, I have more than once had the disappointing experience of encountering established psychoanalysts who have ventured into this field and have bravely written about telepathy, but who balk when faced with parapsychological findings beyond telepathy, although they too have not truly read about or explored these subjects. The findings and the phenomena are just so far outside their belief systems that they dismisses the data often without looking at them. And, in an understandingly self-protective way, they do not want professionally to be consider by fellow psychoanalysts to have questionable grounding in reality, an attack which they are convinced (probably correctly) will occur if they venture beyond telepathy.

This was true, as I have indicated in Chapter Six, of Elizabeth Lloyd Mayer as well as the Israeli analyst Ofra Eshel, who has written so compellingly about telepathy. Eshel was dismissive of precognitive phenomenon, and Mayer of the psychic photography of Ted Serios investigated by Eisenbud (a wall seemed to be instantaneously constructed when I mentioned this work to her as high as the wall that others have erected to defend against telepathy itself). Put in perspective, it is wonderful that such psychoanalysts are willing to go as far as they do when others simply dismiss the entire field, including telepathy, without a moment's hesitation. Yet it is also disappointing to find such a reaction to some of the wider psi phenomena.

More About Psychoanalytic Training

Psychoanalysts often discuss and debate psychoanalytic theory over and over, but too often fail to wonder about aspects of the stuff of life that their patients experience and bring to them, of which psi phenomena are a part. Let me expand further about the training of psychoanalysts to which I have previously alluded. I am familiar with how, at least in the United States, training of psychoanalysts occurs, having been president of an old and well-regarded psychoanalytic institute and in touch with psychoanalysts from other psychoanalytic institutes. Psychic phenomena are neither taught nor generally discussed at psychoanalytic training institutes. They are not brought up with regard to the analytic control cases that candidates are required to undertake and report upon in order to fulfill the requirements of becoming an analyst. In point of fact, a candidate who reports on psi phenomenon with regard to a control case might risk serious questioning as to competence.

Despite the fact that some of the parapsychological case material from my professional practice which I recount in this book derives from control cases, I never wrote about this material during my training, although I was fortunate enough to have one supervisor who, when I hesitantly mentioned it, was open to the possibility of telepathy which made a tremendous difference to me in my personal analysis (another requirement of training) with my more skeptical analyst. In general, then it is also not likely that psi phenomena are brought up in the candidate's *own* analysis or if brought up are met with a sense that the training analyst is familiar with such material.

One would think that in the area of transference and countertransference, at the very least, this topic would be touched upon, given the tendency for telepathy to take place between patient and psychoanalyst. Generally, it is not. For that matter, the challenges telepathy offers on how to do treatment are not engaged. Psychoanalysts, who are attuned to their patients in many ways, are considerably less attuned to listening for these things. For those that counter that "these things never come up in treatment," I would query whether, in a sense, we psychoanalysts hear what we are trained to hear. The concept of "coincidence" covers a vast territory; it can obscure that wonderful element of surprise that occurs for the analyst when a psi event takes place; it is easy and safe; and it can tend to act as a barrier, seemingly a sensible one, to dynamic exploration that might challenge a sense of how the world is put together.

As significantly, patient anxieties that might arise in these areas too often receive short shrift. The psychoanalyst Stoller felt that he was losing his mind when he experienced telepathy, or at the least, if the phenomena existed, something was wrong with him that he experienced them. It is not unusual for patients to experience these phenomena, and often introduce them, if they are trusting enough of the analyst to do so, by beginning: "You will think I am crazy, but…" Even more so, patients from cultures and segments of our society far from the Western educated and professional culture of psychoanalytic institutes, may entertain a belief in psychic phenomena—in ghosts, hauntings, precognition, telepathy for example. Failure of the analyst to accept that, after all, there may be something to the beliefs of such patients can result in a less successful treatment (see my discussion of the folk beliefs of a black mother and her adolescent son from North Carolina [Reichbart, 2006]).

Last, parapsychological issues may come up in the treatment of elderly patients. Of course, we do not understand the nature of our existence on this planet, or the nature of life and reality. Sometimes we move along as if we do; yet in psychoanalysis these issues can come up in compelling fashion and with searching questions. And parapsychological phenomena such as telepathy necessarily bring up just such questions of how our reality is constructed and where "mind" is in this entire fabric of our universe and lastly what happens when we die. It may be clear from what I have written about in these chapters, that I do not favor the concept of "spirit," in the way popularly meant, that is as an entity of some form surviving death, nor for that matter reincarnation (although I would urge anyone interested in the fascinating data from this area to read the carefully researched work of Stevenson [1974]); and I have little patience for the tendency to conflate the study of parapsychology and psychoanalysis with New Age or similarly amorphous or mystical concepts. But I do think that the super-telepathy hypothesis accounts for much of what passes for "spirit" in paranormal events such as ghosts and hauntings. (In the Afterword, incidentally, Michael Prescott, tantalizingly explores the link between psi phenomena and the nature of reality.) As an elderly patient gets closer to death, questions about the nature of life and death can have great valence. Psychoanalysts very much need to be open to parapsychological explorations or questions by these patients. Not that we have the answers, but that we do have available to us parapsychological data and understanding that may help.

A Defense of Eisenbud and Going Further

There are, as I have indicated, a variety of psi phenomena beyond telepathy, some of which are likely to appear in clinical work, and some of which are less likely to do so. I have already in the chapter on *Hamlet* discussed the phenomena of apparitions or more popularly known as ghosts (which may appear in clinical work) and attempted to address the popular theoretical misconceptions of these phenomena. In addition, in the chapter on Chesterton and Bergman, I discussed the psychic photography—a form of psychokinesis or telekinesis—of Ted Serios, explored by Eisenbud, and in the appendix I include a memorial statement I made concerning Eisenbud, where I also focused on the Serios data. In both places, I indicated that I believe the psychic photography in the Serios data is incontrovertible, not only the elaborate protocols including numerous scientific observers discussed in the two editions of the book about Serios, but also in the photographs themselves stored at the University of Maryland facilities in Baltimore which are unreproducible by normal means. Of course, the psychoanalyst is unlikely to come upon psychic photography (despite the brief experience that Bach recounts of a patient of his) in clinical work. The psychoanalyst *is* likely in clinical practice to come upon the phenomenon of precognition.

Before discussing precognition, however, I am aware of the extent to which I have brought up the psychoanalyst Eisenbud and his work, which I indicated that I would do at the beginning of Chapter Six. Eisenbud's work extended considerably beyond telepathy. In effect, he answered Freud's fears by saying that he would let the slippery slope take him wherever, in directions that Freud refused to go, even though Freud knew that theoretically there was no justifiable way to hold back from doing so. And this (Freudian) extension by Eisenbud, being true to Freud's theoretical observation even though Freud could not follow through on it himself, ironically had consequences for the full acceptance of Eisenbud's clinical work itself.

In effect, the tendency of psychoanalysts to be resistant to parapsychological phenomena that go beyond telepathy has had an unfortunate consequence: it has lead to the tendency to dismiss or avoid Eisenbud's psychoanalytic clinical work dealing with telepathy itself. If Eisenbud had focused only on psi phenomenon as it occurs in psychoanalytic treatment, and then only on telepathy, his findings and reasoning undoubtedly would have been better accepted in the psychoanalytic field. As I stated at the beginning, if he had only published *Psi and Psychoanalysis*, his groundbreaking book on telepathy and precognition in psychoanalysis, and no other parapsychological work, I believe he would have been less persona non grata among contemporary psychoanalysts.

However, the reaction of most psychoanalysts to the subsequent work that Eisenbud did with psychic photography (with the talented psychic Ted Serios affecting Polaroid camera film in such a way that images appeared on the film that were not actually in front of the camera at the time it was clicked) has been tremendously negative, despite the elaborate protocols and the existence of photographs that cannot otherwise have been produced. Yet, as is so often the case, more often than not these same analysts have not actually read the study of this phenomenon in Eisenbud's book *The World of Ted Serios* and are not actually familiar with the psychic photographs. Invariably, when this work is brought up, psychoanalysts imply that Eisenbud must have "gone off the deep end" (as one well known senior psychoanalyst assured me), in much the manner of the talented Wilhelm Reich, whose "orgone theory" and "orgone box" treatment suggested regression into psychotic process. And so, for some of them, like the thirteenth chime of the clock, Eisenbud's work in psychic photography then calls into question everything he wrote and they are relieved not to entertain the psi hypothesis in any way, or if willing to at least entertain telepathy, they leave out the important data that appear in his ground-breaking book *Psi and Psychoanalysis*.

The implication of those psychoanalysts who readily dismiss Eisenbud's work without bothering to read what he has written is that Eisenbud must have been delusional or naive or even worse—a charlatan. This was not my experience of the man. As to his being naive and thus duped, it has always struck me as fatuous in the extreme that anyone could believe that the bellhop Ted Serios (the talented psychic photographer), who was so frequently drunk and disorganized, could plan the supposedly elaborate machinations and sleights of hand that resulted in such impossibly unique psychic photographs produced in unique situations not of his own making; and that the scientists and academicians who witnessed his spontaneous productions could all be deceived. In fact, no magicians have ever duplicated the Serios phenomenon, despite pretensions otherwise; and if Serios were doing sleight of hand (and as I have indicated in the previous chapter [Chapter Four] on Chesterton and Bergman, most importantly the photographs themselves appear unreproducible by normal means including sleight of hand) he would have had to be a far, far better magician than the Amazing Randi himself.

As to the hypothesis of charlatanism, which would imply that Eisenbud made everything up, despite the doctors and professors who verified the phenomena in their presence, this was not within the possibilities of Eisenbud's personality as I knew him. Eisenbud attempted to practice unwavering honesty: it was that which I learned from him when he was my analyst (from 1970 to 1974); and it is that which is essential to being an effective psychoanalyst of any persuasion. Years later, I learned the same quality of the importance of attempting unfailing honesty from my second analyst, Joyce Steingart, equally talented as a clinician but not at all cognizant of psi processes nor involved in their investigation and more skeptical than otherwise (at least for much of our work together). In fact, it was the capacity for honesty and self-reflection as espoused by both my analysts, so important to analytic work, that informed my desire to become a psychoanalyst. A struggle toward often brutal honesty permeates Eisenbud's oeuvre, whether as a psychoanalyst or as a psychic researcher. Whatever his shortcomings, which I discuss in my obituary celebration of him [see Appendix], lack of honesty was not one of them.

My basic point however is that when Eisenbud went beyond the investigation of psi in clinical processes, to investigate something so extraordinary as psychic photography, the consequence was that it became harder for some psychoanalysts to recognize the contributions that he actually and already had made to clinical psi and psychoanalysis itself. My hope here has been to encourage psychoanalysts to investigate Eisenbud's clinical contributions more fully and to integrate his findings into the psychoanalytic enterprise so that they become part of an organic whole in the investigation of psi in the clinical setting. And then my greatest hope is to have at least some of them go even further, by looking more closely at Eisenbud's discoveries in psychic photography as well as at his speculations about precognition.

The only contemporary psychoanalyst who has written fully about Eisenbud's work is Mikita Brottman in her book "Phantoms in the Clinic" which provides a more complete exposition than I have given here and which I recommend to the psychoanalytic reader, along of course with Eisenbud's work itself. Brottman, who graciously wrote the introduction to this book, although trained as a psychoanalyst is not in clinical practice but is largely an academician and so she is unable to include clinical material of her own, but her exposition is complete and thoughtful. Her writing in some ways came entirely out of "left field" as far as I can determine. Not a parapsychologist, nor intimately involved with a psychoanalytic institute, she nonetheless seemed to have intuited the importance of Eisenbud's entire work, which had not been given any recent attention at all—preceding her book with an unexpected article in the psychoanalytic journal *American Imago* concerning the Serios phenomenon (which to the journal's considerable credit they published) and making a scholarly case for the importance of his findings.

I have often thought that in some ways it would be a much more comfortable world, if parapsychological phenomena did not exist. Personally, I could fall back on the generally approved Western assumption that "mind" cannot affect the outside world. For if we entertain psychokinesis as a phenomenon, we necessarily are brought face to face (will we or won't we) with the danger of unconscious aggressive wishes, to say nothing of the difficulty, as indicated in the chapter on western law and psi, of constructing a social system that incorporates this concept. But having seen the unreproducible (by normal means) Polaroid pictures of Serios, read as much as I have about them, known so intimately one of the players, Eisenbud, and experienced psi in my analysis and my practice, I am then, so to speak, "stuck"—with that very data, with the psychoanalytically informed phenomena, and with the wonder (and fear) of the concepts that explain the data.

Undoubtedly those analysts and others who choose not to really examine the data of parapsychology receive a certain solace. In effect, denial has its rewards. There is a reason we have constructed a scientific world and a legal system that rests on this denial and disregards the data: it feels safer to us. And in some collective way, I have sometimes thought, perhaps it *does* work at times. After all, the famous sheep-goat experiments of Schmeidler suggest that one's positive belief in psi makes it more likely that one will be telepathic, and this might apply as well to being susceptible to unconsciously aggressive telepathic influence and to psi processes in general, including aggressive psychokinesis. And, of course, the enormity, one might say almost the impossibility, of incorporating our understanding of psi—the phenomena of super-psychokinesis or super-telepathy—into a social system that recognizes it as a part of causality (which I discuss in Chapter Ten on western law and parapsychology), suggests how we are embedded in an entire social construct that by denying psi attempts to provide us with emotional comfort.

Precognition

Apparent precognition, which in my experience also clearly occurs, can often be explained by the super-telepathy hypothesis without having to assume that Time alters in some way, as is popularly conceived and which psychoanalysts tend to accept as the only conceptual version of the phenomenon, and which they then—having set up this conceptual strawman—disclaim as an impossibility. Perhaps and unfortunately most psychoanalysts would probably approve of Freud's insistence that patients delude themselves after the fact that a dream was precognitive, misremembering when the dream actually occurred. In addition, and most distressing, one can also invoke a super-psychokinesis hypothesis to explain precognition, again without altering Time. This last hypothesis is chilling; and in my discussion of Western law and parapsychology, I have indicated how utterly difficult it is to consider. Yet given the apparent reality of psychokinesis, it is a much more logical hypothesis than that Time in some way has been altered for the percipient. (It has the virtue of the principle of "parsimony" which is sometimes invoked in determining what theory may be best; that is, one should choose the theory that invokes the least number of variables.) So if one accepts the precognitive data, as I do, then one is confronted with the following reasoning: It is very unlikely that Time can be altered, so the only other explanation would be that there must be some causal relationship between a precognitive experience and the event that takes place subsequently that resembles the experience. Tanagras said this in another way: "It is we ourselves, as integral and autonomous parts of creative power, who by unconsciously intervening according to our relative impressions, act upon our fellowmen." One has to ask whether the increasing tendency in some psychoanalytic quarters to minimize the importance of the unconscious, stems from some unconscious awareness of this power.

Now let me pause. Initially, I was not going to discuss premonitions or precognitive dreams any further—not because the data on precognitive dreams are insufficient. On the contrary, there are more than enough data to indicate that precognitive dreams occur in psychoanalytic treatment of patients, although they seem to be rare and often involve trivial events (Eisenbud, 1975, p. 106; Eisenbud states he only recorded three dozen precognitive dreams in "as many years"). What led me initially to stop discussion here was because Eisenbud's and Tanagras' hypotheses concerning unconscious causation of precognitive events, as logical as they are, ultimately are so "extremely unsettling" as Brottman observes (Brottman, 2011, p. 80). The suggestion that aggressive wishes may sometimes lend themselves to precognitive events made me reluctant—despite my having brought it to up—to continue this exploration. Nowhere is this "unsettling" more apparent than when it comes to a parapsychological phenomenon we have barely mentioned: the precognition not of individual events in one person's life but of mass disasters by one or more persons. We touched upon this briefly in the report of the psychoanalyst Rosenbaum (2011) who while living in Paris had a precognitive vision of debris falling from the sky, featuring the number 346, hours before a DC-10 airplane crashed outside Paris killing 346 people.

In fact, we *do* have striking and well-researched putative examples of precognitions of mass disasters. Two are most notable: the precognitive dreams by children and others of the Aberfan coal disaster and the remarkable novel written by Morgan Robertson, *Futility*, that so chillingly predicted many years later the sinking of the Titanic.

The Aberfan coal disaster in Wales occurred on October 21, 1966. 144 people—128 of them children—were killed when a slag heap from a coal mine collapsed, like a land-slide, into the town of Aberfan, destroying among other structures, the Pantglas Junior school while the school was in session. It was believed that children and others had striking premonitions of the disaster, and so a London psychiatrist, John Barker, appealed through the media for examples of premonitions (Barker, 1967). He received seventy responses, and winnowed them down to twenty four.

Here are some examples, in which in italic letters I indicate how a premonitory dream was shared *before* the disastrous event: The day before, Cheryl Miller dreamt that a flood of blackness was heading toward a school. *She described the dream in front of a group of witnesses at church and then the next morning, forty-five minutes before the disaster, she told her sister of the dream.* Again, Eryl Mai Jones, ten years old, *told her mother on the morning of the disaster that she had a horrible dream* that her school had disappeared and was replaced by a barren wasteland. Similarly, another child had a nightmare that he was suffocating in "deep blackness"; and another that the schoolhouse was buried by an avalanche of coal. *Both these dreams were told to parents before the disaster.* For many more often heart rending examples, look to Barker's article.

Concerning the second disaster, the wrecking of the *Titanic*: Morgan Robertson's *Futility* (published in 1898) and then republished as the *Wreck of the Titan* (1912) strikingly told a story that resembled the sinking of the *Titanic* fourteen years after the novel was first published. The fictional *Titan* was a giant ship of almost the same tonnage, size, horsepower, and speed as the *Titanic* years later, and like the *Titanic*, it hit an iceberg, with the subsequent loss of life of almost all its 2,000 passengers. Even if one assumes that the naming of the *Titanic* was subconsciously influenced by someone who had read Robertson's book, the coincidence of the iceberg disaster is striking.

Fascinatingly, years later Eisenbud examined aspects of Robertson's life and novels and short stories (of which Eisenbud read 60)—some of which are replete with instances of telepathy and hypnotism—to suggest that dynamically Roberston was constantly struggling in an internal Oedipal drama to foresee Fate (and thus perhaps to actually enlist precognition), unable to fully accept the demands of the Oedipus, and wishing to magically overcome it (Eisenbud, 1982, Chapter 6, pp. 88–112). In a more obscure reference, without a real dynamic formulation, the Lacanian theorist Žižek remarks that the Zeitgist of the age combined with the symbolic meaning of the *Titanic*, represented *jouissance*, and somehow contributed to Robertson's parapsychological feat (Žižek, 1989, p. 76).

But what brings me now to discuss precognitions of mass disasters is something particularly contemporary: two attempts to explore whether the terrorist attacks on the twin towers in New York City and the Pentagon in September 2001 have precognitive phenomena that attach to them. The first attempt appears in a popularly written book by a survivor spouse of the terrorist attacks. Bonnie McEneany, whose husband Eamon, died in the twin towers attack, bravely set out to write about the parapsychological-like experiences of victims and survivors of 9/11, prior to and after that terrible event. She took it upon herself to contact survivors. While the data she collected confirmed for her the hypothesis that there was some element of "soul" to explain what she and others experienced of their loved ones who perished, one need not accept this hypothesis to be impressed by some of the data she collected.

McEneany did two things of importance from a parapsychological viewpoint: first, she reported a number of precognitive experiences of victims and survivors in detail and second, she emphasized how important it was to these survivors that their paranormal experiences be accepted, that they not be considered "weird" for having them. Upon reading her account, I wondered once again whether psychoanalysts, or mental health professionals in general, are able to create an atmosphere for a patient similar to what McEneany created for those she interviewed,—that is an atmosphere sufficiently open to overcome the patient's fear that the analyst thinks something is psychologically wrong with the patient who relates such precognitive experiences. In other words, McEneany's efforts echo those of psychoanalysts such as Ira Brenner, Ullman, and Powell who pleaded that psychoanalysts (or for that matter mental health professionals of any theoretical persuasion) listen to the psychic experiences of their patients with an open mind.

Here are three examples of precognitive dreams from McEneany's book (McEneany, 2011, Chapter 6, pp. 119–151) in which again in italic letters I indicate data that tend to substantiate that the precognitive dream indeed took place *before* the event, and not that the individual misremembered the sequence of events.

1. On September 8th, Julia from Park Slope, Brooklyn dreams of a huge truck that suddenly takes off and pierces a house surrounded by tall buildings and leaves a jagged hole; she *records the dream on a piece of paper*, which she places on the passenger seat of her car as she drives to her therapist's office on the morning of September 11th. Suddenly she feels a blast so strong she fears she will lose control of her car and when she stops the car to see what is going on, she sees a hole in the north tower just like the hole in her dream.

2. Janice Green, who had worked at the World Trade Center, but had left—and who knew at least forty people who died in the tragedy—had a dream on September 2, 2001, in which she was looking out of the windows of her apartment in Jersey City, which showed a view of the World Trade Center, when suddenly there was a huge explosion and a mushroom cloud. She turned to her husband in the dream and said that Bin Laden just blew up New York. The dream so distressed her that *she actually told her husband and her parents in addition at the time.* (Curiously, and perhaps in a way that vitiates the precognitive elements of this dream, she had seen a movie on television shortly before that, in which a terrorist involved in the 1993 attack on the World Trade Center vows that next time they will bring both towers down. The movie must have been "Path to Paradise: The Untold Story of the World Trade Center Bombing" HBO, New York City, 1997.)

3. Katherine Wolf *regularly kept a dream journal.* She had accepted a job to work at the World Trade Center on August 9, 2001, and died in the subsequent attack. But on August 10th, she had recorded what was her last entry in her dream journal. She dreamt that she held a long tubular atom bomb that she released. Another bomb was on its way to her home. She told people that she had released both bombs, and she could see their lights on the radar screen. The second bomb did not go off but it hit where she had just been sitting. The bomb was in the shape of a paper plane.

The second attempt to explore whether there were precognitive experiences concerning the attacks of 9/11 was conducted by Nancy Sondow of the American Society for Psychical Research. Sondow requested that people who had a precognitive experience concerning 9/11 contact her. Here are just three examples from many others in her research (incidentally, other examples she documents occurred repeatedly over long periods of time for the dreamer [Sondow, 2017]):

1. P.A. from West Virgnia had recurring dreams for two weeks before 9/11 and *she told them to her husband and mother:* One dream was of planes crashing and burning, straight down into the Earth. The recurring dream was: people running covered with ash like from a volcano, charred people falling from the sky … *I told my husband* of seeing three women crying, running and covered in ash. *And on 9/11/, my mother called many times to say "your dream, your dream." My husband finally got through on the phone and he said the women from my dream were on CNN.*

2. Kat McCath from New Jersey in the early summer of 2001 experienced an elaborate dream of being in a multistoried building in New York City, when there is a loud noise that shakes the building. She thinks it is an earthquake but as she looks around the room, the whole side of the wall was ripped out and some of the people were sucked out with great force. "I thought it was as if an airplane had crashed into the building. I headed for the stairwell." She ran down flights of stairs and "I could smell smoke and feel the building shaking and crumbling from above. I could hear the building coming down, one floor at a time and Knew if I didn't reach the bottom soon, I'd be buried in rubble." *Kat called her sister after the dream and described it to her, including how frightened she had felt. The day of the attacks she immediately called her sister and her sister "said all she kept thinking about was my dream."*

3. A medium, Susan Maxwell-Trumble, *was recorded by a client,* Koren, in January 2001, asking whether Koren worked at the World Trade Center, and then saying that she saw terrible destruction there, people falling out of windows, fires and bodies everywhere. She told Koren that Koren's deceased grandmother told her to "run, run, run" and she would be safe.

   The reading was forgotten by Maxwell-Trumble but the morning of September 11, she received a call from Koren. Koren described having entered Tower One when the first plane hit, not knowing what to do, and then later the second plane hit Tower Two. Remembering the reading at that point and her grandmother saying for her to run, that is exactly what she did. Then she called the medium to thank her.

We may be brought up short that mass disasters at times lend themselves to precognitions. Whatever the nature of such parapsychological causality—Eisenbud, distraught himself about the logical appeal of Tanagras's hypothesis concerning aggressive wishes, does suggest that in the Aberfan disaster the authorities had overlooked and ignored the danger of the coal slag and that people in Aberfan in general had tended to overlook that danger (much like living under a volcano) and that this general unconscious knowledge contributed to the accuracy of the premonitions (Brottman, 2011, pp. 78–79)—but, again, whatever the nature of the parapsychological causality, the fact is that precognitive dreams and visions *do* happen.

How we treat such dreams and visions as psychoanalysts when a patient brings them to us (whether they involve trivial or more frightening events), is important, because in the analysis (unlike any other setting) one can explore dynamically and therapeutically how such dreams and visions dovetail with and reflect the patient's internal life (much as Eisenbud did, albeit historically, with Robertson). Freud of course suggested this, when he treated some precognitive incidents dynamically as telepathy. He simply could not go that extra step of recognizing that precognition does exist.

Not surprisingly, the psychoanalyst who has done the most in exploring precognition in clinical treatment is Eisenbud. Most excitingly, in 1954 he published two consecutive articles in the Psychoanalytic Quarterly (before the classical psychoanalytic community put the kibosh on such publication) which explore precognition, discussing dynamically among other things a vision of the analyst Hitschmann prior to a pilot falling out of a dirigible; an incident in which a patient appears in a dream to precognize the flooding of the lower floors of a hotel as a result of a water main break (apparently attempting unconsciously to impress Eisenbud who had failed to get results in a psi experiment he was conducting); and a patient who precognitively dreams of an automobile exploding. These dreams are analyzed with attention to destructive wishes and with unconscious wishes directed toward the analyst, in the latter case even with regard to a miscarriage of Eisenbud's wife. (Eisenbud, 1954a, 1954b). Curiously, subsequent psychoanalytic commentators who have ventured into psi have tended to render these striking and ground breaking articles invisible: They do not cite them.

Some Examples of Psi from My Practice

I will end this chapter with some examples of psi phenomena from my practice of psychotherapy and psychoanalysis over the past twenty-five years. Again, I would like to make it clear that there is very little new here. In providing these examples, my hope is they will simply add to the weight of the evidence, which I believe has been dispositive for decades. (I provided other examples in Chapter Five on Joyce's Ulysses involving telepathy among multiple patients.) Most of these examples involve telepathic dreams; one—a chilling one—involves precognitive dreams; another involves a psi "symbol"— the L shape or right angle—rarely reported upon.

Eels

Here is an example, involving animals as did my example in the chapter on Joyce involving raccoons. The psi connections involve two analytic patients. At the time of these patient dreams, I was having a series of dreams myself that involve water, which I thought of as probably having to do with the upcoming birth by a stepdaughter of twins, a boy and a girl as it turned out.

First, the dream of Mr. S. He was a European patient in his early forties, who had come here for training, and whose own father was abusive to and distant from him. He had a strong attachment to me as a father figure. He dreamt:

> I am living in your house which is outdoors and near a river. I go out to the river and I teach the fish-
> ermen there how to fish, and I help them to catch two electric eels, except they are not electric, and
> I hold them up and cut the head off the bigger one.

Mr. S. associated to his wish to go fishing with me, a father-son interaction which he deeply craved. He thought of me so much as a father-figure, at this time, that when he lay down on the couch, he said, ceremoniously each time "Hello, father." I could not help, in hearing the dream, wondering if the two eels are girl and boy, where the girl is characterized as castrated. In fact, as I know, Mr. S. despaired of having children, even by adoption, so I also wondered whether there was an unconscious aggression, unbeknownst to him about these upcoming births of my stepdaughter.

Now at the end of the previous week, Ms. L., a professional woman with three children, who was subjected to much sexual overstimulation by her parents growing up, leading to an obsessive but very much hidden fascination with penises as a child (her attempt as a child to master the anxiety of the overstimulation expressed itself in frequent hidden drawings of penises)—dreamt:

> There are a series of aquariums with water going between them, but they are being used to keep food in. I become worried that this may not be safe for the food. Then I see that one of the aquariums is filled with eels.

I wondered to myself: why these psi links and what do they signify? I could see that both dreams had to do with a fascination with penises and perhaps children. I wondered whether Ms. L., who sometimes is overwhelmed by her maternal duties when she is also a full-time professional, despairs in her dream of keeping her children's resources safe.

Now each of these patients is different in the ability to work with psi phenomena in my opinion. Mr. S. is fully familiar from his own life with aspects of psi, and although in this instance I did not chose to inform him about the psi connection in his dream, at other times I have done so. It is already part of our interaction that at times he impresses me with a measure of psi ability. He would not be surprised by the connection here, although I am not sure what it would add to the interpretation, other than he would like to impress me (although he does feel ambivalent about his psi abilities). Now that I further think of it, however, the aggression toward the eel probably gave me pause in opening up the subject to Mr. S. Even this, Mr. S. might have been able to explore because he was comfortable with his aggressive thoughts. But it was a close call and if I erred it was as a consequence of caution. On the other hand, I think it unlikely, certainly at this time in treatment that Ms. L—who was very frightened of her internal wishes—and often hung onto her treatment by a thread, resistant and claiming that fantasy was useless to her and often involved in negative transference, would explore this psi connection with me. It might drive her further away should I mention it.

Butterflies

Just after Thanksgiving, my psychoanalytic patient, Ms. Q, who is a therapist, tells me the following dream: "I am observing a cocoon which is transparent and it is filled with live buttterflies."

Two sessions later, she tells me that "something weird has happened." She was on Skype with one of her patients who imagined that Ms. Q. was holding her like a baby. At that point, Ms. Q remembered that in fact there was a baby in her butterfly dream she had recounted to me previously, which seemed to establish a wish communicated between her and her patient. The additional part of the dream was: "I was holding a baby, that was very pink, but not soft, kind of bony."

In fact, on Thanksgiving, two of our young grandchildren, toddlers both, were at our house. We had bought a new toy, which they were playing with. It was a blue hard plastic elephant, with a large trunk, to which a long cylinder of blue cloth was attached.

When the toy was turned on, a wind was created in the blue cloth and little light cloth butterflies of various pastel colors came shooting out and floated quickly to the ground. Our grandchildren were completely enthralled with this toy, squealing and trying to catch the butterflies with a "butterfly net" before they landed on the floor. I puzzled to myself as to why Ms. Q should pick up so closely from my experience with our grandchildren. There was a magical aspect to both the dream and the event to which it seemed to be associated—live butterflies floating out of a container—and then a peculiar juxtaposition, an elephant made of hard plastic rather than something soft, and a pink but bony baby.

I thought that what was underlying Ms. Q's dream was the wish which she had at that time often expressed to me, for her to come into my lap and for me to hold her. That she should be prompted to remember her dream when her patient, at a distance, expressed a similar wish, seemed revealing of how fraught with ambivalence was her own wish. Ms. Q alternately thought of me as a father figure in the transference and then as a more kindly father-figure than her father, who may have only reluctantly played with her as a toddler, in fact who would not even hold her as a baby. Ms. Q is at her most vibrant when she observes nature outdoors, which she did frequently with a friend, adventuring on her own as a pre-adolescent and adolescent, and often waxing poetic as an adult about wildness, fecundity and animals. What she desired as a child was a parent with whom she could share these experiences, but neither was there. She wishes, in her psi connection, to be with me as my grandchildren are.

However, I could think of no way to completely share this psi connection with Ms. Q, because it involves revealing too fully my own life, and also I was concerned that it would enlist Ms. Q's considerable capacity for competition and envy, particularly with my significant other. Perhaps I underestimated Ms. Q's capacity to work with this material, I thought to myself at that time. Years later, however, in Ms. Q's therapy I was able to speak more fully about psi connections in general when she began to effect a greater psychological separation from her father. At that point, accepting psi connections became a regular part of her treatment.

Water Dripping from Attic

Ms. B, a woman in twice a week treatment (whom I can never get to increase her frequency) from a Spanish background, dreams:

> I am in my house in Majorca. I see there is water on the floor and that water is dripping from the ceiling. I wonder what is going on here and worry that the floor is going to be ruined. So I go up to the attic and see that there is a man there, but it is strange, because he is only partly human; I can't describe it. He is living there. At first I am afraid of him, but then I am no longer afraid and accept the fact that he will stay there.

Ms. B who thought the man might be her married lover, because although he is married, she would like to control him and have him in her house. She thinks of her ex-husband actually as being like an animal to her, where he wanted her to be his slave. When I remark that this is the reverse of her wish to control the man in her dream, she readily agrees, saying that this is how she thinks of things between a man and a woman: one always has to be dominant. She says nothing about the transference to me, however. I wonder to her whether she considers that one of us must be dominant in our relationship. In fact, this is a constant theme but in this instance she denies it.

As it happened the previous evening, I had to go into my attic because there was water dripping from the pan under the air conditioner onto the floor in our bedroom. My significant other was worried that the wooden floor would be ruined. I have to get towels to remove the water from the pan. This was a repeat of a problem, which had taken place the week before, and subsequently we had to get a repair man.

Ms. B's dream suggests her unacknowledged desire to be in my house, and to witness our bedroom and the primal scene. I am in a transferential sense both her ex-husband and her married lover that she wishes to control.

Colonoscopy

Mr. S, the health care professional, whom I already mentioned as having been particularly psychic, dreamt:

> There is an old man, whose intestines are completely exposed, and I have to save him by keeping them wet with saline water. But then I find out that I have for some reason begun to wash them with soap. And I end up killing the man. I feel so terrible. I was just trying to help.

After telling me this dream, where he assumes the old man must be me, he worries that I might have some gastrointestinal problem. This patient in fact was very anxious about my health. He knew that the dream expressed his ambivalence toward me and that it reflected his constant fear that his aggression, of which he might not have sufficient control, would harm me and those he loved in general. He knew too that he thought of me transferentially as his father. In the beginning of analysis, he was always saying, once he lay down on the couch, "Father" to me as a greeting. His own relationship with his actual father, who was abusive in the extreme and terrifying, had made him feel vulnerable in the world. He was worried that his own psychology had incorporated some of his father's sadism and at the same time, he saw me as a benign father-figure, the type of father that he wished he had growing up. Because he was so anxious about my health (he had in the past become extremely so by extrapolating from a little data) and because his dream actually made me anxious in ways that I felt I could not communicate to him, I said to him that no, I have no gastrointestinal problem, which may have been more supportive than I needed to be. Why did his dream make me anxious? Because the next day, I was in fact to have a routine colonoscopy.

So Mr. S. has reached into my life through a psi-mediated dream, and I decided that I should not tell him of the connection. And also I felt very vulnerable both for the evaluation and for the fear that, despite the more or less routine nature of the procedure, they might find something malignant, and I was also embarrassed by the intrusion into my body that was going to take place (as Mr. S's dream itself felt like an intrusion). In addition, unknown to Mr. S., colonoscopies historically had never gone easily for me, which added to my own anxiety. Long and short, my patient never found out the extent to which this dream had a psychic component.

There was, however, a seeming and unexpected sequel to this psi event. Two sessions later, Mr. S. told me of a physical problem of *his own* that he had never spoken to anybody about but his mother, and a physician with whom he consulted. It was one that made him feel physically less than manly and had resulted throughout his life in his reluctance to expose his body. He did not take part in sports since he was a youngster because of this physical problem nor would he go swimming, and even when he went to the gym, he tried not to change in the locker room but instead to shower at home. He often pretended to friends that he just wanted to be alone or needed to do something else by himself when they asked him to accompany them at some activity, such as going to the beach, that might expose the problem. His lover, although clearly aware of the problem, had never spoken to him about it, apparently for fear of embarrassing him. He was so grateful that he felt he could tell me about it. He had also decided that he would now undergo a medical procedure that could actually take care of it, something he had avoided doing in the past.

Now there was some question in my own mind whether his intrusive psi dream into my body, where he made me feel vulnerable, was related to this sudden revelation about a difficulty with his own body, that made *him* feel vulnerable, and which he had never openly talked about to anyone but his mother and a physician. For I could find little evidence of his working on this issue prior to his sudden revelation about it, other than his general comfort with me as someone he trusted, and then the psi dream involving a procedure on my own body. Was he saying, unconsciously, "I know about your physical body, intimately, in a way no one but those closest to you must know; and so now I feel that can tell you about my body intimately?"

The Trees Are Coming Down

On my way to work one morning, which is walking distance from my home, I pass a large home, that was on the market and apparently recently sold. I am astonished because I see that all the old and giant and beautiful trees in front of the home have been cut down, their large dismembered trunks lying on the grass. For a moment, I stop, as have a couple on the sidewalk. The man remarks to me: "It's just terrible." And I agree.

The next day, Ms. Q., whom I mentioned in a previous example, comes into session, with this dream:

> I had a bad dream: I was in a house and outside I could see that some adolescent boys were climbing a tree and pieces of branches, really big pieces, kept on coming down, scaring me. Then there was suddenly a face at the window, looking in. I started to scream and my mouth opened and opened very wide. (I actually did scream, but did not wake up; my husband woke me because I was screaming.)

Ms. Q. thinks the face in the window must be me, but it reminds her of an incident, which she has frequently reported and troubles her, when she was so scared as a child because she thought there was a face looking in her bedroom window, that she ran out of her suburban house in the middle of the night screaming. And her father had to follow her outside and comfort her and calm her down.

In this case, unusually for me, I do indicate to her that yesterday I was astounded by trees having been cut down on a property on my way to work, and how upsetting it was. She is able to accept this apparent psi connection. When we speak further about it, it becomes clear that she recognizes the castrative association to the cutting down of the trees. This has meaning in particular to her, because her father was often unnecessarily seductive toward her as a child. We wondered whether her dream was an aggressive and castrative wish toward her father.

But she then has a different thought that she says she should not be having, given that she is very aware of her anger at her father, and that is she now remembers, that despite her frequent discomfort with her father, how close she felt to him when she had to go to the hospital to have her appendix out as a child. Her father was there already, for a different medical procedure and he was so wonderful to her, giving up his single room so she could have it, and tending to her in a way her mother did not.

As so often happens with psi events, they tend to proliferate among patients and with a patient. What I do not tell Ms. Q. is that there is another psi element here. I took my significant other to the hospital with what we thought might be appendicitis the previous evening; it developed that it was diverticulitis. But I was in the hospital with her, consoling her, that very evening. Thus, in a sense, Ms. Q. wants me to act toward her as I do toward my significant other, and as her father at his best did toward her, and so she invokes a psi connection with me.

The Right Angle or L Shape

Here is an interesting example that involves a patient Ms. A. from a distant foreign country communicating in a psi sense with a patient whom I see in person in psychoanalysis.

On a Monday, Ms. Q. again brings in the following dream:

> I was here but there were two couches. One was like this one I am lying on, but he other one went out that way, perpendicular and forming an L shape. I was lying on that one, but I was facing you, and you were behind a brown hard plastic screen, very ugly, so that I could not see you. It reminded me of "the other room" which I once dreamt about, in the corner here; and for some reason I thought of a "wrinkle in time" and the tesseract.

On Wednesday, Ms. A, the patient from a foreign country who video-teleconferences with me on a two or three times weekly basis (and who is actually rather psychic although we have never discussed this) said: "I had such a strange dream, that my first boyfriend had cancer."

She then said: "It was strange because I actually found out from my girlfriend the next day that her husband has cancer." Then she added:

> And then I dreamt that I bought an L shaped piece of land, for some reason, and decided to plant vegetables on it. It was very dry, and I looked at a pumpkin on it and inside the pumpkin, it is empty inside.

In both instances, the L shape appeared in the context of psi phenomena—the seemingly precognitive dream of Ms. A. involving cancer and the association of a "wrinkle in time" of Ms. Q. I have found through the years that the right angle or L shape symbolizes "psi." I do not know why. Perhaps it has something to do with looking around corners or suddenly changing direction. Eisenbud had found the same thing, which he pointed out to me during my psychoanalysis with him, but he told me that he had never written about it at the time. (Subsequently, however, he made a brief note of it, indicating that he had "no idea" why this symbol of psi-conditioned dreams existed [Eisenbud, 1982, p. 273]) The fact that Ms. A. lives thousands of miles away made no difference to the appearance of psi here. It was in fact commonplace for her to bring psi related dreams that attached to my other patients, whom I saw in person, despite the distance between them. In this case, it was as if these two women were competing for my attention and for closeness, but in each instance there was a dryness and fear involved.

In fact, I have never done therapy with Ms. A. in the same room; it has always been by video teleconferencing (there is little psychoanalytic treatment or training available in her country). Frequently, we have talked about how things might be different *were* she able to come to the United States, in effect were she able to lie on the analytic couch as does Ms. Q. Here the emptiness of the pumpkin and the dryness reflects that unfortunate distance.

At other times, Ms. Q. and Ms. A. competed with each other in a psi fashion. For example, three months before this incident when I tried to contact Ms. Q. by video teleconference, her still picture identifying her no longer appeared; instead there was an animation of a white cat with big dark green eyes that talked. Apparently, Ms. A's account had been hacked. In the next session, she showed me at the beginning of the session a big white, grey rabbit that she had bought for her daughter (she video teleconferenced from her home). She then talked about the animals in her childhood, four dogs, the last one of which would come to pick her up at elementary school. In my session, with Ms. Q. that same day, at the very end of the session, she proceeded for the first time to show me a picture on her cell phone of her own dog, about which she had frequently spoken but had never showed me a picture.

The Wastebasket

Ms. A. again from her distant country could communicate psi-wise with other patients as well (one could hypothesize that psi was particularly important to her [as in the case of Eshel's patient or Papazian's] because she had been traumatically separated from her father for years as a young girl—the first thing she mentioned to me when she began therapy—and she was separated from me by a great distance). She is a mental health professional, lacking any formal academic mental health degree, in training in her country, and recently she had opened a private practice. One session she lamented to me that her suite mates, both of whom rent from her, did not contribute in various ways to keeping the suite clean. Among other things, they did not let their patients use the bathroom because apparently they did not want ever to be responsible for cleaning it and they refused to empty the trash can, which annoyed her. The next session, I see Ms. L, who tells me that she had the following dream:

> As part of a sorority initiation, I am asked by a girl to clean a bathroom and also a wastebasket which is shaped strangely, like a round cylinder, and with some white stuff around it, like shaving cream. I get very angry at the girl who tells me this and I attack her physically.

I really had no idea why this striking conjunction took place, but it was particularly compelling from a psi point of view. Certainly Ms. L. was looking for my attention by invoking psi and apparently quite angry at her unknown if distant rival Ms. A. I did not mention this conjunction to either patient, particularly as Ms. L. was consumed with how angry she had experienced herself in the dream. So we focused on that aspect of the dream because central to her process is the extent to which she denies her anger. She thought of a professional colleague at her work whom she believes is making a mess and which Ms. L then has to "clean up" after. We also analyzed her desire to hurt me because I ask her to look into her own "mess" in her life. In addition, in expressing her anger at me, she contends that she does not want to be psychoanalytic after all; she contends she certainly no longer wants to join *that* sorority.

And yet, more than seven months later, the dream made more sense. Ms. L, was experienced in the psychology field, with an advanced degree, unlike Ms. Q., who had nothing of the kind. Yet Ms. L had never opened a private practice. Apparently, this dichotomy unconsciously incensed her. To her surprise, however, seven months later her long psychoanalysis began to bear fruit (as she talked about some early "messes" of which she had been ashamed), and her masochism dramatically receded. She finally opened a private practice, something about which she had manifestly given up on at the time of the dream. Unconsciously and psi-wise, her wish had remained very active.

Ozzie Osborne and Sharon

Here is an ideal and somewhat amusing example, even if not particularly elaborate, also involving Ms. L, who was improving dramatically in her analysis, as I have said. In general, throughout the analysis, she had adopted a certain formality, always beginning by saying "Hello, Dr. Reichbart." Years ago, she had briefly attempted to call me by my first name, but quickly felt uncomfortable and returned to "Dr. Reichbart." As she began to become much more comfortable with herself, and less anxious, as a result of finally being able to speak more openly to me about early events, I asked her about her need to maintain distance from me. She said among other things that since I would tell her nothing about myself, she felt justified in keeping her distance. "So there," so to speak. For she really wanted to know all about me, but she knew I would never answer her questions: about my family, about what movies I liked, about what I did on vacations. At this time, as her anxieties diminished strikingly and closeness to me was no longer so threatening, she decided once again to address me by my first name. Shortly thereafter, three weeks after Halloween, she had a dream that she was "with Ozzie Osbourne and Sharon."

She had absolutely no associations to this dream. And to this day I have little knowledge of Ozzie Osbourne, a famous British vocalist, once the lead singer of a group called Black Sabbath, who went off on his own and apparently is all but a cult figure. However, unbeknownst to my patient, the last name of a family relation by marriage of mine is the same (except that the spelling is slightly different). Not only that, but every Halloween, for four years now, they—husband and wife—dress up as Ozzie Osbourne and Sharon for a very large Thanksgiving Day parade, in which citizens make costumes and floats in a suburban town half an hour away. The relatives' costumes are so good and convincing that the two are invariably hailed throughout the parade by marchers and people watching, cell phone selfies and photos taken of them, and frequent screams of "Ozzie" and "Sharon" coming from the crowd; so good in fact that one year the couple won the award as "Best Couple Costume." I too take part in this parade, as do others in my family, but I am invariably only a minor character.

The conjunction of my patient's unexplained dream, and the reality, was too striking for me—as I thought about it and felt how close was the correlation—not to share with my patient, which I proceeded to do in our next session. And her reaction, rather than being disturbed by the possible psi manifestation here, was one of simple acceptance and cogent interpretation on her own. "So," she said with amusement, "I told you I wanted to know about you and your family."

I might add one further thing here. A few weeks prior to this, there had been a small social meeting at my home of members of the New Jersey Psychoanalytic Society, an affiliate of the American Psychoanalytic Association, comprised generally of more conservative medical psychoanalysts, an actually lovely group of people, in which a member made a brief presentation about saying something to a patient about a "fantasy" of his own that he had been having about the patient, which he felt had been useful in the treatment to impart to the patient. This member was castigated by a number of the other members for using these words, and thereby breaking the frame of anonymity so dear to classical psychoanalysis. It was suggested that he was either not properly listening to the patient and/or he was not practicing psychoanalysis by revealing so much about himself. All I could think, at the time of my sharing personal information with my patient as a consequence of her psi-mediated Osbourne dream, was that these same members would have had a field day with me, had I mentioned it or something like it, and I would have been all but drummed out of my own house.

Horses in the House

Speaking of houses, here is another example. Psi is not going to confine itself, as we have seen, to an interchange between a patient and an analyst. It can also bring in not just material from the analyst's life but dynamic material from the internal life of those closest to the analyst. For example, one morning, my significant other said that she dreamt in the nighttime about two horses in the house. Then during the day, Ms. Q, whom I previously mentioned. in her session brought me a pillow of hers to keep for her analytic sessions. She had been uncomfortable with the couch pillow and in what I believed was an enactment on my part and yet what I also felt was an important accommodation (for her to be physically comfortable in this new setting during the early part of her treatment), I yielded to her request the previous session to bring her own pillow. Whatever the psychological fall-out, I thought we could analytically address it subsequently. Near the end of the present session, Ms. Q. now told me she read a book that had a horse in the house!

I then mentioned to her that someone brought me a dream that very morning that had a horse in the house. She said, "That is so strange" and then she said,, instinctively (and insightfully as my previous patient example): "You are the common denominator." She then mentioned, holding the pillow she brought, "This is like my horse." She knew that one of the reasons she had brought the pillow into this "analytic house" in addition to comfort was that she wanted me to "think of her," and she understood that she must be competing with my other patients. What I did not reveal at that time is that she was through psi competing with my significant other. Again, Ms. Q. was tapping into my life as she had when my significant other had diverticulitis.

Chilling Precognition

This is an example of a precognitive dream of one of my patients. I have experienced many in my clinical practice. This one is particularly chilling and understandably one might prefer to ignore it or look the other way. In fact, I have hesitated to write about it because it is so disquieting, but then that has been my point all along. So I feel compelled to recount it.

Ms. B, the twice weekly patient, originally from Spain, has previously dreamt that her daughter has been in a car accident. She had also dreamt previously that I am driving a car too fast in which she is a passenger, which we have understood to be a comment that I am "going too fast" in her treatment, which frightened her. Now at the end of one session, she remembered a dream from the previous night:

> I am driving a car and you were driving a car, and I was frustrated because you were going faster than I was, and I kept pushing down on the gas pedal, but my car would not move faster.

This session before this one, Ms. B had expressed how much she loved me, which represented a significant emotional step but she hesitated when she wondered about how I felt about her. At the same time, she has been unusually flirtatious lately. A beautiful woman, ambivalent and confused about her attractiveness, she recounted showing too much of her cleavage in a professional setting and being seductive to a married man whom she very much loved but whom she could not believe would reciprocate to her. In fact, Ms. B. had a history of not being able to pursue available men, which had been the major focus of her treatment, where she seems unable to work through her Oedipal wishes. The dream suggests a competitive wish toward me on the one hand, and a sexualized desire for doing things together on the other. (Curiously, Papazian recounts a similar competitive dream of his psi-consumed patient involving which one of them should drive a fast-moving racing car, a dream that had a destructive telepathic element to it as well [Papazian, 2017, p. 1181].) As has so often happened when Ms. B. felt a closeness toward me, she subsequently became anxious, because of the intrusion of Oedipal longings, which then would lead her to be self-judgmental.

A week later, I received an evening cell phone call from Ms. B. something which had never previously happened. She was distraught and had meant actually to call my office phone. She explained that her daughter was in the hospital and asked for a change in time for the next day, which I provided. When she came in, she told me that her 20-year-old daughter was in a car accident in which another car hit hers, resulting in serious injury to one of her arms. The driver of the other car was an elderly man ("older than you," she added), who sideswiped her daughter's car when she was stopped at an intersection and hit other cars too before finally coming to a standstill. The drive claimed that his brake pedal did not work, but subsequently the policeman tried and it worked fine. The implication was that as an elderly driver he pressed the gas mistakenly when he meant to press the brake.

All of this has a further personal history of Ms. B, which we had often discussed, that relates dynamically to these events. Ms. B when she was herself a teenager, was very much attracted to an uncle who was much more attentive to her than her own father, and considerably more fun. He took her, just the two of them, on a bike trip. She adored being with him; but then on one hill, he sped fast ahead of her. She tried to keep up but ended up not being able to control her bike, and fell, seriously injuring one arm. She never consciously blamed her uncle, but in her dynamics, it often seemed that this event registered as a self-punishment for her interest in him.

The dynamic parallels here are striking, as are the possible psi components. But we never explored the precognitive psi aspect of Ms. B's dream in her treatment. Yes, the focus was on Ms. B's feelings of guilt for her aggressive wishes toward her daughter, which even before this incident had been a continuing focus, but without the psi element added. I did not feel that I could hazard, at a time when Ms. B was particularly emotionally vulnerable, which lasted for a long time, an examination of the precognitive psi elements even though I was acutely aware of them. In this respect, my reaction was very different than Eisenbud's would have been, who claimed there was no circumstance in which introducing psi explanations could not facilitate dynamic understanding. It seemed to me that Ms. B was working with enough guilt as it was without adding to it. My concern was that, if I had focused on the psi elements, Ms. B would then feel even more responsible than she already did, given the possible implications of the precognitive aspect of her dream; and would not be able to entertain an aggressive psi hypothesis as contributing to what had happened. In fact, she told me subsequently that before the accident she had been having dreams of her daughter dying which she had not mentioned to me at the time. Now, after this terrible incident, her dreams often were brutally and graphically sadistic toward men—ostensibly because of the old man who caused her daughter's injury but directed toward men in general based on her experience with her father and uncle growing up and of course transferentially toward me (another older man who at times she believed "drove" too fast and incompetently, and a man toward whom she had expressed Oedipal longing)—as a way of coping with her anxiety about her own aggressiveness.

Psi in Supervision: The Surround Expands

As we have seen, one need not assume that psi in clinical practice will be "well-behaved" confining itself to the boundaries between the analyst and his patient. Unconsciously driven, psi often permits the analyst's other patients to get into the act. And as we have also seen, loved ones in the analyst's own life can figure in the "paranormal surround" to the extent even of having a dream that corresponds psychically and dynamically with a dream experienced by one of the analyst's patients. Even further (as we have also seen) a patient of an analysand of the analyst, may also enter into the mix, presenting psi-mediated material that corresponds to something taking place in the analysand's therapy or even in the analyst's own life; and of course this should be no surprise, given how psi functions. The psi text, so to speak, often can get very elaborate, resembling as Eisenbud has remarked, the elaborate plot of a mystery story with many characters involved, each vying for attention.

For that matter, in supervision (where an analytic candidate at an institute who undertakes an analysis of a patient as part of what we call "control" work, for which she comes to a senior supervising analyst [usually once a week] for on-going guidance during the course of the control analysis) we can find that one of the supervisee's patients unconsciously enters into the psi conversation. "Don't forget about me," he may seem to be saying. Here is an example:

Ms. X is an analytic patient of mine (whom I previously discussed in Chapter Five with regard to the raccoons she saw coming out of the roof of a neighbor's garage), who was subject to sexual abuse as a child and has been trying to work through this experience. Often in session, she experiences momentary hallucinatory images that are related to her attempts to do the dynamic work. Initially quite disturbed by these images, she now views them as part of the treatment and although they do suggest some degree of a psychotic-like organization, I do not emphasize that point but take them very much as one would any type of fantasy, suggesting to her that since she could not speak of her fantasies as a child, she has found this substitutive way of communicating her wishes to herself. At the end of one session, she sees an elephant's head, which I interpret to her as a phallic symbol. She then says that the trunk is "raised up." We understand this as her ambivalent wish to arouse me, reproducing aspects of the historical sexual abuse.

The next day, a female supervisee discusses with me a patient, who himself is phallically obsessed and has been trying to work through his Oedipal sexual longings on the one hand, and on the other hand has been seeking to impress his neophyte but talented analyst with his masculinity, for which as a child he was much demeaned, and about which now he has much self-punitive ideation. The patient constantly shows off his masculinity in dreams and fantasies to his therapist, desiring to be admired and to arouse her, while often at the same time he attacks her femininity, a kind of double whammy for the supervisee. This difficult patient brings in the following dream, which in a sense symbolizes his life.

> I see Jesus Christ on a cross and his penis is very large and painted a different color than the rest of his body.

The following day, yet another patient of mine, Mr. K, in twice a week face-to-face psychotherapy, who tends toward a narcissistic enjoyment of his masculinity, a tendency which has gotten him into considerable legal trouble by rendering him too self-confident and prone to risky decisions where he over-inflates his abilities, brings in the following dream:

> There is an elephant and I am holding one of his tusks, and it is painted red, and it is hollow, so that I can look through it.

The rub here is how to deal with all this, and I am left it seems without many options. As the analyst to these two patients, and a supervisor who learns of another patient, I can see a theme playing out here: the nature of masculinity. I am able to mention to the supervisee, in our next session, that a patient of mine had a similar dream to her patient, with a painted phallus symbol, and comment on the peculiar struggle that her male patient is going through and how important, but challenging, it is for her to recognize her patient's need to feel masculine and strong (and to integrate his masculinity with his sense of himself) given what began as a pre–Oedipal failure of his parents to acknowledge him. And I can think to myself that the narcissistic patient with the "hollow" tusk may be aware of an emptiness, a fragility, at the core of his acting out, which has been difficult to address in his psychotherapy, as opposed to psychoanalysis and that the dream also suggests a homosexual curiosity on his apart about me and whether my masculinity is hollow.

I can wonder to myself (and to my supervisee) at the need of men to feel masculine and strong. And I can think of how the sexually abused patient as a child seemed aware of this need and addresses it to me. And for that matter I can wonder how all of this plays out for me, as the analyst at the center of this elaborate psi story, and my own masculine feelings or desire to feel powerful. But I cannot think of a way to bring this psi interaction to my woman patient, who exhibits psychotic-like features and who has experienced developmentally such awful boundary violations, leading to a fragile sense of her own individuality. To add psi to the mix in her analysis, even though I believe it exists, seems to me too great a threat to her continued development of a separate self. As a result, I say nothing to her about this. Nor do I comment to the narcissistic patient about the psi element in his dream, dealing with the dream as I would if I did not perceive a psi element there. Not only do I think his therapy not in depth sufficiently to address this element, but I fantasy—whether correctly or not—that he would love his newly discovered psi abilities in a narcissistic way to the detriment of his working through, and we might get considerably side-tracked.

In Summary: A Plea

Psi phenomena exist. Once one recognizes the evidence for telepathy, the easiest of the phenomena to observe and the most frequently verified, there is no logical way to rule out entertaining the other phenomena, as much as we might wish to do so. In addition, as we have seen, psi phenomena can both reflect and have an influence on a person's psychology. One would hope that psychoanalysts, fascinated with a person's psychological functioning, would be open to listening fully for these phenomena. The enriching aspect of psychoanalysis, its play upon the intellect and heartstrings of the analyst, lies in listening *without being judgmental,* in effect letting oneself wonder and experience curiosity about how the analysand thinks and feels. Those of us who are fortunate enough to work as therapists with children are perhaps particularly use to permitting childhood logic and explanations to play themselves out, without interruption from supposedly rational judgment; one can find this approach as well in the magnificent work of Piaget in talking to children about their reasoning processes and observing how those processes develop in Western culture, how in effect cultural reasoning is created, and how incidentally psi phenomena are explained away as being delusions. (This reveals a bias of mine, that adult psychoanalysts should have the experience of treating children as part of their training, because it is so informative about the importance of play and childhood development, including the fascinating development of causal thinking [Reichbart, 2005]). In the same way, it has always seemed to me, one must listen for experiences and associations, of oneself as an analyst and of the adult analysand, without preconceived notions. In other words, to listen for telepathy, precognition and apparitions, without a priori assumptions that these phenomena do not exist, is eminently psychoanalytic.

Psychoanalysts are fond of making definitive statements of how to proceed technically under certain circumstances. One might notice that I have not given well-defined technical "instructions" of what to do when one discovers psi in psychoanalytic treatment. Attempts to do so, whether to confine it as Eshel does to one type of phenomena involving trauma and loss, or to widen it to involve every patient who exhibits it, regardless of his or her symptomology or regardless of the complex and subtle aspects of therapeutic development during psychoanalysis, as does Eisenbud, seems to me premature. Clearly, in the examples I give, I often struggle on how to proceed or *whether* to proceed in terms of introducing the psi material to the patient, even though I might get dynamic insight into the patient as a result of the material. I think at this stage of the game, that is inevitable. Unfortunately, even though Freud a century ago entertained telepathy in treatment, we still do not have a sufficient number of psychoanalysts who are comfortable with psi material to discuss technical tactics and approaches to psi when it occurs during psychoanalysis. Hopefully, some day we can agree enough at least on the facts to have meaningful discussions or for that matter meaningful disagreements on technique, which are essential features of psychoanalytic dialogue. My hope is that this chapter and the previous one—and this book—will facilitate that.

Similarly—and probably to the disappointment of some psychoanalysts—I have eschewed elaborate theories which consider that, for individual patients, psi is a consequence of separation anxiety, early separation trauma, or a desire to find once again a symbiotic maternal union. Such theories are fine when applied to individual cases but when they are used to *limit* the existence of psi functioning to those individuals solely and those circumstances only, they completely miss the fact that psi phenomena are a part of the daily life of everyone, to a greater or lesser extent, regardless of character structure or early trauma or early separation anxiety. If psychoanalysts were more open to entertaining the phenomena, they would observe it more often in all of their patients and themselves, to say nothing of recognizing aspects of psi that go beyond telepathy.

Let me close with this thought: As part of curative hope, no matter how brutal and sad the internal world of our patients may be, what our profession ultimate desires for them is not only emotional stability but that they will be moved by our clinical work with them into creativity and wonder, into the ability to enjoy beauty, love and admiration for this existence that we share. To so quickly dismiss such intriguing parapsychological data seems to me an unfortunate defensive maneuver on our part. As psychoanalysts, we have historically been able to go against the grain in our belief of the importance of the unconscious and its power, of dreams, of sex and aggression, and in the process, we have questioned popular conceptions as well as what we so often find are "hard" science misconceptions. Why should we proceed any differently with regard to psi phenomena? For the fact is that we do not know how the world is constructed, how existence takes place. It is more than a little presumptuous of us to contend that we do or that we are such experts in reality testing of this nature. What a wonderful and sometimes terrifying thing are the parapsychological data (and how vast they are if only we look at them). They appear to be part of us and part of our world: part of our "surround." Rather than defending against them, we should be delighted to explore them as we would do with anything psychoanalytic and to bring to them the full range of our psychoanalytic understanding for our patients—and ourselves.

Notes

1. How carefully psychoanalysts divorce themselves from entertaining the psi hypothesis was impressed upon me recently, when at a memorial presentation for a recently deceased fellow psychoanalyst, a psychoanalyst spoke of an event that took place after the death that had an uncanny aspect to it. The psychoanalyst, prominent in her field and a devotee of Charles Brenner, felt compelled to tell the audience of the event because it impressed itself upon her (it actually did not require a psi hypothesis in my opinion) and yet at the same time, she also needed to state that she had no belief in parapsychology. This interesting defense is typical of what psychoanalysts and others do: at one and the same time, they acknowledge a phenomenon as "uncanny," and then quickly refuse to invoke the psi hypothesis, as if they would prefer poetic metaphor to science (not unlike literary critics who comment on Shakespeare's depiction of apparitions or predictions [see Chapter One]).

References

Barker, J. (1967) Premonitions of the Aberfan disaster. *Journal of the Society of Psychical Research*, 44: 169–181.

Brottman, M. (2011) *Phantoms of the clinic: From thought-transference to projective identification*. London: Karnac.

De Peyer, J. (2014) Telepathic entanglements: Where are we today? Commentary on paper by Claudie Massicotte. *Psychoanalytic Dialogues*, 24: 109–121.

De Peyer, J. (2016) Uncanny communication and the porous mind. *Psychoanalytic Dialogues*, 25: 156–174.

Eisenbud, J. (1954a) Behavioral correspondences to normally unpredictable future events—part 1, *Psychoanalytic Quarterly*, 23: 205–233.

Eisenbud, J. (1954b) Behavioral correspondences to normally unpredictable future events—part 2, *Psychoanalytic Quarterly*, 23: 355–389.

Eisenbud, J. (1970) *Psi and psychoanalysis: Studies in the psychoanalysis of psi-conditioned behavior*. New York: Grune & Stratton.

Eisenbud, J. (1975) Research in precognition. In S. Dean (ed.), *Psychiatry and mysticism*, pp. 101–110. Chicago: Nelson Hall.

Eisenbud, J. (1982) *Paranormal foreknowledge*. New York: Human Sciences Press.

Eshel, O. (2006) Where are you my beloved?: On absence, loss and the enigma of telepathic dreams. *International Journal of Psychoanalysis*, 87: 1603–1627.

Gymensi, J. (2009) The problem of demarcation: Psychoanalysis and the occult. *American Imago*, 66: 457–470.

Kakar, S., & Kripal, J.J. (Eds.) (2012) *Seriously strange*. New Delhi: Penguin Books.

Lazar, S.G. (2001) Knowing influencing, and healing: Paranormal phenomena and implications for psycho-analysis and psychotherapy. *Psychoanalytic Inquiry*, 21: 112–131.

Massicotte, C. (2014) Psychical transmissions: Freud, spiritualism and the occult. *Psychoanalytic Dialogues*, 24: 88–102.

McEneany, B. (2011) *Messages: signs, visits, and premonitions from loved ones lost on 9/11*. New York: Harper.

Papazian, B. (2017) Telepathic phenomena and separation anxiety. *International Journal of Psychoanalysis*, 98: 1169–1192.

Reichbart. R. (2005) The child's cognitive struggle to understand damage to an important object: A six-year-old's attempt to deal with the trauma of his father's epilepsy. *Journal of Infant, Child, and Adolescent Psychotherapy*, 4(1), 77–97.

Reichbart, R. (2006) On the convergence of folk belief and psychopathology: A demon as introject in a twelve-year-old African-American boy. *Journal of Infant, Child and Adolescent Psychotherapy*, 2006, 5 (4): 459–485.

Robertson, M. (1912) *Futility*. London: Arthur F. Bird.

Rosenbaum, R. (2011) Exploring the other dark continent: Parallels between psi phenomena and the psy-chotherapeutic process. *Psychoanalytic Review*, 98: 57–90.

Schmeidler, G.R. (1945) Separating the sheep from the goats. *Journal of the American Society for Psychical Research*, 39: 47–49.

Schmeidler, G.R., & McConnell, R.A. (1958) *ESP and personality patterns*. Westport, CT: Greenwood Press.

Sondow, N. (2017) *Psychic dreams: Telepathic dream group and 9/11 premonitions*. Manuscript for presentation at the American Society of Psychic Research on March 2, 2017.

Stevenson, I. (1974) *Twenty cases suggestive of reincarnation*. Charlottesville: University of Virginia Press.

Tart, C. (1984) Acknowledging and dealing with the fear of psi. *Journal of the American Society for Psychical Research*, 78: 133–143.

Tart, C. (1986) Psychics fears of psychic powers. *Journal of the American Society for Psychical Research*, 90, 279–292.

Totton, N. (2003) (Ed) *Psychoanalysis and the paranormal: Lands of darkness*. London: Karnac.

Van Luijtelarr, M. (2017) Ostensible clairvoyant and precognitive experiences related to air crashes. *Mindfield, the Bulletin of the Parapsychological Association*, 9 (3), 113–117.

Žižek, S. (2008) *The sublime object of ideology: The essential Žižek*. London: Verso.

EIGHT

The Navajo Hand Trembler: Multiple Roles of the Psychic in Traditional Navajo Society[1]

Introduction

The anthropologist's wife had lost her handbag so the anthropologist hired Gregorio, a Navajo[2] Indian hand trembler, to locate it. Gregorio washed his hands and arms, rolled up his sleeves to the elbow, and went to the top of a hill. He faced north, the direction in which the handbag had been lost, and sprinkled corn pollen on his right hand. The hand soon started to tremble. Then he rubbed the palm of his left hand with the palm of his right; the left hand started to tremble instead. This alternation continued, and with his eyes shut, Gregorio began to make motions with both hands symbolizing the missing bag. He said that it had been left at a local trading post. Indeed, this is where the bag was apparently subsequently found.

Hand trembling, sometimes referred to as "motion-in-the-hand" or as "search(ing) for something without looking," is a standard form of Navajo Indian divination,[3] in which Gregorio was particularly talented. The incident just recounted took place in 1937, and the anthropologist who hired Gregorio and recorded the results was Clyde Kluckhohn, one of the deans of American anthropology. In fact, the incident appears in a 177-page monograph devoted to a "psychobiological" study of Gregorio, called appropriately *Gregorio, the Hand-Trembler*, by A.H. and D.C. Leighton (with Opler, 1949), a husband-and-wife anthropological team working during the 1940s under the auspices of the Peabody Museum of Harvard University. However, if the parapsychologist hopes to find some hard evidence of psi phenomena in this study, he is in for a rude awakening: despite the devotion of an entire study to this personality in his role as hand trembler and despite the incident just related and others similar to it, the authors manage to entirely ignore the phenomena or imply there is "nothing to them." And they do so without any follow-up investigation of the individual cases to determine whether or not Gregorio *did* use sensory means to get his results. This is an example of that strange resistance to entertaining the psi hypothesis that so often overtakes otherwise sensible, even sensitive, observers of human nature. Moreover, it is an example of the gap which persists between the study of anthropology and the study of parapsychology.

The Navajo Reservation Today

Today, the practice of hand trembling continues to flourish on the Navajo reservation—that isolated, semi-desert, yet strangely beautiful swatch of northeastern Arizona, northwestern New Mexico, and a thin slice of southern Utah, which is the ancestral home of the Navajos. With the Painted Desert and Petrified Forest to the south, the Grand Canyon to the west, and Monument Valley in its midst, the reservation and surrounding area are well known to the American public for their natural scenery. What is not generally known is that the reservation is approximately 25,000 square miles in area (in size comparable to the state of West Virginia), by far the largest reservation in the United States, and that the Navajo tribe is far and away the largest extant North American Indian tribe. The tribe has grown from a relatively small one of some 10,000 persons at the time of its completed capture in 1866 (by Kit Carson and General Carleton) to approximately 120,000 persons at present (*The Navajo Nation*, 1975, p. 117), thus comprising about one ninth of the present North American Indian population. Its extreme isolation has permitted the continuance of traditional Navajo customs, perhaps more so than in the case of the customs of less isolated tribes. While there are certain minor variations in hand trembling (individual and regional idiosyncrasies in the use of prayers, singing, or the sprinkling of material other than corn pollen), the basic technique is the same throughout the reservation. Using this technique, the hand trembler plays a variety of different roles in traditional society and directs his psychic powers toward multiple ends.

The Hand Trembler as a Finder of Lost Objects

The incident recounted by Kluckhohn concerning Gregorio's location of the missing handbag involves a lost inanimate object, but hand tremblers are also consulted to find animate objects (such as strayed horses or sheep, and missing people), and stolen animate and inanimate objects. For example, a sampling of the available recorded anecdotal incidents concerning hand tremblers' attempts to locate such objects includes the following:

> The traders Arthur and Franc Newcomb hire the hand trembler Hosteen Beall to locate three thousand dollars worth of jewelry stolen from their trading post. The hand trembler leads Arthur Newcomb to a cave in which the jewelry has *been* hidden [Newcomb, 1964, p. 143].

> Hosteen Beall is hired by the Newcombs to locate a Navajo man who tried to kill the wife of a neighboring trader, then fled. Hosteen traces him to a mountain hideout [Newcomb, 1964, p. 143].[4]

> Hosteen Beall successfully locates the Newcombs' three missing saddle horses which, it develops, were borrowed by some Navajos to take part in a horse race [Newcomb, 1964, pp. 143–144].

> Gregorio locates through hand trembling some lost horses after the owner had looked for them for several days without success [Leighton & Leighton, with Opler, 1949, p. 160].

> Anthropologist William Morgan hires a hand trembler to locate a stolen necklace. The hand trembler describes where the thief came from, how he entered the hogan, where he went, and what he did. But the hand trembler cannot see the thief's face clearly. A stargazer (another type of diviner who has since largely disappeared) is called in and makes the final identification [Morgan, 1936, p. 30].

Unfortunately, none of the incidents rises to the level of carefully recorded and cross-checked information.

The Hand Trembler as a "Diagnostician"

The hand trembler has another role as well, probably the one for which he is best known: that of the "diagnostician" within the traditional medical system of the Navajos. Within this system there are three types of practitioners: the herbalist, who knows a variety of medicinal plants for symptomatic relief of illness; the hand trembler who in more serious cases divines the cause of illness and makes an appropriate referral; and the Singer or medicine man who cures the seriously ill patient through elaborate and painstaking rituals which center upon the use of a sand painting in a hogan and the singing of traditional chants.

The hand trembler's role as diagnostician is determined by Navajo etiology in which illness can come from a variety of causes. Most frequently, it is assumed to be the result of the violation of some cultural prohibition by the patient or by a close relative. Traditional Navajo society is hedged with rules and strictures concerning every aspect of life, some of the better known being a prohibition on touching anything that has been struck by lightning or on entering a hogan or house in which someone has died. In other instances, illness may result from a "bad" dream experienced by the patient, particularly a dream in which a living relative dies or in which the patient sees a deceased relative. Least often (when the illness is particularly recalcitrant to cure, or when some of its aspects seem strange to the Navajos) the cause may be put down to witchcraft practiced against the patient (Kluckhohn, 1967). Regardless, cure for the illness (or in the case of a "bad" dream, preventive cure) is the appropriate Sing, performed by a medicine man, often at considerable family expense. These Sings,[5] which range from one-day to nine-day ceremonies, include dancing of people in costume, public speaking, chanting, group discussions—all ritualized in nature—and the attendance of the extended family and surrounding community. The Sing ultimately centers upon the medicine man and his patient in the curative hogan (often especially constructed for the occasion).

The training of a medicine man (who during his lifetime may learn two or three Sings) is laborious, sometimes involving 15 years. He must learn great quantities of ritual chant, the production of several detailed sand paintings, and the recitation of the myth connected with the ceremony. The purpose of the ceremony is to restore to "harmony" the ill person whose illness is a manifestation of the fact that he has gotten out of harmony with the forces of nature (Leighton & Leighton, 1942, p. 205). The "group therapy" aspects of the Sing ceremony have been noted by psychiatrists and one analyst has pointed out that the manipulation of the mythic and ritualistic symbols is similar to the manipulation of the manifest content of a dream (Pfister, 1932).

The hand trembler's duty as diagnostician, whether he is consulted initially or, as often happens, when a medicine man's ceremony has not produced the desired result, is to determine what taboo has been violated (or in the alternative, the meaning of the dream or the identity of the person who has bewitched the patient), what ceremony must be held, and to which medicine man the patient should go. Diagnostic hand trembling is not unlike hand trembling for the purpose of finding lost objects. The same ritual with corn pollen and the same trembling of the hand occurs, although the event usually takes place in the hogan. In addition, the hand trembler may sprinkle corn pollen in a ritualized design on the patient and run his hand over him. The trembling hand may draw outlines in the sand, erasing the drawings until the "correct" one is hit upon. The "correct" drawing will resemble some section of a particular sand painting and thus, from it, the hand trembler will know which ceremony to recommend to his patient.

Miscellaneous Roles of the Hand Trembler

In addition, there are other roles which the Navajo hand trembler played in the past or continues to play, although they are less frequently reported. For example, hand trembling was used in the past to find water when a party was in a strange territory, and to predict the outcome of a war raid or hunting venture (Hill, 1935).[6] In certain instances, rather than being an intermediary in the Navajo medical system, the hand trembler will use his technique to perform psychic healing or to prescribe treatment for cure. For example, Gregorio had a specialty of assisting in difficult childbirth by applying his trembling hand to the woman's body. This type of case is recounted a number of times by the Leightons (with Opler, 1949), although they apparently never observed it. In addition, there are indications that the hand trembler is believed to have general precognitive abilities, although these instances are infrequently reported. Lastly, in an area even more difficult to penetrate than the others, the hand trembler acts as a "psychic detective" in cases of bewitchment by locating the (usually buried) witchcraft paraphernalia which has been placed near the residence of the victim as a curse.

The Call to Hand Trembling

Unlike the Navajo medicine man, the hand trembler comes by his power suddenly. He may have "hand trembling sickness," which Gregorio had and which is recognized by the community as a sign that the victim is to be a hand trembler. Gregorio describes his attack of hand trembling sickness during his late adolescence as waking up in the middle of the afternoon, after going to sleep because he was feeling woozy, to discover that "my legs and feet and whole body felt all large, just like when you sit down and your legs go to sleep. I felt that all over my body." Then his hands started shaking and continued to do so all afternoon, stopped, then started again and into the night. "It was dark night, but I thought the sun was shining on me. I felt like the sunshine was coming in the door." The feeling of sunshine disappeared, but he felt a sensation as if something was running through his body, starting at the toes and going on up to the top of his head. After that the sensations disappeared, recommenced briefly during the next day while herding sheep, and then disappeared fully (Leighton & Leighton with Opler, 1949, p. 20). The community took this illness as a sign that Gregorio had "hand trembling" and thus when he was in his early twenties he was asked to practice a skill he had only observed in others before.

In other cases, the hand trembler may come upon his power for the first time spontaneously when he is in attendance at a curing ceremony for someone, in which case the trembling is recognized as a sign and the advice of the new hand trembler is followed. Less frequently, hand trembling may commence for the first time in a patient at a curing ceremony. Regardless, the hand trembler's apprenticeship is short rather than long and arduous like that of the medicine man. He may learn a few prayers, may even improvise some of his own—something which a medicine man bound by strict ritual cannot do, and if his advice begins to bring results, he is almost immediately "in business." As indicated by Kluckhohn (1939), the hand trembler is in the "shamanistic" tradition whereas the medicine man is in the "priestly" tradition; interestingly enough, the two professions in general are mutually exclusive—a full-fledged medicine man does not do hand trembling. Compared to the medicine man, the hand trembler's remuneration is small: in 1937 in a case of miraculous cure, Gregorio received a saddle horse, but usually he received two to five dollars for his services, which supplemented his meager earnings as a shepherd.

Hand Trembling as Trance

What actually is happening in hand trembling? Kluckhohn in observing Gregorio searching for his wife's handbag states: "My *impression* was that he was forcing his arm to move" (Leighton & Leighton with Opler, 1949, p. 160). Nowhere do the Leightons, even though they were both psychiatrists, comment upon the psychological state that the hand trembler was in during the ceremony or the trembling itself, although they do quote Gregorio as saying that "We must go by this trembling hand. Whenever your hand starts trembling, do not try to hold it back, let it go and see what it will do. Just follow your arm, like" (p. 20). Wyman (1936a) states more directly: "It must first be understood that the motion is involuntary—it starts and stops without volition—and that since the diagnostician closes his eyes and turns his face away from the patient, he does not see what his hand is doing" (p. 240). Wyman compares the trembling hand as it draws pictures in the earth to the phenomenon of automatic writing. Only the psychologist Morgan (1931, p. 393) discusses the fact that the hand trembler may be in a trance and compares his performance, with marked ambivalence toward whether the trance is feigned or authentic, to that of a "medium" among white men. However, if the anthropologists are unwilling to fully characterize the nature of hand trembling, the Navajos themselves seem to have no difficulty in recognizing it as an altered state of consciousness, as illustrated by a striking story related by Dr. Robert L. Bergman, Chief Psychiatrist of the Indian Health Service (Bergman, 1973).

In about 1970, Dr. Bergman was demonstrating hypnosis for the first time to a group of Navajo medicine men at a "School for Medicine Men" funded by the federal government (more of which later). He demonstrated depth tests, somnambulism, age regression, positive and negative hallucinations, and posthypnotic suggestion, using a Navajo woman as a subject. The usually laconic and stolid medicine men were deeply impressed. Said one: "I'm 82 years old, and I've seen white people all my life, but this is the first time that one has ever surprised me. I'm not surprised to see something like this happen because we do things like this, but I am surprised that a white man should know anything so worthwhile." But the clincher came when the medicine men pointed out the resemblance of the woman's hypnotic state to the trance state of the hand trembler and then requested that the hypnotized woman diagnose something! Dr. Bergman, caught entirely unprepared by this development and evidently unacquainted with parapsychological literature, at first was reluctant until, after much insistence by the medicine men, he agreed to let the subject do a "weather prediction," as this seemed to him relatively harmless and drought was a cause of much concern at the time. The subject complied, predicting the rainfall for the next six months. Dr. Bergman's comment: "I make no claim other than the truthful reporting of facts: She was precisely correct." What is an interesting aspect of this is that the medicine men assume that an altered state of consciousness, regardless of its particular nature, may facilitate psi phenomena. In addition, this is one of the few reports I have seen in which precognitive ability is considered part of the hand trembler's repertoire.

The Hand Trembling Experience

While the anthropological accounts are not concerned with the evidence for the existence of psi phenomena, they do report at length what the hand trembler experiences in certain cases as he does hand trembling. "While the hand is moving," states Wyman (1936a), "the diagnostician thinks of various diseases or causes of disease. When something tells him that he is thinking of the correct one, he then thinks of various chants which might cure the disease; then, of what medicine man might be the best one to give the chant; then perhaps of plant medicines or other therapeutic measures" (p. 240). Gregorio describes his process more vividly:

> Then start thinking about the Singer, think about the Singers' names, take one at a time. You see you pray already that you going to point the Singer out that will do good for the patient. As you going along, the Hand-trembling kind of pushes the Singer off. When you going along like that, sometime you come to the Singer that the Hand-trembling will push ... right inside the hogan, and the Hand-trembling will kind of point all his medicine, kind of shake it in, bring it in [Leighton & Leighton with Opler, 1949, pp. 54–55].[7]

The process of determining the cause of the illness could be considered a psychic one; that is, a telepathic determination of which prohibition the patient or relative violated in the past. Indeed, the hand trembler runs through such possible causes in his mind. But, as Morgan (1931) has observed, it is difficult to ascertain (regardless of agreement by the patient or relatives) whether the hand trembler's statement about the past is either psychically arrived at or accurate, for it is likely that at some time any Navajo has violated a prohibition in this ritual-oriented society, or believes he has.[8]

Other Aspects of Hand Trembling

Other aspects of hand trembling are of some interest. The first is that the Navajos recognize that excessive hand trembling is related to madness. There is a ceremonial cure of such a condition, and diagnosticians apparently feel that they must have ceremonials at intervals regardless of any organic difficulty. One informant stated in regard to a hand trembler: "He doesn't like to do hand trembling any more. He's afraid he is getting sick from doing it too much without being sung over" (Kluckhohn, 1939, pp. 69–70).

The second aspect is that the Navajos assume that the "gift" of hand trembling runs in family lines, and the evidence indicates that this is true. Says Kluckhohn (1939): "In sum, out of the 16 [hand tremblers] there is but a single one who is not related to at least one other diagnostician" (p. 67). Needless to say, whether this characteristic is genetically determined or the result of the increased exposure of individuals growing up in a family containing a practicing hand trembler (or a combination of these two factors) has not been determined. Lastly, it should be noted that a woman may be a hand trembler, although this happens infrequently, just as on rare occasions a woman may be a "medicine woman."

The Hand Trembler in His Society

The position of the hand trembler in his society is worthy of some thought. To individuals in Navajo culture with psychic talents, a respected place, a partial livelihood, and an opportunity to do some-thing to benefit the society may be accorded. What is most interesting is that the multiple talents of the psychic are used and directed by the society: he is a finder of lost or stolen objects; his precognitive abilities are sought; he is an integral part of a complicated traditional medical system in which his allegedly psychic powers are used to diagnose illness and heal or refer patients; he determines who may be using psychokinetic forces to injure a patient; and in other times, he located water or anticipated where the wild game was. In contrast, in Western society today the psychic has no such place. He survives on the fringes, either eking out a precarious existence or "going public" and giving way to the adulation of the masses; either subjected to testing for testing's sake without using his ability to benefit society in general, or surviving as a kind of extension of an individual parapsychologist's interests and sometimes on his largesse. Perhaps Tenhaeff in Holland has been unusually successful in his work with psychically talented individuals such as Croiset because he (within the context of a country apparently somewhat sympathetic to parapsychological claims) permits these psychics a measure of security, work within the structure of the society directed toward a tangible end rather than a mere exhibition of phenomena, and protection from the assaults of skeptics (Pollack, 1964). There is, of course, another side to this cultural comparison: the societally-approved roles of the Navajo psychic, while admittedly multiple, are nevertheless carefully circumscribed (in terms of technique and purpose) by the society in a way in which the many roles played by psychics in Western cultural history are not.

Psi and Navajo Culture

It should be kept in mind that the hand trembler fits into a cultural matrix in which psi phenomena are readily accepted. Another example of this acceptance is the traditional Navajo view of dreams. Traditional Navajos think of dreams as possibly precognitive and when a "bad" dream occurs (one, for example, in which there is the death of a living relative), they are under a cultural adjuration to communicate the dream to someone, and they may seek out a hand trembler in order to have a Sing to avoid the consequences of the dream (Morgan, 1936). "We do a little something about our dreams," an informant told Lincoln (1970), who extensively recorded Navajo dreams, "things like having to Sing, to avoid our dreams, and what will happen from them in the future." I myself was told by a Navajo informant of a precognitive dream (dreamt on two separate occasions) of a death in her family which she realized, after death struck, involved a classic case of substitution. She had dreamed of a different family member dying, but under the same unusual circumstances—being run over by a car going backwards. She felt that she had failed to do what Navajo tradition taught—that is, rid the dream of its possibly bad effects by relating it to someone, and that her failure to do so had perhaps contributed to the outcome. Nevertheless, as Bergman (1973) has observed, only the surface of Navajo understanding of the subconscious (and one might add of psi processes) has been pierced. The Navajo medicine men with whom Bergman worked were funded by a grant from the National Institute of Mental Health (Luce, 1971) to continue their teachings in part so that this understanding would not disappear in the wake of the cultural changes taking place on the reservation.[9]

North American Indians and Parapsychology

The anthropological hand trembler studies are not scientifically satisfying from the parapsychological viewpoint (although they contain interesting data), but they do raise a question: Why haven't parapsychological studies been done of Navajo hand trembling or, for that matter, of the psi phenomena characteristic of other American Indian tribes? For example, the yuwipi ceremony of the Sioux would be worth investigating for it has certain marked resemblances to a spiritualist séance—a physically confined "medium," a darkened room, manifestations of lights in the air, and other physical phenomena (Lame Deer & Erdoes, 1972). Parapsychological studies have been attempted or carried out of preliterate peoples all over the globe from Africa to Australia (see, e.g., Angoff & Barth, 1974) and it is therefore doubly strange that virtually no attempts have been made to work with North American Indians who are so much closer in terms of distance to the parapsychological centers in the United States. In fact, 1 have been able to find in the literature only one study of North American Indians; it involved an ESP test (using ordinary playing cards) of Western Canadian Plains Indian children, with virtually no reference to the cultural attributes of the subjects (Foster, 1943).[10] Such limited testing (in terms of conception, design, and type of target used) seems bound to fail, particularly when dealing with a cultural group which often has as an attribute an anti-competitive view very much opposed to the rationale of Western psi-testing procedures.

The first active plea to study psi phenomena in preliterate cultural settings from the point of view of their evidential value was probably made by Humphrey (1944). More recently, Van de Castle (1974) has warned that the opportunity for studying psi in these settings is rapidly diminishing as civilization encroaches. The promise of such studies seemed high after Rose's (1956) fascinating account of the psychical practices of Australian aborigine "clever men" or shamans and of the psi tests he carried out with them, but in many ways that promise has not as yet been fulfilled. Recent studies which have provided the most suggestive results and are in this sense most fulfilling have been the least controlled; they involved investigators willing to meet the psi-talented individual on his own cultural ground (Boshier, 1974; Castaneda, 1968). The data from this type of research are phenomenologically fascinating, but the fact remains that only the rare investigator is willing to act as sorcerer's apprentice and subject himself to the hallucinations, fits, hypnotic states, etc., which seem to be a necessary part of the role. Moreover, this approach, although to my mind a valid one, is fundamentally different from and cannot easily be combined with a controlled experimental approach.

In fact, there are good reasons why controlled studies of psi in preliterate cultural settings are few and far between. The difficulties of any psi investigation are great enough to begin with, and when one adds to them the difficulties of cross-cultural investigation (language barrier, problems of cross checking, reluctance of informants to confide, pervasive fear of witchcraft, different concepts of time and causality, inability to bring the phenomena outside the cultural setting, and culture shock[11] on the part of the investigator himself), the task may seem almost impossible. Thus I am not overly optimistic about obtaining the type of "hard data" which parapsychologists seem to want from such studies. Nevertheless, having said all this, I still think there is much to be learned from Navajo and other American Indian informants in semi-controlled settings, and if results were forthcoming in such studies, they would add valuable pieces to the jigsaw puzzle of how psi fits into the universe.

Tentative Proposals for a Parapsychological Study of the Navajo Hand Trembler

I doubt that the Navajo hand trembler is any more "psychic" than the shaman of other American Indian tribes. But there may be certain advantages in studying the hand trembler. One is that the size of the tribe presents a very large sample to choose from and thus a greater likelihood of obtaining meaningful data. A second is that the tribe itself is very much involved in trying to integrate traditional aspects of its culture into modern life on the reservation in terms of educational and institutional programs, and thus such a study might be well received by the Navajo community. The third is that the presence on the reservation of a large number of professionals (teachers, lawyers, doctors, etc.), both Navajo and non–Navajo, represents an important resource for help in gathering data. The fourth and final advantage is that the line of demarcation between the roles of medicine man (as priest) and hand trembler (as shaman) is fairly clear-cut; that is, the psychic activities of the hand trembler are not so tightly integrated into a closed religious structure that gaining access to them would be difficult.

Ideally, a parapsychological study would have to be a long-term one, dependent upon the cooperation of those living on the reservation for observation and follow through. It would, as I see it, follow a pattern set by the early work of the (British) Society for Psychical Research, with collection and analysis of existing data; then location of contemporary hand tremblers with recording and evaluation of their spontaneous performances; and finally, actual testing of hand tremblers. I doubt that the psi the hand trembler apparently exhibits in roles other than that of finder-of-lost-objects would be susceptible to testing under controlled conditions (although I would be glad to be proved wrong on this point). Methods for testing this "finding" ability, however, could rather easily be devised, perhaps along the lines of those reported by Cadoret (1955).[12] But before deciding on specific testing procedures it might be wise to await the results of the first two approaches mentioned above, and also—most importantly—to consult with the hand tremblers themselves as to the methods *they* would find most acceptable.

The Broader Perspective

Despite the exaggerated fears of witchcraft which permeate the Navajo tribe (Kluck-hohn, 1967) and American Indian society in general; there is at heart an acceptance of phenomena which Western society has all but completely rejected. I have talked about this dichotomy with a number of well-educated American Indians and they see it as a key (though little publicized) conflict in making an adjustment to Western culture. For example, when I asked a Sioux Indian attorney, who still attends the yuwipi ceremony as he did in his youth, how he could maintain his belief in the psi phenomena of the ceremony while being subjected to the antithetical teachings of Western schools, he replied: "By pure arrogance!" And another Sioux Indian, who is pursuing an advanced degree and is quite knowledgeable about parapsychology, confided to me in a moment of exuberance that if it were not for the problem of earning a living, he would have preferred to devote himself to the study of psi phenomena in his own culture, phenomena which—he assured me—were simply accepted as part of the way the world worked and were not even given a label to differentiate them from other ways of knowing or interacting with the world.[13] (However, my later attempts to get him to join a parapsychological study group met with abysmal failure because he felt the participants were "too academic.") Lastly, and more to the point, in discussing psi in Navajo culture with me a well-educated Navajo woman concluded with the observation that such phenomena were merely individual instances of a larger dichotomy: the fact that for the Navajo, "mind" could actively affect the way the world operated and what happened in it. For her this meant an individual policy, learned in part from her own culture, of massive attempts at self-control in order not to think injurious thoughts.

I have had some personal experience of the effect of this dichotomy: I lived and worked on the Navajo and Hopi Indian reservations for over a year (1968–1969) and during this period I had very little contact with the "outside" world. When I left I found that I had absorbed, without realizing it, ways of thinking and theories of causality foreign to those of Western culture. No single experience was overwhelmingly significant. Rather, the cumulative effect of my exposure to a series of incidents in my daily contact with Navajos revealed to me a concept of "psychic determinism" vastly different from the one I had learned from my own culture. It was only upon leaving the reservation and getting back to the theories of causality and anti-psi prejudice of my own culture (which I quickly discovered was in some sense still my own prejudice) that I realized I was missing an essential "analytic link" to explain my experiences. It was this, in part, which brought me to the study of parapsychology (about which I knew absolutely nothing prior to my Navajo adventure) in an attempt to assimilate my experiences into my understanding and put "mind" back into the causal picture. (In contrast, my Western culture colleagues on the reservation remained on the whole antagonistic to these ideas.)

I imagine a similar sort of difficulty confronts almost every American Indian, initially exposed to traditional culture, when he attempts to cross the cultural line into our society and is handed the official passport in which is stamped the condition that he leave his belief in psi behind him. This conflict should be (but unfortunately is not) one of the key concerns of ethno psychiatrists—who seem on the whole as impervious to entertaining the psi hypothesis as their single-culture colleagues. No doubt, the introduction of the psi hypothesis would considerably enlighten the cases of individuals who experience difficulties in adjustment when they find themselves immersed in a society which, unlike theirs, is basically antagonistic to psi concepts.[14]

From my own experience, American Indian society tends to over-emphasize the place of psi in the universe, a tendency most tellingly revealed in its obsession with witchcraft. Nevertheless, the study of psi phenomena in American Indian society might well give us, if nothing else, some understanding of how and why Western culture has developed the even more curious cultural anomaly of refusing to believe that such phenomena exist.

Notes

1. Lest the reader be misled, I should mention that, although I am personally familiar with various aspects of Navajo life, I have never had the opportunity to observe a hand trembler at work.

2. I can discover no reason for the use of the two spellings "Navaho" and "Navajo" in publications, sci-

entific or popular. In some instances, the same anthropologist has used different spellings in different publications. I have elected to use "Navajo" because it is the spelling employed by the Navajo Tribal Council and the Navajo people generally.

3. In addition to hand trembling, there is divination by star-gazing, crystal-gazing, and listening (Morgan, 1931), and by the ingestion of *Datura* or jimsonweed (Hill, 1938). What these have in common is that they are methods of inducing trance in the diviner. Some of these forms have apparently disappeared; hand trembling remains the most frequent form.

4. This and the preceding incident are somewhat atypical because the hand trembler evidently led his client to the missing object.

5. According to one estimate, there were once about 60 Sings which fell into various classifications (Wyman and Kluckhohn, 1938). They have considerably dwindled in number with the process of acculturation. How many there are today is uncertain.

6. The Chiricahua Apaches, who lived south of the Navajos, used muscular tremors as a diagnostic sign to indicate whether a situation was good or bad; these tremors occurred to a greater or lesser degree with all tribal members. The greatest agreement among the members as to which tremors were significant involved those on the outside and inside of the legs and above and below the eyes (Opler, 1965, pp. 187–190).

7. In another instance, a hand trembler stated that the revelation comes directly from the Gila Monster (the god responsible for the hand trembling gift). "You can hear his voice afar off," the hand trembler said, "just like over a telephone" (Hill, 1935). Wyman (1936b) discusses the origin legends of hand trembling.

8. The Leightons (1942) have written that the "number of things a Navajo has as possible sources of fear are enormous.... The tabus and regulations are really part of a system for avoiding harm, and by their use a Navajo feels at least partially protected. The trouble is, they work two ways, especially when real misfortunes are plentiful, and pile up additional fears and hazards. The situation is not unlike that of the obsessive patient who by his rituals of washing and not touching things attains a form of comfort and security, but at the same time makes life intolerable in other ways because of the number of things he may not do and because of his constant fear of transgression" (pp. 205–206).

9. The Institute funded the Navajo "School for Medicine Men" despite some apparent trepidation about being involved in the "continuance of superstition" (Bergman, 1973). Another federal agency, the National Science Foundation, has funded the publication of studies of North American Indian witchcraft and sorcery (Walker, 1970), although (again!) there is no reference to parapsychology in any of these studies.

10. In addition, there is Stevenson's (1966) excellent study of cases of the reincarnation type among the Tlingit Indians of Southeastern Alaska.

11. This is a factor which may well explain why anthropologists, inundated by the different culture in which they briefly live, protect themselves from investigating the reality of the psi phenomena with which they come in contact (see La Barre, 1972, p. 52).

12. Interested in the possibility of practical applications of ESP, Cadoret asked his subjects to find an object hidden in one of 25 large squares into which his yard had been sectioned.

13. Eisenbud makes this point eloquently [although his use of the term "primitive" is unfortunate]: "The primitive feels the relationships of his thoughts to the outer world to be pretty much of a piece with his relationship to his own body. He takes it for granted that his thoughts can do things. He would find no need for a special theory to account for the psychically caused movements of objects in the presence of mediums. His medicine men and shamans do these things all the time—but only for serious ritual purposes, like re-establishing a mutually beneficent harmony between the tribe and nature" (Eisenbud, 1989, p. 215). Freud made the argument that psi was "the original, archaic method of communication between individuals and that in the course of phylogenetic evolution it has been replaced by the better method of giving information with the help of signals which are picked up by the sense organs" (Freud, 1932, p. 55), although he contended it remained in the background. Of course, if a child is taught by a culture to ignore psi signals over others (which are supposedly preferable), his ability to be attuned to psi or psi communication will undoubtedly diminish.

14. I observed a characteristic example of this, although in reverse: A young Navajo woman had returned to her home on the reservation after a period of extended contact with Western culture. Shortly after her return, she reported that she had seen an unusually large, man-shaped coyote (a common sign of witchcraft among the Navajos) and that a Navajo friend with her at the time had also seen the coyote. It was painfully clear to her, as she attempted to understand what she had perceived, that her own culture accepted the sight as a sign of witchcraft whereas ours would dismissed as an hallucination or a case of *folie à deux*. Thus, the sight only added to her confusion, prompted by her return to the reservation, as to which cultural version of the way the world works she would accept.

References

Angoff, A., & Barth, D. (Eds.) (1974). *Parapsychology and anthropology.* New York: Parapsychology Foundation.

Bergman, R.L. (1973). A school for medicine men. *American Journal of Psychiatry, 130*, 663–666.

Boshier, A.K. (1974). African apprenticeship. In A. Angoff and D. Barth (eds.), *Parapsychology and anthropology.* New York: Parapsychology Foundation, pp. 273–284.

Cadoret, R.J. (1955). The reliable application of ESP. *Journal of Parapsychology, 19*, 203–227.

Castenada, C. (1968). *The teachings of Don Juan.* Berkeley: University of California Press.

Eisenbud, J. (1989) *The world of Ted Serios.* 2d ed. Jefferson, NC: McFarland.

Freud, S. (1932). Dreams and occultism. *Standard Edition,* XXII: 31–56.

Foster, A.A. (1943). ESP tests with American Indian children. *Journal of Parapsychology, 7*, 94–103.

Hill, W.W. (1935). The hand trembling ceremony of the Navaho. *El Palacio, 38*, 65–68.

Hill, W.W. (1938). Navaho use of jimsonweed. *New Mexico Anthropologist, 3*, 19–21.

Humphrey, B.M. (1944). Paranormal occurrences among preliterate peoples. *Journal of Parapsychology, 8*, 214–229.

Kluckhohn, C. (1939). Some personal and social aspects of Navaho ceremonial practice. *Harvard Theological Review, 32*, 57–82.

Kluckhohn, C. (1967) *Navaho witchcraft.* Boston: Beacon Press.

La Barre, W. (1972). *The Ghost Dance: The origins of religion.* New York: Dell.

Lame Deer, J., & Erdoes, R (1972). *Lame Deer, seeker of visions.* New York: Simon & Schuster.

Leighton, A.H., & Leighton, D.C. (1942). Some types of uneasiness and fear in a Navaho Indian community. *American Anthropologist, 44*, 194–209.

Leighton, A.H., & Leighton, D.C., with Opler, C. (1949). Gregorio, the Hand-Trembler, a psychobiological personality study of a Navaho Indian. *Papers of the Peabody Museum of American Archaeology and Ethnology,* Harvard University, 40, No. 1.

Lincoln, J.S. (1970). *The Dream in primitive cultures.* New York: Johnson Reprint Co.

Luce, G. (1971). The importance of psychic medicine: Training Navaho medicine men. In J. Segal (Ed.), *Mental Health Program Reports—No.* 5, Department of Health, Education and Welfare Publication Number (HSM) 72–9042, pp. 20–43.

Morgan, W. (1931). Navaho treatment of sickness: Diagnosticians. *American Anthropologist, 33*, 390–402.

Morgan, W. (1936). Human-wolves among the Navaho. *Yale University Publications in Anthropology,* No. 11. *The Navajo nation: An American colony* (1975) Washington, D.C.: U.S. Commission on Civil Rights.

Newcomb, F.J. (1964). *Hosteen Klah, Navaho medicine man and sand painter.* Norman: University of Oklahoma Press.

Opler, M.E. (1965) An *Apache life-way: The economic, social and religious institutions of the Chiricahua Indians.* New York: Cooper Square Publishers.

Pfister, O. (1932). Instinctive psychoanalysis among the Navahos. *Journal of Nervous and Mental Disease, 76*, 234–254.

Pollack, J.H. (1964). *Croiset the clairvoyant.* Garden City, NY: Doubleday.

Rose, R. (1956). *Living magic: The realities underlying the psychical practices and beliefs of Australian Aborigines.* Chicago: Rand McNally, 1956.

Stevenson, I. (1966). Cultural patterns in cases suggestive of reincarnation among the Tlingit Indians of Southeastern Alaska. *Journal of the American Society for Psychical Research, 60*, 229–243.

Van de Castle, R.L. (1974). An investigation of psi abilities among the Cuna Indians of Panama. In A. Angoff and D. Barth (Eds.), *Parapsychology and Anthropology.* New York: Parapsychology Foundation, pp. 80–97.

Walker, D.E., Jr. (Ed.). (1970). *Systems of North American witchcraft and sorcery.* Moscow: University of Idaho Press.

Wyman, L.C. (1936). Navaho diagnosticians. *American Anthropologist, 38*, 236–246. (a)

Wyman, L.C. (1936b). Origin legends of Navaho divinatory rites. *Journal of American Folk-Lore, 49*, 134–142.

Wyman, L. C., & Kluckhohn, C. (1938). Navaho classification of their song ceremonials. *Memoirs of the American Anthropological Association,* No. 50. Menasha, WI.

NINE

Magic and Psi: Some Speculations on Their Relationship

Introduction

The word *magic* has so many meanings, often contradictory, that I must begin with a definition of the sense in which I shall use the term in this paper: the conscious attempt of an individual to imitate through ordinary sensorimotor means the operation of psi phenomena.[1] Under the term I subsume such practices as legerdemain or sleight of hand, illusion, and the presentation of normally acquired information as psychically obtained. As such, magic has been the bane of parapsychologists since the scientific study of the paranormal began in the late nineteenth century. Much of the work of parapsychology can be seen as an attempt to separate legitimate psi phenomena from phenomena which are the product of sensory cues or normal motor activity. In this separation process, perhaps nothing offends us more than the discovery of an alleged psychic who exclusively practices magic—unless it is the discovery of a genuine psychic who resorts to magic when, for whatever reason, his psi abilities do not operate on schedule. It has been contended that the presence of such magic in the actions of both alleged and genuine psychics has discouraged many scientific investigators from becoming involved in a study which has such a "seamy" side to it. And, however unscientific it may be in theory, it is evident that for some parapsychologists the revelation that a genuine psychic has on occasion resorted to magic is enough to render unreliable any evidence of genuine psi phenomena on other occasions by the same psychic, no matter how carefully witnessed and controlled. In part, it was the spate of mediums or alleged mediums who resorted to magic during the height of Spiritualism which led J.B. Rhine in the 1930s to apply stringent controls in psi experiments so that parapsychology might begin to gain acceptance from the scientific community.

But the general urgency of parapsychologists, particularly in the United States, to get their findings accepted by the scientific establishment, and to isolate psi in pure and unadulterated form, has had an unfortunate consequence: assorted types of magic have been pulled out of the experimental garden like so many weeds and thrown into a trash heap where they tend to be indiscriminately labeled "fraud." In fact, however, in terms of psychological dynamics these "weeds" are often very different from one another: there is the magic practiced by the primitive shaman, that of the contemporary stage magician, that of the con-artist posing as psychic, and that of the talented psychic who, given the opportunity, is not above resorting to magic in his performance. In effect, parapsychologists have failed to realize that these different types of magic are psychological phenomena too, as deserving of examination as the lush and more digestible varieties of psi, and perhaps in some instances even serving in a dynamic relationship to psi phenomena. The glaring fact that magic in the distant past was always associated with apparently genuine psi phenomena and that the attempt to separate the two has been only a fairly recent activity in man's history, should prompt us to take a closer look at the relationship between magic and psi.

The Shaman: Magician and Psychic

The logical place to begin an examination of the relationship between magic and psi is in the psychic practices of preliterate man. From our more secure perspective, it is difficult to realize the extent to which preliterate man considers psi manifestations to be a matter of life and death. Unfortunately, we have done far too few controlled psi experiments among preliterate peoples to know how effectively they are able to direct their psi abilities, but we do know that all preliterate, and by inference prehistoric, societies select an individual, or individuals, with more publicly acknowledged psychic powers than the other members of the society. These individuals occupy the role of shamans, and around their powers, particularly at times when survival is at stake, center the hopes of the entire community.

One of the duties of the shaman in man's earliest hunting societies was to psychically control the movements of game animals, upon which man was entirely dependent for food, so that they could be hunted and killed. We have evidence of this role of the shaman in the caves of southern France and northern Spain in which Paleolithic man held his hunting rituals. On walls and ceilings, prehistoric man drew or incised countless horses, ibex, bison, deer, and other animals; drew projectiles in these images in a form of sympathetic magic; and depicted the shaman dressed as an animal in his role as bringer-of-the-game. We have further evidence of this duty of the shaman in data gathered from Eskimo society, so brutally dependent upon the vagaries of sea and land animals for its sustenance. For example, an Eskimo shaman recounted the origin of his profession as follows:

> In very early times there were no wizards, and people generally were ignorant of many things pertaining to their welfare. Then it came about that there was great famine ... and many died of starvation. One day, many being assembled in one house, a man there present declared that he would go down to the Mother of the Sea. None of those present knew what he meant by that. But he insisted.... And he went down to the Mother of Sea, and brought back her good will and the grant of game for the hunters, so that thenceforward there was no longer dearth, but great abundance of food, and all were happy once more. Since then, the angakoqs [shamans] have learned much more about hidden things, and aided their fellows in many ways [Rasmussen, 1969, pp. 125–126].

The shamanistic ceremony to seek the good will of the Mother of the Sea in times of dearth continued full force until the Eskimo made contact with the technology of Western civilization, and one shaman correctly pointed out what undoubtedly was the most important factor leading to the subsequent loss of power of the shaman:

> Young hunters nowadays have too easy a time of it to trouble about consulting wizards. In the olden days when our food for the whole winter depended on the autumn hunting at the sacred fords, it was a very different matter; all the regular observances and many particular ones in addition were dictated by the angakoqs who knew all about such things [Rasmussen, 1969, p. 198].

In addition to this crucial, early role as bringer-of-the-animals, the shaman is healer, finder-of-lost-objects, weather-predictor-and-controller, and a host of other things, all of which represent activities upon which individual or community survival may depend.[2]

Shamans use certain techniques in these assorted roles to bring psi under control. Many of these techniques, such as singing by the participants in the ritual the shaman performs or the holding of such a ritual in darkness, also play a part in a psychic ritual of Western culture, namely, the mediumistic séance. And other of these techniques, such as the use of drugs by the shaman or the requirement that he go into trance, have been examined by parapsychologists as psi-conducive in laboratory experiments with drugs, hypnosis, ganzfeld stimulation, etc. (see, e.g., Honorton, 1977; Tart, 1977). But, in addition, almost universally shamans are trained in and skilled at the use of magic: sleight of hand and the use of normally-acquired information which they pretend they have obtained psychically. Many reasons for the shaman's reliance on these magical techniques have been suggested: that he uses them to maintain his political power among the gullible; that they reflect the primitive's mistaken belief in the power of sympathetic magic; that when used in healing ceremonies, they are actually beneficial because they are suggestive to the patient; and so on—all of which is perfectly valid, as far as it goes.

But parapsychologists, confronted by this universal presence of magic in the techniques of shamans, have generally managed to miss or avoid the crucial conclusion: that magic is used by the shaman as a psi-conducive technique (as are drugs or trance), a technique which I would suggest actually works given the proper circumstances; and, further, that it is to this psi-conducive element which magic, even the magic of the modern stage magician (so often similar in its particulars yet so different in its purpose), must trace its very origin.

It is in light of the origin of magic as a psi-conducive technique that I have emphasized the life-and-death nature of the attempt to control psi in preliterate societies. For we must remember that we look at the activities of the shaman through Western eyes and with numerous technological alternatives, the product of centuries of Western thinking, comfortably within our reach. And thus we tend to .view the primitive in his dependence on magic as desperate and often pathetic in his attempt to gain control over forces which are so much more powerful than he is. However, why should the primitive, who knows no easy technological escape route when he is confronted by danger, hesitate to gain whatever edge he can over the forces that control survival? And if shamanistic exercises bring results only infrequently, what does it matter? In those instances, he survives to enjoy another day. The point is that our scientific and ethical niceties which lead us to label magic as "fraud" are hardly relevant to the psi activities of the shaman, and are luxuries which he can neither comprehend nor afford. He must use whatever means he can to invoke psi powers, and if sleight of hand sometimes works why should he give up a viable method? From his own perspective, the shaman could equally well accuse the parapsychologist, with his false feedback techniques and his deceptions in describing the real purposes of his experiments, of practicing fraud upon his gullible subjects, and doing so without nearly as much justification as the shaman has.

Elements in Shamanistic Exercises

Before elaborating on my contention that magic began in man's history as a psi-conducive technique which sometimes actually works, let me turn to the various elements in shamanistic exercises and the circumstances under which they appear in preliterate societies. I am speaking of exercises conducted for a variety of purposes, including healing,[3] and circumstances which seem to be particularly relevant to the interaction of magic and psi; I do not contend, however, that any single one of them is universal or necessary. I will merely describe the general design of the shamanistic ceremony and attempt to show the way in which magic as a psi-conducive technique is a part of this design.

The Shaman Is Aware of the Importance of Faith in All Participants

The native participants in the shamanistic ceremony are, in general, of a single affirmative cast of mind concerning the reality of psi, in sharp contrast to the general skepticism of Western man (Van de Castle, 1974). In addition, the shaman himself is very aware that participants in the ceremony should be "believers" in psi phenomena in general and in the shaman's psi ability in particular. For example, the Apache shaman "insists upon the impossibility of curing one who is skeptical of the efficacy of the ceremony to be performed or unconvinced of the integrity of the practitioner" (Opler, 1936, p. 1375). To ensure that the patient does believe, the shaman gives him a series of tasks to perform preparatory to the ceremony. He must bring four ceremonial gifts, such as a downy eagle feather, a piece of turquoise, a pouch of pollen, and buckskin. The alacrity with which he meets these tasks is considered evidence of his faith. Nor is the requirement of faith confined to the patient; it applies to all those in attendance at the curing rite. Apache shamans "have been known to refuse the benefits of their rite," says Opler (1936), "until … persons with a marked tendency to scoff at the supernatural claims of others, have been requested to depart" (p. 1376).

Similarly, the Greenland Eskimo shaman Sorqaq began a performance by walking up pointedly to the outsider Freuchen and asking him to leave. "This is nothing," Sorqaq said, "for a man like you to look at. I am only a big liar, and even if these idiots are stupid enough to believe in me, I never expected you to stand for it. I am only a foolish old man, and what happens here has nothing to do with the truth." In this evidently culturally-determined way, he sought to eliminate a possible doubter in the group, but when Freuchen insisted upon staying to listen to the shaman's wisdom, he reluctantly acceded, saying, "Well, well, if a man is born white he may still be born stupid" (Freuchen, 1935, p. 133).[4]

The Participants Believe That the Magic Performed by the Shaman Is Psi Activity

The native participants fully believe that the shaman's magic tricks are legitimate psi manifestations. The shaman does not inform them that he is "doing magic only." Whereas this aspect of things may appear obvious, the importance of it will become apparent later on in my discussion.

The Shaman Believes in the Efficacy and Importance of Using Magic

Many commentators have discussed the shaman's attitude toward his use of magic in which he expresses, to the trusted anthropologist although not to his people, complete awareness of what he is doing and its justification (see, for example, Elkin, 1948, p. 217, and Opler, 1936, pp. 1376–1377). But perhaps no more vivid example of this exists than Rose's (1956) confrontation with the Australian aborigine "clever man" Fred Cowlin. Rose notes that the clever man pretended to remove physical objects from the body of the patient, but that "'extracting' objects with his fingers is simple sleight of hand; 'sucking' objects out, he secretes them in his mouth beforehand; the blood that he spits out he gets by lacerating his gums." And then Rose confronts Cowlin:

> Bluntly I put it to Fred Cowlin that these were the methods he used, emphasizing my charge by "extracting" a twig from the doctor's [Cowlin's] own arm. Smilingly, he agreed, but immediately stressed the psychological point of view. "They bin get better all the same," he said [pp. 94–95].

And Cowlin's point of view is also expressed in another, even more curious, fact: When the shaman himself is ill, he will go to another shaman, knowing perfectly well the magical techniques employed, but with full belief in their efficacy. As Rose (1956) states: "To the doctor [shaman] the methods are not merely trickery; he sees clearly the psychology involved, and the symbolism, he believes, *aids him in exercising mental forces he genuinely believes himself to possess*" [my emphasis] (p. 95).

The Shaman Has a Flair for the Dramatic

It has been observed that many talented psychics, such as Serios, Croiset, and Geller, have a flair for the dramatic. Similarly, the shaman often is a showman par excellence. For example, Sorqaq, the Greenland Eskimo described by Freuchen (1935), entered the shamanistic setting in the following manner: "Like a stage star making an appearance ... Sorqaq was the last man to enter the house, and he was announced three times before he finally arrived" (p. 133). Another shaman was described by Rasmussen (1969) in a spur-of-the-moment, dramatic attempt to quiet a distressed child:

> He dashed out into the darkness and returned some time later covered with blood and with great rents in his clothing, having fought and defeated the "evil Spirits" that were seeking to harm the child. No one suspected that he snatched up a lump of half frozen seal's blood from the kitchen and with this, and a few self-inflicted wounds upon his garments, supplied the needful evidence to impress his fellow villagers ... [pp. 122–123].

A variety of other magic tricks used by the shaman are theatrical to say the least. The Sioux Indian shaman is tightly bound at the beginning of the yuwipi ceremony, but at the end has become "miraculously" untied (Lame Deer and Erdoes, 1972). The Greenland Eskimo shaman performs the same trick, even disappearing in the course of his ceremony (Freuchen, 1935, p. 134), when he supposedly descends to visit the Mother of the Sea. The Copper Eskimo shaman surreptitiously inserts large teeth into his mouth in the midst of his performance so that he looks like a wild animal (Jenness, 1922, p. 194). The Copper Eskimo also is credited with various feats with sharp implements that appear to be conjuring tricks. For example, he drives a knife into the back wall of a hut, stands in the middle of the floor, removes his coat, and picks up the knife from the ground at his feet; or he thrusts a spear through a man and pulls it out without leaving a mark (Jenness, 1922, p. 199). Ingenious devices—the collapsing arrow of the Navajo, the bag disguised as a piece of cloth of the Menominee—often contribute to the shaman's special effects (Stone, 1962). Ventriloquism is a technique practiced by many shamans in the course of their ceremonies, including those of the Eyak Indian tribe in Alaska (Birket-Smith and de Laguna, 1938, p. 216) and of the Chuckchee tribe (Bogoras, 1960, p. 325). An Eskimo shaman from Wales, Alaska, swallows a foot and a half of a smooth stick he carries prior to conducting a curing ceremony (Thornton, 1931, p. 102), and the Winnebago Indian shamans are trained to feign death from psychic causes in their "shooting ritual" ceremony (Radin, 1920, p. 402). One can see, in most of these magical techniques, analogies to the practices of modern stage magicians.

Similarly, the settings chosen for shamanistic exercises are often dramatic. After all, few settings could equal that selected by prehistoric man for his hunting rituals: the deep underground cave, difficult to locate, dangerous to reach, dark except for the light thrown by torches, and lacking in sensory input. In the same way, the shamanistic setting of pre-literate man may be the interior of a tent, hut, or igloo, darkened for the occasion.[5]

The Shaman Does Not Believe His Power Is Omnipotent

Although preliterate man may overestimate the place of psi in the world, the shaman does not believe he is psychically omnipotent. On the contrary, he is painfully aware of his limitations, and when confronted by a case of illness in which the individual appears too far gone for hope of recovery, he may resort to magic to indicate the hopelessness of the situation. Opler (1936) makes this point in reference to Apache shamans:

> For one thing the Apache shaman is not a credulous dupe of his own supernaturalistic claims and boastings, who undertakes to cure any ailment, no matter how hopeless. Such an indiscriminate practitioner soon finds himself without honor or clients. The seasoned shaman is a shrewd and wary person who has witnessed enough of suffering and death to recognize serious organic disturbances when he sees them, and he is often very reluctant to accept responsibility for the cure of these. In many cases the shaman will simply tell the patient, "You waited too long to call me," or, "The good in you is mostly dead already: I can't help you." One shaman, finding the youth he had been called upon to cure suffering from a most serious case of tuberculosis, resorted to legerdemain to demonstrate to those present that he was unable to be of any assistance. He thrust two eagle tail feathers down the throat of the sick boy and then shook worms from their ends. These worms were large and active. This indicated, he claimed, that they were hungry, that they had already eaten up the youth's lungs and that recovery was therefore unthinkable. Another shaman, correctly gauging the unlikelihood of success in undertaking a cure, appealed to his "power" to tell him what the outcome would be. He was instructed to touch the quill end of a downy feather to the patient's bared chest and to withdraw from the case if the feather should fall. The feather did fall, and the shaman made his exit solemnly but with every evidence of relief [pp. 1372–1373].

The Rationale for Magic

Certain principles of shamanistic exercises can be extrapolated from the elements in these exercises which I have already discussed above. The shaman is aware that he is not entirely in control of psychic phenomena. Not only does he recognize that there are certain limits to his power, he also recognizes that everyone present—whether principal or observer—may contribute to the result. Parapsychologists are familiar with this concept. The results of mediumistic sittings, for example, are often as dependent upon the sitters as the medium, or may be as much a product of a sitter as of the medium (see, e.g., Eisenbud's [1975] study of the "professional" sitter, Florence Marryat). And the outcome of laboratory experiments on psi may be a product of the paranormal influence not only of the experimenter, but also of the observers, the assistant who checks the data, the investigator who designs but does not conduct the tests, and so on (Kennedy and Taddonio, 1976; White, 1976).

The shaman is also aware of another, closely related principle: the beliefs of those present (including himself) as to the possibility of producing psi phenomena may affect the results. As a consequence, the shaman is usually reluctant to permit even a single skeptic to be present on the ground that a skeptic is likely to act as a deterrent to the successful expression of psi. Parapsychologists have of course been familiar with this concept since Schmeidler conducted her now-classic "sheep-goat" experiments in which subjects who believed in the existence of ESP (the sheep) tended to score higher on ESP tests than did subjects who did not believe in ESP (the goats) (Palmer, 1971; Schmeidler and McConnell, 1958). Therefore, to use parapsychological terminology, the shaman generally insists that his audience be composed entirely of sheep.[6]

Finally, the shaman is intent upon creating a dramatic atmosphere, heightening the emotions of those present and focusing their attention as a means of inducing psi. One can see in this shamanistic emphasis upon the dramatic the beginnings of our modern drama. We are well aware of how such drama creates what has been termed "suspension of disbelief": we weep at a death which we realize is entirely fictitious, and shiver in terror at a horror movie when observing what we know to be mere images thrown on a screen. For that matter, the great actor, too, appears to believe, at some level, in the reality of his role, for it leads him to the expression of emotions associated with "real-life" situations. (Or, as Hamlet says, "What's Hecuba to him or he to Hecuba that he should weep for her?") We enjoy such drama because it releases our emotions, permits us to live vicariously, and helps us to ponder life; but the shaman produces a dramatic situation with another intent: to help the group in the expression of psi phenomena.

Parapsychologists have on occasion made use of this concept in designing research. For example, experiments have been conducted (with positive results) which assume that a sense of drama on the part of the telepathic sender will aid in the transmission of a target picture to a dreaming percipient. These experiments create a multi-sensory, emotionally-loaded experience associated with elements of the target picture for the sender to transmit (Ullman and Krippner, with Vaughan, 1973). Moreover, psi phenomena tend to be associated, at least most strikingly, with life-and-death situations, and thus one might assume that the artificial or not-so-artificial creation of danger (the prehistoric cave after all was not exactly a safe refuge) would encourage the emergence of the more striking forms of psi.

The point is that through the use of elements such as these (participants who are believers in psi, a sense of drama, and so on), the shaman creates a situation in which those attending the ceremony are primed for psi production. If then, through his use of magic, the shaman convinces them that psi phenomena are indeed taking place at that very moment, he may succeed in liberating them from any last vestiges of resistance to the actual occurrence of psi. Moreover, the shaman himself may be affected by his own use of magic, for in the same auto hypnotic manner in which the actor convinces himself at some level that his actions are "real," the shaman seeks to convince himself that psi, not magic, is taking place even though he knows otherwise (Jenness, 1922, p. 217). There is, of course, no guarantee that the use of one or all of the elements of the shamanistic setting, combined with magic, will produce psi in any given instance, but the point is that magic was developed by man as a psi-conducive technique designed to tip the scales in favor of psi production.[7]

Magic and Modern Parapsychological Theory

The use of magic as a psi-conducive technique fits readily into established parapsychological theory. For example, the "sheep-goat" effect, which relates to the way in which ESP is expressed, basically involves one element: the attitude or belief of the individual as to whether or not psi exists. But for all the investigator knows, the sheep may be believers in psi on bases which are totally irrational and "unscientific." Their beliefs may rest on having mistaken as psychic an event which is explainable in normal terms; they may have been taken in by outright fraud; they may be adherents of pseudo-parapsychological fads which manifestly have no validity; certainly they are not likely to have read the vast but little known professional literature upon which parapsychologists generally rest their own beliefs. But the point is that the rationality of the sheep's belief, the way they arrive at their belief, is not the determining factor as to whether they are likely to evince ESP. Their belief alone apparently is the determining factor. (Another aspect of this principle is that the belief of the goats, though manifestly a mistaken one, can nevertheless also be a determining factor in the way they may express psi: missing the target to an extent which indicates the operation of psi, though in a direction opposite to that called for by the testing procedure.) Thus, one can see that the shaman who convinces the participants in his ceremony that he is performing psychically when he is actually doing magic may have created a climate for the production of psi which is just as favorable as if he had produced psi rather than magic in the first place.

Further, parapsychologists have experimented with various techniques to influence the subjects' attitudes toward ESP prior to testing on the assumption that a favorable attitude or expectancy will result in psi-hitting. For example, investigators have told one group of subjects that a certain ESP task was highly psi-conducive, while another group was told that the same task was not psi-conducive (Taddonio, 1975); they have made a preliminary presentation favorable to ESP to one group, to another group a presentation unfavorable to ESP (Akolkar, 1968); they have exposed the experimenters themselves to lectures prior to their conducting tests, one group of experimenters who believed in ESP to a favorable lecture, another non-believing group to a negative lecture (Parker, 1975). And in many such instances (though not all), the finding was that the preliminary presentation seemed to affect the psi results on the subsequent tests.

To cite one case in particular: L.E. Rhine (1968) found that, in an atmosphere which "seemed quite restrained and formal" (p. 49), members of a college psychology club scored significantly better on an ESP test after she presented a lecture on ESP than they had before she presented her lecture. She hypothesized that her presentation brought about a "relaxation of tension" and an openness in the club members toward the possibility of ESP, and thus, on the second test their scores reflected the consequences of their "loosening up" and increased expectancy of success. But there is no reason to suppose that the same result, given a similar setting, could not have been obtained if a charlatan succeeded in convincing a group of the validity of his data; or—and this is the point— if a magician convinced the group of the reality of psi by conducting magic, then and there. Again, the key variable is apparently the belief of the subjects, not the validity of the data upon which their belief is based.

Examples from Contemporary Literature

The suggestion that magic serves a function as a psi-conducive technique is not new. On the contrary, it has appeared here and there in the past, but without elaboration of the historical origin of magic that I am stressing here. Unfortunately, most of the references to the concept have been cursory and incomplete. For example, Owen (1975, pp. 153–154) refers to an alleged "electrostatic pseudo-psychokinetic" technique adopted by Russian researchers to permit psychics to practice seemingly psychokinetic activity before trying for true psychokinesis, and Rauscher (with Spraggett, 1975) quotes some interesting correspondence from Humphry Osmond in which Osmond contends that psi "of a genuine kind can probably be primed, started up, with what amounts to a bit of fraud" (p. 126). However, as far as I can determine, credit for the first systematic articulation of the concept of magic as a psi-conducive force (although using different terminology) should go to the British clinical psychologist and researcher, K.J. Batcheldor, in his work, both published and unpublished, that he carried out during the last decade. I offer below a synopsis of his experiments and findings, and those of his colleague Colin Brookes-Smith.

Batcheldor's Findings

In 1966 Batcheldor published a description of his initial experiments with a group of sitters (none of whom were known to have any special psychic ability) who ostensibly achieved table levitations and related phenomena. The group usually sat in darkness so that, from a strictly evidentiary viewpoint, the experiments were of limited value; but at the outset Batcheldor was less concerned with evidentiary data than he was with developing a theoretical understanding of psychokinetic phenomena and techniques for enhancing them. Continuing his work with the original and other groups, Batcheldor noticed that certain accidental normal events were sometimes miss-taken by the sitters for paranormal events, and that these were apparently psi conducive. He reasoned that the same effect could be brought about deliberately by the use of carefully planned "trickery," and in 1968 he incorporated his data on the use of this technique, which he called the "deliberate deception" technique, and an accompanying theory in a long paper which has not been published.[8] Some of the pertinent background concerning the "deliberate deception" technique follows:

At this time, Batcheldor was working with more than one group of sitters. The original group, whose meetings began in 1964, continued to obtain ostensibly paranormal phenomena (until it disbanded in 1967) without any evidence of a falling off of activity, so that Batcheldor felt there was no need to experiment with the "deliberate deception" technique or other induction techniques with this group. But he had also established a "novice" group with different members in an attempt to locate and control factors which might contribute to the spontaneous development of psychokinetic phenomena in group sittings or, in his words, to the understanding of "the factors responsible for induction as far as possible" (Batcheldor, personal communication, 1977). Thus, to this novice group, which had been obtaining only very slight, erratic paranormal effects since April 1967, he suggested (at a sitting held on January 9, 1968) that perhaps deliberate deception (in addition to unconscious muscular action or illusion mistaken for paranormal activity) could induce the "real thing"; however, having suggested the idea, he thought the group had been so alerted that deception would not work in that particular sitting. But:

> Two days later (on 11th January, 1968), it occurred to me that if I now produced a fake effect, provided I confessed afterwards, the group would probably agree that the experiment had been justified.... There were several requirements for success to be likely: first, the faked movement must not be so large or peculiar that it would seem incongruous with the movements already taking place, or it would be suspected; second, the deception must not be confessed until after an (ostensible) genuine effect (if any) had followed the fake effect; and third, the confession must in any case be made before the end of the sitting ... [Batcheldor, 1968, p. 19].

At the sitting of January 11, Batcheldor produced a sideways drag of the trumpet (of about two inches) which was quickly followed by ostensibly paranormal movement of the trumpet. On January 17, a similar experiment with the trumpet was attempted without success by another member of the group, the lack of success being attributed to the fact that he was seen in his deception. However, on January 27, a third member of the group (with one new member) in the midst of "vigorous" table movement succeeded in faking a table levitation which was quickly followed by ostensibly paranormal levitation. This was the first time that the novice group had obtained an ostensibly paranormal levitation.

Clearly, the "deliberate deception" technique is fraught with danger—a fact of which Batcheldor was well aware. He had never claimed, even in his first paper (1966) published before the technique was used, that he had satisfied evidentiary criteria, and he was always careful to use the term "ostensibly paranormal." But now, having introduced the conception of intentional faking, the already fragile credibility of the entire affair was shaken even further. It was for this reason that he developed the idea of a "delayed invalidation system" which would permit detection of artifact activity such as unconscious muscular action or faking, but which would not interrupt the induction process achieved by these techniques at the time they were applied.

Brookes-Smith's Findings

It remained for the British instrument engineer Colin Brookes-Smith to actually devise and use a delayed invalidation system to attempt to put Batcheldor's theory of deliberate deception as a psi-conducive technique[9] to its first evidentiary test. Brookes-Smith constructed a table, auxiliary devices, and a data-tape system which recorded any hand contact applied on the lower surface of the table and also measured the mechanical upward force producing a levitation. The data-tape recording can be transcribed to a polygraph chart at any later time, thus permitting a delayed invalidation of upward table movements which may be attributable to normal motor activities of the sitters on the lower surface of the table. Brookes-Smith (1973) explains the theory of Batcheldor which he attempted to test and his "Joker" technique for doing so as follows:

> Batcheldor had deduced theoretically and then confirmed experimentally that deliberate deception ... secretly applied in the dark by one sitter was psychologically beneficial to the induction process. It created amongst the sitters an illusion of paranormal activity and provided that the "fake" was not so advanced in character as to strain credulity at the time, it generated sufficiently intense and synchronous expectation to trigger a genuine display.... At some of the later sittings this deliberate deception technique was agreed to and permitted to one sitter secretly chosen before the sitting by drawing a Joker (appropriately) from a pack of cards [pp. 75–76].

The group with which Brookes-Smith worked had been getting table levitations during several sittings for many weeks before sitting No. 57 (held on July 14, 1972), of which a data-tape record is reproduced in his paper (Figure 6, p. 87). According to Brookes-Smith (personal communication, 1977), the group, which had not experienced any levitations since a week before, began this sitting, as was usual, with a "warming up" exercise which consisted of the (apparently normal) rocking of the table and stopping it on command, then sliding and tilting the table. Following this, the group took a brief break to permit hooking up the equipment and then experienced ostensibly paranormal table levitation immediately following secretly applied "aid" which was identified by the invalidation system.

Certain problems are involved in the interpretation of these data: First, it cannot be "proved" that ostensible paranormal levitation would not have occurred anyway, without the use of deliberate deception; secondly, Brookes-Smith's equipment does not register very weak signals (see, e.g., Brookes-Smith, 1974) and it records finger contact rather than finger pressure; and lastly, when monitoring psychokinetic forces, there is no conceivable way of insuring that psi is not directly affecting the recording mechanism itself. (From what we know of psi dynamics, we would expect that how-ever ingenious our methods, psi will be equally ingenious in evading our attempts to pin it down.) Nonetheless, Brookes-Smith's findings apparently represent the first reported experimental attempt to verify the use of magic as a psi-induction technique.

Why Parapsychologists Have Avoided the Subject of Magic and Psi

It should be apparent at this point why parapsychologists have not looked as closely as they should have at magic as a psi-conducive technique either historically or in the case of "mixed" mediums or psychics—those who sometimes practice magic "to get things going." Since Henry Sidgwick (1882, p. 12) made the point in his first Presidential Address to the Society for Psychical Research, it has often been restated that the hope of the field lies in the presentation of so much compelling evidence for psi that the skeptic must fall back on the final, desperate contention that the investigator himself is party to a fraud. But here, by suggesting that magic may have a definite psi-conducive effect, I risk donating ammunition to the inveterate skeptic, who may now contend that parapsychologists *must* be party to fraud for they openly encourage its use in their studies. Of course, I am *not* recommending that magic in an allegedly psychic performance be overlooked, that we go back to the dark ages when no distinction between magic and psi was drawn, or that we lower the standards by which we judge an event to be paranormal. What I *am* suggesting is that if parapsychologists are to probe the dynamics of psi, they cannot avoid dealing with its interrelationship with magic. If parapsychologists entirely ignore this interrelationship for fear that it exposes a flank to attack, the opponents of our field will have registered a *real* victory.

The Stage Magician: Magic Without Psi

Perhaps another reason why parapsychologists have missed the important historical relationship between magic and psi is that the practitioner of magic with whom we are most familiar, the modern stage magician, plays an entirely different role from that of his ancestor, the shaman. Through history, the activities of the shaman have gradually diverged until today we have two characteristic individuals in place of one: the medium or psychic, who is expected to practice psi without magic, and the stage magician, who is expected to practice magic without psi. It is with this modern-day magician that we associate magical techniques which actually began as psi-conducive techniques. Sleight of hand and illusion, seemingly miraculous escapes from the tight bondage of ropes, the apparent thrusting of sharp implements through people without injury, and other such techniques were first developed by the shaman as devices to elicit psi. But today they are the staples of the stage magician in whose hands their use represents an about-face, a parody of the original driving force which led to their development. For, while the shaman practices magic to help in the production of psychic phenomena, the stage magician in practicing magic actually seeks to *deny* the possibility of the paranormal.

There are striking differences in the circumstances surrounding the performance of the stage magician compared to that of the shaman which should alert us to the extent to which the psychological dynamics of the two performances are different. For one, the audience of the shaman is naive—it accepts his magical techniques as true psychic phenomena. In contrast, virtually all the members of a stage magician's audience take it for granted that the seemingly psychic feats he performs are sleight of hand and illusion. Further, the shaman pretends that the magic he performs is a manifestation of psi; the stage magician does not generally claim that any psychic powers are involved in his magic.[10] Given these differences, the questions become: For what purpose does the stage magician practice *his* magic? What are the psychological motives which drive him to perform his illusions and an audience to watch?

We might assume that what holds the audience is admiration of the craftsmanship of the magician in producing seeming miracles, as well as the desire to play detective and discover how the miracles were produced. This is well and good, but more is at stake here. Over and over the magician imitates psychical acts which momentarily "tease" the audience, momentarily provoke the possibility that psi phenomena are actually occurring; But at the same time he relieves both himself and his audience of the anxiety prompted by such a possibility, for everyone knows that in fact he has full sensorimotor control of the elements in his act, and that what they have witnessed is "only magic." Thus, he assures himself and the audience that, however much it might appear otherwise, nothing uncontrollably psychic is occurring—at least in this instance.

But it is exactly this uncontrollability of our psychic wishes, arising from the deep and often vindictive reaches of our subconscious, which lies at the core of the resistance in our society to the acceptance of psi phenomena. For to grant reality to psi is to come face to face (as commentators such as Eisenbud [1972] have hypothesized) with the possibility that our spontaneous, subconscious death wishes directed toward loved objects can be effective. This possibility is something which we do not wish to entertain. Thus, watching a magician's act is analogous to watching a horror movie: during both types of performances we experience twinges of excitement and fear as the anxiety-laden possibilities are before us, and then—afterward—we can assure ourselves that, after all, what we saw as not real and reality itself is not half so bad. In case there is any doubt that our aggressive psychic desires are invoked by the magician's performance, we need only examine what is considered today to be the magician's standard repertoire: the (usually male) magician deftly sticks knives in a beautiful woman assistant (sometimes his wife), saws her in half, makes her disappear—and in each instance magically resurrects her intact. In this way, he acts out, in a kind of repetition compulsion, his homicidal desire toward and his need to psychically control the mother figure (the original figure with whom during childhood he shared close psi communication) without any apparent harm. And we share in this display, indulging in our own psychic fantasies without apparent harm as well. Other magical performances, of course, are not so obviously aggressive, but the point is that any performance openly masquerading as psychic cannot help but invoke and then lay to rest the anxiety associated with psychic aggression.

This brings us to the conscious attitude of the stage magician toward parapsychological data. Not all, but most magicians have an anti-psi bias. The depth of this bias has often been overlooked. The real threat to such a magician is one against which he feels compelled to guard himself over and over again by performing magic; the threat that he himself has psychic power. In fact, the magicians very choice of profession may be testimony to his resistance to the psi hypothesis. To cite a current example: the stage magician Milbourne Christopher (1975), who devotes the greater part of his recent book on the "occult" to debunking paranormal phenomena, recounts an incident in which, in the process of a planned magic trick to deliver an unmarked letter to the right address, he unaccountably asks his cab driver to stop at a railway station where he later discovers the addressee had been at the time. Says Christopher: "Although I know exactly how I delivered the unmarked letter to the right address, I still don't know why I asked the cab to stop at the railway station. But I don't think that I have any superhuman powers" (p. 233). And, while he goes on to admit that any magician who performs mental magic "has had similar experiences" and that perhaps there is "something to what parapsychologist call spontaneous telepathy" this brief lapse into sensibility does not deter him from his debunking mission. It is evident that the thought which disturbs him and leads him to deny psychic abilities in general, is that *he* might be psychic!

In his use of the term "superhuman powers" Christopher may have unwittingly put his finger on another aspect of the psychological dynamics leading an individual to the profession of magic. Rauscher (with Spraggett, 1975) also touches near this point when he states: "There is a theory I favor about magicians as a breed. They have a Jehovah complex. They want to be able to perform real magic, and they secretly resent the fact that they can't.... Inside every magician is a nine-year-old boy who has never gotten over his luciferian ambition to be God" (pp. 9–10).

Of course, we all believed in our omnipotence when were children (this finding is one of the cornerstones of psychoanalytic theory), but in the process of growth we discovered—only too well—our lack of omnipotence in reality, although subconsciously we retain an unrepentant wish for godhead. But magicians such as Christopher and "the Amazing Randi" appear to have resolved the loss of their wished-for omnipotence in a unique manner: They turn to magic in a kind of cynical parody of their former desire, and they deny that psi ability *of any kind* exists. In effect, they are unable to settle for the fact that, from everything we know, psi ability is neither superhuman nor omnipotent; rather, as without other human abilities, it exists to a greater or lesser extent in all of us and is subject to apparent, if little understood, limits. In other word, the stage magician is unwilling to settle for the half-a-loaf which reality offers: for him, psychic ability must be "all or nothing."

Magicians as a group are hardly unique in their resistant to the psi hypothesis. In fact, their attitude might not be significant to psychical research at all if it were not for the fact that their knowledge of deceptive techniques is sometimes deemed necessary to distinguish fraud from genuine psychic performance. Yet many parapsychologists, and others, who blithely invite magicians to comment on allegedly psychic events are extremely naive about the possible psychological depth of a magician's resistance to accept parapsychological data no matter how convincing. Or, put in another way, many individuals have retained the remnants of the historical role played by the participants in a shamanistic ceremony: they believe unquestioningly in the magician's testimony. As anyone who has watched a magician perform must be aware, this adulatory role is easy to adopt despite the fact that one knows rationally that only magic is performed. And this for several reasons: First, the magician has kept and even elaborated upon certain elements in the performance of his distant ancestor, the shaman, which are designed to compel just such adulation from his audience, the most crucial of these elements being his position of unquestioned authority and the great sense of drama which accompanies his presentation. And second, we all have tendency when provoked by a magical display to regress to our childhood, when we believed in the magical power of parental figures. In fact, this regressive tendency is something which the magician often depends upon for his effects.

But this tendency becomes a definite liability when it spills over from the stage to the parapsychological arena. To cite an illustrative example: Eisenbud (1975) reports that after a statement by The Amazing Randi attacking the thoughtographic phenomena of Ted Serios and alleging that Serios had publicly confessed to fraud appeared in a popular magazine, Eisenbud received communications from many persons demanding an explanation, "as if feeling personally betrayed after having taken the Serios data seriously" (p. 94). Even more disturbing was the fact that the colleagues of many years standing, who were familiar with the extent of the Serios data (see Eisenbud, 1967) and the caliber of the witnesses to them, wrote to Eisenbud to ask "whether there *was* any truth to the story." The point I am making here is that such a simplistic attack as Randi's, when weighted against the overwhelming evidence to the contrary, would probably have been discounted by these same individuals if it had been delivered by any body *other than a magician!* And the more so, considering the transparent bias of Randi, who leaves Christopher far behind in his psychological need to deny the existence of psi (see Randi, 1975; but compare with Dingwall, 1976). I am suggesting that parapsychologists should examine more closely the psychological reasons for the unwritten "ground rules" whereby the evidence presented by a professional magician need not be as solid or as well attested as that presented by a non-magician.

Summary and Conclusions

I have suggested that the shaman is the historical forebear of, on the one hand, the modern stage magician, and on the other, the modern medium or psychic. Magic (among its functions both good and bad) was a technique originally developed and used by the shaman to help induce psi phenomena, which were considered crucial to the survival of the individual and of the tribe. The shaman created a variety of conditions in which his magic was likely to be effective; these conditions included the requirement that the participants in the ceremony have "faith" in its efficacy, the creation of a dramatic and emotionally stirring performance, and the careful selection of those events which the shaman felt he could actually influence. Magic served to convince the participants that psi was taking place, thus dissipating any vestiges of resistance among them, and in the shaman himself, to the emergence of genuine psi phenomena. Only in fairly recent times has magic lost its social attributes as a psi-conducive technique and tended, in an about-face revealing of the orientation of contemporary society, to be used as a parody of genuine psi phenomena in order to relieve modern audiences of the anxiety created by the idea of the paranormal.

This chapter represents a cross-fertilization between two disciplines, parapsychology and anthropology. A knowledge of parapsychological data and theory succeeds in bringing to anthropology a more complete explanation of the origin, development, and rationale of magical techniques and their attendant institutions than anthropology is capable of alone. But in addition this type of study cannot help but bring to parapsychology itself (which has an unfortunate tendency toward insularity) a better understanding of the dynamics of psi, in this case of the frequent (and often distressing) contiguity of magic and genuine psi phenomena. In no way does this study relieve parapsychologists of their continuing responsibility for separating magic from genuine psi, but it does suggest that such evidentiary excision be made with greater appreciation of the surrounding circumstances which may influence the production of psi.

Notes

1. I wish to thank Kenneth J. Batcheldor and Colin Brookes-Smith for helpful suggestions concerning various aspects of this chapter.

2. For reasons of space, I have barely touched upon here the plethora of roles played by the shaman in preliterate societies (see, e.g., Reichbart, 1976; Van de Castle, 1974), and have stressed only the hunting tribes and other tribes in which the shaman followed what I suspect was the most primordial psychic model—that of the trance medium.

3. Since in our present state of knowledge it is difficult to separate out paranormal factors from suggestive factors in cases of ostensible cures which occur during healing ceremonies, the area of healing is not an ideal one from which to draw conclusions about the relations between magic and psi; but neither can this area be ignored.

4. As few other commentators, Freuchen captures the Eskimo sense of humor, which in my experience has a characteristic resemblance to that of the American Indian. Other commentators have, I suspect, been led astray by the dryness of this wit as to the true depth of native beliefs.

5. The Mackenzie River Eskimo shaman provides an interesting combination of dramatic setting replete with danger and a lack of sensory input for the participants: A hammer or axe blade is tied to a long thong and the shaman is bound with the remaining rope so that, in theory, it is impossible for him to move. The participants sit in the darkness and then they hear the whizzing of the axe or hammer in centrifugal motion, signifying the fact that the shaman is now flying in circles above them. They must keep their eyes shut, for if anyone "were to open his eyes even a little to try to see what was going on, the hammer would strike him in the head, killing him instantly" (Stefansson, 1913, p. 404).

6. Thus we see that the reluctance with which shamans permit Western anthropologists to observe their ceremonies may in fact have a legitimate basis in "reality": that the usually skeptical anthropologist is more likely to be a deterrent to the expression of psi than the believing native. In addition, one can see in this primitive "exclusion" principle what may well be an underlying and very real basis for religious exclusion and prejudice—with their myriad, often tragic elaborations throughout the course of man's history (Reichbart, 1977).

7. I am not implying that primitive man could analyze the reasons why he used magic or the other elements of shamanistic ceremonies; his discoveries were intuitive, not analytical.

8. I am indebted to Mr. Batcheldor for his willingness to share his unpublished material with me. His theory, which is too complex to describe here, involves what he calls "artifact induction"; this includes spontaneous artifacts (such as illusion or unconscious muscular action) and deliberate artifacts (such as deception or sleight of hand) which may facilitate psychokinetic manifestations.

9. Stanford (1974, p. 341) has discussed the deliberate deception technique employed by Batcheldor and Brookes-Smith in relation to his psi-mediated instrumental response (PMIR) theory.

10. There are, of course, exceptions to this general rule. Some stage magicians, such as the American magician Kreskin, play upon the uncertainty and anxiety of the audience as to whether or not psi is involved in their magic productions, never quite committing themselves either way (see, e.g., Cox, 1974).

References

Akolkar, V.V. (1968) Experimentally induced shifts in attitude to ESP and their effects on scoring. *Journal of Parapsychology, 32,* 63. (Abstract).

Batcheldor, K.J. (1966) Report on a case of table levitation and associated phenomena. *Journal of the Society for Psychical Research, 43,* 339–356.

Batcheldor, K.J. (1968) Macro-PK in group sittings: Theoretical and practical aspects. Unpublished paper.

Batcheldor, K.J. (1977) Personal communication.

Birket-Smith, K., & De Laguna, F. (1938) *The Eyak Indians of the Copper River Delta, Alaska.* Copenhagen: Levin and Munksgaard.

Bogoras, W. (1960) The Chuckchee. In M. Mead & R.L. Bunzel (eds.), *The golden age of American Anthropology.* New York: Braziller, pp. 320–330.

Brookes-Smith, C. (1973) Data-tape recorded experimental PK phenomena. *Journal of the Society for Psychical Research, 47,* 69–89.

Brookes-Smith, C. (1974) Correspondence. *Journal of the Society for Psychical Research, 47,* 392–396.

Brookes-Smith, C. (1977) Personal communication.

Christopher M. (1975) *Mediums, mystics, and the occult.* New York: Crowell.

Cox, W.E. (1974) Parapsychology and magicians. *Parapsychology Review, 5,* 12–14.

Dingwall, E.J. (1976) The magic of Uri Geller. (Book review) *Parapsychology Review, 7,* 14–15.

Eisenbud, J. (1967) *The world of Ted Serios.* New York: Morrow.

Eisenbud, J. (1972) Some notes on the psychology of the paranormal. *Journal of the American Society for Psychical Research, 66,* 27–41.

Eisenbud, J. (1975a) Correspondence: On Ted Serios' alleged "confession." *Journal of the American Society for Psychical Research, 69,* 94–96.

Eisenbud, J. (1975b) The case of Florence Marryat. *Journal of the American Society for Psychical Research, 69,* 215–233.

Elkin, A.P. (1948) *The Australian aborigines: How to understand them.* 2d ed. Sydney, Australia: Angus and Robertson.

Freuchen, P. (1935) *Arctic adventure: My life in the frozen north.* New York: Farrar & Rinehart.

Honorton, C. (1977) Psi and internal attention states. In B.B. Wolman (ed.), *Handbook of Parapsychology.* New York: Van Nostrand Reinhold, pp. 435–472.

Jenness, D. (1922) *The life of the Copper Eskimos.* Report of the Canadian Arctic Expedition, 1913–18 (Vol. XII). Ottawa: F.A. Acland.

Kennedy, J.E., & Taddonio, J.L. (1976) Experimenter effects in parapsychological research. *Journal of Parapsychology, 40,* 1–33.

Lame Deer, J., & Erdoes, R. (1972) *Lame Deer, seeker of visions.* New York: Simon & Schuster.

Opler, M.E. (1936) Some points of comparison and contrast between the treatment of functional disorders by Apache shamans and modern psychiatric practice. *American Journal of Psychiatry, 92,* 1371–1387.

Owen, A.R.G. (1975) *Psychic Mysteries of the North.* New York: Harper & Row.

Palmer, J. (1971) Scoring in ESP tests as a function of belief in ESP. Part I. The sheep-goat effect. *Journal of the American Society for Psychical Research, 65,* 373–408.

Parker A. (1975) A pilot study of the influence of experimenter expectancy on ESP scores. In J.D. Morris, W.G. Roll & R.L. Morris (eds.), *Research in Parapsychology 1974.* Metuchen, NJ: Scarecrow Press, pp. 42–44.

Radin, P. (1920) The autobiography of a Winnebago Indian. *University of California Publications in American Archaeology and Ethnology, 16,* 381–473.

Randi, J. (1975) *The Magic of Uri Geller.* New York: Ballantine Books.

Rasmussen, K. (1969) *Across Arctic America: Narrative of the Fifth Thule Expedition.* Westport, CT: Greenwood Press.

Rauscher, W.V., with Spraggett, A. (1975) *The Spiritual Frontier.* Garden City, NY: Doubleday.

Reichbart, R. (1976) The Navajo hand trembler: Multiple roles of the psychic in traditional Navajo society. *Journal of the American Society for Psychical Research, 70,* 381–396.

Reichbart, R. (1977) Group psi: Comments on the recent Toronto PK experiment as recounted in *Conjuring Up Philip. Journal of the American Society for Psychical Research, 71,* 201–212.

Rhine, L.E. (1968) Note on an informal group test of ESP. *Journal of Parapsychology, 32,* 47–53.

Rose, R. (1956) *Living Magic: The realities underlying the psychical practices and beliefs of Australian Aborigines.* Chicago: Rand McNally.

Schmeidler, G.R., & Mcconnell R.A. (1958) *ESP and personality patterns.* New Haven, CT: Yale University Press.

Sidgwick. (1882) The president's address. *Proceedings of the Society for Psychical Research, 1,* 7–12.

Stanford, R.G. (1974) An experimentally testable model for spontaneous psi events. II. Psychokinetic events. *Journal of the American Society for Psychical Research, 68,* 321–356.

Stefannson, V. (1913) *My life with the Eskimo.* New York: Macmillan.

Stone, E. (1962) *Medicine among the American Indians.* New York: Hafner.

Taddonio, J.L. (1975) Attitudes and expectancies in ESP scoring. *Journal of Parapsychology,* 39, 289–296.

Tart, C.T. (1977) Drug-induced states of consciousness. In B.B. Wolman (ed.), *Handbook of Parapsychology.* New York: Van Nostrand Reinhold, pp. 500–525.

Thornton, H.R. (1931) *Among the Eskimos of Wales, Alaska, 1890–1893.* Baltimore: Johns Hopkins University Press.

Ullman, M., & Krippner, S., with Vaughan, A. (1973) *Dream telepathy.* New York: Macmillan.

Van De Castle, R.L. (1974) Anthropology and psychic research. In E.D. Mitchell et al. (ed. by J. White), *Psychic Exploration.* New York: Putnam's, pp. 269–287.

White, R.A. (1976) The limits of experimenter influence on psi test results: Can any be set? *Journal of the American Society for Psychical Research,* 70, 333–369.

TEN

Western Law and Parapsychology

Introduction

In 1978, I published an article entitled "Western Law and Parapsychology," to which I have referred in previous chapters. This is an updated introduction to that article. I had then and I still have a great deal of trepidation presenting this article because it contains a somewhat chilling thesis. Yet the thesis follows very logically from the acceptance of a premise that was first suggested by Tanagras (1967), then adopted by Eisenbud (1982), as well as by subsequent parapsychologists such as Braude (1986) as well as elaborated by the psychoanalyst Brottman (2011).

The thesis is that as soon as one entertains the possibility of psychokinesis, as in the Serios thoughtographic phenomenon in which Polaroid film appeared to be affected by mind alone, one then is faced with the problem that psi might be used aggressively. Put differently, if a physical object can be controlled just by mind, then any object, such as a crucial piece of a car's machinery, or any part of another person's body can conceivably be controlled by a person's mind, in the service of unconscious or conceivably conscious aggression. Eisenbud contends that this possibility or hypothesis is the principle reason that psi phenomena are denied and resisted (to such an extent that the hypothesis itself is entirely avoided even though logically it should be entertained). The hypothesis is simply too frightening. It shakes our assumption of how the world is put together. It is too similar to the concept of "omnipotence of thought" which Freud and psychoanalysts in general use to characterize psychotic process in a patient. Put differently, it brings into question whether the "reality testing"—a term which in common understanding assumes that such things are not possible—of those who espouse the hypothesis is lacking. Moreover, the hypothesis strikes at the very heart of clinical psychoanalytic technique where the patient is assured, repeatedly, that fantasy, no matter how aggressive, is after all just fantasy and therefore harmless. In fact, it reflects on more than just psychoanalytic diagnosis or technique: one could describe psychoanalysis as a process that progressively modulates the primitive superego of a patient who has been unable to accept his aggressive or libidinal wishes, who tends toward self-punitive or guilty ideation as a way to defend against and control these fantasies. If one's unconscious wishes might in some cases not necessarily be harmless, the entire structure (and a very therapeutic and successful structure at that) of psychoanalysis is called into question.

In fact, incidentally, one does not need to go *quite* as far as accepting psychokinesis to encounter this theoretical problem; one need only go as far as telepathy. That is, if there is indeed telepathy unconsciously existing at times between individuals, does that not mean that one person can unconsciously affect another person cognitively or emotionally at a distance through "mind," including conceivably by conveying aggressive thoughts or feelings? As an example of that, I have previously highlighted the Dorothy Burlingham vignette of a mother whose son tries to throw hot water on his sister, after the mother has the angry thought of throwing boiling water on someone else—an example studiously ignored by Freud and subsequent commentators who have nonetheless approvingly cited Burlingham's other examples of psi (Burlingham, 1953). Despite Freud's interest in telepathy, as well as his fear of where entertaining it would lead, he never quite made the point explicitly that acceptance of telepathy necessarily carried with it acceptance of the idea that mind could influence mind at a distance (despite his apparent awareness of this fact), nor do most of those psychoanalysts who have subsequently presented data suggestive of telepathy convey this inevitable conclusion.

In the text that follows, I *do* entertain the hypothesis of unconscious aggressive psi, and then examine what acceptance of this hypothesis would mean to the system of causality that is embodied in our Western law. We do not, I believe, generally recognize how much Western law contains a social construct about causality similar to the psychological construct that mind cannot directly affect the external world. In fact, such causality is embedded in the way we think about a person's motivation and often how we teach our children about motivation, from early development onward. It becomes a part of us, without our quite realizing it. I remember many years ago, when I was a young and rather naive student at Yale Law School, I had a conversation in class with Thomas Emerson, a wonderful professor of law—short of stature, white-haired, gentlemanly, soft-spoken—who was a leading expert of constitutional law and first amendment rights. He asked our class: What is constitutional law about when it is always subject to change and new interpretations by the Supreme Court? How could it possibly express the truth if it is so malleable? I found myself answering the question, afraid that my answer would be ridiculed as not legal-sounding, by saying somewhat to my own surprise that law was a social construct that provided a system for society to function. When I said that, and when he—also to my surprise—agreed entirely, I suddenly realized that I had also said that there was no "truth" in the sense I as a young man tended to think; and that what I said applied as well to criminal law, where laymen and sometimes lawyers like to speak of evidence, proof, and gradations of guilty actions as if they are concepts fashioned in stone.

As psychoanalysts in particular we know that legal concepts of causality, legal principles of guilt and innocence (or "not proven"—innocence actually not favored as a concept in criminal law), do not approach the complexity of a person's motivations and functioning. We understand that often "all is not what it seems" on the surface or to a court of law, and that unconscious motivation can explain much of a person's functioning. Legal causality is like a conceptual straitjacket, placed on a person's shoulders; it is used to determine whether a person will be held *responsible by society or by the State* for his actions and whether the State can prove its case (not whether a person is "innocent"); but the emotional developmental history, ambivalence, and complexity that psychoanalysts know contribute to a person's ultimate actions are never fully considered in a Western court. They are generally and purposefully left out. Western law is a necessity that permits our society to function properly. One might be impressed by the wonderful system this Western democratic law creates, how it helps us to flourish in relative peace, but the justice it renders is also (by necessity) always going to be "rough" and inexact.

To illustrate my point, let me turn to a contrasting and very different system of law than that of our Western culture, the traditional legal system of the Navajo tribe, whose traditional mental health system, which embraces psi phenomena, I discussed in Chapter Eight on the Navajo hand trembler. To turn to this may seem at first a diversion, but bear with me because I think the elaboration will make my point.

When I lived and worked as a legal services attorney on the Navajo reservation, I became very aware how parochial is Western law (as is every society's law). In a sense, as a colonial power vis-à-vis Native Americans, the United States imposed a Western legal system upon all tribes. Most particularly, we set up "tribal governments" that did not resemble at all native and tribal legal systems prior to our conquest nor did they embody each tribes' traditional sense of justice. In doing so, what interested us most was to create executive and legislative branches for tribes, branches that could negotiate treaties and contracts with state, local and federal authorities, and with outsiders. We did not bother with imposing all of our democratic principles, which apparently seemed extraneous to our needs.

Thus, it was as late as 1968, that the Indian Civil Rights Act was passed by Congress, courtesy incidentally of Senator Sam Ervin, its principal sponsor (later of fame in his role in the Senate Watergate investigation that led to President Nixon's resignation). Simplifying greatly, this Act provided on all Native American reservations for the very first time a Bill of Rights comparable to the Bill of Rights of our constitution. Prior to its passage, for example, there was no federally mandated freedom of speech nor freedom of religion on Native American reservations. But the Indian Civil Rights Act was not and has not been greeted with universal acclaim by Native American tribes; it was often resisted, for a number of reasons one of which was that concepts such as individual "freedom of speech" or "freedom of religion" as they are defined in federal jurisprudence were not part of traditional law (Carpenter, 2012; Fletcher, 2012). In addition, justice traditionally would not have been meted out by an authoritarian court anyway, but would have been decided as part of a group process in which tribal elders and medicine men played crucial roles. For example, in traditional Navajo society the ultimate goal of justice was for the individual and the community to be "in harmony." Individual freedom was not a standard for justice; group accommodation and the welfare of the group that required harmonious functioning *were* the standard. A Navajo judge explains this in very direct terms:

> Traditional Navajo tort law is based on nalyeeh, which is a demand that the victim be made whole for an injury. In the law of nalyeeh, one who is hurt is not concerned with intent, causation, fault, or negligence. If I am hurt, all I know is that I hurt: that makes me feel bad and makes those around me feel bad too. I want the hurt to stop, and I want others to acknowledge that I am in pain. The maxim for nalyeeh is that there must be compensation so that there will be no hard feelings. This is restorative justice. Returning people to good relations with each other in a community is an important focus. Before good relations can be restored, the community must arrive at a consensus about the problem [Yazzie, 2005].

Even in its present form, the laws of the Navajo tribe attempt to preserve traditional understanding of such process and causality, and involve the medicine men in the process. For example, Section G of Navajo Tribal law (in which the traditional name for the Navajo, Dine, meaning "the people" is used) states:

> Our elders and our medicine people, the teachers of traditional laws, values and principles must always be respected and honored if the people and the government are to persevere and thrive; the teachings of the elders and medicine people, their participation in government and their contributions of the traditional values and principles of Dine' life way will ensure growth of the Navajo Nation; and from

time to time, the elders and medicine people must be requested to provide the cleansing, protection prayers, and blessing ceremonies necessary for securing healthy leadership and the operation of the government in harmony with traditional law [Transcript of the fundamental laws of the Dine, 2002, Title I,1.ii G].

For the Navajo diagnostician (as discussed in the chapter on the Navajo Hand Trembler) who makes referrals to the appropriate medicine man for treatment as well as for the medicine man himself, psi phenomena are considered an intimate part of causality. Indeed, for the entire traditional Navajo culture, psi phenomena are to be considered as part of the process of reaching a "harmonious" conclusion. Thus, the social construct that permitted and still permits this society to function is very different than ours.

In fact, in 1982, rebelling against the imposition of Western law on the Navajo legal system, the Navajo tribal court, in a procedure characterized as "going back to the future" instituted a "Peacemaker Court" that formally incorporated principles of mediation and arbitration using traditional Navajo values. As stated by commentators explaining the need for this new court:

The alien Navajo Court of Indian Offenses (1892–1959) and Bureau of Indian Affairs (BIA) Law and Order Code (written in 1934 and adopted by the Navajo Nation in 1959) made Navajos judge others, using power and force to control. That arrangement is repugnant to Navajo morals [Bluehouse & Zion, 2005, p. 157].

Rather than using an authoritarian system, Navajos think of their peace planning system of justice as "horizontal." It uses : "Navajo norms, values, moral principles as law. K'e and k'ei are only two of these precepts. There are many others, which are expressed in Navajo creation and journey scripture, songs, ceremonies and prayers." The failure to follow these precepts means that one "acts as if he has no relatives" (Bluehouse& Zion, 2005, p. 159). These precepts are directed toward issues of harmony which require spiritual input. Navajo common law:

builds on k'e solidarity in a procedure to summon assistance from the Holy People and humans to diagnose how people are distant from k è or their k'ei relations (to identify the disharmony that creates disputes), teach how Navajo values apply to the problem, and restore the continuing relationship of the parties in their community. It is in fact a justice ceremony [Bluehouse & Zion, 2005, p. 159].

And here is an interesting aspect of that construct, as it functions today in the contemporary world: whereas Western culture seeks to control aggressive psi, apparently, by collectively *denying* its power, in fact denying its very existence, the Navajo system of justice accepts the fact that mind in and of itself can affect events, but uses social group control (very unlike Western culture) to limit that effect. As the same Navajo commentators go on to say, in criticizing the authoritarianism of Western courts: "Just as authoritarianism is an abuse of authority, an abuse of supernatural coercive power is witchcraft, one of the most feared evils" (Bluehouse and Zion, 2005, pp. 160–161). They thereby acknowledge that in the Navajo system of justice, aggressive psi is recognized; and in its conscious form, that is as the practice of witchcraft, it is frowned upon and feared. In effect, the Navajo legal system acknowledges that mind can operate in the world, and that thought in itself can be harmful. Yet as I suggest in the article which follows, it is questionable whether this Native American social way of dealing with aggressive psi actually works. Is it as problematic as the Western culture's approach?

Western law, of course, does not go in this direction at all. But what if it did? What if it tried in its own way to *accept* the existence of psi, at least in so far as its unconscious form? What follows in the cogitation I wrote many years ago is an exploration of this question. In it, I suggest that causality and legal responsibility can become very complex if one accepts that psi exists. This exercise explains in another way and in very concrete terms why the acceptance of psi phenomena in Western culture is so strongly resisted.

A Cogitation on Western Law and Parapsychology

I am frequently asked why I left the legal profession to enter that of clinical psychology—sometimes my interrogator framing his question in such a manner that the implication is unavoidable that I am a man with a great future behind him. Over the years, I have settled on a stock answer which, while admittedly incomplete, has a distinct virtue: it seems to forestall additional questions. I simply say that I became "bored" with law as a profession. In this manner, I seem able to avoid hearing disquisitions on how a lawyer can help people, which occur to the noble-minded, or on how he can gain wealth and power, which occur to the more mercenary; and I need not enter into a disquisition of my own on the philosophical concerns which contributed to my decision to change careers. In fact, many of my interlocutors seem to be caught up short by my response, as if they thought that anyone who makes enjoyment a prime criterion for choosing a profession probably deserves to be a clinical psychologist. For such as these, usually I can guarantee an abrupt end to our conversation and the look of one whose worst fears have been confirmed, should I mention that one of my interests happens to be parapsychology. On the other hand, once in a while in the course of these casual conversations, someone strikes upon the philosophical quintessence of my change of career. For example, the other day, I dropped into a local gift shop to say hello to the proprietor, long a family friend, and mentioned to him that I often am uncertain whether I should inform my psychotherapy patients that I have a law degree. "Well," my friend observed after a moment of thought, "a patient might consider it an advantage to go to you. Not only can you analyze his dream, but afterward you can tell him it is illegal in 17 states."

Now, my friend's remark provides a perfect introduction to the subject 1 want to address, namely the interrelationship between two fields: Western law and parapsychology. Although this subject has not exactly flooded the pages of parapsychological journals (and I can almost hear some parapsychologists saying "What relationship?"), the subject is so broad that I cannot do justice to it in this space, and will confine myself to two areas of it, which even then I will cover cursorily: the role of the victim and psychic aggression. Of course, it is true that if one contemplates the gross maintenance function which our system of law, like any other, provides to society—the business of government, of regulation, of commerce—the subject matter of parapsychology *is* far removed. On the other hand, when one contemplates the Western legal concept of cause—of guilt and innocence, of appropriate evidence, of "reasonable" actions as a standard of conduct—-which pervades our thinking not only in the courtroom, but in our daily lives, one confronts a system of thought which appears to relate to parapsychology by being fundamentally at odds with it. For a basic tenet of Western law, at present, is that "mind" in and of itself has no effect upon the world. You cannot be held accountable for your dreams, wishes, or subconscious desires unless you act upon them sensorimotorally—a state of affairs which provides the humor for my friend's joke about illegal dreams. From the point of view of parapsychology, however, this legal version of causality is, in its limitation, false. The question is not whether "mind" affects the world, but how and how much.

Even then, many parapsychologists would be willing to concede this distinction without considering it of any importance, largely because they implicitly answer the question of "how much" as "not very." Put differently, they cannot conceive of the likelihood of the parapsychological data they study marching off the research laboratory table to marshal themselves in the closing argument of some defense attorney in court. Given the type of research that many parapsychologists prefer, the study of what has been termed "micro-events," such as those which yield to the fine statistical tests which accompany random number generators or Zener card runs, rather than "macro-events," such as mediumistic productions, psychic photography, or precognitive dreams, it is perhaps understandable that they cannot conceive of parapsychological phenomena having much impact upon the social interactions and structures, including the legal system of our society. In this I think they are wrong. The implications of psychic phenomena reach considerably further than the front door to the mansion of Western science: in fact, it is just because the data challenge our "commonsense" notions of daily interactions in life that many scientists, unconscious of the reason for their opposition, are so vehemently resistant to permitting parapsychology a room of its own. The fact is that the psi hypothesis tugs directly on ourselves and the fabric of our society: on such things as our responsibility for events in the world, what we teach our children about causality, and our concepts of fair play and justice which are reflected, however roughly, in our legal system.

Let me give a number of examples of what I am talking about. In doing so, I hope to be provocative, for situations such as these frequently intrigued and troubled me in my process of changing careers and continue to do so. I should state one of my suppositions in these examples explicitly: that psi abilities are more or less common to each individual, although disguised, and are not confined to those individuals, whom we call psychics or mediums, who admittedly have extraordinary control over their psi functioning.

The Role of the Victim

Simplifying considerably (and disregarding the distinction between criminal and civil actions), most litigation is essentially directed toward the question of who is "at fault" or, to turn the question around, who has been victimized and how badly. The evidence which may be introduced to determine the question of fault or victimization, however, is carefully circumscribed by law. For example, let us take a hypothetical case, one which appears to be "open and shut." Mr. Jones, driving with a green light in his appropriate lane and at a legal speed, is struck broadside one morning on the way to work by Mr. Smith, who has driven through a red light. Now from a legal viewpoint, evidence which is relevant to a determination of guilt or responsibility will be confined as to time, namely the time of the accident, and as to content, namely the physical actions which took place at that time (assuming no atypical event such as a malfunction of brakes or a heart attack while Mr. Smith was driving). More to the point, the court is not about to permit an inquiry as to the responsibility of the apparent victim of this accident, Mr. Jones, beyond a determination that he was legally where he was entitled to be when his car was struck. But what if we were to open *our* inquiry further, and discovered that Mr. Jones seemed to have a history of being in the wrong place at the wrong time, having been in three very similar accidents recently, and that these accidents always seemed to take place at times of emotional stress, particularly when he had arguments with his wife, and that the morning of the accident he had such an argument with his wife just before leaving the house? In fact, all of us probably know people who seem to suffer just such unexpected accidents with regularity, usually appearing to be innocent victims of circumstance, and we *do* tend to make certain vague connections between the person's character and his "bad luck." Further, what constantly surprises me, many psychotherapists uninformed about or opposed to parapsychology would nevertheless have little hesitancy, were Mr. Jones in therapy, to explore with him the psychodynamic relationship between his "accident proneness" and his personality, even though he appeared to be innocent of any sensorimotor responsibility. But what if, in a case like this, one were to add a discrete parapsychological event to the mix, the kind of thing which never could be introduced in court, namely that Mr. Jones had an apparently precognitive dream of the accident the previous night, one which (just to nail things down) he communicated to members of his family and his next door neighbor before he got into his car? Here, of course, is the rub. For it is perfectly possible that a precognitive experience reveals or is part of the process of causality of the subsequent event—perhaps is simply the manifest extrusion of an underlying psychic interrelatedness; or to put it differently, that Mr. Jones had a need to appear to be the innocent, and righteous, victim—a role perhaps tied into his perception of his marital relationship—and acted out this need psychically and symbolically with a third party whom he had never met (through telepathic influence, for example.) However, our legal system slams the door on the introduction of such thinking concerning causality as if fearful of the consequences, no matter how compelling the evidence for psi interaction might be.

One might hypothesize that countless incidents which come before our legal system, in which the victim and the aggressor seem clear, would reveal a more questionable causality if one were permitted to examine beneath the surface of the legally relevant events. Or, to take it a step further, it may be that a legal system such as ours, by its very denial of psi-mediated causality, serves to shape the subconscious expression of psi in a certain manner: That is, it encourages those who wish to appear to themselves or to their peers as the "innocent" victims of chance, to use their unacknowledged psi capacities to obtain just such seeming results. For a number of reasons, this thought is disturbing. It is, after all, a concept much easier to entertain when the misfortune is the other fellow's rather than our own—in which instance, we often cherish all the sympathy we can get, and it is difficult to know, even when we sense some possible responsibility for a seeming "accident," how to share that information or act upon it in a society where to admit a partial responsibility of any kind (not to say one involving a psi dimension) is generally dealt with most punitively. In addition, the thought is disturbing because concepts such as this one can be readily abused to justify oppressive social conditions where the victim is a member of a discriminated group, whether racial, religious, political or—as in the example of a woman in our often sexually exploitive society—gender. Perhaps the most that can be said is that a cultural pattern of victimization, terribly unjust as it may be, may only be one determinant of how a particular person psychodynamically and in some cases psi-dynamically chooses to participate at a particular time.

Psychic Aggression

There is another side to this question of how our legal system considers evidence in cases of injury and seeming accident, this time involving the hypothesis that psychokinesis or telepathy may be employed subconsciously not to victimize oneself but to inflict injury upon another. In our hypothetical car accident, we need only change the facts slightly, or add to them, to reach the question of whether the victim's wife, Mrs. Jones, took part in the subconscious dynamics which led to the accident. Let us say, for example, that Mrs. Jones, rather than her husband, had a precognitive dream of the accident and that—opening up our inquiry still further—she has a history of close members of her family being involved in accidents, of which they are apparently victims, at the time of strained relations with her, and—just to add a piquant note—her first husband died in such an accident which followed directly on a terrific marital spat. Obviously, the "case" gets stranger and more complex, and begins to look like one of those detective stories in which the at-first-obvious solution to the crime recedes further and further into the distance. In fact, our fascination with the detective story is probably based upon the anxiety produced by the concept that a host of people, or some "supernatural" agency, could be responsible for the crime (as if to scare the reader by implying "even you, dear reader, could be involved") and then relief of the reader's anxiety with the usual revelation that only one individual, of a .dark and nefarious nature, plotted the victim's end in an ingenious, but—mind you—purely sensorimotor fashion. Regardless, this hypothesis of psychic aggression by Mrs. Jones against her husband resulting in an accident in which Mr. Smith's car collides with Mr. Jones', is similar to the hypotheses put forward in "real-life" situations by such parapsychological investigators as Eisenbud—and at considerably greater length than I wish to do here. My main point is that our legal system would not begin to entertain the notion of dragging Mrs. Jones and her precognitive dream into court, much less the concept of malevolent psi.

Here it is appropriate to point out that the manner in which our legal system deals with human aggression is unique among cultures, and often leads to strange results. Succinctly stated, Western law holds that the closer an aggression is to consciousness, the more responsible one becomes for the consequences of his sensorimotor actions. It is this hierarchical concept which makes for such legal distinctions as "degrees of intention" or "degrees of homicide," and which serves to punish more severely an aggression committed with "malice aforethought" than an action resulting in "accidental" injury. However, as students of psychoanalysis have recognized, since Freud began to plumb the depths of human personality, the absence of aggressive intent does not mean that an individual is not responsible for his action. Quite the contrary, for, by probing beneath the conscious level of personality, we often discover that seeming sensorimotor accidents, whether resulting from slips of memory, speech, or physical movement, are the consequences of quite hostile motivation which the individual has hidden from himself. But our legal system—acting in a fashion antithetical to psychological understanding of causality—will hold more responsible, for example, the person who kills his lover with premeditation than the person who shoots his lover with a hunting rifle he forgot was loaded. In other words, our legal system offers to the individual who succeeds in expressing his aggression in a manner in which his intention is not apparent to himself or to others, a convenient "pay off."

What does this have to do with subconscious malevolent psi? Clearly, as the system presently works, the most effective way to be aggressive without appearing responsible for the consequences, is to be psychically aggressive, for the simple reason that this type of aggression is not only (usually) subconscious, it has no sensorimotor concomitant and thus does not even merit a place on the hierarchal ladder. Its existence, in short, is denied. Thus, psychic aggression, subconsciously delivered and disguised as accident, misfortune, or illness is guaranteed to go undetected in our culture by perpetrator, victim, and society alike.[2] Is it possible, too, that the denial of this causality by our legal system does more: that is, actively encourages, as in the hypothetical case of Mrs. Jones, the expression of sub-conscious malevolent psi.

Conclusion

Having posed these questions, I do not hope to do more than disturb our complacency concerning causality in day-to-day life. I cannot offer answers as to how our legal system, alternatively, should function except to observe that the legal system is only one element in a societal matrix—much of which would have to change should the full implications of the psi hypothesis be accepted. However, those legal systems which have attempted to incorporate the psi hypothesis (if not exactly by this name), that is, the legal systems of tribal societies and of Western culture at times in the past, have failed abysmally—exaggerating the potency of any one individual's psi abilities and creating unpleasant systems of witch hunt and witchcraft. In fact, it is very likely that the complexities of an in-depth inquiry into causality are far beyond the rough justice that any legal system creates; or, put differently, perhaps our very concepts of personal "guilt" and "innocence," the very fabric of our Western civilization, are inadequate to accommodate a concept of causality which acknowledges fully the intertwined threads of circumstance, including psi causation, that lead to the misfortunes and accidents we are all prone to. If that is so, one must accept the fact that our legal system (as any legal system) is a construct only, mutually created and designed, one of whose unacknowledged purposes is to guide and channel the workings of self-destructive and malevolent psi in our culture rather than to explore such causality.

References

Bluehouse, P., and Zion, J.W. (2005) The Navajo justice and harmony ceremony. In M.O. Nielsen and J.W. Zion (eds.) *Navajo nation peacemaking: Living traditional justice.* Tucson: University of Arizona Press, pp. 156–164.

Braude, S. (1986) *The limits of influence.* New York: Routledge & Kegan Paul.

Brottman, M. (2011) *Phantoms of the clinic.* London: Karnac Books.

Burlingham, D. (1935) Child analysis and the mother. *Psychoanalytic Quarterly,* 4: 69–92.

Carpenter, K.A. (2012) Individual religious freedoms in American Indian tribal constitutional law. *In* K.A. Carpenter & M.L.M. Fletcher (eds.) *The Indian Civil Rights Act at forty.* Los Angeles: University of California American Indian Studies Center, pp. 159–210.

Eisenbud, J. (1982) *Paranormal foreknowledge.* New York: Human Sciences Press.

Fletcher, M.L.M. (2012) Resisting congress: free speech and tribal law. *In* K.A. Carpenter & M.L.M. Fletcher (eds.) *The Indian Civil Rights Act at forty.* Los Angeles: University of California American Indian Studies Center, pp. 133–158.

Tanagras, A. (1967) *Psychophysical elements in parapsychological traditions.* New York: Parapsychological Foundation.

Transcript of fundamental laws of the Dine (Nov. 8, 2002) Retrieved from: http://www.nativeweb.org/pages/legal/navajo_law.html

Yazzie, R. (2005). "Life comes from it": Navajo justice concepts. In M.O. Nielsen and J.W. Zion (eds.) *Navajo nation peacemaking: Living traditional justice.* Tucson: University of Arizona Press, pp. 42–58.

Conclusion

My hope in putting together this book has been tempered by the realization that significant findings in the field of parapsychology as it intersects with psychoanalysis, literature and culture, invariably have been consigned to the dust-heap of history, no matter their intrinsic worth, one might cynically say, the more likely their intrinsic worth given the resistance to psi data of which I have spoken in this book. I have the following sense of the effect of a book such as this on the various fields to which it is addressed.

For the field of psychoanalysis and psi, I do not have a sanguine view of the possibilities of applying our understanding of psi processes in psychoanalytic clinical practice. The pioneering work of the greats in this field, from Freud to Eisenbud (including such names as Ehrenwald, Servadio, Ullman) as well as forays by such formidable names as Derrida, Stoller and Burlingham, have more or less been forgotten. The newcomers who have ventured here, such as Eshel, I. Brenner, Brottman, Rosenbaum, and de Peyer have singularly tried to resurrect aspects of this field, but it seems to me unlikely, given the conservative nature of psychoanalytic institutions, that their work will get much concentrated traction. I believe unfortunately that the same will hold true for this work.

For the field of literature, of which I am not an academic, I sense the possibility that the academic field may on the whole be less rigidly bound and less resistant than the psychoanalytic community, and so I am much more hopeful. Perhaps some in this field will explore more fully the type of work I have suggested here. It would be particularly important if the study of Western literature was accompanied by an informed understanding of parapsychological data.

For the field of culture, anthropologists have at times struggled with the issues that I have discussed here. Again, I do not know enough about where the field stands today (although the heyday of the linking of psychoanalysis and anthropology appears to have come and gone) to judge whether the parapsychological issues I touch upon here will be elaborated in more detail some day by the professionals in the field. But of this field I also remain hopeful.

For the field of parapsychology, I am afraid this work—which makes no effort to provide typical experimental data—will suffer the same fate as the much more compelling work of Eisenbud, both the psychoanalytic work and the experimental data from the Serios phenomenon. It will be minimized. I think this is unfortunate particularly given the opportunities that exist for parapsychology to claim a more prominent place in natural and scientific studies. It is in the interest of parapsychology, as a science, to realize that our great writers, film-makers and playwrights, have often made psi phenomena a central part of the stories that characterize our culture and have done so in an intuitively informed manner. A greater celebration of this fact in parapsychological circles could only improve acceptance of the field. For great Western creative thinkers, parapsychological phenomena are not marginal to life; they are more often than not central.

My notable pessimism is a consequence of my seeing that the resistance to entertaining the psi hypothesis is enormous. It is much easier to avoid the hypothesis entirely. Why then attempt to introduce this book at all? My fundamental hope is that it will reach to a few, who will take it to heart—perhaps even those who are just general readers— and who will as a consequence explore what is a fascinating if sometimes disconcerting subject.

And for those who are psychoanalysts, let me observe that we believe too often we know how things work, how people function, what unconscious process is about. We expound upon our successful cases often forgetting those where we could not engage the patient or where we missed significant connections with the patient. We also not only tend to worship Freud but we seem to need to worship psychoanalysts in general, whether Lacan or Ferenczi or Bion or Klein, and in the process, we too often forget to look at the data of human functioning itself, and in particular the data of psi functioning. In effect, we forget to *wonder*, that crucial aspect of free association in which we ask our patients to indulge as a way to reveal psychoanalytic dynamics and in which we ask ourselves to partake when we apply "free floating attention" to our listening. To wonder involves the questioning of assumptions—always. And so, if as a result of presenting this work, I have managed to shake a few of you a bit, made you question the assumptions of how we function, and encouraged you to wonder again about how the world is put together, then I will have succeeded.

Afterword

by Michael Prescott

As we've seen in Richard Reichbart's important book, there are multiple points of intersection between paranormal phenomena and culture, law, and literature—yet they all converge on the mysterious meeting place of parapsychology and psychology, psi and psyche. And no one ever explored this boundary with more penetrating discernment than the late Jule Eisenbud, Richard's mentor and colleague.

In his tribute to Eisenbud, Richard writes, "He would let his curiosity take him wherever, giving himself fully up to it, irrespective of the initial subject matter, as if giving himself up to a river; and it would take him from a vernacular comment by someone, perhaps uneducated as was Ted, to some psychoanalytic insight to some anthropological observation or observation about prehistoric man, all in one sentence." This free-flowing facility of thought was all too easy to mock and to misrepresent. Who better to illustrate this point than the master of mockery and misrepresentation, the professional escape artist/debunker James ("the Amazing") Randi?

Back in 1980, Randi published his most famous book, *Flim-Flam!*, which remains in print to this day. In a chapter charmingly titled "Off the Deep End," Randi confronts the Ted Serios case. Serios, Randi says, "discovered that by using a simple little device and gathering a few simple minds around him, he could work magic." He gives the example of an instance where Serios was asked to produce a photo of a nuclear sub, the Thresher, and instead produced a photo of Queen Elizabeth. Randi sarcastically summarizes Eisenbud's lengthy speculation that the words "Elizabeth Regina," when analyzed from the point of view of unconscious associations, could translate into "Thresher." "What? You didn't see it?" Randi jeers. "You'll never be a parapsychologist at that rate!"

Eisenbud's analysis of the alleged Elizabeth-Thresher connection is in fact just one example of his nimbleness of mind and his willingness to consider any interpretation, no matter how arcane. What it most definitely is *not*, however, is an example of Eisenbud's willingness to score a miss as a hit. Here is what Eisenbud wrote, in a passage not quoted by Randi: "Without question this [i.e., the Elizabeth photo] would be judged, as in fact it was, a completely inappropriate response, a clear miss in relation to the target asked for."

To repeat: it would be judged, *as in fact it was,* a clear miss. Randi's commentary notwithstanding, Eisenbud did not score the Elizabeth photo as a hit.

Now, Randi is too crafty to say explicitly that Eisenbud did call the photo a hit. He merely implies this conclusion, blissfully certain that his readers have not read Eisenbud and will not know any better. Thus, by implication, he impugns the whole catalog of hits that actually were ascribed to Serios.

Randi goes on to cite a certain Dr. Boris Lofgren, who "described parapsychology enthusiasts as 'decaying minds' with 'thinking defects and disturbed relations to reality' … At the very least," Randi graciously concludes, "it seems Dr. Eisenbud is not rowing with both oars in the water."

Sadly, this is the kind of treatment that Eisenbud and everyone else with a serious interest in parapsychology must expect to receive. Perhaps partly in an effort to avoid being victimized by such empty cleverness, some proponents of psi have labored to develop methodologies that would largely take the psychology out of parapsychology, ostensibly placing the field on an more objective basis.

Decades ago, the inventor George Meek, holder of several important patents, set out to design a mechanical device that would allow direct communication between the living and the dead. He called it Spiricom. Essential to the project was engineer Bill O'Neil, who translated Meek's ideas into a working prototype. Spiricom, according to some reports, actually did produce communications inexplicable in non-paranormal terms.

But there was a hitch. The device worked only when Bill O'Neil was operating it. Without O'Neil, it was useless. O'Neil, it appears, possessed unsuspected mediumistic capabilities of his own, and it was via these talents that voices could be coaxed from Spiricom. Subtract Bill O'Neil's psyche from the mix, and there was no ghost in the machine. Meek's hope—to build a device that would make after-death communications as commonplace as telephone calls—proved chimerical. A purely mechanistic solution to the problem wasn't feasible.

Or consider the field of electronic voice phenomena, or EVP, in which an experimenter records the silence of an empty room, then plays back the audio, listening for snippets of speech. Ghost voices caught on tape—what could be more objective? The trouble is that most (though not quite all) EVP fragments scarcely qualify as speech. A trained ear is required to decipher these mysterious pops and buzzes and interpret them as words. It's hard to escape the inference that the EVP explorer himself, primed to tease out messages from the ether, hears what he wants, needs, or expects to hear—and almost always, conveniently enough, in his own language. In practice, this supposedly most objective of techniques becomes largely subjective, with the EVP recordings serving as the audio equivalents of Rorschach blots. Once again, human psychology is an inextricable part of the mix.

Beyond what an investigator hopes to find, there's the issue of what he may be *afraid* to find. Charles Tart has written about the "fear of psi"—the tendency even among parapsychologists to draw back from evidence that is too compelling, too unsettling. Tart himself may have been an unwitting victim of fear of psi when he blithely allowed a promising test subject, known in the literature as Miss Z, to move away from his lab. His one startlingly successful experiment with Miss Z, if replicated under progressively tighter test conditions, might have revolutionized the entire field of parapsychology. Yet Tart made no effort to persuade Miss Z to stay or to arrange for her occasional return. Today he seems a bit perplexed by his own indifference to a potentially paradigm-shifting study.

But psi is like that, always just out of reach, always retreating from view. It's not surprising that Miss Z moved away; it would be surprising if she hadn't. The best experimental subjects grow bored and quit, or suddenly lose their powers, or are discovered cheating even though their earlier successes can't possibly be explained that way. The medium Daniel Dunglas Hume inexplicably lost his talents for a year, got them back, then saw them fade away as he grew older. Another medium, Arthur Ford, turned to drink as his powers waned—or perhaps his powers waned because he turned to drink. The Fox sisters confessed to fraud, then recanted; their careers appear to have been a mixture of genuine and phony phenomena, and neither the confession nor the retraction can be taken at face value. Young children may report past lives in convincing detail, but when they are a few years older, the memories are gone.

This elusiveness is an aspect of what George P. Hansen has called "the trickster and the paranormal" in his book of the same name. Hansen's point is that psi is inherently liminal, peripheral—whether in pre-technological societies where the shaman lives apart from the community and conducts himself in a comically antisocial manner, or in modern societies where psi is safely relegated to horror movies, ghost-hunter TV fare, and Halloween parties. Psi is always marginalized, or perhaps more accurately, it marginalizes itself and those who are drawn to it. It is an embarrassment to be scrubbed out of approved biographies; William James' lifelong fascination with mediums is mentioned only grudgingly, while his contemporary F.W.H. Myers, another pioneer of psychological and parapsychological theory, is nearly forgotten.

The trickster also makes himself known in a kind of personal amnesia attendant on psi events. I've learned to make note of premonitions and synchronicities at once; if I don't, I find them impossible to recall even an hour later. Sitters investigating Eusapia Palladino in 1905 found that within a day or two they'd forgotten the most spectacular parts of her séances; only by reading stenographic transcripts of the sessions could they recover these details. Far from embellishing paranormal episodes, our minds often seem to downplay, discount, and forget them. Remembering a bona fide experience of the paranormal may be as difficult as holding on to the memory of a dream.

Just possibly, we are not meant to remember. Our amnesia could be a self-protective measure. In episodes of transcendent mystical insight or "cosmic consciousness" (a term coined by Richard Maurice Bucke), as well as in some near-death experiences, a person feels he has come face to face with a new, higher reality that makes physical life seem dreamlike by comparison—a plane of being that is "realer than real." Maybe, as Aldous Huxley suggested, the complex architecture of the brain is meant to filter out the excess of information that would wake us from slumber. The brain, going full tilt, may be actively at work keeping us asleep and dreaming. Too much wakefulness—too much reality—could prove overwhelming. "No live organism can continue for long to exist sanely under conditions of absolute reality," Shirley Jackson mused.

Some studies of mindfulness, a meditation technique, report that a minority of participants suffer unexpected negative consequences that can persist for months or years—panic attacks, depression, feelings of depersonalization and unreality. Is it possible that meditation, which quiets the brain, opens the filter a little too wide for some of us, letting in an understanding that we find disorienting and terrifying? To see the self as a persona, the physical world as an illusion, and memory as myth, might prove destabilizing to someone unprepared for it. Perhaps not everybody is ready for cosmic consciousness.

There's a well-known connection between psychosis and religious mania. To the atheist, this is because religious belief originates in madness. An alternative explanation is that as the malfunctioning brain fails in its role as filter, it lets in a rush of cosmic consciousness that both inspires and destabilizes. The psychotic may be sure he's heard the voice of God because he has, in fact, been in touch with higher powers (God, the higher self, or what-have-you), and this very contact has thrown him permanently off balance. It's not surprising that the distinction between madman and seer—and poet, and vision-ary—is so often blurred, or that behavior that would get a modern-day American insti-tutionalized can mark a member of a pre-technological community as a savant.

To maintain an iron grip on the rationality and orderliness of the world, one must expel any deviant phenomena, sometimes by sheer force of Randiesque bluster. Clear vision is preserved at the cost of wearing blinders that limit vision's scope. Remove the blinders, and the world is larger but murkier, offering both more opportunities and fresh terrors.

A common mistake made by those who've never taken psi seriously is to say that its proponents are motivated by fear and seeking comfort—fear of death or of the mean-inglessness of life in a purely materialistic world; comfort by way of ghost stories and fairytales. The larger reality hinted at by psi phenomena, however, is not comforting but disturbing; it undercuts our preconceptions; it hints at the deep strangeness at the margins of things, or—even more unsettling—at the vital center. And it defies easy answers, either from the proponent or the doubter. It obliges us to cultivate composure in the face of ambiguity.

Few people can maintain a state of partial belief and partial doubt—or more accu-rately, parallel states of belief and doubt, existing side by side, with the focus of attention shifting nimbly from one to the other. It places a strain on the mind. It cries out for a resolution, a final, definitive answer, either yea or nay.

But we may not be meant to have a final answer. It might spoil the game, pull down the curtain on the show. "This is all an elaborate hoax," Roger Ebert told his wife shortly before he died. He meant reality—life, the universe, and everything. More and more, I think he was right. Like the virtual reality of a computer game, the "real world" may be no more than a rendered environment, "a stubbornly persistent illusion" (Einstein's description of the conceptual categories of past, present, and future) constructed out of a substrate of information and the information-processing powers of consciousness itself. Kant may not have been far wrong when he contrasted an inaccessible noumenal dimen-sion with a mentally constructed phenomenal realm. The phenomenal world is the ren-dered landscape of tangible images; the noumenal world is the source code that runs the game.

Some people become upset when I compare life to a game. Don't I know how much suffering there is in the world? How can it be a mere game? A less contentious metaphor might be that of a play—a tragedy, if you like. No one doubts that Lear, Oedipus, and Willy Loman suffer dreadfully. And an actor feels everything much more deeply when he loses himself in his role. If life is a game, it's a fully immersive game, one that requires our total commitment.

So perhaps we aren't allowed to go backstage and see the cardboard props, or peel away the graphic images to read the constantly recalculated strings of ones and zeros underneath. Perhaps the taboos against magic, the marginalization of the occult, the elu-siveness of paranormal phenomena, the proliferation of fraud, the fear of psi, our own forgetfulness and doubts, even the shrill mockery of debunkers—perhaps *all* of it is simply a defense against seeing the game for what it is, and a protection against the anx-iety, depersonalization, and even madness that may follow such a dangerous epiphany.

And so we return to the meeting place between psyche and psi. How many patients find themselves in psychiatrists' offices because they've glimpsed, even fleetingly, a larger reality that threatens the structure of their egos? How much of modern angst and anomie derives from an awakening realization of the larger dimensions of life?

It's just possible—though I wouldn't insist on it—that we're currently passing through a transitional phase in human development, and that these first glimmers of deeper awareness are a prelude to a larger awakening that will transform our science and our civilization.

If this future comes to pass, the writings of Jule Eisenbud—and a few rare books like the one you've just read—will be seen, if only in retrospect, as signposts pointing the way.

Michael Prescott is the author of 26 novels of psychological suspense (Chasing Omega *deals with parapsychological research). He hosts a widely read blog dealing with the persistence of the human personality after death (michaelprescott.typepad.com/).*

Appendix A:
Jule Eisenbud: Explorer

I was privileged to know Jule Eisenbud. Ultimately, I became his colleague, both as a psychoanalyst and as a parapsychologist, but that was later. When I first saw Jule in early 1970, I was 27 years old; he was in his early 60s. I was a recent graduate of an Eastern law school and had the dust of the Navajo and Hopi reservations of Arizona on my shoes, where I had spent a year and a half as a legal services attorney, and where among other things I had fallen deeply in love and lost. When I arrived on Jule's doorstep in Denver as a patient, he took one look at me and said that if he had known from my phone call that I was "on the ragged edge," he would have seen me sooner.

He was right, of course. Over the next two and a half years with an eight-month hiatus at one point, beginning at six times a week on the couch, not only did he save my life in a very real sense, but he opened a new world to me that I had no idea existed—one of immense possibility and excitement. It was not a world outside but a world inside, where the explorations were as daring and dangerous as any I had sought as a young man. Completely unfamiliar with things psychoanalytic, much less parapsychological, I had not the faintest clue when I stepped over his thresh-old—desperate and in psychological pain—of the extent to which I had indeed arrived.

I hope here to give an impression of Jule from my vantage point on the couch, so to speak, as well as from my perspective of the two disciplines that I entered, leaving the practice of law, because he showed me how intellectually and emotionally satisfying they were. I did not know Jule when he was younger, and I will leave it to others (e.g., Pilkington, 1999), who know first hand the battles he fought then, to speak of their memories of him. One of the most important things I learned from Jule was how dearly he held to intellectual honesty; and so I hope here to give a sense of him as he would have it: his brilliance, his courage, and also his flaws. If there was one thing Jule could not abide, it was sentiment that obscured. His understanding of parapsychology was characterized by a conception of how human emotions, particularly sexual wishes and aggressive feelings, figured in psi manifestations and in our reluctance to fully investigate psi. The need to "pretty up" psi—as if we suddenly became saintly rather than human when it occurred—had no appeal to him. Nor would such a tribute to him.

At the outset, let me put my cards on the table. I believe that Jule's work in parapsychology, particularly the psychic photography data produced by Ted Serios (Eisenbud, 1967, 1989) and his theories concerning how psi functions in daily life, to be far and away the most important evidential and theoretical work in the history of parapsychology. I believe that their dismal fate—which he himself predicted—in parapsychological circles today is a testament to how troubling is the very nature of psi to parapsychologists. In addition, I believe his work in psychoanalysis is without precedence in terms of exploration of psi (Eisenbud, 1970).

On the other hand, I also believe that he failed terribly, from the point of view of psychoanalytic technique, to find a benign and appropriate way to make use of psi data to help patients in psychoanalytic treatment; nor did he ever acknowledge the shortcomings of his technique. I make these statements from the perspective of my subsequent much fuller psychoanalysis and my own work as a psychoanalyst. However, I should add that the reception of the psi data from Jule's psychoanalytic work (leaving aside the technical problems about how to handle the data) has been even worse in psychoanalytic circles than in parapsychological ones. To be interested in these data in psychoanalysis today [written in 1998] is more of a professional kiss of death, if possible, than it was in the 1950s when Jule became involved. Again, I believe this is a consequence of how terribly troubling psi is, not only to parapsychologists but also to psychoanalysts. One of the tragedies in psychoanalysis is that there has been no way to talk about how psi data could be integrated into psychoanalytic technique, if at all. There has never been adequate discussion of what Jule attempted to do, because for almost all psychoanalysts (leaving aside Ehrenwald, 1955; Fodor, 1947; Servadio, 1955; Ullman, 1959; and a few others) it was beyond the pale.

My conclusion from all of this is that Jule's work, if it survives at all, will do so a hundred years hence, when it will be rediscovered in some fashion. For now, there seems to be no way to fit the data he found or his theories concerning them into how we think about causality. They are simply too threatening to our current belief systems.

In character, Jule was a man of extraordinary charm and intellectual quickness. His style of writing, as in *The World of Ted Serios* (1967), was in fact his style of speaking: it was marked not only by a breadth of knowledge but by such intellectual curiosity that he often dazzled. He would let his curiosity take him wherever, giving himself fully up to it, irrespective of the initial subject matter, as if surrendering himself to a river current; and it would take him from a vernacular comment by someone, perhaps uneducated as was Ted, to some psychoanalytic insight to some anthropological observation or a note about prehistoric man, all in one sentence.

By following Jule's example, I learned how to think for the first time; in fact, I had to unlearn what high school, college, and graduate school had taught me with their strictures on subject matter. In effect, I went to school with *The World of Ted Serios* (Eisenbud, 1967) and *Psi and Psychoanalysis* (Eisenbud, 1970) all over again, going through all the references I could locate. I re-found my curiosity, and for that I will be forever grateful to him.

For Jule loved life, and he communicated that. He made his adopted home in Colorado for his wife and three children, where he loved the mountains, a special place. Believing that one should follow Voltaire's advice to "cultivate your garden," he constructed a Spanish-style fountain surrounded by a wall that protected his house. He found life endlessly fascinating, and he prided himself on making no a priori assumptions about what aspect of it could be investigated, whether it be precognition, physical mediumship, UFO phenomena, or psychic photography (which to his chagrin, he at first rejected). To my mind, what he found in psychic photography by Ted Serios is apparently too evidentiary for parapsychologists or others to accept. In all the useless searching since for the repeatable experiment, the palpable, physical evidence of one of Ted's photographs, often an amalgam of the past and the present or of different events or of impossible perspectives, with the extensive protocols and the numerous scientific witnesses, is as firm evidence as we have ever had or maybe that we will ever get, and by far it is the most fascinating. It is to the shame of parapsychology that the discipline has all but abandoned these data, or in some places, approved the observations of one or two cynics at the time. All the resources of parapsychology should be put toward an examination of the Serios data, which has yet to be done, and to argue for them.

In psychoanalysis, Jule (Eisenbud, 1970, 1982) tried to extend the theory that Freud ambivalently had proposed in his seminal work on how telepathic data could enter the unconscious mind and be transformed (like a day residue) in the manifest content of a person's dream (Freud, 1922/1955). But what Jule did by sharing with the patient ostensible psi data from other patient's dreams or from their lives or from Jule's own life was to make it impossible for the transference to develop in a full-blown way or to be explored fully. Often Jule ran the risk of seeming to be more interested in acquiring psi data for his own interest than in the patient himself; certainly, my own analysis with him suffered from this focus. In addition, Jule ignored the findings of ego psychology and exercised a kind of interpretive control over the patient, where his tendency to shine intellectually became a liability. Although Jule was open, in a way that some present day psychoanalysts only now appear willing to be (e.g., Renik, 1993) about his counter-transferential reactions in psychoanalysis, he so violated the frame of psychoanalysis to explore psi reactions— justifying his procedure as the only way to understand what the patient was experiencing (although the patient usually had no idea of the psi determinants of his productions)— that the patient's sense of being understood as an entity or being understood in the *here and now emotionally* was sacrificed. Even should psychoanalysts become open to psi, Jule's relentless focus would create immense problems in our understanding of how to cure patients.

I do not know what the solution to this problem is. In my own psychoanalytic work, I am left with Jule's type of data, but no framework in which to use it, other than to inform myself. Let me close with an example, which seems fitting in this tribute to Jule, of what happened two days ago, just after arranging with the editor to write this piece. I had just seen a middle-aged patient who has struggled terrifically with the internal effects of a seductive and emotionally abusive mother upon whom he was utterly depend-ent as a child, and who oscillates between paroxysms of rage and the most awful sadistic wishes toward her, which he finds sexually exciting, on one hand, and the wish for her to protect him from ever having to engage life, on the other. The patient also constantly struggles, because of guilty incestuous feelings, with his sense of his own gender. When he was an adolescent, for example, he punished himself for his incestuous fantasies by truly believing he had the breasts of a woman. His transferential relationship to me is the same as toward his mother, one minute wanting to kill or maim me, which drives him also to desire to isolate himself entirely from me and from everyone who knows him, and in the next, wanting me to hold him, encourage him, tell him what to do as his mother might. In depicting his rage toward me, he said that he thought of himself as a polar bear, with a wall between us, who would look over the wall at me; and if I dared get too close to him, he would maim and kill me. Why a polar bear was unclear.

Shortly after seeing the patient, I sat down to enjoy my lunch, opening the current issue of a psychoanalytic journal that I had been looking forward to reading. I began an article that examined why Amundsen, the determined explorer and discoverer of the South Pole, when attacked, beaten, and seemingly about to be killed by a polar bear had this inconsequential thought: "I lay wondering how many hairpins were swept up on the sidewalks of Regent Street in London on Monday morning" (Anthi, 1999). Sigmund Freud subsequently expressed an interest in what provoked this seeming last thought of the explorer and in this article, the author, Per Anthi, examined the possible determinants of the thought, evaluating how Amundsen throughout his life tried to escape (to the far-thest poles) the clutches of his mother and struggled with guilty incestuous and com-petitive wishes. He suggested that Amundsen also punished himself by denying his masculinity and his power toward the end of his life, as evidenced by his seeming last thought of women's hairpins. To tie matters together, Eisenbud has written in a number of places (e.g., 1982, pp. 140–141; 1983, pp. 221–222) about the bear as a mother-symbol, a fact of which I was well aware. For me, the Amundsen piece helps me to understand my patient better. His ostensible need to enlist psi certainly suggests his wish to stay in contact with me after a session, an issue we have been working on (and for that matter, Amundsen's near miraculous escape from an attacking bear suggests my own under-standable wish with regard to this patient). But I know no way that I could even suggest to this patient, whose reality testing is fragile and who has tremendous boundary prob-lems, that his fantasy about being a polar bear might be psi determined and predictive of something I would come upon later in the day.

  Of course, Jule would have loved to explore exactly this type of ostensible psi man-ifestation. As a result, those of us who have been affected by his work find our eyes and hearts open to seeing the world in ways we never would have, except for him. He was truly an explorer, intrepid and persevering, in an inhospitable climate of which he never really complained. We will miss him.

References

Anthi, P.R. (1999) Roald Amundsen: A study in rivalry, masochism and paranoia. *International Journal of Psychoanalysis*, 80, 995–1010.

Ehrenwald, J. (1955) *New dimensions of deep analysis: A study of telepathy in interpersonal relationships.* New York: Grune & Stratton.

Eisenbud, J. (1967) *The world of Ted Serios.* New York: Morrow.

Eisenbud, J. (1970) *Psi and psychoanalysis: Studies in the psychoanalysis of psi-conditioned behavior.* New York: Grune & Stratton.

Eisenbud, J. (1982) *Paranormal foreknowledge.* New York: Human Sciences Press.

Eisenbud, J. (1983) *Parapsychology and the unconscious.* Berkeley, CA: North Atlantic Press.

Eisenbud, J. (1989) *The world of Ted Serios.* 2d ed. Jefferson, NC: McFarland.

Appendix B: Correspondence with Elizabeth Lloyd Mayer

A. Initial correspondence to editor Arnold Richards of the *Journal of the American Psychoanalytic Association* concerning Elizabeth Lloyd Mayer's article on Stoller's telepathic experiences

Richard Reichbart, Ph.D.
60 West Ridgewood Avenue
Ridgewood, N.J. 07450

October 3, 2001

To: Arnold Richards, Editor, *JAPA*
    Historical perspective on telepathy in psychoanalysis

I commend Elizabeth Lloyd Mayer (Mayer, 2001) for her write-up of Robert Stoller's draft of a paper on telepathy in psychoanalysis, as well as for the decision of *JAPA* to publish this material. Historically, it should be noted that *JAPA* has never, as far as I can determine, had a piece that entertained the possibility of telepathic phenomenon in psychoanalysis. In 1973, it published a scathing review by Lofgren of eleven books on parapsychology (including the Devereux collection on psi and psychoanalysis [Devereux, 1953]) which concluded that editors who publish parapsychological papers "have no defense against the accusation of actively supporting superstition in a rather insidious and invidious manner" (Lofgren, 1973, p. 177); and in 1987 it published a memoir by Brenner who claimed that his 1957 refutation of the parapsychological hypotheses of Eisenbud had the beneficent result that nothing of a parapsychological nature since had been published in a "reputable" psychoanalytic journal (Brenner, 1987, p. 554). Of course, if material on ostensible telepathy in psychoanalysis cannot be openly published, it is also unlikely that it will be openly discussed.

Thus, it is a wonderful development that a prominent analyst such as Mayer has been willing to put her imprimatur on investigating this aspect of psychoanalytic process, and that *JAPA* has published it. What I object to in Mayer's presentation of Stoller's material, however, is that in her effort to open up this subject anew, she divorces it somewhat from its previous history, as if by doing so she can avoid the anathema to which those who have published in this area have been subject in the past, despite Freud's own interest in it (e.g., Freud, 1922). To begin with, she fails to fully convey the extent to which there is nothing new in what Stoller experienced, and that this material has been presented in a similar detailed fashion throughout the literature on telepathy in psychoanalysis, including in the very articles she cites (and often at considerable professional cost) (cf. e.g., Eisenbud, 1970; Pederson-Krag, 1947). What *is* remarkable is that such a prominent and in other respects daring psychoanalyst as Stoller became frightened for his own sanity, did not publish this material in his lifetime for fear of consequences to his professional standing, and at least as far as can be ascertained from what has been presented seemed unaware of or took no consolation in what had already been published on the subject.

In addition, Mayer also does not fully convey the extent to which from the very beginning those psychoanalysts brave (or foolhardy) enough to explore this area have suggested at some length a variety of theories to explain the psychodynamics that might contribute to a patient or analyst exhibiting telepathy, including that the patient picks up on repressed or countertransferential issues of the psychoanalyst (Hollos, 1933) or attempts to compete unconsciously with other patients who have the psychoanalyst's attention (Eisenbud, 1970, pp. 323–329). We can learn a great deal from these previous theoretical forays rather than seeming to approach the material de novo.

But most importantly the premise with which Mayer introduces Stoller's material is misleading. It is true that most psychoanalysts in the past were reluctant to tell a patient that something ostensibly telepathic had occurred, in part for fear of breaching anonymity. However, the issue was certainly openly broached and discussed in the literature (see, e.g., Gillespie, 1953, pp. 380–381), particularly by Eisenbud, who argued forcefully and repeatedly for introducing to the patient the possibility that a telepathic communication had occurred and discussed many examples of having done so, such as informing the patient that a dream appeared to pick up telepathically on an otherwise hidden aspect of the psychoanalyst's own life. He contended that telling of an ostensible telepathic communication not only never did any harm, but actually helped the patient to explore psychodynamics and transference otherwise not apparent (Eisenbud, 1946, p. 81). I strongly believe that from a technical viewpoint, his approach could be disastrous: it gave ostensible telepathy undue importance, encouraged the patient to focus too much on the psychoanalyst's actual life, and rather than encouraging the development of transference tended to interfere with it (Reichbart, 1998). But his struggles, and those of others, to know what to do with ostensible telepathic material were valiant, and by not giving them their due, Mayer risks the very openness she invokes.

I hope as does she that today's generally greater appreciation of transference and countertransference, as well as the technical changes that have occurred as a consequence of considering more fully the relationship between analyst and patient, may permit us to discuss more openly this type of ostensible telepathic experience among ourselves without fear of reprobation, and perhaps help us to figure out how (if at all) to handle it technically. I applaud her very considerable courage in asking us to do so.

References

Brenner, C. (1987) Notes on psychoanalysis by a participant observer: a personal chronicle. *Journal of the American Psychoanalytic Association*, 35: 539–556.

Devereux, G., ed. (1953) *Psychoanalysis and the Occult*. New York: International Universities Press.

Eisenbud, J. (1946) Telepathy and problems of psychoanalysis. *Psychoanalytic Quarterly* 15:32–87.

Eisenbud, J. (1970) *Psi and psychoanalysis*. New York: Grune & Stratton.

Freud, S. (1922) Dreams and telepathy. *Standard Edition* 18: 197–220.

Gillespie, W. (1953) Extrasensory elements in dream interpretation. In Psychoanalysis and the Occult, ed. G. Devereux. New York: International Universities Press, 1953, pp. 373–382.

Hollos, I. (1933) Psychopathologie alltaglicher telepathischer Erscheinungen. Imago 19:529–546.

Lofgren, L.B. (1968) Recent publications on parapsychology. *Journal of the American Psychoanalytic Association* 16:146–178.

Mayer, E.L. (2001) "On ATelepathic dreams?": an unpublished paper by Robert J. Stoller. *Journal of the American Psychoanalytic Association*, 49: 629–657.

Pederson-Krag, G. (1947) Telepathy and repression. Psychoanalytic Quarterly 16: 61–68.

Reichbart, R. (1998): Jule Eisenbud: explorer. *Journal of the American Society for Psychical Research* 92:427–431.

B. Elizabeth Lloyd Mayer's response to initial letter forwarded to Richard Reichbart with her permission by Arnold Richards, former editor of JAPA

From: Elizabeth Lloyd Mayer, Ph.D.
2435 Russell Street
Berkeley, California 94705

Date: February 8, 2002

To: Arnold Richards, M.D.
    Response to 'Richard Reichbart, Ph.D.

I am pleased that Dr. Reichbart has responded so thoughtfully and helpfully to my introduction and epilogue to Robert Stoller's paper, "Telepathic Dreams?" He is certainly correct that these are issues anything but new to psychoanalysis. Though he feels that my citing of past literature didn't do justice to its extent and significance, he'll note that I did, in a long list of relevant articles, cite all the sources he highlights (with the exception of his own excellent obituary piece on Jule Eisenbud which, while informative, is not to the point in referencing original literature on the topic of "telepathy" and unconscious communication). And I fully agree with him that it would be a mistake to approach the overall topic "de novo," given our psychoanalytic history. However, in reviewing the psychoanalytic literature that does exist, I remain frankly less satisfied than he appears to be with the level of both prior theorizing as well as the degree of disclosure by most analysts of purportedly telepathic experiences with patients.

But there is no question we are in general hoping for the same thing: increased scientific and psychoanalytic attention to unconscious communication and how it may actually happen. He is to be commended for his own attention to the topic.

C. Second Letter in Response to Elizabeth Lloyd Mayer

Richard Reichbart, Ph.D.
60 West Ridgewood Avenue
Ridgewood, N.J. 07450

March 27, 2002

Elizabeth Lloyd Mayer is very gracious. But we disagree. I am much more impressed than she is by the attempts of analysts in the past to deal with ostensible telepathy in psychoanalysis. To my mind, because of the nature of the phenomena, there has been a *greater* tendency, at least by a few analysts, to disclose information to a patient than customary and certainly *more* revelation in subsequent clinical reports about events—often highly personal ones—concerning the analyst outside the consulting room. And especially I believe that theorizing about telepathy in analysis, given the small number of psychoanalysts who have entertained the topic, has been considerable.

It was Freud, after all, who—although deeply ambivalent (at one point he wrote in correspondence that if he were to be at the beginning of his career again, he would become a psychical researcher [Freud, 1921/1957])—applied psychodynamic formulations to alleged telepathy, suggesting that if an unconscious telepathic communication took place it underwent the same psychodynamically determined distortion as a day residue when it appeared in a manifest dream (Freud, 1933, p. 38) and breaking an accustomed frame to explore telepathy in psychoanalytic treatment by disclosing an event from his own life to an analysand. In this last instance, when a patient said to Freud that he was a *"Herr von Vorsicht"* [gentleman of foresight], a term that a female admirer used for him, Freud immediately showed the patient the calling card of his prior visitor, a Dr. Forsyth, whom this patient ostensibly could not have known just had an interview. And in his clinical report Freud discussed the importance Dr. Forsyth's visit held for him, for it was a sign of new professional activities that would probably result in hastening the end of this particular patient's treatment, the manner in which the patient wove the name into treatment, and other actions of his own outside the clinical setting that he felt in an over determined way contributed to the patient's telepathy. He speculated that the patient, experiencing great jealousy, had unconsciously invoked telepathy to compete for attention from Freud equal to that which Dr. Forsyth had just received (Freud, 1933, pp. 47–54).

Other analysts have reported more personal and often painful events sometimes remarking that the depth to which the patient's ostensible telepathy had touched their own lives and countertransferences made it difficult for them to make a full clinical report. Pederson-Krag commented that when ostensible telepathy with her occurred the "...manifest content of the patients' dreams relating to my life all had unpleasant connections to me, and I had decided to suppress each of them" (Pederson-Krag, 1947, p. 67) and included such things as lacking silverware for dinner guests and arguing with a male colleague about who should pay for dinner, with attendant associations. Deutsch (1926) became aware that a patient was picking up on her eighth wedding anniversary plans in a telepathic bid for equal attention.

Eisenbud explicitly stated that "the outstanding characteristics of practically all telepathic occurrences as seen in analysis is the involvement of the analyst himself to the extent that his repressed, affect-laden material therein relates itself dynamically to the repressed material of the patient" (Eisenbud, 1946, p. 73), an idea articulated also by Hollos (1933), Servadio (1934) and Fodor (1942). Eisenbud believed that only when the analyst explored the telepathic components when they appeared (either in his self-analysis or with the patient) could one get to the heart of a patient's transference or the analyst's countertransference. As a consequence, Eisenbud's clinical reports contain innumerable personal revelations including such things as an eroticized dream about the wife of a colleague, thoughts about his father, tension with his wife about having another child, issues of potency or self-esteem tied to his choice of clothing or automobile unknown to the patient—all of which seemed to be telepathically brought up when a patient bid for attention or understanding, or expressed feelings ranging from anger to competition to love (Eisenbud, 1970, pp. 125–127, pp. 158–160, pp. 200–234; Eisenbud, 1946, pp. 240–242). Although Eisenbud did not disclose all of these things to his patients (and one can see the profound difficulties of doing so), he did go so far at one point in his celebrated argument with Albert Ellis concerning telepathy in psychoanalysis, as to have a patient sign a document that recounted their mutual telepathic interaction (Eisenbud, 1948), which to my mind goes far beyond the therapeutic pale. Roheim shared with a patient that a dream of hers appeared to have unconsciously picked up on his attendance of a lecture by Hollos on the same evening on the subject of telepathy, and discussed it in terms of her magical desire to be included in the primal scene (Roheim, 1932). Gillespie shared information with a patient about his being near the same location as she had been earlier in the day, and having a similar associations at the time, but drew the line on sharing a dream of his he felt had telepathic elements coinciding with her dream (Gillespie, 1953). Devereux wrote about the rationale for different technical approaches to disclosures concerning telepathy (Devereux, 1953). These are just some examples of the self-revelations in clinical reports, the theorizing, and the technical issues concerning disclosure articulated in the past with regard to ostensible telepathy in psychoanalysis and do not begin to do justice to the extensive literature.

I agree with Dr. Mayer that new views on countertransference raise the question of whether the analyst can pursue ostensible telepathic data in treatment in some mutual way with an analysand, but I am frankly much more skeptical than she appears to be that this can be done in a manner that will preserve the transference. However, I prefer to put her efforts within the context of a long, varied and neglected tradition. She has chosen to publicly keep alive the spirit of Freud's gentle adjuration from eight decades ago, "...I must urge you to have kindlier thoughts on the objective possibility of thought-transference and at the same time of telepathy as well" (Freud, 1933, p. 54). In this regard, I wish there were more like her.

References

Deutsch, H. (1926) Occult process occurring during psychoanalysis. In *Psychoanalysis and the occult*, ed. G. Devereux. New York: International Universities Press, 1953.
Devereux G. (1953) Technique of analyzing occult occurrences. In *Psychoanalysis and the occult*, ed. G. Devereux. New York: International Universities Press, 1953, pp. 373–417.
Eisenbud, J. (1946) Telepathy and problems of psychoanalysis. *Psychoanalytic Quarterly* 15: 32–87.
Eisenbud, J. (1948) Analysis of a presumptively telepathic dream. *Psychiatric Quarterly* 22: 103–135.
Eisenbud, J. (1970) *Psi and Psychoanalysis*. New York: Grune & Stratton.
Fodor, N. (1942) Telepathic dreams. *American Imago* 3: 61–87.
Freud, S. (1922) Dreams and telepathy. *Standard Edition* 18: 197–220.
Freud, S. (1933) Dreams and occultism. *Standard Edition* 22: 31–56.
Freud, S. (1957) Letter to Hereward Carrington, 1921. In *Psychoanalysis and the Future*, ed. B. Nelson. New York: National Psychological Association for Psychoanalysis, Inc., 1957, pp. 12–13.
Gillespie, W. (1953) Extrasensory elements in dream interpretation. In *Psychoanalysis and the Occult*, ed. G. Devereux. New York: International Universities Press, 1953, pp. 373–382.

Hollos, I. (1933) Psychopathologie alltaglicher telepathischer Erscheinungen. *Imago* 19: 529–546.

Pederson-Krag, G. (1947) Telepathy and repression. *Psychoanalytic Quarterly* 16: 61–68.

Roheim, G. (1932) Telepathy in a dream. *Psychoanalytic Quarterly* 1: 227–291.

Servadio, E. (1934) Psychoanalysis and telepathy. In *Psychoanalysis and the occult*, ed. G. Devereux. New York: International Universities Press, 1953, pp. 210–220.

Appendix C: A Cloak
and Dagger Psi Mystery Story

Whereas psychoanalysts generally are unfamiliar with and deeply skeptical about the existence of psi phenomena, there were others I discovered who apparently were quite familiar with the field, in a way that I could only wish did not exist—and quite familiar with me and my involvement in it.

In December 1977, my wife Paige Hooper-Reichbart and I were running a small art gallery in Denver, called Jasper Gallery (the name actually was chosen because the *Journal of the American Society for Psychical Research* in which I had by then published a number of parapsychological articles has the acronym JASPR, but the gallery was a modern art gallery—only someone very familiar with my parapsychological writings would have known of this association). One day, my wife was approached by a man who came into the gallery and said that he knew me. He said his name was "John Connors" and that he had been in my class at Yale Law School. He said that maybe he would return at another time.

Now each class at Yale Law School back then was not much over one hundred students in number. When I heard about this "John Connors," I told my wife that I certainly did not know him nor was there any one by that name in my class. For that matter, I did not recognize the name from other classes at Yale Law during the time I attended (I graduated in 1968). Strange we thought.

But return he did. And now it got stranger. This time he proceeded to tell my wife that he knew all about us. He knew that my psychoanalyst was the parapsychologist Jule Eisenbud and that I was supposedly "working with him" on parapsychological matters. He wondered about what we might be doing together. In addition, he knew of all the parapsychological meetings my wife had attended in New York City (some at the American Society for Psychical Research) years before she and I had met and before I myself even had an interest in the field; and about the course I was then teaching in parapsychology at the University of Colorado at Denver. He also knew of my Yale law school roommate, Peter Rindskopf, who became an outstanding civil rights attorney, working in the South, and had died in a tragic car accident in 1971; he also knew of distant Russian relatives of mine whom I had located through HIAS ("Hebrew Immigrant Aid Society" that aids and keeps track of Jewish refugees) in doing a "roots" search in 1976 and one of whom had emigrated to Canada; he knew of my arrest in 1964 for participation in the Free Speech Movement in Berkeley; he knew of my work as an attorney for the Navajo Indians; he knew of my work for Martin Luther King's SCLC; and a variety of other personal information, including accurate aspects of my prior love life. He did miss some anti–Vietnam war work that Paige had done, but there was not much he left out in his account.

I might not know "Connors," but it appeared he was right: he certainly did know me. He refused to tell Paige with what agency he was working but he did say that his information about us was "confirmed by F.B.I. files." He said he could meet with us. Paige declined. Thankfully, we heard no more from him, although we of course speculated. Was he from the F.B.I. or from another government agency or even from the Russian government, a possibility at which he appeared to hint when he met with Paige? Unfortunately, the matter did not seem to be entirely over—for from then on, we found that we received innumerable hang-up calls on our home phone. They were constant for two years.

Sometimes one's paranoia is well founded. In 1979, my wife and I had moved to Schwab House, a large apartment complex between 73rd and 74th streets on the West Side of New York City, and our daughter, Nicole, was one year old. Early one morning, when my wife was out shopping with our daughter and I had gone off to psychology classes at the graduate school of the City University of New York (returning briefly because I had forgotten something and passing an unfamiliar man conspicuously eating an apple— so I could not quite see his face—as I approached my apartment door) our apartment was broken into, although with no evidence of forced entry. Our dog was locked in the closet. No valuables were taken and the apartment was more or less untouched, but my files in my file cabinet had been obviously rifled through, including those involving parapsychology. Almost all my files about my Russian relatives were taken. The robber had also removed a series of tape recordings, which were actually of a book on which my wife was working, concerning our daughter who was born with spina bifida.

We reported the break-in and then had a two-hour meeting with the Russian Section of the F.B.I. in New York City, on February 8, 1980. The F.B.I. claimed it was not their agency at work in Denver and they knew nothing about any of it; and all the information they had on me had been communicated to me previously in an FOIA request I had made (there was, in essence, nothing there). They themselves seemed to wonder if it were the Russians, which rather startled us. Regardless, the harassing phone calls continued. My father, an attorney himself, enlisted the aid of a friend of his, Congressman Steven Solarz who represented the 13th district (our district) in New York City, in May of that year (Reichbart, 1980) but although Solarz also approached the F.B.I., there was still no explanation. My father then hired a private investigator. Still the phone calls continued. Finally, my father—an eminently honest man but one very familiar with the ways of the world and with the mob as a consequence of his union work—told the private investigator to put out the word that my father had underground connections and that harassing us should cease. All I know is that from then on, the phone calls stopped!

So somebody took my work with Eisenbud and Eisenbud's work itself quite seriously.

Perhaps this is not as surprising as it at first seems—at least in hindsight. Ted Serios did not just produce innocuous thoughtography of buildings or people. He also produced (on his own, not as part of his protocol with Eisenbud) two psychic photographs of the Russian Vostok rockets, apparently in space (Eisenbud, 1967, pp. 226–227)—which could not be found in any of the literature on the rockets. (Note also, the very first hidden photograph Eisenbud hoped Ted would psychically reproduce was of a Kremlin structure, the Dormiton Cathedral, for which Serios arguably got a "hit" by association [Eisenbud, 1967, pp. 27, 205].) For that matter, unbeknownst to most people, since 1972 a variety of

United States government intelligence (such as the C.I.A.) and military agencies in the United States had been secretly funding highly classified programs exploring in particular "remote viewing," that is the ability of a talented subject to get impressions of a distant target, through extrasensory perception (clearly of interest to intelligence agencies but as with all psychic abilities, difficult to definitively "bottle" so that it might be consistently useful). It became eventually a twenty-year multi-million-dollar secret project, now known by its nickname, STAR GATE, that was only fully declassified in the 1990s, most famously run by the Stanford Research Institute (SRI). Russia was believed to be doing something similar. (For a summary of this work which has been made publicly available courtesy of the CIA electronic reading room, cf. May [2012] and Stargate CIA FOIA.)

Whatever agencies or governments thought of Serios's work (in 1980 Eisenbud claimed—not overly convincingly in my opinion—that one of Serios's pictures actually showed Ganymede, a moon of Jupiter, which had not yet been filmed at the time that Serios produced the photo [Eisenbud, 1983b]), I suppose the conjunction of my politics, my search for distant Russian relatives, my psychoanalysis with Eisenbud, and my publishing in parapsychology, was just too much for them to ignore. However, whomever they were, they caused long and unnecessary distress on my family for many years. For a time, these events succeeded in adding to my reluctance to continue to explore this field.

Two further things. First: my recent reading in a different area has reminded me of aspects of what happened. In a political book on the role of Russia in the United States elections, Harding describes that the KGB and then the FSB had a method of worrying those in whom it was interested. On the one hand, they would find out about the person's love life, attempting to procure compromising information, as well as of course harassing and electronically "bugging" the person, and on the other, they would break into apartments while the owners were away, and leave "demonstrable clues" such as "stolen shoes, women's tights knotted together, cigarette butts stomped out" (Harding, 1917, p. 15; see also pp. 76–77). Our dog at the time of the break-in would have been as friendly to a burglar as to an invited guest, neither barking nor aggressive. Why so obviously put her in the closet or was this another example of a "demonstrable clue"?

Second: looking back, I remember two gentlemen in the parapsychology class whom I taught at the University of Colorado at Denver, who always came to class dressed in jackets and ties and always sat together, never saying anything. I never could quite understand their interest in my course, but they came to it religiously, never missing a class and never really taking part. And if this had been in a more controversial political setting, given their careful attire and their impenetrability, I would have been more suspicious of them. Perhaps they too were explainable … but I will never know.

References

Eisenbud, J. (1967) *The world of Ted Serios*. New York: William Morrow & Co.

Eisenbud, J. (1983) Postscript: Ganymede observed. In J. Eisenbud *Parapsychology and the unconscious*, pp. 131–135. Berkeley: North Atlantic Books.

Harding, L. (2017) *Collusion: Secret meetings, dirty money and how Russia helped Donald Trump win*. New York: Vintage Books.

May, E.C. (2012) PsiSpy: Recollections from a psychic spying programme. In S. Kakar & J.J. Kripal (eds.) *Seriously strange: Thinking anew about psychical experiences*. New York: Penguin, pp. 87–125.

Reichbart, J. (1980) Letter to congressman Steven Solarz, from the law firm Reichbart & Reichbart, May 13, 1980.

Stargate CIA FOIA https://www.cia.gov/library/readingroom/collection/stargate

Glossary

Because I attempt to bridge the gap between parapsychology and other areas of study, namely literature, culture, and psychoanalysis—whose researchers, scholars, professionals and enthusiasts may not be familiar with parapsychological terms—I am including this glossary which I hope might be helpful. The definitions here are accompanied by comments which reflect my perspective. In parapsychology, often the same phenomena are described by different terms, which can be confusing. Thus, I also hope that I can to clarify this tendency here.

Anomalous Experiences   A most unfortunate term, introduced in the 1970s with the misguided hope that by widening the field to include a variety of phenomena, the insularity of parapsychology from the scientific community would be overcome. The consequence has been that experiences which are not parapsychological have been mixed with those which are in some scientific journals and the nomenclature of parapsychology as well as the field itself has become watered-down. Anomalous, as in occult and the uncanny (see below), also implies that psi is unusual. I contend throughout this book that psi phenomena are a common and natural occurrence of our lives, neither anomalous nor occult, toward which we, in Western and scientific culture, have developed a resistance to recognizing.

Apparition   Also referred to as "ghost." Often thought of in the past as the ghosts of departed "spirits" but in fact there are apparitions of living persons as well. There is no need to invoke a spiritist hypothesis to explain this phenomenon as I have indicated extensively in this book, particularly in my discussion of *Hamlet*. An apparition is usually a visual sense of a person (although it may be accompanied by an auditory sense as well) who is not actually present. Apparitions may be shared by more than one person.

Clairvoyance   A misused term. Technically, this refers to the ability to cognize through the mind an event or object at a distance (not a person) as contrasted with telepathy, in which the psi communication is between persons. However, the term has been so generalized in practice that it has come to denote a slew of parapsychological phenomena.

Macro and Micro Psi   The terms "macro" and "micro" are usually used to differentiate between different types of psychokinesis or PK. In a general sense, it is used as the difference between statistical experimental tests that show statistically small changes versus larger and also more spontaneous PK events. I use it to refer to small and large changes in psi events in general, the small changes associated with parapsychological experiments. However, as Braude suggests, from the point of view of causation (rather than of psychodynamic interest in which spontaneous macro psi is by far more compelling) there is no distinction to be made between these types of psi (Braude, 1986, pp. 224–226).

Occult   Not a term that I favor at all because its meaning on its face is "unknown" and I contend that these phenomena are not so much unknown or unusual as unacknowledged in Western culture. Frequently however "occult phenomena" is a term used interchangeably with "psychic phenomena." The term is popular in the public mind, where it gets much attention and tends to have cachet; and it is sometimes used in psychoanalytic studies as in Freud (Freud,) and in Devereux's book Psychoanalysis and the Occult (Devereux, 1953).

Out of Body Experience   Also referred to as astral projection. The phenomenon of a person having the sense of being outside his body, and looking down upon it. Most strikingly occurs when the person is unconscious, as under anesthesia, and yet accurately observes things that take place. The term "astral projection" was used previously implying that the soul left the body. The most complete studies of this phenomenon, with voluminous data, are the works of Crookall (1970) and Monroe (1971).

Parapsychology   Also referred to as psychic research or psychical research. The term used to indicate the study of psychic phenomena. Introduced in an article in the German periodical Spinx in 1889 by Max Desoir, a member of the Society for Psychical Research, it did not come into common use until J.B. Rhine adopted it in the 1930s to replace the previous term psychic research or psychical research, again with the hope of gaining greater acceptance from the scientific community. The term is probably unfortunate as "para" can imply "less than" the full study of psychology (as in legal and "para-legal") but it is the common term in use today.

Premonition   The apparent precognizing of an event before it takes place either in a dream or in a thought. Explanations for this phenomenon remain various, but—again—some of the hypotheses do not entail overcoming the linear movement of time, but suggest that the most economical explanation is that psi works in elaborate ways, involving psychokinesis or telepathic suggestion (sometimes referred to as "super-psi")to account for the phenomenon.

Psi   Also referred to as psi phenomena, psychic phenomenon or paranormal phenomena. This is the umbrella term that I favor as do most parapsychologists, although it is often not recognized in other disciplines, to describe psychic phenomena of any kind. However, the general public is more familiar with other terms. Hence, I have entitled this book with the word "paranormal" although in the content of the book I often have preferred to use "psi."

Psychic Photography   Also referred to as thoughtography and in the past as spirit photography. The apparent ability to influence the image that appears on film. Originally occurred at the beginning of photography when people who had sittings with early photographers (who advertised as spirit photographers) hoped that an image of a deceased loved one, a spirit, would show up—as indeed appears to have happened in some cases. However, all indications are that this a form of psychokinesis and is not confined to images of deceased persons or "spirits." The most famous modern study of psychic photography is that of the psychic Ted Serios, who tended to get images of buildings and whose abilities were extensively documented by Jule Eisenbud and which is a primary focus of this book (Eisenbud, 1967, 1989).

Psychokinesis   Also referred to as PK and telekinesis. The apparent ability of mind to influence the material world with no sensorimotor intervention.

Reincarnation   The ability of a child to remember detailed aspects of the life of a deceased person that he has not known, or to have physical characteristics of that person, common in certain cultures, such as the Indian, which suggests to some that a spirit has been passed from the deceased to the new incarnation of the child. Extensive studies with fascinating data were performed by Ian Stevenson, M.D. (e.g., Stevenson, 1966), although explanations do not necessarily support a reincarnation hypothesis.

Sheep-Goat experiment   The famous experimental studies of the parapsychologist Gertrude Schmeidler, Ph.D. which showed that people who believed in the possibility of "psi"—the sheep—tended to perform better on experiments testing for telepathy than those who did not hold such beliefs—the goats (Schmeidler & McConnell, 1958).

Super-Psi   Encompassing super-telepathy and super-psychokinesis. This term states that a variety of phenomena—popularly thought of as evidence of spirits, such as ghosts or hauntings, or as evidence of the ability to be influenced by events that have not yet occurred, sometimes referred to as "retrocausation," resulting in apparent precognition—are in fact much more economically explained as a consequence of the intricate workings of telepathy or psychokinesis.

For a discussion of this, with reference to precognition, turn to Braude (1986, pp. 266–277).

Telepathic Drawing Experiments Experiments in which a "sender" who is obscured from the "receiver" draws a picture, usually indicating verbally what he or she is drawing, and the receiver tries to draw a similar picture, also usually indicating to what he or she associates in making the drawing. Distance does not appear to matter when there are "hits," that is when the receiver makes a drawing similar to the sender. The most famous experiments, as I indicate in this text, were by Warcollier (Warcollier, 1938) and Upton Sinclair (Sinclair, 1971).

Telepathy Also referred to as extrasensory perception, ESP, and thought transference. Often psychoanalysts have favored the term thought transference in their literature. There is no indication that this phenomenon is based upon waves, and there is little indication that the distance between two (or more) people is a factor when it takes place. In other words, whether the participants are far or near to each other, it takes place, with no evidence that distance produces a lag in time. Nor is there any indication that the communication must take place at the exact same time as the thought or event to which it relates. In other words, time is not a factor, although sometimes the thought is shared or received simultaneously for both parties.

Uncanny In my opinion, a most unfortunate association takes place when psi phenomena are labeled "uncanny." The term came into use in psychoanalysis because of Freud's paper on "the uncanny" (Freud, 1919), in which he lumped together a variety of different phenomena and labeled them all as frightening as well as unreal. In this famous paper, he threw in everything but the kitchen sink (which if it became animate would no doubt have been included). Automatons that seem human, coincidences, "omnipotence of thought," ghosts, the "evil eye," doubles, being buried alive, madness and epilepsy—were all thrown together as examples of the uncanny. Unfortunately, many psychoanalysts have continued to do the same, without examining the parapsychological and psychoanalytic literature on telepathy (including Freud's own work) and ghosts, as well as on psi phenomena in general. As with the use of the word "occult," the term "uncanny" to describe psi phenomena provides a kind of thrill. But it almost invariably risks obscuring an understanding of the ubiquity and psychodynamics of the phenomena.

References

Braude, S. (1986) *The limits of influence: Psychokinesis and the philosophy of science.* New York: Routledge & Kegan Paul.

Crookall, R. (1970) *Out of the body experience.* New York: University Books.

Devereux, G. (1953) *Psychoanalysis and the occult.* New York: International Universities Press.

Eisenbud, J. (1967) *The world of Ted Serios.* New York: William Morrow & Co.

Eisenbud, J. (1989) *The world of Ted Serios.* 2d ed. Jefferson, NC: McFarland.

Freud, S. (1919) The uncanny. In An infantile neurosis and other works. *Standard Edition,* 17, 217–256.

Freud, S. (1925) The occult significance of dreams. In Some additional notes on dream interpretation as a whole. *Standard Edition* 19,125–138.

Freud, S. (1933) Lecture XXX: Dreams and occultism. In New introductory lectures on psychoanalysis, *Standard Edition,* 22, 31–56.

Monroe, R.A. (1971) *Journeys out of the body.* Garden City, NY: Anchor.

Schmeidler, G.R. & McConnell R.A. (1958) *ESP and personality patterns.* New York: Yale University Press.

Sinclair, U. (1971) *Mental radio.* New York: Collier Books.

Stevenson, I. (1974) *Twenty cases suggestive of reincarnation.* Charlottesville: University of Virgnia Press.

Warcollier, R. (1938) *Experiments in telepathy.* New York: Harper & Brothers.

Index

Dream Telepathy (Ullman) 102
Dukhobors 30

early development 117, 135, 138–
139, 160, 188; *see also* abuse;
trauma or loss
Eastern culture 36, 64–65; *see
also A Passage to India*
(Forster)
ectoplasm 29
Ehrenwald, Jan 58*n*3, 74, 85, 99,
116, 117, 136, 210
Einstein, Albert 74, 93, 100, 102,
109, 113, 128*n*1, 210
Eisenbud, Jule; *see also* Brenner,
C.; *Psi and Psychoanalysis;*
Serios, Ted
on aggressive wishes 147, 186,
192, 209
Amundsen article and 69
author and 5–6, 58*n*8, 209, 220
on causality 210
Chesterton and Bergman and
57
"Connors" and 218
dark skinned lady and 68, 112
defense of 141–143
F.B.I. and 219–220
forgetting of 74, 75–76
Freud and 211
importance of 209–210
L shape and 153
Marryat and 29
Mayer and 106
mesmerism and 47–48
on mother symbols 212
overviews 10, 52
precognition and 75, 89–90,
141–142, 143, 148
on precognitive dreams 144, 210
on "primitives" 173*n*13
psi correspondence and 26
on psychoanalysts' dreams or
personal life 75, 99, 111, 216
psychoanalysts' sharing of psi
and 87, 114–116, 157, 160, 211,
214, 216
psychoanalytic work and 210,
211
Randi and 55–56
recent literature on 133
resistance to 135, 137
on resistance to psi 39, 118, 135,
186, 188, 192
on Robertson 145, 148
Russia and 219–220
surround, telepathic and 112,
158
on transference/countertrans-
ference 116, 216
video of 58*n*6
Western law and 192
Eisendrath, D.B. 53
Eissler, K.R. 14

Eitingon, Max 107
11 (number) 62, 65–66
Elliotson, John 47, 81
Ellis, A. 52, 216
Ellman, R. 121
Emerson, Thomas 193
Ereto 61
Ervin, Sam 194
Esdaile, James 47, 81
Eshel, O. 79–80, 84, 95–96, 112,
120, 134–135, 139
Eskimo shamans 176–177, 178,
179, 180, 189*n*4, 189*n*5
ESP 223; *see also* psi
everyday occurrences; *see also*
Western law
Bach and 120–121
Freud on 86, 87
Hamlet and 13
parent-child telepathy and 118
Psi and Psychoanalysis and 136
Stoller and 104–105
terminology and 78, 221, 223
trauma *versus* 95–96, 99, 105,
134–135, 159–160
Ulysses and 60–61, 65
Western law and 200
evolution 87
exorcism 39, 41
Experiments in Telepathy (War-
collier) 93
Extraordinary Knowing (Mayer)
105–106

"Facts, Coincidence, and the Psi
Hypothesis" (C. Brenner) 101
Farrell, D. 101, 108, 127
fathers and sons 63, 103, 148–
149, 151; *see also* Shakespeare,
Hamnet
F.B.I. 219
fear; *see also* denial or resistance to psi
aggressive wishes and 192
author's 108–109
Chesterton and 44, 46–47
contemporary psychoanalysts
and 102
of Eisenbud's work 135
Navajos and 173*n*8
of our aggression 117–119
patients' 123, 125
slippery slope and 85
Stoller and 103, 104
terminology and 78
Ferenczi 74–75, 84, 90–91, 102,
107, 108
Fiedler, L.A. 35
finding missing objects 105, 139,
163, 164, 171, 173*n*4, 173*n*12
First International Congress of
Physiological Psychology 83
Fischer, Doris 40, 124
Fleiss, Wilhelm 84

Fodor, N. 74, 216
Forster, E.M. 35–41, 41*n*2
Forsyth case 86–87, 97–98, 107,
108, 109–111, 114, 120, 136,
155–156, 215
fortune tellers' prophecies 84–
85, 99
Fox sisters 81
frauds, charlatans, and swind-
lers 45, 48–49, 56, 58*n*5, 142,
175, 177, 182, 185; *see also*
"deliberate deception"
free association 90–91, 92, 94,
98, 123, 124
freedom, individual 194
Free Speech Movement 218
Freuchen, P. 178, 179, 189*n*4
Freud, Sigmund; *see also* denial
or resistance to psi; Forsyth
case; omnipotence of
thought; principles of psi
on aggressive wishes 192
Amundsen article and 212
Charcot and 82
on common occurrence of psi
117
on day residue and psi 215
Derrida and 107
distortions and 94
dreams and 96
Eisenbud and 211
Ferenczi and 84, 90–91, 107
Joyce and 62
letters on psi of 88–91, 107
literature on 10, 23
"occult" and 222
parapsychology and 52, 61
on psi 173*n*13
psi phenomena and 73, 74, 78,
80, 83–85
psychic research and 81, 83
publications on psi of 84–88
recent literature on 135–136
on Shakespeare 14
telepathy experiments and 91–
92
time and 113–114
the "uncanny" and 77, 223
FSB 220
Futility (Robertson) 144, 145

Ganymede (moon of Jupiter)
220
Gardner, M. 53
Getting Married (Shaw) 58*n*3
ghosts (apparitions) (poltergeist);
see also deceased person's
spirit; knocking; *Phantasms
of the Living* (Gurney, Myers
and Podmore); spirits; super-
telepathy hypothesis
Chesterton and 44
dismissal of 35
Freud and 80, 85, 89